# INFORMATION WARFARE IN THE AGE OF CYBER CONFLICT

This book examines the shape, sources and dangers of information warfare (IW) as it pertains to military, diplomatic and civilian stakeholders.

Cyber warfare and information warfare are different beasts. Both concern information, but where the former does so exclusively in its digitized and operationalized form, the latter does so in a much broader sense: with IW, information itself is the weapon. The present work aims to help scholars, analysts and policymakers understand IW within the context of cyber conflict. Specifically, the chapters in the volume address the shape of influence campaigns waged across digital infrastructure and in the psychology of democratic populations in recent years by belligerent state actors, from the Russian Federation to the Islamic Republic of Iran. In marshalling evidence on the shape and evolution of IW as a broad-scoped phenomenon aimed at societies writ large, the authors in this book present timely empirical investigations into the global landscape of influence operations, legal and strategic analyses of their role in international politics, and insightful examinations of the potential for democratic process to overcome pervasive foreign manipulation.

This book will be of much interest to students of cybersecurity, national security, strategic studies, defence studies and International Relations in general.

**Christopher Whyte** is an Assistant Professor at Virginia Commonwealth University, USA.

**A. Trevor Thrall** is Associate Professor in the Schar School of Policy and Government at George Mason University, USA, and a Senior Fellow at the Cato Institute, USA.

**Brian M. Mazanec** is a researcher of cyber conflict, strategic warfare, and intelligence and teaches in the Department of Defense and Strategic Studies at Missouri State University, USA, and in the Schar School of Policy and Government at George Mason University, USA.

# Routledge Studies in Conflict, Security and Technology

Series Editors: Mark Lacy, *Lancaster University*, Dan Prince, *Lancaster University*, and Sean Lawson, *University of Utah*

The *Routledge Studies in Conflict, Technology and Security* series aims to publish challenging studies that map the terrain of technology and security from a range of disciplinary perspectives, offering critical perspectives on the issues that concern publics, business and policymakers in a time of rapid and disruptive technological change.

**Conflict in Cyber Space**
Theoretical, strategic and legal perspectives
*Edited by Karsten Friis and Jens Ringsmose*

**US National Cybersecurity**
International Politics, Concepts and Organization
*Edited by Damien Van Puyvelde and Aaron F. Brantly*

**Cybersecurity Discourse in the United States**
Cyber-Doom Rhetoric and Beyond
*Sean T. Lawson*

**National Cyber Emergencies**
The Return to Civil Defence
*Edited by Greg Austin*

**Information Warfare in the Age of Cyber Conflict**
*Edited by Christopher Whyte, A. Trevor Thrall, and Brian M. Mazanec*

**Emerging Security Technologies and EU Governance**
Actors, Practices and Processes
*Edited by Antonio Calcara, Raluca Csernatoni and Chantal Lavallée*

**Cyber-Security Education**
Principles and Policies
*Edited by Greg Austin*

For more information about this series, please visit: https://www.routledge.com/Routledge-Studies-in-Conflict-Security-and-Technology/book-series/CST

# INFORMATION WARFARE IN THE AGE OF CYBER CONFLICT

*Edited by Christopher Whyte, A. Trevor Thrall, and Brian M. Mazanec*

LONDON AND NEW YORK

First published 2021
by Routledge
2 Park Square, Milton Park, Abingdon, Oxon OX14 4RN

and by Routledge
52 Vanderbilt Avenue, New York, NY 10017

*Routledge is an imprint of the Taylor & Francis Group, an informa business*

© 2021 selection and editorial matter, Christopher Whyte, A. Trevor Thrall, and Brian M. Mazanec individual chapters, the contributors

The right of Christopher Whyte, A. Trevor Thrall, and Brian M. Mazanec to be identified as the authors of the editorial material, and of the authors for their individual chapters, has been asserted in accordance with sections 77 and 78 of the Copyright, Designs and Patents Act 1988.

All rights reserved. No part of this book may be reprinted or reproduced or utilised in any form or by any electronic, mechanical, or other means, now known or hereafter invented, including photocopying and recording, or in any information storage or retrieval system, without permission in writing from the publishers.

*Trademark notice*: Product or corporate names may be trademarks or registered trademarks, and are used only for identification and explanation without intent to infringe.

*British Library Cataloguing-in-Publication Data*
A catalogue record for this book is available from the British Library

*Library of Congress Cataloging-in-Publication Data*
Names: Whyte, Christopher, 1988- editor. | Thrall, A. Trevor, editor. |
Mazanec, Brian M., editor.
Title: Information warfare in the age of cyber conflict / edited by
Christopher Whyte, A. Trevor Thrall, and Brian M. Mazanec.
Description: London ; New York : Routledge/Taylor & Francis Group, 2020. |
Series: Routledge studies in conflict, security and technology |
Includes bibliographical references and index.
Identifiers: LCCN 2020012491 (print) | LCCN 2020012492 (ebook) | ISBN
9781138600911 (hardback) | ISBN 9781138600935 (paperback) | ISBN
9780429470509 (ebook)
Subjects: LCSH: Information warfare. | Disinformation. |
Propaganda–Technological innovations. | Propaganda,
International–History–21st century. | Disinformation–United
States–History–21st century. | Democracy. | Social media–Political
aspects. | Cyberspace–Political aspects. | Disinformation–Government
policy. | United States–Politics and government–21st century.
Classification: LCC UB275 .I5465 2020 (print) | LCC UB275 (ebook) | DDC
355.3/43–dc23
LC record available at https://lccn.loc.gov/2020012491
LC ebook record available at https://lccn.loc.gov/2020012492

ISBN: 978-1-138-60091-1 (hbk)
ISBN: 978-1-138-60093-5 (pbk)
ISBN: 978-0-429-47050-9 (ebk)

Typeset in Bembo
by MPS Limited, Dehradun

# CONTENTS

| | |
|---|---|
| *List of figures* | viii |
| *List of tables* | ix |
| *Contributors* | x |
| *Acknowledgments* | xvi |
| *List of acronyms* | xvii |

| | |
|---|---|
| 1 Introduction<br>*Christopher Whyte, A. Trevor Thrall, and Brian M. Mazanec* | 1 |

**PART I**
**The nature, history and correlates of information warfare in the age of cyber conflict** 	**13**

| | |
|---|---|
| 2 The convergence of information warfare<br>*Martin C. Libicki* | 15 |
| 3 A brief history of fake: Surveying Russian disinformation from the Russian Empire through the Cold War and to the present<br>*Aaron F. Brantly* | 27 |
| 4 The ideological battlefield: China's approach to political warfare and propaganda in an age of cyber conflict<br>*Elsa B. Kania* | 42 |

**vi** Contents

5 Cyber conflict at the intersection of information operations: Cyber-enabled information operations, 2000–2016 — 54
*Colin Foote, Ryan C. Maness, Benjamin Jensen, and Brandon Valeriano*

## PART II
## (Cyber-enabled) Information at war — 71

6 Bear market? Grizzly steppe and the American marketplace of ideas — 73
*A. Trevor Thrall and Andrew Armstrong*

7 Commanding the trend: Social media as information warfare — 88
*Jarred Prier*

8 Cyber by a different logic: Using an information warfare kill chain to understand cyber-enabled influence operations — 114
*Christopher Whyte and Ugochukwu Etudo*

9 Cyber-enabled information warfare and influence operations: A revolution in technique? — 132
*Miguel Alberto Gomez*

## PART III
## Building resilience: Questions of legality, diplomacy and society — 147

10 Might or byte(s): On the safeguarding of democracy in the digital age — 149
*Christopher Colligan*

11 On the organization of the U.S. government for responding to adversarial information warfare and influence operations — 166
*Herbert Lin*

12 Virtual disenfranchisement: Cyber election meddling in the grey zones of international law — 186
*Michael Schmitt*

13 Stigmatizing cyber and information warfare: Mission impossible? — 215
*Brian M. Mazanec and Patricia Shamai*

Contents **vii**

**PART IV**
**The fluid shape of modern information warfare** **229**

14 How deep the rabbit hole goes: Escalation, deterrence and
the "deeper" challenges of information warfare in the age of
the Internet 231
*Christopher Whyte*

*Index* 241

# FIGURES

| | | |
|---|---|---|
| 5.1 | Russian Hacking Group Fancy Bear propaganda | 63 |
| 7.1 | Illustration of a bot network | 91 |
| 7.2 | Model of individual opinion formation | 93 |
| 7.3 | Process map of how propaganda spreads via the trend | 94 |
| 7.4 | Total Facebook engagements for top 20 election stories | 95 |
| 8.1 | Anthony Soules' "Commandments" of disinformation (updated by Bruce Schneier) | 120 |
| 8.2 | An information operations kill chain | 126 |
| 11.1 | Bubble Chart for U.S. government cybersecurity roles and responsibilities | 179 |

# TABLES

| | | |
|---|---|---:|
| 5.1 | Crosstabulations of state actors who launch cyber-enabled information operations with Pearson residuals | 59 |
| 5.2 | Crosstabulations of cyber operation strategic objective and cyber-enabled information operations with Pearson residuals | 60 |
| 5.3 | Crosstabulations of cyber method and cyber-enabled information operations with Pearson residuals | 61 |
| 7.1 | Snapshot of IS Twitter activity | 97 |
| 7.2 | IS case study analysis | 99 |
| 7.3 | Russia case study analysis in 2016 election | 105 |

# CONTRIBUTORS

**Miguel Alberto Gomez** is a senior researcher at the Center for Security Studies. He holds a Masters degree in International Security from the *Institut Barcelona d'Estudis Internacionals*. He has previously worked as a lecturer at both the De La Salle University and the College of St. Benilde in the Philippines and has worked in the Information Security industry for the past eight years. His area of research is centered around cybersecurity. Specifically, he is interested in the strategic use of cyberspace as an instrument of national power as well the emergence of norms surrounding the use of this domain.

**Andrew Armstrong** is a PhD candidate in political science at George Mason University. His research focuses on the intersection of epistemology, politics, and the media. Armstrong earned a BA in psychology from Haverford College and an MA in political science from the University of California, Davis.

**Aaron Brantly** is an Assistant Professor in the Department of Political Science at Virginia Tech and an affiliated faculty member of the Hume Center for National Security and Technology, the Alliance for Social, Political, Ethical, and Cultural Thought and the Information, Trust and Society Initiative at Virginia Tech. He is also a cyber policy fellow and senior research scientist for the U.S. Army Cyber Institute at West Point. Alongside colleagues in Virginia Tech's Integrated Security Destination Area, Integrated Security Education Research Center, The Army Cyber Institute and the Combating Terrorism Center at the United States Military Academy, Dr. Brantly picks apart complex problems and attempts to provide policy and technically feasible solutions to the State of Virginia, The United States Army and the Nation. As a member of these teams, he specifically engages problems through the disciplines of Political Science (International Relations and Comparative Politics) and Computer Science, with research specifically focusing on issues related to cyber conflict, deterrence, parallel computing, human rights, big data, artificial intelligence, terrorism, encryption and more.

**Christopher Colligan** is a doctoral candidate at the University of Washington, where his research focuses on civil–military relations and sociological approaches to military innovation. In this role, he has presented research at several academic conferences and was appointed the 2018–2020 Richard B. Wesley Chair of the University of Washington International Security Colloquium.

**Ugochukwu Etudo**, PhD, is an assistant professor at the University of Connecticut's School of Business. Dr. Etudo's research focuses on the application of ontology and knowledge engineering towards the provision of solutions to various business and social problems. He has successfully used these techniques to provide several computational solutions to the problem of interoperability in XBRL financial statements in the United States. Dr. Etudo also studies machine learning for text analytics focusing on named entity recognition and relation extraction. An applied researcher, he studies how these techniques can be used to track the propagation of organizational messaging on the Web with a special focus on terrorist organizations.

**Major Colin J. Foote** is a Psychological Operations Officer in the United States Army Special Operations Command. He has a Master of Science degree from the Department of Defense Analysis at the Naval Postgraduate School.

**Benjamin Jensen** is a nonresident senior fellow at the Atlantic Council's Scowcroft Center for Strategy and Security and a professor holding dual appointments at the Marine Corps University and American University, School of International Service. At American University, Dr. Jensen is the program coordinator for the peace, global security and conflict resolution undergraduate thematic area. His teaching and research explore the changing character of political violence and strategy. At the Marine Corps University, Command and Staff College, he is an assistant professor running the Advanced Studies Program. The program integrates student research with long-range studies on future warfighting concepts and competitive strategies in the U.S. defense and intelligence communities. During his career, Dr. Jensen has supported multiple U.S. government agencies including contributing to Joint Staff studies and war games on transnational threats and great power competition, counterinsurgency doctrine, intelligence community scenarios on the future of Afghanistan, studies on cyber operational art, and red team assessments for the NATO headquarters in Afghanistan. Dr. Jensen is also an officer in the U.S. Army Reserves with multiple deployments including Kosovo (2006) and Afghanistan (2011). Dr. Jensen has authored or co-authored three books, *Forging the Sword: U.S. Army Doctrinal Innovation*, *Cyber Strategy* and *The Human Domain: Breaking Series of Failures*. He is a prolific writer who has published numerous articles and editorials, presented numerous conference papers and has regular columns on War on the Rocks. Dr. Jensen received his bachelor's degree in English and communications from the University of Wisconsin, Madison, an MA in international affairs, international peace and conflict resolution from American University, School of International Service, a master's of science in strategic intelligence from the National Defense Intelligence College (Defense Intelligence Agency) and his PhD in international relations (international politics, international security) from American University, School of International Service.

**Elsa B. Kania** is an Adjunct Senior Fellow with the Technology and National Security Program at the Center for a New American Security (CNAS). Her research focuses on Chinese military innovation in emerging technologies in support of the Artificial Intelligence and Global Security Initiative at CNAS, where she also acts as a member of the research team for the new Task Force on Artificial Intelligence and National Security. Her analytic interests include Chinese military modernization, information warfare, and defense science and technology. She has been invited to testify before the U.S. House of Representatives Permanent Select Committee on Intelligence (HPSCI) and the U.S.–China Economic and Security Review Commission (USCC). Elsa is an independent analyst, consultant and co-founder of the China Cyber and Intelligence Studies Institute. She was a 2018 Fulbright Specialist and is a Non-Resident Fellow with the Australian Strategic Policy Institute's International Cyber Policy Centre. Elsa works in support of the China Aerospace Studies Institute through its Associates Program, and she is a policy advisor for the non-profit Technology for Global Security. Elsa has also been named an official "Mad Scientist" by the U.S. Army's Training and Doctrine Command. Elsa is a PhD student in Harvard University's Department of Government, and she is a graduate of Harvard College (summa cum laude, Phi Beta Kappa). Her thesis on the evolution of the PLA's strategic thinking on information warfare was awarded the James Gordon Bennett Prize. Her prior professional experience includes time with the Department of Defense, the Long Term Strategy Group, FireEye, Inc. and the Carnegie-Tsinghua Center for Global Policy. While at Harvard, she has worked as a research assistant at the Belfer Center for Science and International Affairs and the Weatherhead Center for International Affairs. Elsa was a Boren Scholar in Beijing, China, and she has professional proficiency in Mandarin Chinese.

**Martin Libicki** (PhD, U.C. Berkeley 1978) holds the Keyser Chair of cybersecurity studies at the U.S. Naval Academy. In addition to teaching, he carries out research in cyberwar and the general impact of information technology on domestic and national security. He is the author of a 2016 textbook on cyberwar, *Cyberspace in Peace and War*, as well as two other commercially published books, *Conquest in Cyberspace: National Security and Information Warfare*, and *Information Technology Standards: Quest for the Common Byte*. He is also the author of numerous RAND monographs, notably *Defender's Dilemma, Brandishing Cyberattack Capabilities, Crisis and Escalation in Cyberspace, Global Demographic Change and its Implications for Military Power, Cyberdeterrence and Cyberwar, How Insurgencies End* (with Ben Connable), and *How Terrorist Groups End* (with Seth Jones). Prior employment includes 12 years at the National Defense University, three years on the Navy Staff as program sponsor for industrial preparedness, and three years for the GAO.

**Herbert Lin** is senior research scholar for cyber policy and security at the Center for International Security and Cooperation and Hank J. Holland Fellow in Cyber Policy and Security at the Hoover Institution, both at Stanford University. His research interests relate broadly to policy-related dimensions of cybersecurity and cyberspace, and he is particularly interested in the use of offensive operations in cyberspace as instruments of national policy and in the security dimensions of information warfare and influence operations on national security. In addition to his positions at Stanford University, he is Chief Scientist, Emeritus for the Computer Science and Telecommunications Board, National Research Council (NRC) of the National Academies, where he served from 1990 through 2014 as study director of major projects on public policy and information technology, and Adjunct Senior Research Scholar and Senior Fellow in Cybersecurity (not in residence) at the Saltzman Institute for War and Peace Studies in the School for International and Public Affairs at Columbia

University; and a member of the Science and Security Board of the Bulletin of Atomic Scientists. In 2016, he served on President Obama's Commission on Enhancing National Cybersecurity. Prior to his NRC service, he was a professional staff member and staff scientist for the House Armed Services Committee (1986–1990), where his portfolio included defense policy and arms control issues. He received his doctorate in physics from MIT.

**Ryan Maness** is an American cybersecurity expert and an assistant professor at the Defense Analysis Department of the Naval Postgraduate School. He is the co-author of Cyber War Versus Cyber Realities: Cyber Conflict in the International System, which won widespread critical acclaim.

**Brian M. Mazanec**, PhD, is an Adjunct Professor at George Mason University and Missouri State University and a Director with the U.S. Government where he leads analysis on intelligence community management, personnel security clearances, artificial intelligence, sensitive activities, space policy/operations, and other emerging warfare issues. Dr. Mazanec earned a PhD in International Security from George Mason University. He also has a master's degree in Defense and Strategic Studies from Missouri State University and a bachelor's degree in Political Science from the University of Richmond. He is the author of *The Evolution of Cyber War* (2015) and co-author of *Understanding Cyber Warfare* (2018) and *Deterring Cyber Warfare* (2014).

**Lt Col Jarred Prier**, USAF, currently serves as director of operations for the 20th Bomb Squadron. He completed a USAF fellowship at the Walsh School of Foreign Service at Georgetown University and earned a master's degree from the School of Advanced Air and Space Studies at Air University, Maxwell Air Force Base, Alabama. Prier also holds a master of science degree in international relations from Troy University, Alabama. This article evolved from his thesis.

**Michael Schmitt** is Professor of Public International Law at Exeter Law School. Additionally, he is the Francis Lieber Distinguished Scholar at the Lieber Institute of the United States Military Academy at West Point; a Strauss Center Distinguished Scholar and Visiting Professor at the University of Texas; and professor emeritus at the U.S. Naval War College. Professor Schmitt is a Senior Fellow at the NATO Cyber Defence Centre of Excellence, Senior Research Associate at Hebrew University, Affiliate at Harvard's Program on International Law and Armed Conflict, and General Editor of both *International Law Studies* and the Lieber Studies series (OUP). Previously he was Professor of International Law at Durham University, Dean of the George C. Marshall European Center for Security Studies in Germany, and General Editor of the *Yearbook of International Humanitarian Law*. He served 20 years in the United States Air Force as a judge advocate specializing in operational and international law. Professor Schmitt has been an invited visiting scholar at Melbourne University, Australian National University, Yale Law School and Emory University, and has delivered the James Crawford Biennial Lecture at Adelaide Law School, Sir Ninian Stephen Lecture at Melbourne University, Hilaire McCoubrey Lecture at Hull University and the Waldemar Solf Lecture at the U.S. Army's Judge Advocate General's Legal Center and School. He serves on many boards of institutions, learned and professional societies, and publications dealing with international law. The author of over 160 scholarly publications, he is a life member of the Council on Foreign Relations and a Fellow of the Royal Society of the Arts. Also a member of the Secretary of State's Advisory Committee on International Law, in 2017 he was awarded the Order of the Cross of Terra Mariana by the President of Estonia for his work in promoting cyber defence and in 2018 was named the Naval War College's Research Scholar of the year.

**Patricia Shamai** is a Senior Lecturer at Portsmouth University. Her research specializes in nuclear, chemical and biological proliferation and security issues. She has published on these subjects and was shortlisted in 2016 for the Taylor & Francis Bernard Brodie prize for Contemporary Security Policy article "Name and Shame: Unravelling the Stigmatisation of Weapons of Mass Destruction." Patricia has presented to a wide range of audiences in the UK and abroad on these subjects. Patricia is a member of a number of groups encouraging dialogue between academia and the policy community. Recently, she has been working to support the development of a UK based Deterrence and Assurance Academic Alliance (DAAA). Patricia has recently completed research on stigma and cyber security and is involved in a research project exploring knowledge exchange between government decisionmakers and academia in the area of deterrence.

**A. Trevor Thrall** is an associate professor at George Mason University's Schar School of Policy and Government where he teaches courses in international security and political communication. He is also a senior fellow for the Cato Institute's Defense and Foreign Policy Department. He is the author most recently of *Fuel to the Fire: How Trump Made America's Broken Foreign Policy Even Worse* (2019). He received his PhD in political science from MIT.

**Brandon Valeriano** (PhD Vanderbilt University) is the Donald Bren Chair of Armed Politics at the Marine Corps University. He also serves as a Senior Fellow in cyber security for the Niskanen Center in Washington DC. Dr. Valeriano has published 94 publications during the duration of his career, including four books with one more forthcoming, 21 peer reviewed articles, 27 other scholarly articles, and 41 public articles for such outlets as *Washington Post*, *Slate*, *Lawfare* and *Foreign Affairs*. His three most recent co-authored books are *Cyber Strategy and Cyber War vs. Cyber Reality* from Oxford University Press (2018; 2015) and *Russian Coercive Diplomacy* from Palgrave (2015). Ongoing research explores creating comprehensive cyber conflict data, Russian foreign policy behavior, biological and psychological examinations of national security threats, and digital repression. Dr. Valeriano recently provided testimony in front of both the United States Senate and the Parliament of the United Kingdom on the dynamics of modern conflict. In his spare professional time, he focuses on engaging policymakers and government officials on the changing character of war.

**Christopher Whyte** is an Assistant Professor in the program on Homeland Security & Emergency Preparedness at the L. Douglas Wilder School of Government & Public Affairs at Virginia Commonwealth University. His research focuses on decision-making in cyber operations, the dynamics of influence operations, the prospective impacts of emerging information technologies (such as blockchain and AI) on international security, and the determinants of decision-making among fringe non-state actors that employ ICT for subversion. His work has appeared or is forthcoming in several publications including *International Studies Quarterly*, *Studies in Conflict & Terrorism*, *International Studies Review*,

*Comparative Strategy, Strategic Studies Quarterly, Institute of Electrical and Electronics Engineers (IEEE)* and *New Media & Society*. He is also co-author of a volume on international security and cyberspace – entitled *Understanding Cyber Warfare: Politics, Policy and Strategy* – with Brian Mazanec. He received his PhD in Political Science from the Schar School of Policy & Government at George Mason University. He also holds a BA in International Relations and Economics from the College of William and Mary and an MA in Political Science from George Mason University.

# ACKNOWLEDGMENTS

Chris would like to thank both of his co-editors, Trevor Thrall and Brian Mazanec, for their support and input on the construction and execution of this project. They have, here and in other ventures, consistently proven to be reliable and insightful collaborators. He would also like to thank his wife, Susan, who is an unending source of optimism and encouragement.

Trevor would like to thank his recent PhD students (including his co-authors and co-editors!) and the past several years' worth of students from his Politics and Media course who have helped him sharpen his thinking about information warfare.

Brian would like to thank his co-editors, Trevor Thrall and Chris Whyte, for their efforts and leadership of this project. Far and away they did the heavy lifting and brought this volume to life. He would also like to thank his co-author, Patricia Shamai, for her insightful perspectives on stigma and information warfare. Finally, Brian would like to thank his family for tolerating inconvenient diversions of time and random musings on information operations and the future of warfare.

# ACRONYMS

| | |
|---|---|
| AI | Artificial intelligence |
| APN | Novosti Press Agency |
| BBG | Broadcasting Board of Governors |
| BDA | Battle damage assessment |
| BLM | Black Lives Matter |
| C2W | counter-command/control warfare |
| CBW | Chemical and biological weapons |
| CCP | Chinese Communist Party |
| CDC | Centers for Disease Control |
| CHBC | China Huayi Broadcasting Corporation |
| CIA | Central Intelligence Agency |
| CIO | Cyber-enabled information operations |
| CNA | Computer network attack |
| CND | Computer network defense |
| CNE | Computer network exploitation |
| CPC | Christian Peace Conference |
| CPSU | Communist Party of the Soviet Union |
| DCCC | Democratic Congressional Campaign Committee |
| DCI | Defense for Children, International |
| DCID | Dyadic Cyber Incident and Campaign Dataset |
| DDOS | Distributed denial of service |
| DHS | Department of Homeland Security |
| DNC | Democratic National Committee |
| DOD | Department of Defense |
| DOJ | Department of Justice |
| DPT | Dual Process Theory |
| EAC | Election Assistance Commission |
| ED | Department of Education |
| EW | Electronic warfare |

| | |
|---|---|
| FBI | Federal Bureau of Investigation |
| FCC | Federal Communications Commission |
| FEC | Federal Election Commission |
| FOR | Feeling of Rightness |
| FSB | Federal'naya sluzhba bezopasnosti Rossiyskoy Federatsii/Federal Security Service of the Russian Federation |
| FTC | Federal Trade Commission |
| GEC | Global Engagement Center (U.S. State Department) |
| GPD | General Political Department |
| GPS | Global positioning system |
| GRU | Glavnoye razvedyvatel'noye upravleniye/Main Intelligence Directorate |
| HAV | Hauptabteilung Aufklarung/Department of Disinformation |
| ICCPR | International Covenant on Economic, Social and Cultural Rights |
| ICJ | International Court of Justice |
| ICT | Information communication technologies |
| IGE | International Group of Experts |
| IIP | International Information Programs (U.S. State Department) |
| IMLS | Institute of Museum and Library Services |
| IO | Information operations |
| IOC | International Olympic Committee |
| IOJ | International Organization of Journalists |
| IRA | Internet Research Agency |
| IRC | Information-related capabilities |
| IS | Islamic State |
| ISIS | Islamic State of Iraq and Syria |
| ISP | Internet service provider |
| ISR | Intelligence, surveillance and reconnaissance |
| IT | Information technology |
| IW | Information warfare |
| IW/IO | Information warfare/information operations |
| IWIO | Information warfare and information operations |
| JTF-CND | Joint Task Force Computer Network Defense |
| KGB | Komitet Gosudarstvennoy Bezopasnosti/Committee for State Security |
| KKK | Ku Klux Klan |
| MAD | Mutually assured destruction |
| MOI | Marketplace of ideas |
| NATO | North Atlantic Treaty Organization |
| NEH | National Endowment for the Humanities |
| NGO | Nongovernmental organization |
| NSA | National Security Agency |
| NSF | National Science Foundation |
| NSPD | National Security Presidential Directive |
| NSSM-59 | National Security Study Memorandum |
| OCO | Offensive cyber operations |
| ODNI | Office of the Director of National Intelligence |
| OODA | Observe, orientate, decide, act |

| | |
|---|---|
| OPM | Office of Personnel Management |
| PA | Bureau of Public Affairs (U.S. State Department) |
| PAC | Political action committee |
| PCI | Press Club of India |
| PLA | People's Liberation Army |
| PLASSF | People's Liberation Army Strategic Support Force |
| PPP | Pakistani Peoples Party |
| PSYOP | Psychological operations |
| RF | Radio frequency |
| RMA | Revolution in military affairs |
| RT | Russia Today |
| SQL | Structured Query Language |
| SVR | Sluzhba vneshney razvedki/Foreign Intelligence Service of the Russian Federation |
| TASS | Soviet news bureau |
| TTP | Tactics, techniques, and procedures |
| UN GGE | United Nations Group of Governmental Experts |
| UN | United Nations |
| USAID | U.S. Agency for International Development |
| USCYBERCOM | U.S. Cyber Command |
| USIA | United States Information Agency |
| USNORTHCOM | U.S. Northern Command |
| USSR | United Soviet Socialist Republics |
| WADA | World Anti-Doping Agency |
| WMD | Weapons of mass destruction |
| WPC | World Peace Council |

# 1

# INTRODUCTION

*Christopher Whyte, A. Trevor Thrall, and Brian M. Mazanec*

If prompted, technologists, military practitioners and scholars alike might all repeat the oft-cited maxim that cyber conflict is something both old and new. It has been three-and-a-half decades since the United States and other Western countries faced their first crises of national security born of the malicious use of networked computer systems. At the same time, cyber-enabled or -augmented threats to national security continue to manifest in new – often unpredicted – forms to this day. The past several decades have seen an evolving panoply of threats to national and international security that might be said to be of a cyber nature. From the broad-scoped theft of intellectual property to the disruptive targeting of commercial ventures, critical infrastructure and military systems, the era in which the Internet has become globally significant has been defined by a consistent broadening and diversification of vectors by which national security might be assailed. Arguably, there are few areas where this is clearer than with the scope and practice of information warfare (IW).

Cyber warfare and information warfare are different beasts. To be sure, the two are consistently held by experts to be adjacent concepts or approaches to contestation. Both concern information; but where the former does so exclusively in its digitized and oper-ationalized form, the latter does so in a much broader sense. With IW, information itself is the weapon. In cyber conflict, information systems are leveraged as terrain over which di-verse effects might be realized. Even given such a distinction, however, the space between cyber and IW has often seemed minimal to the point of negligible. Early Western experi-ences with cyber conflict through the 1980s and into the 1990s led experts like John Arquilla and David Ronfeldt to describe the threat to the West from cyberspace as one of counter-command/control warfare (C2W), where adversaries would infiltrate military and govern-ment networks to interfere with the function of decision-making processes and operational communications. Though not all cyber engagement is information warfare, C2W waged via cyber means certainly is. After all, C2W constitutes a process by which the value and credibility of information is degraded by the interference of digital saboteurs.

Today, the question of how cyber instruments aid and abet – and even constitute – information warfare activities is murkier than it ever has been. In the West, approaches to thinking about and operationalizing cyber-conflict processes have not much focused on or been nested in the context of information warfare beyond C2W. Elsewhere in the world, however, different lessons have been learned and mentalities adopted. Specifically, adversarial, authoritarian governments have consistently linked the potentialities of digital infrastructure to mechanisms of societal manipulation and control – i.e. to the informational substrates of modern society beyond the singular shape of new digital infrastructure. In China, for instance, early encounters with online dissidence through the 1990s inspired the rapid rise of a sophisticated digital censor. Thus, alongside efforts to develop an information economy, Chinese interest in mitigating sources of societal unrest has led to cyber strategy focused on how the information revolution has altered *both* the technical basis of international interactions and the ideational content of politics. By contrast, recent incidents have demonstrated that IW remains an underexplored strategic concept among scholars in the West, particularly in the United States. Cyber operations employed by the Russian Federation as part of a sophisticated campaign to influence political processes in Ukraine, the United Kingdom, the United States, France and nearly twenty other Western countries since 2013 indicate that national strategies for success in cyber conflict *must* adapt to focus on defeating a broader IW threat than has previously been imagined.

This book aims to help scholars, analysts and policymakers think smarter about IW – which we define broadly as "the deliberate manipulation or use of information by one party on an adversary to influence the choices and decisions that the adversary makes in order for military or strategic gain" – within the context of cyber conflict.[1] Twenty years ago, such a book may have focused exclusively on the informational impact of cyber intrusion on military decision-making and operational process. In the 2020s, such a book faces a different threat landscape that is defined by the blended manipulation of digital systems – i.e. by the use of cyber alongside the exploitation of mechanisms of discourse and communication online – by Western adversaries to achieve large-scale disruptive, psychological impacts.

Editors of this kind of volume typically begin their introductions with an attempt to establish the importance of the topic at hand. In this case, however, that is hardly necessary. Even the most casual observer of the world today recognizes the growing importance of IW, whether they recognize it as trolling, hacking, disinformation, propaganda or any other of a number of popular terms. In the United States, unless one has been living under a rock, it has been impossible to escape the extended outcry, investigations and debate over the aforementioned Russian 2016 election interference that has recently elevated the subject of IW from niche issue to center stage in the national security realm.

If we *were* going to try to convince readers that this topic is worth investigating – now more than ever – we might make any of three related arguments. First, thanks to the convergence of digital technologies, IW of the style increasingly encountered over the past decade – i.e. the blended use of cyber intrusions alongside multifaceted interferences in the form and function of digital media platforms – is easier to conduct, especially over great distances, than at any previous point in history, and as a result is more popular than ever. Ubiquitous tools of outreach like Twitter, Reddit and Facebook in the West join the ecosystems of Weibo and RenRen and others elsewhere in the world as growing, self-replicating and natural venues for the conduct of IW.

Second, thanks to the migration of much of the world's population onto the Internet via social media, online news sites, etc., more of the world is targetable with information operations than ever before. The Internet is estimated to be growing at the rate of more than eleven users per second, or 1 million new users each day, with 57% (4.4 billion) of the global population online with a year-over-year growth rate of 9%.[2] That translates to about 4.4 billion people, which is a 9% growth from 2018. In reality, of course, the argument about the "onlining" of the world's population as a reason why IW is more relevant today than it may have been in decades past is conditioned on our first point above. It is not just that so many global citizens are now using the Internet; it is that their digital lives are governed by the systematic algorithmic, commercial and sometimes governmental correlates of new information environments.

Third, there are the subsequent implications of all of the above for impact at scale. Thanks to the rapidly increasing reliance of individuals, businesses and governments on networks and digital tools to do more or less everything, the potential impact of IW is higher than ever. It is also much of the time less direct in its pressure on social and political processes. The attack surface of IW – meaning the sum of vulnerabilities of a system, in this case entire national societies, to exploit – is immense and multilayered. As such, IW effects can manifest extremely broadly and across diverse targets, often without obvious patterns of interconnection. Information warfare is also partly more prospectively impactful and diffuse in its shape due – at least where the two things intersect – to the inherent unpredictability and potential for collateral damage associated with cyber operations. The ever-changing innovations in enterprise architecture and network operations, as well as any IT interdependencies, makes predicting the precise effects of cyber operation – including cyber-enabled IW – very difficult.

While cyber warfare itself is mere decades old, IW is age old. In his *Art of War*, Sun Tzu famously stated that "all warfare is deception," a game of information perception and misperception understanding of which determines victors and losers more assuredly than does simple amassment of military resources. In the modern era, world history is replete with instances of famous military campaigns preceded or augmented by IW in the form of C2W, military deception and psychological warfare. George Washington, at the time a General commanding the Continental forces of the American revolution, began his historic Valley Forge attack with an information operation intended to mislead his counterpart, General Howe. Specifically, Washington deftly manipulated circumstances so that Howe rushed the bulk of his forces back to Philadelphia and away from major elements of America's fledgling military forces.[3] Prior to the D-Day landings, Allied forces deceived German intelligence operations by staging blow-up tanks and other fabricated troop emplacements at alternative invasion launch sites away in southern England. And both Louis XIV and Ivan the Terrible conducted widespread propaganda operations against populations in Central and Eastern Europe ahead of military campaigns in order to ease the path to conquest.

In the age of the Internet, the list of notable IW campaigns sponsored by national governments is not only long, but striking insofar as it lines up so neatly with a list of major foreign policy incidents over the course of the 2010s. Such incidents and operations might notably include:

- Russian efforts to influence Western democratic processes across more than twenty countries (Way and Casey 2019) since 2013. In the best-known example of such efforts – against the United States' presidential election process – it was concluded by the Office of the Director of National Intelligence (ODNI) with high confidence that Russian President Vladimir Putin "ordered an influence campaign in 2016 aimed at the

U.S. presidential election" in order to "undermine public faith in the U.S. democratic process, denigrate Clinton, and harm her electability and potential presidency";[4]
- China's use of fake social media accounts to manipulate political discourse in Taiwan through 2018 and the parallel promulgation of disinformation during the protests in Hong Kong in the summer of 2019;
- The efforts of the Islamic Republic of Iran to utilize Twitter, Facebook and other platforms to shape conversation about American foreign policy between 2016 and 2019;
- Russia's pairing of social media manipulation with other unconventional tactics in its direct prosecution of civil conflict in Ukraine since 2014; and
- The use of social media by the so-called Islamic State of Iraq and Syria (ISIS) to spread information, to recruit and to amplify the effects of terror.

It is these incidents and others in the same vein that we and the authors whose work is represented in this volume seek to explore in greater detail. The 21st century has seen a dramatic increase in incidence of IW, much of the time linked with some use of cyber operations. In many cases, it is that element of the thing – cyber activity – that consumes the focus of pundits and commentators who report on such incidents. We argue that, while understandable, this is a fundamentally misleading and disadvantageous perspective on what is unique about IW in the age of cyber conflict, and so devote the proceeding sections and chapters to rectifying this imbalance.

## Defining information warfare in the age of cyber conflict

Even if readers accept the importance of IW, what this introductory chapter yet needs to make clear is exactly what we mean – and don't mean – when we use the term IW. Our first task in doing so is to define and situate IW with respect to cyber conflict and other things Internet-related. Thanks to the rapid proliferation of new technologies and humanity's love of catchy new labels, keeping track of what various terms mean and how they relate to one another in the digital world is difficult. With respect to national security alone, the Internet has brought us cyberspace, cyberwar, cyber-attacks, cyber crime, cyber espionage, cyberterrorism – the list goes on and on.

Unfortunately, as with all buzzwords, the word "cyber," though certainly sexy, quickly lost whatever meaning it may have once had after it got attached to everything. In the 1980s and 1990s, after the word was introduced first into popular culture in the book *Neuromancer* and then into national security parlance in reports like the Marsh Commission document that followed the Oklahoma City bombings, calling something "cyber" was usually an effort to make something sound both new and more important than it used to be, whether it was or not. In particular, the word "cyber" appealed to anyone trying to promote a threat as new and, because of the implied Internet tie-in, uniquely dynamic. Labelling a problem "cyber" evoked a sense of the vast, the unpredictable, and certainly of negative consequences. What it didn't do, however, was help people understand what whatever the nature of the problem being described really was.

Cyber's overuse as a marketing term well into the new century does not, of course, mean that there is nothing new, different or threatening about developments in cyberspace. After all, there is a reason that terms like "cyberwar," "cyberspace" and "cyber conflict" persist and now define entire fields of study and industry. To a greater extent even than television, the

Internet and its associated technologies have disrupted old patterns of behavior in every realm, laying waste to traditional forms of communication, governance and economics while simultaneously creating new forms. Policymakers must clearly respond to associated threats and researchers must attempt to better understand how conflict and security are continuing to evolve in the digital age.

The rise of the cyber age in the latter years of the 20th century, in fact, led many observers to believe that fundamental concepts of strategy and conflict would have to be rethought, in much the same way that the nuclear revolution affected strategic thinking in the 1950s and 1960s. It was in part this sort of thinking that led the United States, alongside other institutional and cultural pressures, to create U.S. Cyber Command. There, the assumption was that cyber was not only generically new and important, but that cyber principles were somehow new enough and cyber effects ubiquitous enough that a single Department of Defense (DoD) component should be put in charge of dealing with it.

In contrast with such perspective, many scholars decided – after the initial excitement over all things cyber wore off – that most cyber issues were in fact mostly old wine in new bottles, and that their digital nature had done little to alter fundamental dynamics of conflict or espionage.[5] A second wave of research that followed initial alarmist writings was critical of any broad-brush approach to cyber issues. Some argued that attempting to combine electronic warfare, psychological operations, surveillance, etc. under a single cyber umbrella did more harm than good.

Given all the light and heat surrounding cyber conflict, a good place for us to start here is to contrast what most people mean by "cyber conflict" with what we mean in this volume by "information warfare". Though there are probably as many published definitions of cyber conflict as there are of terrorism, a useful working definition might simply be that cyber conflict consists of offensive cyber operations (OCO) comprised of computer network attack (CNA) leveraged towards digital disruption, effects beyond cyberspace and espionage. Such a definition leaves out any question of effects and limits the scope of cyber conflict only to instances where offensive digital instruments are employed for malicious purpose. Operations that center on the use of such instruments, OCO, are the employment of cyber capabilities over Internet infrastructure against a network-connected target for some objective. Such objectives might involve disruption, degradation of adversary capabilities, espionage or an attempt to enable one of the preceding objectives via a secondary action. The capabilities themselves are multiform and multipurpose. Cyber actions taken to enable espionage – most often differentiated as computer network exploitations (CNE) – often go hand-in-hand with intrusions aimed at disruption or degradation. After all, CNE is often conducted to collect information and conduct reconnaissance for a future assault. As such, in a very real sense, cyber techniques are difficult to categorize via some understanding of potential effects. Tom Gjelten described this phenomenon when he said that

> the difference between cyber crime, cyber-espionage and cyber war is a couple of keystrokes. The same technique that gets you in to steal money, patented blueprint information, or chemical formulas is the same technique that a nation-state would use to get in and destroy things.[6]

By contrast, as noted previously, we define IW in broad terms as the *deliberate manipulation or use of information by one party on an adversary to influence the choices and decisions that the adversary makes in order for military or strategic gain.* This definition is quite similar to the one adopted recently by DOD, which calls it "the integrated employment, during military operations, of information-related capabilities in concert with other lines of operation to influence, disrupt, corrupt, or usurp the decision making of adversaries and potential adversaries while protecting our own."[7] Both of these definitions capture the core activity of information operations and avoid the focus on different mechanisms – from electronic warfare to C2W, economic warfare, psychological operations and propaganda – that is so common amongst national security professionals.

Our definition of IW avoids mention of cyber or digital means for a simple reason: the aims of IW and the fundamental mechanisms of influence have not changed throughout history. Propaganda, deception and subversion have been with humanity as long as people have had speech. The brain's ability to process information and the processes by which ideas and information influence attitudes, opinions and decisions, also have not changed much, if at all, over time. That the dominant media through which people receive most of their information about the social and political world has changed over time has not changed the underlying concepts and processes of persuasion, for example.

Following this definition, IW differs from cyber conflict in a fundamental way – IW is platform agnostic, not defined by the physical tools or medium with which it is carried out. Rather, IW is defined by the impact of information manipulating and employed as weaponry against or amongst a target audience. In this sense, IW is a much broader concept than is cyber conflict. In some instances, cyber engagement might entirely constitute the practice of IW. In other cases, cyber conflict is only IW insofar as all warfighting activities distort information environments. As a result, it seems far more reasonable to think of the intersection of cyber instruments and information operations as augmentative – of information warfare that is cyber-*enabled*.

Even understanding this key difference between IW and cyber conflict, the confusion between both is easy to understand because, as Martin Libicki discusses in the following chapter, IW and cyber conflict use many of the same tools and IW has become a central component in a great deal of cyber conflict.

## Information warfare's increasing pervasiveness and importance

With a better grasp of the conceptual differences between IW and cyber conflict, we come back to the fundamental assumption underpinning this volume: that the digital age has transformed the practice and the potential of IW. Grappling with this assumption requires untangling the influence of technology, tactics and the changing times. Is the Russian trolling of recent years just old tactics in a new medium, or does it represent an entirely new mechanism for influence? Does the sheer volume of computer-enabled IW represent increasing danger, or does it merely add to the background noise of modern society? If, as Marshall McLuhan argued, the medium is the message, then is IW via new social message more worrisome than via previous mainstream media? And how much of what we see of new IW threats is really, as the over-cited meme goes, "cyberwar?"

On the technology front, there can be little question that the digital age has changed the IW landscape in dramatic fashion. Perhaps most fundamentally, the Internet and digital technologies have literally reshaped the public sphere, changing how people engage the social and political worlds. A world that contained hierarchical national communication networks and a few major media outlets has become a world with an incredibly dense array of outlets connected to each other in a horizontal network of incredible complexity. Even countries that attempt to restrict their citizens' access to the Internet have witnessed the rise of domestic social networks, bloggers and alternate information sources.

As a result, new media and new tactics of influence are possible today that simply were not available even ten or fifteen years ago. At the same time, the cost to use the Internet for IW has dropped precipitously over roughly the same period. Though governments and non-state actors alike were happily conducting IW through various media (radio, film, television, newspapers, etc.) before the emergence of the Internet, there has clearly been an explosion in the variety and the volume of IW activity in the past decade thanks to the cheap and powerful new computers, software and other tools at the disposal of an increasing number of people. Indeed, by all research accounts, state and non-state IW activities and operations are increasing due to these aforementioned reasons. Studies now report more than two dozen state-sponsored interference efforts focused on cyber actions and manipulation of social media since 2014 (Way and Casey 2019). Twitter, in 2017 and 2018, released data on millions of social media postings and linked content verified as coming from representatives of the Russian Federation and Iran. Recent non-profit reporting has shed light on a booming underground market for fake news and media manipulation across East Asia. And work in this volume by Valeriano, Maness, Jensen and Foote demonstrates that information operations have been increasingly linked to cyber campaigns since 2000.

One important result of the erosion of the major gatekeeper media organizations has been an increase in the permeability of national public spheres to external information campaigns. During the Cold War, for example, thanks to the dominant role of news organizations in providing information to the American public, the Soviet Union had difficulty waging a mass information campaign in the United States. Fast forward to 2016, and the Russians benefitted from the simple fact that news organizations no longer controlled everything Americans learned about the world around them. Thanks to social media, the Russians could use fake accounts to spread misleading or provocative information online to potentially millions of people, information that never would have reached them through traditional news outlets.

The feasibility and lower costs of such campaigns, in turn, has allowed nations with smaller budgets to get in on the action. Iran and North Korea are better equipped and positioned to launch IW against the U.S and other western nations with proliferating cyber-enabled platforms and applications that can be used to reach their populations.

Additionally, the lack of robust international norms for IW (and cyber conflict) can further increase the attractiveness and increased occurrence of IW in the international arena. Norms, which are shared expectations of appropriate behavior, exist at various levels and can apply to different actors.[8] In the international arena, these nonbinding shared expectations can, to some degree, constrain and regulate the behavior of international actors and, in that sense, have a structural impact on the international system as a whole. However, there is a lack of a consensus on what red lines should exist as it pertains to IW, increasing the prospects for miscalculations and escalation.

But while few would argue that the practice of IW has changed dramatically, there is yet less agreement about whether its impact has grown, and why or why not. On the general question of impact, the most popular opinion today is probably that the impact of IW – and thus the threat it represents – is greater today than it was in the pre-digital era. In her postmortem of the 2016 election, for example, the scholar Kathleen Hall Jamieson concludes that "We will never know for sure, but Russia's hacking probably won the election for

Donald Trump." While this may or may not be the case, the fact that serious scholars are even making the argument underscores the importance of IW and the kind of effects it can achieve in a cyber-based world.

And finally, in light of the need for policymakers to craft effective strategies for IW (both offensive and defensive), we must address the question of why modern IW works, or doesn't work. On this issue there remains considerable debate between at least three schools of thought. The first school, advocated by Miguel Gomez in Chapter 10, holds that modern IW is more powerful today thanks to "medium effects," that is, the way that new technologies present information to people. The second school holds that little has changed about the process of winning hearts and minds, but that the sheer volume of IW enabled by new technologies has resulted in new tactics (social bots, e.g.) that have dramatically increased its impact. Finally, the third school takes a more sanguine perspective and holds that the digital public sphere, though certainly a more permissive environment for IW, is also a correspondingly noisier and more fragmented public sphere, thus damping the impact of modern tactics under most circumstances.

We cannot claim to resolve these debates in this volume. But by defining terms, articulating key questions and debates, and assembling useful analytical frameworks and evidence for thinking about IW, we believe that our authors have made a significant contribution.

## Plan of the book

This volume will marshal evidence and discuss the implications of changing digital developments for security institutions and perspectives. In line with the need to explore IW as a strategic concept that informs cyber policy and practice over various arenas of international politics, the book will be split into three sections.

Section I of the book sets the stage for discussion by providing historical context. As we have just noted, the digital age has made new things possible, but it has also simply made old things more visible. To some extent, then, grappling with IW is simply a matter of recognizing old wine in new bottles. At the same time, however, the digital revolution has introduced new dynamics and new capabilities, for which new strategies must be created. As a result, an important first step in any conversation about IW today is to ask: What is new, and what is not so new about IW today?

Chapter 2 kicks off this discussion as Martin Libicki explores the evolution of IW and makes the case that what were once quite disparate elements – including electronic warfare, psychological operations ("psyops"), intelligence, surveillance and reconnaissance (ISR), subversion, and more – are now converging due to technological advances related mostly (though not entirely) to the Internet. Libicki warns, in particular, that the United States – and, by extension, her Western partners – face a future where combating cyber threats must inevitably entail defeating broader IW initiatives.

Aaron Brantly follows in Chapter 3 by tracing the historical evolution of Russian disinformation and related IW efforts, arguing that today's social media trolling and other disinformation campaigns are not new, but in fact bear a striking resemblance to information strategies used in the 19th century. In Chapter 4, Elsa Kania contrasts this offered perspective by providing an assessment of China's approach to political warfare, noting that China also has a long history of viewing information as a strategic tool. A key question for China, she points out, is whether the government can continue to make effective use of the tools for IW abroad without risking their use by domestic opponents.

In Chapter 5, Colin Foote, Ryan C. Maness, Benjamin Jensen, and Brandon Valeriano bring a wealth of data to bear on several fundamental questions about international cyber conflict – who initiates it, for what ends, and with what level of success? Using a novel dataset with data from 2000 to 2016, they argue that there has been a steady rise in cyber-enabled information operations, or efforts to "control the message the masses or a target receives" during a cyber operation. They also find, however, that such efforts remain relatively rare and that most of them take place between nations that are already engaged in rivalry.

Part II of the book examines the modern conduct and effects of IW. Since the dawn of the age of the Internet, overly optimistic optimists have battled overly pessimistic pessimists in debate over the impact of new technologies on society and politics. In part, the lack of progress in such debates stems from a consistent tendency to frame debates in the broadest possible terms (i.e. will the Internet save us or does it spell doom for all?). This volume does not look to settle that debate. Instead, our authors take a range of perspectives on a set of more narrowly framed questions and offer a mix of answers.

In Chapter 6, Andrew Armstrong and Trevor Thrall ask what "Grizzly Steppe," the malicious cyber compromise of Democratic assets and associated influence efforts undertaken by Russia against the United States in 2016, can tell us about the resilience of the American marketplace of ideas. They argue that although 2016 may have represented a perfect storm, Russia's efforts did not in fact reveal any fundamental new weaknesses and that the marketplace of ideas, as imperfect as it certainly is, remains quite resilient to external influence.

In Chapter 7, Jarred Prier assesses the use of social media for influence operations and offers a categorical perspective on how malicious foreign actors hijack popular platforms for discourse and bend engagement to their will. Then, in Chapter 8, Christopher Whyte and Ugochukwu Etudo assess the role of cyber instruments in sophisticated information warfare campaigns that are themselves shaped by certain terms of engagement from afar. Specifically, the authors offer a threat model that describes IW operators' attempts to hijack organic discourse, activate prospective dissidents and then take steps to "capture" and grow audiences. Given the model, cyber operations might be thought of as particularly useful to IW operations in line with three specific functions – the provision of private information that enriches informational manipulations, opportunities for tailored data collection and opportunities to garner increased audience via lateral means.

In Chapter 9, Miguel Gomez acknowledges that most of today's tactics of propaganda and IW remain unchanged in form from the pre-digital age, but argues that cyberspace exploits human psychology more effectively than other communication media. The result, he argues, is that under the right circumstances IW is now a more powerful tool than ever.

In Part III, our volume turns to questions of resilience, policy and law. How should governments organize to cope with cyber threats? What efforts should be made to control the spread and use of IW?

Chris Colligan frames Part III in Chapter 10 by exploring the applicability of civil-military relations theories to rising cyber conflict and IW threats. He argues that the Internet adds a nested paradox to the traditional problematic at the heart of civil–military relations research. Authors in that tradition address the challenge of civilian control vs. military capability – how can democracies empower their militaries to be as effective as possible whilst ensuring that the military does not use that power to overthrow the polity? Given the manner in which most of the physical infrastructure, logical processes and informational apparatus of the global Internet is privately owned, civilian governments must consider private stakeholders when they act to empower the military to respond to cyber and cyber-enabled threats. The problem is that doing so in any substantial fashion risks limiting the economic, social and political freedoms of the civil society that government represents. And yet, government cannot simply accept limitations on empowering the military to act in cyberspace, as doing so would fundamentally mean accepting a situation of compromised sovereignty. Instead, governments must figure out how to coordinate with and, if possible, co-opt relevant private actors so as to maximize both oversight capabilities and coercive power online.

In Chapter 11, Herbert Lin discusses the role of the U.S. government and its various subcomponents in combating threats of cyber-enabled information warfare. In particular, Lin draws attention to prospective challenges the United States faces in addressing threats from IW given both the diverse landscape of potentially relevant stakeholders that must be coordinated and the constitutional backdrop of any policy debate along such lines.

In Chapter 12, Michael Schmitt considers the recourse of nations concerned with cyber-enabled IW under international law. He concludes that unsettled issues and pervasive attribution challenges constitute a "grey area" in international law that must be settled before statutory recourse becomes a viable option for victims of IW in the 21st century. Brian Mazanec and Patricia Shamai then take up this point in Chapter 13 in discussing prospects for the development of international norms to restrain the use of IW. Central to developing such norms, they argue, is stigmatizing the use of IW. Unfortunately, they note, few norms and little stigma constrain cyber and IW today, in part because they lack clear definitions, typically get used in secret, and their effects are less obvious (and less dreaded) than those of other weapons. Moreover, they conclude, at present there seems to be little interest within the United States, China, or Russia for creating constraining norms, making them unlikely to emerge anytime soon.

Christopher Whyte concludes our volume in Chapter 14 by asking the question of "just how deep the rabbit hole goes?" Cyber-enabled IW, he argues, does not bring with it existential challenges for democratic states; rather, it implies significant lateral opportunities for foreign interference, disruption of sociopolitical process and even conflict escalation. That said, there *is* a pathway towards deterrence to be found in the logic of recent work on deterring cyber operations. Information operations are often characterized by many of the same peculiar features that make cyber operations difficult to deter. However, not all interference is undesirable and, unlike with cyber conflict, some singular and far-reaching defensive measures against information manipulation may be possible, under the right circumstances. If opportunities for diffuse IW operation can be neutralized, then states might narrow the playing field of learned adversary behaviors such that conventional deterrence by punishment is possible. However, particularly given the specter of disinformation powered by artificial intelligence, national governments must act quickly to make defensive progress.

With these three sections taken together, we believe this book provides an in-depth empirical and conceptual exploration of evolving perspectives on IW in the context of cyber conflict while also exploring the implications for both the United States and the international community. This focus on cyber-enabled IW is particularly timely as senior U.S. leaders begin to more seriously consider this dynamic. For example, in August 2019, Lt. Gen. Fogarty, commander of U.S. Army Cyber Command, called for renaming his organization "Army IW Command" as an acknowledgement of the relationship between IW and cyber operations.[9] We expect this nexus to garner increasing focus as both IW and cyber conflict grow in pervasiveness and importance to international relations and global security. This primer will help arm the reader for this complex new dynamic.

## Notes

1 *Information Warfare and Information Operations (IW/IO): A Bibliography*, www.hsdl.org/?view&did= 443229.
2 Jeannie Dougherty, ClickZ, May 1, 2019. www.clickz.com/internet-growth-usage-stats-2019-time-online-devices-users/235102/.
3 Bob Drury and Tom Clavin, "Valley Forge: George Washington's Most Dismal Christmas Ever," June 7, 2019. History.com. www.history.com/news/valley-forge-george-washington-worst-christmas.
4 Office of the Director of National Intelligence, "Assessing Russian Activities and Intentions in Recent US Elections," January 6, 2017.
5 Thomas Rid, "Cyber War Will Not Take Place," *Journal of Strategic Studies*, 35:1 (2011): 5–32; Martin Libicki, *Cyberspace in Peace and War* (Naval Institute Press, 2016).
6 Tom Gjelten, "Cyber Insecurity: U.S. Struggles to Confront Threat," *NPR.org*, April 6, 2012. www.npr.org/tem,lates/story/story.php?storyId=125578576.
7 Department of Defense, Joint Publication 3–13.
8 P.J. Katzenstein, A. Wendt, and R.L. Jepperson, "Norms, Identity, and Culture in National Security," *The Culture of National Security: Norms and Identity in World Politics*, edited by P.J. Katzenstein, 34–75 (New York: Columbia University Press, 1996), 54.
9 Shannon Vavra, "Army Cyber Command is trying to become an information warfare force," CyberScoop, www.cyberscoop.com/cyber-command-information-warfare/.

## Reference

Way, L.A., and Casey, A.E. (2019) *How can we know if Russia is a threat to western democracy? Understanding the impact of Russia's second wave of election interference.* Conference paper. Retrieved April 28, 2020 from https://fsi-live.s3.us-west-1.amazonaws.com/s3fs-public/way-casey_russia_stanford_memo_2019-sentb.pdf.

**PART I**

# The nature, history and correlates of information warfare in the age of cyber conflict

# 2

# THE CONVERGENCE OF INFORMATION WARFARE

*Martin C. Libicki*

In the 1990s, information warfare (IW) burst on the scene and subsequently left with a whimper. It came to prominence when a community of military strategists, citing the works of John Boyd, the Tofflers, and Sun Tzu, argued that competition over information would be the high ground of warfare.[1] In this struggle, some would collect ever-more pieces of information intelligence, surveillance, and reconnaissance (ISR) systems. Others would use the tools of electronic warfare (EW), psychological operations (PSYOP), and cyber operations to degrade what the other side knew or could control. Many felt there had to be a unified theory of information warfare out there to integrate these various elements.

Information warfare receded when people realized there was no such unified theory and hence no good reason to organize militaries as if there were.[2] The ISR community kept building and operating systems of greater acuity and range. Electronic warriors went back to mastering their magic in support of air operations, counter-improvised explosive devices, and other combat specialties. Psychological operators continued to refine the arts of persuasion and apply them to an increasing roster of disparate groups. Cyber warriors bounced through the space community before getting their own subunified command within which they could practice their craft. This refusal to coalesce happened for good reason. Although the *ends* of each of these separate activities—to gain the information advantage—were similar, the *means* by which these separate activities were carried out were very different. Expertise in sensors, emitters, content, and code (for ISR, EW, PSYOPs, and cyber operations, respectively) hardly resembled one another. Each called for different equipment and training; there was scant reason for them to be organized together.

However, given today's circumstances, in contrast to those that existed when information warfare was first mooted, the various elements of IW should now increasingly be considered elements of a larger whole rather than separate specialties that individually support kinetic military operations. This claim is supported by three emerging circumstances. First, the various elements can use many of the same techniques, starting with the subversion of computers, systems, and networks, to allow them to work. Second, as a partial result of the first circumstance, the strategic aspects of these elements are converging. This makes it more likely that in circumstances where one element of IW can be used, other elements can also be used. Hence, they can be used together. Third, as a partial result of the second circumstance, countries—notably Russia, but, to a lesser extent, North Korea, Iran, and China—are starting to combine IW elements, with each element used as part of a broader whole.

Taken together, these emerging circumstances create challenging implications for the future of US information warfare. Simply put: if information technology trends continue and, more importantly, if other countries begin to exploit these trends, then as a general rule, the US focus on defeating a cyber war threat will have to evolve into a focus on defeating a broader IW threat. Perceptions of cyber war will likely need rethinking. One could debate plausibility of a determined cyber attack campaign unaccompanied by physical violence and destruction. It is becoming far less plausible to imagine a cyber attack campaign unaccompanied by other elements of information warfare. Preparations to retain resilience and accelerate recovery after a cyber attack campaign would also do well to address the complications that could arise if other IW elements were used in conjunction with such cyber attacks.

## Computer subversion as information warfare

Subversion can be the starting point for multiple IW elements. The point of subversion is to usurp the normal state in which systems do only what their owners want. Instead, they do things hackers want. In some cases, hackers can get systems to react to inputs in unexpected ways, and in other cases such systems can execute an arbitrary set of commands provided by hackers.

Once hackers compromise a system they have many options. These days the most common is to collect information. When national intelligence agencies do this, it is called cyber espionage, a subset of intelligence collection. Whereas human intelligence takes place one person at a time, cyber espionage can take place millions of records at a time. A prime example is the Office of Personnel Management (OPM) hack—22 million personnel records were stolen. It showed how one side's voluminous data keeping can be another side's intelligence mother lode. It can be a lot easier to find those who collect information and steal from them than it is to collect the information afresh. The advantage of piggybacking can be applied to the many ways that individual data are generated, with the theft of information already ordered in databases (as with OPM) as the clearest case of leveraging the other side's work. Indeed, imagine what could be done with the Chinese database of political "creditworthiness."[3] But there are other targets, notably the large compilations created via web transactions and surveillance systems.[4] For overhead images, consider the burgeoning market for gyrocopters or other types of unmanned aerial vehicles; for ground imagery, there are cell phone snaps—which could wind up in an intelligence database by being donated, posted, offered, aggregated, and handed over—or simply stolen. If the Internet of Things evolves as it appears to be doing, homes could leak information from sources almost too many to keep track of.[5] Again, why collect what can be stolen?

In many cases, the purpose of stealing all the haystacks is to find the few needles of particular interest. But one can also make hay with such information. Once collected, data-mining techniques permit analyses and exquisite tailoring of such information.[6] The ability to build increasingly realistic simulations of individuals, indeed perhaps of most of a population, could arise from integrating data streams with enormous cloud-based storage, powerful processing, and a dash of artificial intelligence. Such simulations may be used to test every individual's reaction to events (both virtual and real), advertising, political campaigns, and psychological operations, and even guess what might go viral through person-to-person interactions.

One way to use information on individuals gathered through a combination of ISR (albeit often third-party ISR) and cyber operations is through exquisite psychological operations, messages tailored to one person at a time. The trend to "micro-appeals" is already obvious in US domestic political campaigns and advertising.[7] As long as psychological operators grasp the essentials of the cultures of those they wish to influence, there is every reason to believe that a data-mining campaign to characterize individuals precisely can help in crafting the message most likely to resonate with them. The messages do not have to convince (e.g., buy this, believe that); in a conflict context, their point may be to induce fear or at least anxiety and thus paralyze resistance one person at a time; tailoring messages to each person erodes the solidarity enjoyed by groups all facing the same threat. Doxing individuals, which is posting the results of hacking to embarrass or blacken their reputation through randomly found (as in the Ashley-Madison hack) or deliberately selected (as in the Democratic National Committee hack) information, is increasingly common.

Cyber operations can enhance PSYOPs in other ways. Devices and websites both can be infected to introduce users to propaganda that shows up in unexpected places or carries unexpected credentials.[8] Compromising systems can also aid psychological operations by directing people to sites they had not intended to go or to sites that falsely purport to be where they had intended to go. Similar techniques can and are being used to enhance the credibility and page rankings of favored sites. Spam-bots can be engineered to dominate online debates.[9] Troves of material stolen from political opponents can be seasoned with concocted documents with appropriate levels of verisimilitude.[10] Overall, the shift from more-curated mass media to less-curated Internet websites and uncurated social media permits outright falsehoods to spread much faster and farther.

Other harvests from compromised systems—notably the other side's—are the classic ones of disruption, corruption, and, possibly, destruction. Websites can be knocked offline when computers (and, one day, kitchen appliances?) of web users are converted into bots and herded into bot-nets. To date, the damage from all cyber attacks combined (as distinct from cyber espionage) has been modest, but it is an open question whether the threat will stay contained. Can increasingly sophisticated defenders withstand assaults from increasingly sophisticated attackers? How much will growing digitization and networking increase a country's attack surface?

The Internet of Things is another new playground for hackers, which could harm not only such things but also whatever they could come into contact with. To date, it has been difficult for hackers to hurt people and break things, in large part because the major industrial facilities, having seen others attacked through cyberspace, are taking information security more seriously. But most of the Internet of Things will be owned by people unable or unwilling to pay requisite attention to security; many of those who build these networked things seem to have ignored the security lessons that information system makers have painfully learned. Many of the things that are becoming networked (notably, cars and drones) are capable of causing serious harm to their owners and worse, third parties, if their controls are usurped. Even if wholesale chaos is unlikely, there will be new ways of heightening anxiety or targeting individuals from afar.[11]

To a partial extent, electronic warfare can also be carried out by controlling devices that emit radio-frequency (RF) energy. New forms of RF signals pervade homes and cities: Bluetooth, Wi-Fi, 5G, keyless entry systems, and GPS to name a few. The coming Internet of Things is essentially an Internet of RF-connected items. If software-defined radios (those capable of broadcasting or receiving signals over an arbitrarily selected frequency) become ubiquitous, they could be hijacked to jam or spoof targets hitherto inaccessible using traditional EW boxes.[12]

In sum, systems compromise is becoming a core technique across all IW elements. It remains the key element of cyber attack. Cyber espionage itself is a growing element in ISR. Subverting sensors or the data repository allows harvesting of surveillance collected by others. Similar subversion can allow data collection at such high resolution as to permit individuals to be simulated; this knowledge permits PSYOPs to be optimized; compromising media creates new conduits for persuasion or the manipulation of fear. Hijacking the Internet of Things can create new ways to create physical harm. Finally, some forms of EW can be carried out by subverting RF-transmitting devices. Opportunities abound.

## IW in the niche of cyber war

The second basis for arguing that the various elements of information warfare should be considered parts of a greater whole results from four propositions. First, cyberspace operations differ in key respects from kinetic operations. Second, other elements of IW differ from kinetic operations in similar ways. Consequently, third, these various elements can all be used for operations where these characteristics are important or even essential (or where opposing characteristics make using kinetic operations impractical or unwise). And, fourth, for such operations, the use of IW elements should therefore be considered together rather than separately. Consider that the first two positive propositions now ground the last two propositions (what is versus what could or should be).

Several broad characteristics differentiate cyber from kinetic operations: the variance of their effects, their nonlethality, their ambiguity, and the persistence of the war-fighting community. Take each in turn.

Higher degrees of variance are more likely to characterize cyber attacks than kinetic attacks. Most cyber attacks cause temporary or at least reversible effects whose extent depends on the technical details of the target systems (many of which change in ways attackers cannot expect), the services such systems provide (often opaque to attackers), how such services are used (also opaque), and how quickly the attacked system can be restored (often unclear even to defenders, much less attackers). Outcomes can easily vary from expectations in such an environment. Even estimating battle damage assessment (BDA), not to mention collateral damage, can be unreliable particularly if defenders isolate an attacked system from the rest of the world to restore it. Because systems have to be penetrated before they are attacked, the timing of success in going after hard targets is often unpredictable (with Stuxnet, for instance, effects had to await some unknown person inserting a USB device into a computer inside the closed network).

Insofar as other IW operations start with compromising systems, they consequently would wait until those systems are sufficiently compromised; thus these IW operations can also start with large degrees of unpredictability. But even after this unpredictability is taken into account, the IW effects are, to a further extent, unpredictable. PSYOPs, for instance, entail persuasion in that one hears echoes of retail tycoon John Wanamaker: "Half the money I spend on advertising is wasted; the trouble is I don't know which half." Unpredictability is higher if leveraging social media rather than mass media, because the former depends on the willingness of those receiving the message to pass it on and thus have it go viral. Although

EW and ISR have features that allow predictability, their ultimate effectiveness often depends on the tricks the other side has or lacks: do war fighters know what frequency-protection measures are being used; will spoofing be successful or will the other side see through some tricks; how well does the other side camouflage itself, hide itself, or use denial and deception techniques? Even if one side sees what it sees (or thinks it sees) it can only guess at what it cannot see.

One obviously different effect is the general nonlethality of information operations vis-à-vis kinetic operations. Rarely do cyber attacks in particular or other IW techniques in general create casualties. After nearly a quarter-century of alarm over the lethality of cyber attacks, no one has yet been hurt in a cyber attack, and there are only two known occasions of serious physical destruction (Stuxnet and a blast furnace in Germany).[13] EW is even more benign (electronics can be fried, but this generally requires either close range or nuclear effects). This has several implications. IW can rarely disarm (even if it can temporarily disable equipment or at least discourage its use) or make others realistically fear for their lives. It can be used in circumstances where causing casualties may yield condemnation or beget an overreaction.

Ambiguity entails doubt over who is doing what and for what purpose. Cyberspace operations unfold in a dense fog of ambiguity (even as certain fogs that have bedeviled kinetic operations are lifting). In the wake of a cyber attack, although context may provide a strong clue of who did what, attribution can be a problem if and when attackers take pains to mask their involvement. Adding ambiguity to IW means that the global reach of the Internet widens the number of potential attackers because small states and nonstate actors can threaten large ones. It does not take a large state apparatus to hack computers or devices, exploit borrowed ISR, or generate propaganda—although it does take clever people to do this well. Countries can use IW elements to harass countries they cannot hope to touch in traditional kinetic ways—as long as they aim for societal effects rather than those requiring kinetic follow-up (e.g., that would exploit the other side's confusion when its information turns to mush).

In some cases even the effects may be less than obvious (e.g., a subtle intermittent corruption of data), particularly if the attack is halted midway. Discovering a penetration into a system does not indicate whether its purpose was to spy on or to interfere with a system and, if the latter, when the system would go awry—if the penetration is discovered, which often takes months or years if it takes place at all. Thus, intentions cannot always be inferred from actions, and indications and warnings have yet to be terribly useful;[14] there are, for example, few if any steps that must precede a cyber attack by x hours and whose discovery can be used to predict when a cyber attack is coming. Inasmuch as cyber attack techniques are unlikely to work if their particulars are exposed, these particulars are deep secrets. No one really knows what others can do in cyberspace. Few show what they themselves can do; past attacks may be demonstrative but not necessarily repeatable—hence they are better indicators of what was rather than what will be.

Other IW elements would be colored by such ambiguity if they worked by first subverting systems. To the extent that the source of such subversion was not obvious, then neither would be the identification of what element of information warfare (e.g., surveillance, messaging, manipulating RF emissions) was the purpose. Similarly, to the extent that the purpose of such subversion was not obvious, it complicates drawing inferences once such subversion is discovered.

But again, many information warfare elements would have ambiguous features even if carried out through non-cyber means. It can be hard to locate the source of a transmitter that moves and broadcasts infrequently. People often do not know they are under surveillance or even if they do, from where and using what means. And even if these are known, the use to which such information is put can be little better than a guess. The origins of a meme or a rumor circulating within social media can be easily obscured. The ultimate target of surveillance, emission, or disinformation may not be the proximate one.

Finally, information warriors—notably cyber warriors—may persist longer than their kinetic counterparts because they work as small units or even individuals without expensive, bulky, or otherwise telltale equipment. Information warriors rarely need be in harm's way nor need their operations have any obvious signature that distinguishes them from civilians. Their ability to generate instant worldwide effects from anywhere gives them plenty of places to hide in relative safety. Thus it is hard to put them out of commission by attacks (and certainly not by cyber attacks). Because hacking looks like typing it can escape casual oversight. Because their efforts need little specialized equipment, hackers may even survive their country's demise. This latter characteristic does not extend to forms of IW that use expensive organic assets like aircraft-mounted jamming pods, surveillance satellites, or mass media outlets. But a force that can no longer count on such assets may be able to leverage subverted systems to make up some of what these assets supplied. Such a force can persist in fighting even if dispersed.

## Implications of variance, non-lethality, ambiguity, and persistence

These characteristics of information war shape how countries might want to use (and not use) information warfare. Take each characteristic in turn.

*Variance* complicates the use of IW elements to support modern kinetic combat or various forms of irregular warfare, all of which represent a highly complex and synchronized affair dependent on the careful integration of effects. On such battlefields, IW is used almost entirely in support of kinetic operations. Although militaries favor efforts with high degrees of effectiveness, many, perhaps most, military operations are predicated on the finite and bounded success of discrete, well-defined support efforts (e.g., radars are jammed to permit aircraft to reach a target and return home safely). While exceeding objectives is nice, it is usually not worth the risk of *not* meeting objectives. So although IW elements may be included in operational plans, they are more likely to be nice-to-have but not need-to-have tools—apart from traditional and more predictable (i.e., measurable and discrete) aspects of EW or ISR. Conversely, unpredictability matters less if IW is the main event where the point is to achieve an agglomeration of effects so that overachievement in one endeavor can compensate for underachievement in another, particularly if done to support strategic narratives that shape decisions or actions. There is a big difference between (1) needing A to work in order that B would work and (2) knowing that if A and B both work they reinforce the message that each other is sending. Arguably, cumulative rather than coordinated effects are what better characterize the use of IW against societies in comparison to its use against militaries.

In any event, civilian targets are softer targets for IW than are their military counterparts. Civilian systems are less well protected and are more often exposed to outside networks. Civilians rarely practice operational security. Security is still an afterthought for the Internet of Things. Civilian RF signals rarely use antijamming or antispoofing techniques. Civilians themselves are often softer targets than war fighters, who are trained to be inured to most IW. So IW is likely to have a different target than kinetic warfare.

Nonlethality and ambiguity, for their part, may be exploited to modulate the risk of reprisals—notably, violent reprisals—for having carried out information operations. Information warriors may well doubt that target countries will mount a kinetic response, which can break things and kill people, to an IW campaign that does neither. Indeed, it is unclear whether countries would mount a kinetic response to an information warfare campaign that happens to wreak some damage and hurts a few people. Similarly, there is little precedent for responding to propaganda with force.

If the target cannot be sure who is causing its suffering it may have to forego both disarming and deterring the attacker. Even if the target later concludes that it knows who is doing what or at least cannot afford to remain passive (doubts notwithstanding), it may not be able to do so easily. Having accepted continued harassment as the new normal puts the onus on the defender to risk escalation to end harassment; it has to shift from deterrence to the much harder art of compulsion.

Nevertheless, an IW campaign that wants to avoid triggering a violent reaction from the target requires knowing where the latter's thresholds lie,[15] and it may have little better than a guess to work with. The true threshold will depend on personalities, politics, and foreign pressure. Injury may be, alternatively, likened to a boiling frog (leading to underreaction) or the straw that broke the camel's back (leading to an unexpected reaction). An attack that passes notice may be only subtly different from one that excites retaliation. The target state may deem something put at risk to be more sensitive than outsiders realize even as it assumes that its own sensitivities are known and understood by others. The threshold may also vary by information war element. Cyber war can levy large costs (it may take $1 billion to replace South Korea's national identification system[16]) without anything actually breaking. Broad foreign surveillance can be scary without much cost in life and property, but it can also be shrugged off. EW, however, can interfere with transportation operations by making them unsafe, but if there is damage, fingers may point to those who choose to operate in the face of risks.[17]

These days, countries appear to be mindful that there are limits. Although Russia took territory, tried to interfere with Ukrainian elections, and disrupted Ukraine's parliamentary sites with a distributed denial of service (DDOS) attack, it has refrained from all-out cyber attack or EW against civilian targets and is not trying to foment disorder in core Ukrainian areas, which may now be out of reach for Russia. It probably does not want Ukraine to feel under existential threat unless and until Ukraine reacts forcefully to Russian incursions.

Persistence means that IW can be hard to disable even as kinetic forces are being targeted for destruction. Much as ambiguity makes it hard to figure out if information warfare has started, persistence means that the end itself may not be declared unless someone concedes and perhaps not even then—persistence can be a two-edged sword for a country that turns such tools on but cannot credibly promise to turn them off. President Kennedy's phrase "a long twilight struggle" may become apropos when discussing information warfare.[18] Indeed, were the Cold War to have taken place in the modern era, its day-to-day activities may well have included many such elements.

In many ways, we have already seen this kind of war before: terrorism combines high levels of variance (many would-be terrorist attempts fail or are thwarted), modest levels of

## Co-mingling IW elements

The third reason to take the convergence of IW seriously is because the Russians and others are doing so in theory and in practice (i.e., Ukraine). Russia's "hybrid warfare" campaign features an admixture of specialized units (*speznats* and artillery), logistical support of local insurgents—and copious amounts of IW. The latter has included DDOS attacks on Ukrainian sites, an attack on Ukraine's power grid, near-successful attempts to corrupt Ukrainian election reporting, heavy electronic warfare in combat areas, the severing of electronic links between Ukraine and Crimea, the physical destruction of communications links, and heavy amounts of propaganda directed at Russian-speaking Ukrainians among others.[19] Russian cyber espionage against Western targets appears to have grown; they are certainly being detected more often. Examples include NATO and the unclassified e-mail systems of the White House, the US State Department, the Joint Chiefs of Staff, the Democratic National Committee, and the German Parliament.

Russian theory underlies its practice. As security specialist Keir Giles has observed, "the Russian definition [is] all-encompassing, and not limited to wartime … [and] much broader than simply sowing lies and denial, for instance maintaining that Russian troops and equipment are not where they plainly are. Instead, Russian state and non-state actors have exploited history, culture, language, nationalism, and more to carry out cyber-enhanced disinformation campaigns with much wider objectives."[20] Others note that, "Cyberspace is a primary theater of Russia's asymmetrical activity … because … [it] offers a way to easily combine fighting arenas, including espionage, information operations, and conventional combat, and to do so behind a curtain of plausible deniability."[21] Russian military doctrine argues,

> military dangers and threats have gradually shifted into the information space and internal sphere of the Russian Federation … [requiring military forces to] create conditions, that will reduce the risks that information and communication technologies will be used [by others] to achieve military-political goals.[22]

Russia expert Dmitry Adamsky argues,

> It is difficult to overemphasize the role that Russian official doctrine attributes to … informational struggle in modern conflicts … [which] comprises both technological and psychological components designed to manipulate the adversary's picture of reality, misinform it, and … forces the adversary to act according to a false picture of reality in a predictable way…. Moral-psychological suppression and manipulation of social consciousness aim to make the population cease resistance, even supporting the attacker, due to … disillusionment and discontent."[23]

Similar beliefs may motivate North Korea, which has carried out cyber attacks against South Korea, notably its banks, media companies, and national identification system. It also engages

The convergence of information warfare **23**

in intermittent electronic warfare (GPS jamming directed at passing aircraft[24]) and directs propaganda south (which the South Korean government takes seriously enough to censor). China for its part has pressed on with a more tactical approach to IW; in late 2015 it merged its integrated network electronic warfare activities with its space and ISR activities.

Russians and to a lesser extent others believe that IW should be approached holistically for two reasons. First, IW should not be dismissed out of hand—and Russia seems satisfied that it worked in Ukraine. Second, to the extent that the United States has to contend with Russian operations, it helps to grasp how IW elements fit together.

## The future of US information warfare

Given the trends and convergence of information warfare, how might the United States exploit these trends? On the face of it, no country is better positioned to carry out information war. US skills at cyber war have no equal. US institutions lead the world in the commercialized arts of persuasion, and the collection and analysis of personal information for commercial and political purposes have proceeded farther in the United States than anywhere else. No country is more advanced in digitizing and networking things. US expertise in systems integration is unchallenged. But figuring out how to effectively harass another country's citizens one at a time does not seem like an urgent or important, much less permissible, US national security problem to solve.

Nevertheless, because other countries are interested in figuring out how to combine these elements of information warfare into a unified whole, the United States ought to understand how to do so itself. First, there may be useful techniques learned even if the larger idea is unacceptable. Second, even though the prospect of operating a harassment campaign based on IW is unpalatable, one cannot rule out occasions in which the only way to stop others from doing so (short of armed conflict) may be a credible offensive capability. Third, just as the Defense Advanced Research Projects Agency was established shortly after *Sputnik* launched for the purposes of preventing surprise—and then went ahead to develop technology that surprised others—dabbling in the arts of IW could help prevent external developments from surprising the United States.

If the United States were to embed cyber operations within a broader context of IW, then the mission and organization of US Cyber Command would have to change. Today it boggles the mind to ask an organization (deservedly) wrapped in great secrecy to take the lead for influence operations, which are ineluctably public. But in time, the choice to overlook the psychological effects of cyber operations or the potential synergy between psychological operations and cyber operations would make just as little sense.[25] Serious thought may be needed on how to build an information warfare authority, whether housed under one organization or achieved through intense coordination among the various communities: cyber warriors, cyber intelligence collectors, electronic warriors, psychological operators, and, in some cases, special operators.

Perceptions of cyber war might also need rethinking. One could debate the plausibility of a determined cyber attack campaign unaccompanied by violence. However, it is harder to imagine a cyber attack campaign unaccompanied by other elements of information warfare, in large part because almost all situations where cyber attacks are useful are also those which offer no good reason not to use other elements of IW. For instance, if another country is trying to exhaust US will by conducting cyber attacks on information systems that underlie

US commerce, they would not necessarily try to blow up trucks. Rather, cyber attacks that compromise trucks, to reduce confidence in their safe operation, are more plausible, if achievable. It is also quite likely that in a systematic campaign, attackers would try to jam GPS or override satellite uplinks, using cyber espionage to create the impression that they are watching Americans and are prepared to dox particular individuals, or letting a thousand trolls bloom to create a news environment that would pit Americans against each other. The latter activities have attributes of nonlethality, unpredictability, ambiguity, and persistence that allow them to fit the strategic niche occupied by cyber attacks. Preparations to retain resilience and accelerate recovery after a cyber attack campaign would also do well to address the complications that could arise if other elements of IW were used in conjunction with cyber attacks.

Against such a campaign how should countries respond? The terms war and warfare suggest a military response, and one cannot completely rule out circumstances in which the only way to reduce suffering from an IW campaign to within reasonable levels is to threaten force. But many characteristics of IW—nonlethality, ambiguity, and persistence—suggest using the same mindset, tools, and rules used against crime. Much crime fighting involves changing the environment. The moral environment affects an individual's propensity to join a fight; it includes ethical norms and the social influences that arise when communities alternatively applaud, excuse, or shun criminals. The physical environment can also be changed. Cyber attacks can be countered by cybersecurity standards, air-gapping (e.g., isolating controls from the grid), and information sharing (making it as mandatory as accident investigations). EW threats may be mitigated through spectrum and transmission-device controls (which make it easier to identify attacking devices). ISR exploitation may be frustrated by policies such as restricting unmanned aerial vehicles, surveillance cameras, data collection, and data retention (so that there is less data to steal). Ultimately, it has been the evolution of the information economy that has provided the means by which hostile others can run a pervasive harassment campaign. There is little evidence that others have been willing to invest enough time and trouble to make a comprehensive campaign work and no evidence yet that such a campaign could work, in the sense of shifting the balance of power among various actors. But it would not hurt to ask to what extent the collection and connection of personal information in modern economies provides more raw material than it should for someone else's hostile IW campaign.

Even if defeating information warfare through conventional war is unrealistic, the prospect of managing it down to tolerable levels need not be. Treating IW like crime rather than state acts shows a refusal to accept it as "acceptable" behavior but does not signal a commitment to violence as an appropriate response. Such a strategy requires a narrative that calls on the public for both less and more: less in that conscious mobilization is deliberately eschewed and more in that managing such a conflict may require fundamental and lasting changes in how people go about their daily lives.

## Notes

1 John Boyd's briefing "Winning and Losing" exists only in summary form. For more on his work, see, for instance, Frans Osinga, *Science, Strategy and War: The Strategic Theory of John Boyd* (London: Routledge, 2006); Alvin and Heidi Toffler, *War and Anti-War, Survival at the Dawn of the 21st Century* (New York: Little, Brown & Co., 1993); Sun Tzu, *The Art of War*, ancient.

2 The author's contribution to this process is *What Is Information Warfare?* (Washington, DC: National Defense University Press), 1995.

3 Celia Hatton, "China 'social credit': Beijing sets up huge system," BBC, 26 October 2015, www.bbc.com/news/world-asia-china-34592186. FireEye's William Glass observed that "a centralized system would be both vulnerable and immensely attractive to hackers. 'There is a big market for this stuff, and as soon as this system sets up, there is great incentive for cybercriminals and even state-backed actors to go in, whether to steal information or even to alter it.'" Simon Denyer, "China's Plan to Organize Its Society Relies on 'Big Data' to Rate Everyone," *Washington Post*, 22 October 2016, www.washingtonpost.com/world/asia_pacific/chinas-plan-to-organize-its-whole-society-around-big-data-a-rating-for-everyone/2016/10/20/1cd0dd9c-9516-11e6-ae9d-0030ac1899cd_story.html.

4 Ludwig Siegele, "The Signal and the Noise," *Economist*, 26 March 2016, 10, www.economist.com/news/special-report/21695198-ever-easier-communications-and-ever-growing-data-mountains-are-transforming-politics. "Facebook and Google … know much more about people than any official agency does and hold all this information in one virtual place. It may not be in their commercial interest to use that knowledge to influence political outcomes, as some people fear, but they certainly have the wherewithal."

5 Law Enforcement Cyber Center, "Internet of Things Infographic," accessed 8 December 2016, www.iacpcybercenter.org/officers/iot/.

6 Adm Michael Rogers, National Security Agency director, has opined that the Office of Personnel Management attack is a signal of what may become an emerging trend in network attacks by other nation states: because of the proliferation of tools that can readily perform detailed analytics on large data sets, adversaries will increasingly seek to purloin entire haystacks of data all at once and search for the needles later. See Jared Serbu, "Cyber Command Chief Frustrated by Lack of Industry Participation," Federal News Radio, 8 July 2015, http://federalnewsradio.com/cybersecurity/2015/07/cyber-command-chief-frustrated-lack-industry-participation-u-s-tries-build-early-warning-system-cyber-attacks.

7 "Ted Cruz Took a Position on Iowa Firework Sales to Try and Sway 60 Voters," *The Week*, 2 February 2016, http://theweek.com/speedreads/603059/ted-cruz-took-position-iowa-firework-sales-try-sway-60-voters.

8 Apparently, so can airport public address systems. See "The Alleged Chinese Hacking at Vietnam's Airports Shows that the South China Sea Battle Isn't Just in the Water," *Huffington Post*, 6 August 2016, www.huffingtonpost.com/helen_clark/china-hack-vietnam-south-china-sea_b_11357330.html.

9 Siegele, "The Signal and the Noise," 9. "During the Maidan protests in Ukraine in 2013–2014, Russian 'spam bots' had a much larger presence in Ukraine's Twittersphere than tweets by the Russian political opposition."

10 Cory Bennett, "Democrats' New Warning: Leaks Could Include Russian Lies," 17 August 2016, www.politico.com/story/2016/08/democrats-cyberhack-russia-lies-227080.

11 What may be highly implausible *in toto* is not necessarily implausible considered one incident at a time; see, for instance, Reeves Wiedeman, "The Big Hack," *New York Magazine*, 19 June 2016, http://nymag.com/daily/intelligencer/2016/06/the-hack-that-could-take-down-nyc.html.

12 Inasmuch as traffic lights are normally accessible only through wired connections and Bluetooth devices, they might seem immune to mass remote hacking—until the population of infected Bluetooth devices crosses some threshold to where nearly every control box is within range of some such device.

13 Several major cyber attacks, most notably at Saudi Aramco and Sony, have rendered computers inoperable, but that was as a result of hard-to-reverse changes in software, not damaged hardware.

14 The FBI supposedly warned the Democratic National Committee (DNC) that their systems could be hacked but not with enough specificity to do anything much about it; see Even Perez, "Sources: US Officials Warned DNC of Hack Months before the Party Acted," CNN, 26 July 2016, www.cnn.com/2016/07/25/politics/democratic-convention-dnc-emails-russia/.

15 The concept of "grey zone" is one specifically below the threshold of conventional conflict; see, for instance, Michael J. Mazarr, *Mastering the Gray Zone: Understanding a Changing Era of Conflict* (Carlisle, PA: US Army War College Strategic Studies Institute, 2 December 2015), http://strategicstudiesinstitute.army.mil/pubs/display.cfm?pubID=1303.

16 Iain Thomson, "South Korea Faces $1bn Bill after Hackers Raid National ID Database," *The Register,* 14 October 2014, www.theregister.co.uk/2014/10/14/south_korea_national_identity_system_hacked/.

17 Mary-Ann Russon, "Russia Blamed for Crashing Swedish Air Traffic Control to Test Electronic Warfare Capabilities," *International Business Times,* 14 April 2016, www.ibtimes.co.uk/russia-blamed-bringing-down-swedish-air-traffic-control-test-electronic-warfare-capabilities-1554895.

18 Pres. John F. Kennedy, "Inaugural Address," 20 January 1961, www.presidency.ucsb.edu/ws/?pid=8032.

19 "Russia jammed and intercepted Kiev signals and communications, hampering the other side's operations, and effectively detaching the peninsula from Ukraine's information space," quoted from Pasi Eronen, "Russian Hybrid Warfare: How to Confront a New Challenge to the West" (Washington, DC: Foundation for Defense of Democracies, June 2016), 6, 8, www.defenddemocracy.org/content/uploads/documents/Russian_Hybrid_Warfare.pdf.

20 Kier Giles, *The Next Phase of Russian Information Warfare*, NATO Strategic Communications Centre of Excellence, 20 May 2016, 2, www.stratcomcoe.org/next-phase-russian-information-warfare-keir-giles.

21 Margaret Coker and Paul Sonne, "Ukraine: Cyber war's Hottest Front," *Wall Street Journal,* 10 November 2015, www.wsj.com/articles/ukraine-cyber wars-hottestfront-1447121671.

22 *Voyennaya Doctrina Rossiiskoy Federatsii* (2014), rg.ru/2014/12/30/doktrina-dok.html (citation courtesy of Olesya Tkacheva).

23 Dmitry Adamsky, "Cross-Domain Coercion: the Current Russian Art of Strategy," *Proliferation Papers*, no. 54 (November 2015), 26–27, www.ifri.org/sites/default/files/atoms/files/pp54adamsky.pdf.

24 Choe Sanghun, "North Korea Tried Jamming GPS Signals across Border, South Korea Says," *New York Times,* 1 April 2016, www.nytimes.com/2016/04/02/world/asia/north-korea-jams-gps-signals.html. Although that particular attempt disrupted little, earlier attempts in 2012 had forced incoming aircraft to use alternative navigation methods.

25 The broad psychological ramifications of cyber operations, which this paragraph talks about, should be distinguished from the use of psychology to assist cyber operations by, for instance, enhancing social engineering or understanding how mucking with an adversary's C2 systems will change how its forces are commanded.

# 3

# A BRIEF HISTORY OF FAKE

## Surveying Russian disinformation from the Russian Empire through the Cold War and to the present

*Aaron F. Brantly*

The use of information in warfare is nothing new. While the volume and penetration of information into the handheld devices we carry every day brings new relevance and impact, the practice itself dates back to before Sun Tzu in his writings that "all warfare is based on deception" in 450 BC and most assuredly predates him as well.[1] For as long as states or principalities have engaged one another they have sought to influence each other and those around them. This influence occurs both through the overt use of diplomacy and propaganda, but also through the use of covert means of information manipulation. The history of information manipulation to alter the perceptions and policies of others remains a consistent feature in international politics in the present era of fake news. The history of modern information manipulation is not unique to any one country; however, there are certain states, most notably the Russian Empire, followed by the Soviet Union and subsequently the Russian Federation who have elevated information manipulation to an art form and in so doing coined several key phrases that serve to highlight its impact and true nature. This chapter surveys the history and evolution of the Russian and Soviet thought and practice on information manipulation and highlights the value and impact its use has on shaping international politics as well as its failings.

Dezinformatsiya (disinformation, дезынформáция) is the deliberate promulgation of false information by a person, entity or state. Disinformation is often combined in strategic or tactical configurations to engage in operations known as active measures (активные мероприятия). Active measures are comprised of activities that include disinformation, propaganda, forgery and in some cases assassination. Active measures and disinformation more narrowly both originate within the Russian lexicon and made their way into the English vernacular only in the late 1970s and early 1980s.

Russian and Soviet skillsets associated with the development and utilization of active measures and by extension disinformation extend well back into Tsarist times, yet the modern concepts used by the successors to the KGB (Komitet Gosudarstvennoy Bezopasnosti, Committee for State Security) and Soviet GRU (Glavnoye razvedyvatel'noye upravleniye, Main Intelligence Directorate), to include the SVR (Sluzhba vneshney razvedki, Foreign Intelligence Service of the Russian Federation), the FSB (Federal'naya sluzhba bezopasnosti

Rossiyskoy Federatsii, Federal Security Service of the Russian Federation), and GRU (Glavnoye razvedyvatel'noye upravleniye, Main intelligence Directorate, Military of Russia) can trace their roots back to the secret police employed by the Tsars, known as the Okhrana. The progression from Tsarist secret police to modern intelligence services is sordid and filled with numerous successes and failures, yet the evolution highlights a community of practice within the present day Russian Federation that extends well beyond what most commentators on recent events including Russia's invasion of Georgia in 2008, Russia's Annexation of Crimea and subsequent war in Eastern Ukraine in 2014, Russia's involvement in Syria, or their involvement in the 2016 United States Presidential elections indicate. Russian active measures are a skillset that has been honed over time and across technologies. It is a body of practice well-suited to the current international political environment. Active measures pose a perplexing challenge to liberal democracies and to societies whose moral, ethical and legal constraints limit the creativity and willingness of their intelligence agencies to take risks.

## The Okhrana and the birth of modern active measures

Twenty-first-century Russian active measures have a decidedly 19th-century origin story. In the mid to late 19th century with the invention of the rotary printing press and dynamite the Russian Empire came under increasing stress from violent extremists internal to the state.[2] To address these rising concerns, the Interior Ministry of the Russian Empire sought to establish a subdivision within the national police forces staffed by loyal and specially trained gendarmes.[3] These special police, a subsection of the Russian Imperial Police, known as the Okhrana were tasked with engaging in intelligence activities against revolutionaries both within and external to the territory of Russia.[4] The overall scale of the Okhrana was quite small, yet they were remarkably productive based on evidence found within the archives of the Okhrana stored at Stanford's Hoover Archives. Founded in 1881 with its core mission being to protect the Tsar, it opened its principal foreign section in Paris in 1883.[5] Of importance to the study of modern active measures are the skills that were developed by the Okhrana and its agents over a 40-year period. These skills include the development of assets, the tracking of assets, the dissemination of information and propaganda about state adversaries to foreign governments, notably the French, and the development of a systematized set of methods that were used by subsequent post-revolutionary Soviet Intelligence services such as the Cheka, NKVD and the KGB up until the end of the Cold War in 1991.[6]

Interestingly, the main targets of the Okhrana were Russian nationals engaged in revolutionary activities both living abroad and within the empire. The honing of intelligence skills such as active measures was not primarily intended to safeguard or reinforce the power of the Russian Empire in relation to foreign adversaries but rather designed to protect itself from its own citizenry. The tactics, techniques and procedures of the Okhrana were novel and built to infiltrate and undermine the organizations and structures that sought to overthrow the Tsar. Many of these tactics are detailed both within the Okhrana Hoover Archives at Stanford University; however, a first-hand account of being in the Okhrana was published by Aleksieĭ Tīkhonovīch Vasīlév. Vasīlév provides a robust and detailed account of how early methods of espionage and active measures were developed.[7] In some instances, Okhrana agents used misinformation and disinformation to convince revolutionaries to turn out for meetings at which they were arrested or convinced them to return back to Russian soil where they were executed.[8] The Okhrana also collaborated with the French police to

A brief history of fake **29**

provide information and justifications for their actions. While ultimately unable to succeed in stemming the tide of revolutionary fervor and overwhelmed by a world war, the Okhrana set the stage for early Leninist methods and later strategies employed by Soviet intelligence services.

## Early post-revolutionary disinformation and propaganda

The Russian Civil War from 1917 to 1927 and the early periods of Bolshevik governance within the Soviet Union in many ways established a test bed for information control and manipulation. Just as in Tsarist times, the primary concern of the Soviet State was internal rather than external. The establishment of control over information required the development of active measures and the honing of processes, organizations and concepts to enable the directed mobilization of domestic populations in pursuit of Bolshevik strategies. As noted by Peter Kenez, early Bolshevik leadership inverted the calls for liberalization of the press under revolutionary periods and sought to close the information environment of the Soviet Union as they continued to consolidate political power.[9] Bolshevik leadership in the early civil war period pushed to establish control over a variety of publishing houses and confiscated more than 90 presses by July 1918.[10] However, the consolidation of the press into Bolshevik hands was also constrained by economics and the lack of paper.[11] Whereas a free press had enabled the rise of Bolshevik presses such as *Novoe vremia* (New Times), *Pravda* (Truth), *Soldatskaia Pravda* (Soldiers Truth), *Ekonomicheskaia Zhizn'* (Economic Life), *Kommunistka* (Women Communist), *Bednota* (village poor), *Rabotnitsa* (Worker Woman), *Voennoe delo* (Military Affairs), albeit with some creative and often frequent name changes over the revolutionary period, a lack of paper and increasing political control resulted in a consolidation of publications, the closure of others and a general decline in both the quality and circulation of the press.[12]

Other problems plagued early efforts at propaganda and disinformation within the Soviet Union, in particular poor infrastructure, resulted in a general inability to distribute materials to outside of major urban areas. Also challenging the propaganda efforts of the incoming Bolsheviks were extremely low literacy rates throughout the country.[13] By the time of the revolution only about 42.3% of the population was literate and the highest concentrations of literacy were in Urban areas.[14] Low literacy rates gave rise to the use of theater and movies as a means of propagandizing and promoting party lines.[15] Beyond challenges associated with the production and dissemination of propaganda and disinformation was the content itself. In establishing a new system of government and disseminating and materials that did not counter the party line, the Bolsheviks faced a dilemma in how to generate content that was sufficiently interesting and yet did not upset the goals of the revolution. Early forays into mass appeal were dull and resulted in the consistent circulation of party speeches. Subsequent forays into embedding journalists into local communities also turned out to be dangerous with many journalists being killed as they reported on corruption or violations of party doctrine.[16]

The solution turned out to be quite innovative and hints at a precursor to today's use of social media. Individuals were encouraged to submit letters to major publications in which they identified good and bad practices. These juicy tidbits began the process of creating an information network fed at the local level and resulted in changes in behavior.[17] Presses could then service the needs of the state while also developing and encouraging readership. Kenez notes that in 1927 alone letters resulted in 461 firings, 522 judicial proceedings and 65 party exclusions.[18]

In addition to the learning curve associated with managing the press within the newly forming Soviet state, the developing communist structure also managed the publication of books, official publications and began forming a codified set of practices that would form the foundation of later active measures. What is most important to take away from both the late imperial and early communist period is the formation of the skills and strategies, developed not against a foreign adversary but rather tested and utilized against its own citizenry with remarkable success. Many of the same information control and manipulation strategies that arose during these two periods informed how the KGB and the SVR, FSB and GRU manage and run active measures both domestically and within adversary nations.

## The post-war period and rise of modern active measures

What are often considered modern tactics, techniques and procedures (TTPs) associated with active measures arose in the post World War II period. As the Soviet Union expanded into Eastern and Central Europe and began encountering the challenges of managing the populations within these newly Sovietized states, they simultaneously sought to expand their new-found influence within the developing world. The Soviet Union beginning in late 1940s and early 1950s was engaged in an ideological, and at times kinetic battle with foreign adversaries, the most prominent of whom was the United States. Reeling from the loss of more than 20 million citizens and yet concurrently arriving as a power on the global stage necessitated a new approach, one that played to its ideological and material strengths, while attacking the weaknesses of their primary adversary.

The history of Soviet active measures following the World War II is replete with successes and failures, comedy and moral and ethical deprivations that have had lasting effects to this day. At their core, Soviet Active Measures were run out of the KGB First Chief Directorate, Department D, later changed to Department A. Department D was created in 1959 and by 1961, was already producing forgeries and engaging in disinformation operations.[19] Early indications of modern ideological warfare and education can be found in documents such as a CIA intelligence report entitled "Prometheus Bound" which indicates that, as early as 1946, a series of Party Central Committee decrees began to reemphasize the role of various forms of literature, theatre and art in the ideological education of individuals and how these products should become weapons of the state.[20] The creation and collection of numerous forgeries of documents from this early period combined with overall disinformation and propaganda efforts gave rise to the modern concept of active measures. It was in the early 1960s that the Department changed its name from D to A in line with its function and its longer more functionally accurate name, known as the "Active Measures Department."[21]

Concurrent to the rise of the Active Measures Department was the creation of overt communications channels specializing in propaganda. Initial overt messaging campaigns were managed via the Department of Agitation and Propaganda (Agitprop) of the Central Committee of the Communist Party of the Soviet Union (CPSU) beginning in 1947. Agitprop was responsible for the supervision of propaganda campaigns, ideological enforcement, journalistic and cultural endeavors and foreign communist party relations.[22] The organization of activities was not isolated to Agitprop and also included functions within the International Department and by extension the International Information Department of the CPSU and the KGB. Early CIA reports on Agitprop highlight a degree of confusion over its organizational and functional structures yet provide a rough sketch of the propaganda functions of the department both domestically within the USSR and more broadly outside of it including collaborations with the ministry of Foreign Affairs.[23] In addition to Agitprop was the creation of foreign affairs sections that related to the control and manipulation of foreign communist delegations.

Active measures aimed at propaganda, disinformation and influence with substantial international implications arose during the late 1940s and the 1950s through the development of organizations purporting to foster international peace, global trade, youth and democracy or a variety of other activities. Between August 25 and 28, 1948 at World Congress of Intellectuals in Defense of Peace there are indications of Soviet Active Measures within the dialogue of delegates.[24] These proceedings leaned heavily in favor of Soviet ideology and intentions and sought to portray the West and the United States in particular as undermining global peace. The World Congress of Intellectuals in Defense of Peace was a precursor to the World Peace Council (WPC) founded in 1950. A 1954 CIA intelligence report estimated that the WPC was a propaganda and disinformation arm of the Soviet Union, organized and placed directly in Vienna with the intent to "exploit the universal desire for peace to serve Soviet aims."[25] The intelligence report goes on to state "this 'peace movement' attempts to confuse 'peace' with 'peace' on Soviet Terms."[26] By altering the conversations surrounding common topics, infiltrating existing organizations, constructing new organizations, or manipulating insiders within the media, the WPC and similar organizations engaged sought to actively change conversations and subvert Western political messaging. Specifically, the WPC and a variety of similar organizations were leveraged by the USSR to, in the terms of Richard Shultz and Roy Godson:

> (1) Preserve, enhance, and expand security in those areas under the influence of the USSR. (2) Divide the Western opponents of the Soviet Union by driving wedges between them and disrupting the alliance systems. (3) Retain the primacy of the USSR in the Communist world. (4) promote "proletarian internationalism," and those "national liberation movements" which are under Communist control or serve Soviet Interests. (5) Minimize risks and avoid serious involvements on more than one front at any given time.[27]

Shultz and Godson go on to state that Soviet political warfare ambitions were virtually unlimited.[28] Much of the emphasis for this construct arises out of early Soviet concepts derived from Leninist philosophy emphasizing an ideological struggle and the justification of often violent or repressive means.[29] Framing the contest between states as an ideological struggle opens the door for an inclusive and permissive set of behaviors under political warfare that include a range of options that later become termed active measures. It should be noted at the outset that propaganda and disinformation are not mutually exclusive and the practices of the more overt forms of influence, propaganda, can and often do receive assistance via the promotion of disinformation or forgery.

It is believed that the organization and development of active measures and their authorities stemmed directly from the Central Committee of the Communist Party of the Soviet Union.[30] These assessments are largely in-line with the firsthand accounts of Ladislav Bittman, a former Officer in the Czechosolvak StB.[31] Leveraging data and testimony,

Christopher Andrew and Vasili Mtrokhin write that KGB information operations were "radically different" than those of their Western counterparts.[32] Whereas the United States leveraged Radio Free Europe and Radio Liberty, the Soviet Union leveraged Novosti Press Agency (APN), TASS and other news agencies to achieve substantial global political reach, particularly within foreign presses. By the 1970s Soviet influence over foreign presses had grown to 300 foreign press agencies/services in 93 countries.[33]

By 1983 it is estimated that Department A had about 300 staff and was organized along regional lines.[34] These 300 staff were not working in isolation, but rather served as co-ordinators of disinformation across KGB regional and country desks globally. They were in effect technical specialists providing substantial assistance to KGB officers in the field who were engaged in active measures. Department A also coordinated the active measures of regional and country desks with internal Soviet organizations including the International Information Department of the CPSU, the International Department of the CPSU and other committees across the directorates of the KGB.[35]

CIA reports and academic reports and articles indicate the high degree of functional co-ordination achieved across Soviet activities ranging from propaganda to disinformation. Major fronts for the dissemination of both overt and covert information were accomplished via news organizations, journalists, scholars, non-governmental organizations and more. Many of the organization names involved in the dissemination of propaganda and disinformation were remarkably innocuous. Names such as International Union of Students, World Federation of Democratic Youth, The Christian Peace Conference, International Organization of Journalists, Afro-Asian People's Solidary Organization and many more offered robust vectors for the in-fluencing of foreign societies and by extension their governments.[36]

A 1973 analysis of the World Federation of Democratic Youth identified organizational festivals as "a perfecting of a kind of mass psychological technique."[37] CIA analysts' reports comment almost approvingly on the quality and character of these events and highlight that they are "superior technical achievements."[38] Moreover, the reports note "a real effort has been made to influence non-Communist youth in positions of responsibility in youth and student organizations in non-Communist countries."[39]

Subverting the ideological nature of societies was not limited to youth or even peace organizations. In a precursor to contemporary active measures, Soviet agents established and funded the Christian Peace Conference (CPC) in 1958. The CPC fostered a long-view approach towards ideological subversion. CIA intelligence reports on the CPC note ex-plicitly its role as "aktivnyye meropiryatiya" (active measures).[40] By 1982 the CPC had membership in more than 80 countries globally and was able to secure participation from the Reverend Billy Graham in events such as the World Peace Conference of Religious Workers.[41] This conference was sponsored by the Moscow Patriarch Pimen and was or-ganized under the theme of "Religious Workers for Saving the Sacred Gift of Life from Nuclear Catastrophe."[42] The CPC activities highlight the way in which a government can engage non-traditional organizations with substantive effect. By engaging through covert and overt means with religious institutions Soviet active measures dramatically expanded their reach. A 1987 report by the US Department of State comments that "One of the most important tools used in furthering Soviet foreign policy objectives, particularly in the areas of defense and arms control, is religion."[43] This type of organizational outreach parallels the organizational inroads attempted in the post-Cold War era and contextualizes their success in achieving influence within and across communities within the US.

Active measures also sought to undermine the fundamental means by which liberal democracies achieve information transparency. The Soviet Union created the International Organization of Journalists (IOJ) in 1946 as a front organization, not to be confused with the International Federation of Journalists. The IOJ's stated goal was "freedom of the press, promotion of international friendship and understanding through free interchange of information, promotion of trade unionism among journalists, support of "persecuted" journalists."[44] The IOJ sought to inject itself into legitimate discussions on free press and convey Soviet concepts of press freedom. These efforts extended into the United Nations and other international organizations. The IOJ was able to build an organization of journalists capable of facilitating active measures initiatives both knowingly and unknowingly. In an era predating the Internet, the IOJ filled a valuable role in Soviet active measures and enabled the creation and dissemination of content globally.

Shultz and Godson in studying the evolution of propaganda over a 20-year period from the 1960s to the 1980s identified several core themes that each of the organizations and overt as well as covert propaganda efforts sought to highlight. While the consistency across themes changed over time and the relative volume fluctuated based on perceived Soviet needs, the general themes highlight the approach undertaken by the Soviet Union in undermining the West. The themes they identified were: Aggressiveness, Militarism, Opposition to Negotiations, Crises in the West (Social, Economic or Political), Threatening Behaviors, Realism, NATO Alliance Problems, US Unreliability, Collusion with Soviet Enemies, and Human Rights Violations.[45] What becomes readily apparent when examining these thematic issues is their relevant organizational and operational parallels in the form of forged documents, Soviet sponsored NGOs such as the CPC WFDY, or the IOJ, the dissemination or placement of false or misleading news stories in foreign presses and more.

The scale, diversity and intent of active measures far exceeds anything undertaken by the United States or its intelligence agencies including the US Information Agency (USIA). Department A, as will be described in the next section leveraged the organizational structures developed under the auspices of a number of different ministries including Agitprop, the KGB, Ministry of Foreign Affairs and more to engage in innovative and damaging active measures campaigns developed using a variety of technical and human means that matured over the course of years to achieve impact. It is in these combinations of instruments of active measures that the foundations for modern Russian active measure TTPs arise.

## Building fake: infektions and body parts

US Biological weapons programs were halted in November 1969 by President Richard Nixon. Until that time US Biological Weapons programs were primarily run out of Fort Detrick, MD. The US had, through its research at Ft. Detrick, developed several offensive biological weapons, including weaponized strains of anthrax, tularemia, brucellosis and Q-fever, botulinum toxin, staphylococcus enterotoxin B and several anti-crop biological weapons.[46] In part the ban was due to congressional testimony following a failed 1968 test of the nerve agent VX gas which escaped the controlled test site resulting in agricultural losses and additional publicly released information indicating that the US Army had been secretly transporting damaging chemical and biological agents and subsequently disposing of them at sea.[47] The Nixon administration implemented a review of chemical and biological weapons (CBW) under National Security Study Memorandum 59 (NSSM-59) in May of 1969 to be conducted across multiple agencies and departments.[48] While the review was under way, Press reports indicate further security lapses in the management of CBWs resulting in low exposures to Army Personnel and civilians on Okinawa.[49] The Results of interdepartmental research into CBW programs resulted in the recommendation that all offensive programs be halted and that purely defensive programs be instituted to "hedge against strategic surprise."[50]

Active measures are a combination of truth and lies. And in the case of Soviet active measures pertaining to biological weapons, the lies were borne out of historical truth. The more believable a lie, the more damaging it can become in the overall process of information manipulation. Disinformation is corrosive to the public opinion of nations and their people. The proliferation of disinformation within networks breaks apart the trust of societies and harms diplomatic, civil, military and humanitarian interactions. While the history of soviet active measures is replete with instances of forged documents, false press stories and influence operations of all shapes and sizes, likely none were more extensive and have had a longer and more far-reaching impact than Soviet efforts to implicate the United States in the creation of the HIV-1 virus. The disinformation campaign and its subsequent analysis by the US Department of State and by the Central Intelligence Agency provide a ground level view for how active measures function and how difficult it is for the average journalist, consumer of news or even government official to separate fact from fiction. Soviet disinformation on HIV, while entirely fiction, was rooted in the historical fact that prior to Nixon's closure of US CBW programs, the US actively engaged in CBW research for offensive purposes.

Andrew and Mitrokhin write that one of the most successful active measures campaigns of Gorbachev's first couple years in office was *Operation Infektion*.[51] The episode marks both one of the most successful campaigns and one that has had lingering effects to the present day. An official Department of State report from August 1987 provides a brief timeline of the methods used to develop this campaign and further highlights the fundamental challenges associated with combating it. Both CIA and State Department reporting indicates that the origin point for Operation Infektion likely arose out of an interactions between the International Department (ID), KGB First Chief Directorate Department A and the propaganda department.[52] Operation Infektion as it has become known began with an article placed on July 13, 1983 as a letter to the editor of an Indian publication, known to have been established with Soviet assistance. *The Patriot* published an article purporting to be from an anonymous source, a "well-known American Scientist," claiming that HIV arose out of Fort Detrick and the Centers for Disease Control (CDC) collaborations on biological warfare.[53]

This disinformation campaign did not arise out of the blue, but rather was in line with previous disinformation efforts that occurred over the preceding decades attempting to implicate the United States both acts of biological and chemical warfare and the sustainment of biological warfare programs in violation of Geneva Conventions.[54] The slow burn of disinformation provided a foundation for the continuity of doubt regarding American intentions. Moreover, the initial publication of the article "AIDS may invade India: Mystery disease caused by US experiments" closely mirrors the rhetorical style of much of the media conspiracies seen today on Russian sponsored media. A 2009 article in *Studies in Intelligence*, further indicates that the Soviets recognized American sensitivity to their government's behavior.[55] Because only 15 years prior the US did in fact shutter its CBW program as it was highly susceptible to manipulations. Moreover, the US did have a history of experimenting with biological and chemical agents as in the case of the CIA LSD trials or medical experiments assessing the impact of penicillin on African American farm workers in Tuskegee, Alabama.[56]

However, the initial article appearing in *The Patriot* was not immediately followed by subsequent propaganda and disinformation; rather, Soviet active measures engaged in a patient long-game and waited until October 30, 1985 to follow up. The delayed follow-up by Valentin Zapevalov in the weekly *Literaturnaya Gazeta* leveraged the obscurity of the original source as a backstop to the credibility of the revitalized disinformation effort. This tactic is not unique to this case, but rather is illustrative of active measures more broadly. Again, the rhetorical title of the article sought to introduce ambiguity "Panic in West or What is Hidden Behind the Sensation About AIDs" sought to cast doubt on American activities related to CBW. Zapevalov's article began a cascade of articles in newspapers, on the radio and eventually on television, including on CBS News with Dan Rather on March 30, 1987. The story was further bolstered by agents of influence or witting fools in the form of Professor Jacob Segal, a 76-year-old retired East German biophysicist and his wife Dr. Lili Segal.[57]

Segal and his wife were identified for their role within the disinformation scheme by the department of disinformation HAV (Hauptabteilung Aufklärung) within the Stasi according to reports from both the CIA and State Department based on reporting of former Stasi officers.[58] The report the Segals produced is believed to have been initially released in Harare, Zimbabwe at a Soviet sponsored summit of non-aligned states. The release of the report in a third-party nation, sought to further distance the hand of KGB active measures and further strengthened the credibility of the report within third world media. The combination of the Zapevalov article and the Segal Report created a perfect storm of disinformation that was increasingly divorced from its purveyors. State Department documentation on the incident highlights the "viral" nature of the story, in which interviews with Segal, while quickly dismissed by the international medical community, were requoted and published in other newspapers around the world. Further assistance from TASS (the Soviet news bureau) further assisted its dissemination globally. As the stories spread, a game of telephone transpired in which the details associated with the initial release continued to worsen while the fidelity to even its false beginnings deteriorated. By late 1986 and early 1987 stories of US violations of the Geneva Conventions were prevalent. Perhaps equally as damaging, stories about the prevalence of HIV/AIDS in proximity to US military facilities in many nations including Korea and Europe began to proliferate.[59]

Although eventually the United States, with substantial evidence from the medical community, a robust tracing of Soviet propaganda and disinformation efforts, and substantial political pressure was able to secure a public statement from Gorbachev claiming credit for the disinformation campaign,[60] the impact of this campaign continues to be felt more than 30 years later. The persistence of the conspiracy theories surrounding HIV and AIDS persists to this day. In 2008 Presidential candidate Barack Obama had to address concerns raised by his Pastor Jeremiah Wright who indicated that the HIV was created to harm blacks.[61] In 2010 Nobel Prize winning Kenyan environmentalist Wangari Maathai was forced to walk back statements in which she implied US responsibility for the HIV virus.[62] Yet, the most devastating aspects of the conspiracy have been its impact on HIV/AIDS policy in many African nations. South African President Thabo Mbeki and his health minister Manto Tshabalala-Msimang citing the disinformation associated with Operation Infektion refused certain drugs and treatments associated with HIV/AIDS.[63]

36  Aaron F. Brantly

Operation Infektion was not an isolated incident. While its success and damage have been largely unrivaled, they are not unique. Beginning in April of 1987, reports of US trafficking in the organs and body parts of children around the world began to circulate. Initial reports of these activities were heavily spread by *Pravda, Izvestia, TASS, Novosti, Trud, Sovetskaya Kultura, Sotsialistichekaya Industriya Sovetskaya Rossiya* and on Moscow Radio.[64] According to a US Information Agency (USIA) report the starting point for these disinformation stories arose on January 2, in the *Tecugigalpa La Tribuna*.[65] The aggressive nature of the quotations within the article and their intent to deceive is visible at the outset. One individual quoted by the USIA reportedly said:

> Many parents came to adopt children with physical defects. At first, it was believed that they were well-intentioned people who took the children away because they really cared for them, but in time it was discovered that they wanted to sell them for parts. For example, they would take out their eyes for other children who needed them.

Although the quotations were later retracted, the fuse had been lit and the story began to spread globally, aided by Soviet information outlets. Within months other newspapers in Latin America began to pick up the story. The progression of stories began to extend beyond and reach into European, North American, Indian and Asian presses. The reports eventually made their way to international children's rights NGOs including the Defense for Children, International (DCI) which issued a statement expressing skepticism in its quarterly journal.[66]

Rumors of theft or adoptions of children for the purposes of obtaining body parts gained in credibility in 1993 with the airing of a Canadian/British Production: "The Body Parts Business." More credibility was lent to rumors when United Nations Commission on Human Rights addressed the rumors specifically by declaring:

> Perhaps the most insidious issue to appear on the international scene in recent years is the question of organ transplants affecting children. Are children being sold for this purpose? The rumours abound, and the denials are equally abundant. A 1990 report of the World Health Organization notes as follows:

> "A feature of organ transplantation since its commencement has been the shortage of available organs. Supply has never satisfied demand, and this has led to the continuous development in many countries of procedures and systems to increase supply. Rational argument can be made to the effect that shortage has led to the rise of commercial traffic in human organs, particularly from living donors who are unrelated to recipients. There is clear evidence of such traffic in recent years, and fears have arisen of the possibility of related traffic in human beings."
>
> *(Human Organ Transplantation, ED 87/12,*
> *19 November 1990, World Health Organization, p. 4)*

Whatever the facts of the case, it is submitted that safeguards are required to protect children from such threat. In this regard it is interesting to note that the World Health Organization has taken up the issue concretely. It is currently drafting a set of guiding principles on human organ transplantation which have direct import on children, including the following:

"No organ should be removed from the body of a living minor for the purpose of transplantation. Exceptions may be made under national law in the case of regenerative tissues."

"The human body and its parts cannot be the subject of commercial transactions. Accordingly, giving or receiving payment (including any other compensation or reward) for organs should be prohibited."

"It should be prohibited for any person or facility involved in organ transplantation procedures to receive any payment that exceeds a justifiable fee for the services rendered."

*(Human Organ Transplantation, supra, pp. 4–5)*[67]

Body party theft rumors led to the targeting of American women by a mob who burned down the police station in which they sought refuge in Guatemala.[68] Other mob attacks occurred targeting westerners in Guatemala and El Salvador. The rumors spread, though Soviet active measures persist and continue to impact national level laws on adoption, including the laws of adoption in many developing world countries. In 2012 Svetland Goryacheva, a member of the Russian State Duma was quoted as saying:

Even if one-tenth of (60,000) orphans will be tortured, used for organs transplanting or for sexual exploitation, given that there are 9 million same-sex marriages in the United States, the remaining 50,000 may be used in the future to be recruited for war, maybe even with Russia.[69]

As of 2012, almost 10% of Russians surveyed indicated that they believed banning US adoptions would prevent the exploitation of children for the purposes of forced labor or the harvesting of their organs.[70] These fears are not unique to the Russian Federation and have found a home in the policies and opinions of many countries around the world. The success of active measures related to such a seemingly implausible story, related to the murder and harvesting of organs remains stubbornly persistent. The active measures that led to the diffusion of rumors of body organ harvesting carry over into similar stories that have arisen in recent years. One such story arose in 2016 and came to be known as Pizzagate. Pizzagate was a 2016 Russian inspired active measures campaign purporting that democratic leaders engaged in a satanic child sex ring in the basement of the Comet Ping Pong pizza restaurant in Washington, DC led to an attack by an AR-15 wielding Edgar Maddison Welch.[71]

Both Operation Infektion and the active measures supporting rumors around the harvesting of children's body parts are but the tip of the iceberg of a long line of Soviet and now post-Soviet campaigns to wage what is best described as an information war on the West and in particular the United States. A survey of different reports from the USIA, CIA, Department of State and others indicate that there were hundreds if not thousands of concurrent campaigns all under way from the 1960s through the early 1990s. While many of these campaigns failed, many did not. The damage these campaigns sought to achieve is at its very core a form of political warfare that seeks to undermine adversary nations and keep them from achieving their political goals by forcing them into informationally defensive positions.

## Offensive information: defensive counter-information

This chapter has outlined, in brief, the long and sordid history of Russian active measures. The history of Russian active measures is in many respects unique to the Russian experience. The skills and practices initially developed and used by the Tsar's secret police were adapted and modified within early Bolshevik political life not for the manipulation of foreign nations but for domestic control. As early manipulations of media and the press became increasingly successful, the skills necessary to engage in effective active measures against foreign populations likewise increased. Each iteration both organizationally and functionally enhanced the capacity and skills of Soviet and subsequently Russian state organs to use information to undermine and manipulate foreign states, while insulating their own population to some degree. Active measures are a long-game activity. Their success is not direct and the causal linkage between any given activity and a specific outcome is uncertain. Their goal at the most basic level is the subversion of reality.[72] Through the subversion of objective reality and fact Russian active measures place their targets in a perpetually defensive counter-information environment.

Within this counter-information environment defenders are in the awkward position of having to defend or prove the negative. Even when done successfully as in the case of Operation Infektion, the lingering effect of active measures often requires consistent and sustained counter-information operations. All of the active measures examined within this chapter occurred prior to the widespread use of the Internet and required robust organizational structures, spies, agents of influence, witting and unwitting fools. Despite all of these challenges it is hard not to assess Soviet active measures in the pre-Internet age as quite successful. Although they did not result in a Cold War victory, the disinformation and lies spread around the world continue to resurface or morph in political, social, scientific, economic and other discussions long after the demise of the Soviet Union.

Of greatest relevance to the current challenges posed by information operations, the development of Russian active measures highlights how information was used to undermine foreign adversaries. Many of the tactics used have subsequently morphed or hybridized within the modern information environment. In nearly every way the organizational and functional capacity associated with active measures developed under the Soviet Union have become enhanced by cyberspace and computers more broadly. Whereas forgeries used to be difficult to produce, they are now easy to generate, adapt and obfuscate. Hiding the sourcing of information has become increasingly easy in an era of blogs and social media. Moreover, agents of influence can be replaced by bots of influence as was seen to a great extent during the 2016 US Presidential elections. If history holds, true to form, the presence of Russian active measures is likely to remain a consistent feature of Russian foreign policy in the decades to come. The sophistication and impact of active measures will vary from issue to issue, but the practice itself will continue and Western nations, in particular, the United States, should understand and begin the process of developing strategies to both build societal resilience as well as re-establish robust organizational capacity such as the US Information Agency to counter the challenges of both the present and the future.

## Notes

1 Griffith, Samuel B, and Sun Tzu. 1971. *The Art of War*. New York: Oxford University Press.
2 Lauchlan, Iain. 2005. "Security Policing in Late Imperial Russia." In *Late Imperial Russia Problems and Prospects. Essays in Honour of R.B. McKean*, edited by Robert B. McKean and Ian D. Thatcher. Manchester: Manchester University Press. 44–63.
3 Ibid.
4 Fischer, Ben B. 1997. "Okhrana: the Paris Operations of the Russian Imperial Police." *Cia.Gov*. Washington, D.C. www.cia.gov/library/center-for-the-study-of-intelligence/csi-publications/books-and-monographs/okhrana-the-paris-operations-of-the-russian-imperial-police/5474-1.html.
5 Ibid.
6 Andrew, Christopher, and V. N. Mitrokhin. 2001. *The Sword and the Shield: the Mitrokhin Archive and the Secret History of the KGB*. New York, NY: Basic Books.
7 Vasil ev, A. T., and René Fülöp-Miller. 1930. *The Ochrana, the Russian Secret Police*. Philadelphia, PA: J.B. Lippincott.
8 Fischer, Ben B. 1997. *Okhrana: the Paris Operations of the Russian Imperial Police*. Washington, DC: Central Intelligence Agency.
9 Kenez, Peter. 1986. *The Birth of the Propaganda State: Soviet Methods of Mass Mobilization, 1917–1929*. Cambridge; New York: Cambridge University Press.
10 Ibid. 44.
11 Ibid.
12 Ibid. 44–47.
13 Mironov, Boris N. 1991. "The Development of Literacy in Russia and the USSR from the Tenth to the Twentieth Centuries." *History of Education Quarterly* 31 (2): 229–52.
14 Ibid. 240.
15 Kenez. *The Birth of the Propaganda State*.
16 Ibid.
17 Ibid. 225.
18 Ibid. 237.
19 Kux, Dennis. 1985. "Soviet Active Measures and Disinformation: Overview and Assessment." *Parameters* 15 (4), 19.
20 Central Intelligence Agency, "Prometheus Bound" 1999. (Obtained under the freedom of information act from the Central Intelligence Agency Aug. 28, 1999) www.cia.gov/library/readingroom/docs/CIA-RDP78-02771R000500500004-5.pdf.
21 Ibid.
22 Shultz, Richard H, and Roy Godson. 1986. *Dezinformatsia: Active Measures in Soviet Strategy*. New York: Berkley Books. 28–29.
23 Central Intelligence Agency, "The Apparatus of the Central Committee of the CPSU" 1959. (Obtained under the freedom of information act from the Central Intelligence Agency Sept. 09, 2010) https://www.cia.gov/library/readingroom/docs/CIA-RDP78-00915R000300040001-3.pdf.
24 Dobrenko, Vladimir. 2016. "Conspiracy of Peace: the Cold War, the International Peace Movement, and the Soviet Peace Campaign, 1946–1956." London: The London School of Economics and Political Science.
25 Central Intelligence Agency, "The World Peace Council" 1954. (Obtained under the freedom of information act from the Central Intelligence Agency Jul. 09, 1998) www.cia.gov/library/readingroom/docs/CIA-RDP78-00915R000300040001-3.pdf.
26 Ibid.
27 Shultz, Richard H., and Roy Godson. 1986. *Dezinformatsia: Active Measures in Soviet Strategy*. New York: Berkley Books.
28 Ibid. 16.
29 Ryan, James. 2011. "'Revolution Is War'": the Development of the Thought of V. I. Lenin on Violence, 1899–1907." *The Slavonic and East European Review* 89 (2): 248–27.
30 Ibid. 19.
31 Bittman, Ladislav. 1985. *The KGB and Soviet Disinformation: an Insider's View*. Washington, DC: Pergamon-Brassey's.
32 Andrew, Christopher M., and Vasili Mitrokhin. 2007. *The World Was Going Our Way: the KGB and the Battle for the Third World*. New York: Basic Books.

33 Shultz and Godson, *Dezinformatsia.*
34 Kux, "Soviet Active Measures and Disinformation."
35 Shultz and Godson, *Dezinformatsia*; Kux, "Soviet Active Measures and Disinformation."
36 Ibid;
37 Central Intelligence Agency, "World Youth Festivals" 1973. (Obtained under the freedom of information act from the Central Intelligence Agency Sept. 09, 1999) www.cia.gov/library/readingroom/docs/CIA-RDP79-01194A000200030001-1.pdf.
38 Ibid.
39 Ibid.
40 Central Intelligence Agency, "Christian Peace Conference" 1982. (Obtained under the freedom of information act from the Central Intelligence Agency Apr. 26, 2007) www.cia.gov/library/readingroom/docs/CIA-RDP83M00914R001200110031-7.pdf.
41 Ibid.
42 Ibid.
43 US Department of State. 1987. *Soviet Influence Activities: A Report on Active Measures and Propaganda, 1986–87.* ix.
44 Central Intelligence Agency, "A Study of the International Organization of Journalists (IOJ)" 1995. (Obtained under the freedom of information act from the Central Intelligence Agency Aug. 28, 2000) https://www.cia.gov/library/readingroom/docs/CIA-RDP78-00915R000400220001-2.pdf.
45 Shultz and Godson, *Dezinformatsia.* 50–52.
46 Tucker, Jonathan B., and Erin R. Mahan. 2009. *President Nixon's Decision to Renounce the U.S. Offensive Biological Weapons Program.* Washington, D.C.
47 Ibid.
48 1969. *National Security Study Memorandum 59.* National Security Council. https://fas.org/irp/offdocs/nssm-nixon/nssm_059.pdf.
49 Central Intelligence Agency, "Nerve Gas Incident on Okinawa" July 18, 1969. (Obtained under the freedom of information act from the Central Intelligence Agency Dec. 12, 2016) www.cia.gov/library/readingroom/docs/CIA-RDP80B01439R000500090021-7.pdf.
50 Tucker and Mahan. *President Nixon's Decision to Renounce the U.S. Offensive Biological Weapons Program.*
51 Andrew and Mitrokhin. *The World Was Going Our Way.*
52 US Department of State. 1987. *Soviet Influence Activities: A Report on Active Measures and Propaganda, 1986–87.* 30–43; Central Intelligence Agency, "USSR: INCREASING DISINFORMATION ABOUT AIDS" 1987. (Obtained under the freedom of information act from the Central Intelligence Agency N.D.) www.cia.gov/library/readingroom/docs/DOC_0000367991.pdf.
53 US Department of State. 1987. *Soviet Influence Activities: A Report on Active Measures and Propaganda, 1986–87.* 30–43.
54 Central Intelligence Agency, "Project Truth" Oct. 27, 1981. (Obtained under the freedom of information act from the Central Intelligence Agency May 14, 2008) www.cia.gov/library/readingroom/docs/CIA-RDP83M00914R002100120069-5.pdf.
55 Boghardt, Thomas. 2009. "Soviet Bloc Intelligence and Its AIDS Disinformation Campaign." *Studies in Intelligence* 53 (4): 1–24.
56 Jeppsson, Anders. 2017. "How East Germany Fabricated the Myth of HIV Being Man-Made." *Journal of the International Association of Providers of AIDS Care (JIAPAC)* 16 (6): 519–22.
57 US Department of State. *Soviet Influence Activities.* 35.
58 Jeppsson. "How East Germany Fabricated the Myth of HIV Being Man-Made."
59 US Department of State. *Soviet Influence Activities.* 39.
60 Ellick, Adam B., and Adam Westbrook. 2018. "Operation Infektion: A Three-Part Video Series on Russian Disinformation." *The New York Times.* November 12. www.nytimes.com/2018/11/12/opinion/russia-meddling-disinformation-fake-news-elections.html.
61 Hagerty, Barbara Bradley. 2008. "Does Jeremiah Wright Speak for All Black Churches?" *NPR.* January 5. www.npr.org/templates/story/story.php?storyId=90111137.
62 Gibbs, Walter. 2004. "Nobel Peace Laureate Seeks to Explain Remarks About AIDS." *The New York Times.* December 10. www.nytimes.com/2004/12/10/world/nobel-peace-laureate-seeks-to-explain-remarks-about-aids.html.
63 Nattrass, Nicoli. 2012. *The AIDS Conspiracy: Science Fights Back.* New York: Columbia University Press. Accessed February 18, 2019. ProQuest Ebook Central. 2.

A brief history of fake **41**

64 1988. *Soviet Active Measures in the Era of Glasnost.* Washington, DC. 32.
65 Ibid. 34.
66 Ibid. 35.
67 1991. "Question of the Violation of Human Rights and Fundamental Freedoms, in Any Part of the World with Particular Reference to Colonial and Other Dependent Countries and Territories." E/CN.4/1991/51. New York: Commission on Human Rights.
68 Leventhal, Todd. 1994. *The Child Organ Trafficking Rumor: a Modern "Urban Legend."* Washington, DC.
69 Schepp, Matthias. 2012. "Picking on the Weakest: Religious Leaders Condemn Putin's Adoption Ban." *Spiegel Online.* December 31. www.spiegel.de/international/world/putin-move-to-ban-us-adoptions-leaves-children-further-isolated-a-875220.html.
70 Fisher, Max. 2012. "The Real Reason Russia Wants to Ban Adoptions by 'Dangerous' American Families." *The Washington Post.* December 28. www.washingtonpost.com/news/worldviews/wp/2012/12/28/the-real-reason-russia-wants-to-ban-adoptions-by-dangerous-american-families/.
71 Douglas, William, and Mark Washburn. 2016. "Religious Zeal Drives N.C. Man in 'Pizzagate'." *The Courier-Tirbune.* December 6. https://web.archive.org/web/20161208131816/http://www.courier-tribune.com/news/20161206/religious-zeal-drives-nc-man-in-8216pizzagate8217.
72 Fitzgerald, Chad W., and Aaron F. Brantly. 2017. "Subverting Reality: The Role of Propaganda in 21st Century Intelligence." *International Journal of Intelligence and CounterIntelligence* 30 (2): 215–40.

# 4

# THE IDEOLOGICAL BATTLEFIELD

## China's approach to political warfare and propaganda in an age of cyber conflict

*Elsa B. Kania*

China's Party-state and its military sees the Internet as an ideological battlefield. For the Chinese Communist Party (CCP), the advent of the Internet has presented a threat to its survival that is perceived as nearly existential in nature. In response to this potential vulnerability, the CCP has sought to control content and dominate discourse in China's online environment, including through censorship and propaganda that is both internal and external in its focus. Increasingly, cyber sovereignty is recognized as a critical component of national sovereignty. This traditional conceptualization of information as a "double-edged sword" to be leveraged for strategic purposes may provide China an advantage relative to democracies in exploiting the cyber domain and global information ecosystem as a means to advance its national interests. Moreover, China's diplomacy and activities aimed to exercise influence have exploited methods informed by a tradition of political work and warfare, which appear to be starting to expand into and be enabled by cyberspace.

For the People's Liberation Army (PLA), psychological warfare is an integral element of information operations, in conjunction with cyber and electronic warfare, to be undertaken continuously throughout peacetime and wartime across all domains. The PLA sees these "intangible" domains as integral to modern "informatized" warfare, in which seizing information dominance (制信息权) is vital to victory on the battlefield. Similarly, psychological warfare, along with legal warfare and public opinion warfare, known as the "three warfares" (三种战法) are seen as critical to seizing "discourse dominance" (话语权) in future political and military struggles. Recent changes in the PLA's force structure could facilitate the integration of capabilities for cyber and psychological operations through the creation of a PLA Strategic Support Force. These ideological dimensions of competition are integral to China's ambitions to become a "cyber superpower" (网络强国).

## The existential challenge and emerging opportunities

Chinese concepts of cyber security and cyber conflict are inextricable from the ideological considerations that shape threat perceptions. The CCP's approach to the cyber domain starts from a recognition of acute, even existential challenge. Infamously, as Document 9, a communiqué leaked from the CCP Central Committee's General Office in 2013 highlighted, the "ideological situation" is a "complicated, intense struggle."[1] From the CCP's perspective, "Western anti-China forces" are "actively trying to infiltrate China's ideological sphere," threatening China with "the spearhead of Westernizing, splitting, and 'Color Revolutions,'" for which the blame is often placed upon the influence of the Internet and social media. The very notion of Internet freedom is seen as a direct challenge to China's model of "Internet management." In response to threats, the Party must "conscientiously strengthen its management of the ideological battlefield." In practice, this requires that the CCP develop the capability to "strengthen guidance of public opinion on the Internet." The CCP has devoted great attention and resources to tracking and monitoring opinion online, including in an attempt to have early warning of unrest or potential threats to social stability.

Xi Jinping's oft-quoted declaration, "without cyber security, there is no national security," aptly reflects these core concerns. As one authoritative commentary from researchers with the Cyberspace Administration of China gravely declared, "If our Party cannot traverse the hurdle represented by the Internet, it cannot traverse the hurdle of remaining in power for the long term."[2] The stakes are high for the CCP, and cyber security is recognized as integral to the regime's security and survival.[3] Specifically, according to China's National Security Law, state/national security involves the capability of the state to "maintain its ideological domination," taking "political security as the fundamental" requirement.[4] For that reason, any contestation of the Party-state's control and ideological influence in cyberspace often provokes a forceful response.[5] Consequently, Xi Jinping's agenda to build China into a powerful cyber nation or "cyber superpower" (网络强国) has included an emphasis on "online public opinion work" as an integral element of its broader agenda for propaganda and ideological work, linking online and offline efforts.[6] These efforts involve an extensive apparatus for censorship that is starting to become more sophisticated with the introduction of more automated techniques,[7] yet still confronts the challenge of adaptations and countermeasures deployed by Chinese netizens to evade detection.[8]

Beyond defensive measures, China's Party-state actively attempts to shape online public opinion in a favorable direction through methods that are often clumsy in practice but starting to become more sophisticated. Beyond its responsibility for cybersecurity, the Cyberspace Administration of China, which is closely linked to the propaganda apparatus,[9] has actively attempted to propagate "positive propaganda (宣传)" online.[10] Such attempts to shape public opinion are seen as critical to state security in terms of maintaining the primacy of the Party's ideology within a "favorable cyber environment."[11] This 'new era' of propaganda has taken online public opinion as the highest of priorities, not only through a reshaping of the system for propaganda but also exploring more 'innovative' techniques for propaganda that are more engaging and intended to promote pride and nationalism.[12] The intention is often explicitly described as undertaking an "online public opinion struggle" in seeking to "correctly guide" public opinion in order to ensure "unity and stability."[13] These efforts should be contextualized as an agenda of "social management" that seeks to shape incentives and behavior, including through the social credit system,[14] which may have not merely domestic but also potentially international implications.[15] Inherently, these activities and techniques can be considered a dual-use capability with relevance to information/influence operations that China might undertake.

In the course of its rise, China is seeking to exercise global influence that is commensurate with its increased capabilities. In practice, Chinese leaders see a multi-dimensional conceptualization of comprehensive national power (综合国力) that not only takes into account the hard power of economic and military capabilities but also attempts to increase its "soft power."[16] In practice, these state-driven and often heavy-handed attempts to generate and exercise "soft" power concentrated on expanding the reach of its media and propaganda, investing perhaps upwards of $10 billion a year in this endeavor.[17] In practice, China's approach to and exercise of soft power often depart from the original notion,[18] in ways that have invited the coining of the concept of "sharp power" to characterize Chinese activities and engagement in the world.[19] In the aggregate, Beijing's efforts have been since criticized as a new model of "authoritarian influence,"[20] characterized as "sharp power," which can be bullying or coercive.[21] These activities of China's Party-state on the global "ideological battlefield" have often leveraged online media and cyberspace as key fronts.

Within and beyond cyberspace, Xi Jinping has called for China to concentrate on pursuing the "right to speak" or "discourse power" (话语权, *huayuquan*).[22] Despite the extensive writings on *huayuquan* in the Chinese social science literature, there have been only limited writings in English-language scholarship that consider this concept to date.[23,24,25] However, China's attempts to increase its discourse power have confronted real constraints and limitations in practice. Consistently, Xi Jinping has called for China not only to redouble its efforts to increase soft power but also to contest "discourse power." Speaking in 2012, Xi declared, "We should increase China's soft power, give a good Chinese narrative, and better communicate China's messages to the world." This active promotion of the "China model" is often framed as a way to counter the "hegemony of universal values."[26] At a Party conference on public opinion work in February 2016, Xi Jinping emphasized the necessity of China's "constructing an external discourse system" and "enhancing its discourse power internationally."[27] As one apt analysis describes it, *huayuquan* involves "the power to lead and guide debate, or to set the parameters of acceptable discourse," including to exercise influence in international institutions.[28] In practice, this process has involved the construction of concepts, such as a redefinition of the notion of human rights, seen as capable of countering prevalent Western ideas and values.[29]

## Political warfare in current and historical perspective

The core concept in CCP/PLA political warfare is that of "disintegrating enemy forces" (瓦解敌军) through non-kinetic measures. These approaches and techniques date back to the earliest days of the Red Army and draw upon traditional aspects of Marxist-Leninist ideology. Over time, the PLA has progressively developed a more systematic framework for the three warfares, under the aegis of wartime political work (战时政治工作). The 2003 Political Work Regulations (政治工作條例) incorporated public opinion warfare, psychological warfare, and legal warfare, which were the responsibility of the former General Political Department (总政治部). These three warfares were described as including carrying out "disintegration of enemy forces work," anti-psychological warfare (反心战), and anti-instigation work (反策反工作). Of course, it is important to note that the concept of political work can be applied both defensively and offensively, to ideological indoctrination of PLA personnel and the exploitation of psychological vulnerabilities of enemy forces.[30]

Notably, in 2005, the PLA's Central Military Commission ratified and the former General Staff Department, General Political Department, General Logistics Department, and General Armaments Department jointly promulgated official guidelines (*gangyao*, 綱要, literally "outline" or "essentials") for public opinion warfare, psychological warfare, and legal warfare.[31] Through these *gangyao*, the concepts thus were officially incorporated into the PLA's education and training and its "preparation for military struggle." While the *gangyao* are not publicly available, their release at that point indicated the PLA's continued progression towards ensuring that the three warfares were not merely a rhetorical device but corresponded with a concrete set of techniques and expertise that could be taught in the classroom and utilized on the battlefield. Indeed, in response to these new policy measures, the PLA sought to engage in more systematic research and training, and force development in support of the three warfares, particularly at its National Defense University and Xi'an and Nanjing Political Institutes, which have pioneered new concepts on these issues.[32,33] For instance, at the Xi'an Political Institute, prominent theorists, such as Ma Zhong (马忠), affiliated with its Psychological Warfare Teaching and Research Office (心理战教研室), have focused on advancing "theoretical innovation" in the PLA's approach to political warfare, pursuing research that have involved "cyber political work" and "hostile forces' cyber psychological warfare."[34]

## Information Operations in Chinese Military Strategy

The challenge of contesting discourse power has emerged as an important element of Chinese military strategic thinking. For instance, as described in *The Science of Military Strategy*, a text seen as authoritative that is authored by the PLA Academy of Military Science, "discourse power" involves the use of information, belief, and mentality (信息—信仰—心智), implying the capability to capability to control the narrative in a military contingency.[35] According to this text, the contestation of *huayuaquan* requires "the integrated employment" of public opinion warfare, legal warfare, and psychological warfare, known as the three warfares (三种战法), to be undertaken across peace and wartime in a manner that is integrated with conventional operations. These three warfare operations, based on such principles as public opinion control (舆论控制) and legal restriction (法律制约), are intended to be complementary and mutually reinforcing in future wars or in political and diplomatic struggle, thus acting as a force multiplier to material capabilities.[36] The undertaking of the three warfares is seen as critical to increasing the PLA's "soft power" and contributing to its success in future warfare, particularly through weakening the adversary's "will to fight" (战斗意志), from the perspective of defense academics from the PLA's National Defense University.[37] In practice, this traditional concentration on opportunities for "winning without fighting" could result in great interest to manipulating American public opinion.[38]

In today's "informatized" (信息化) warfare, the PLA's contestation of information dominance would be the tip of the spear for Chinese military power. Evidently, the PLA recognizes space and cyberspace as "strategic frontiers" (战略边疆) and the "commanding heights" (制高点) of future warfare. Although there are noteworthy consistencies in the Chinese military's strategic thinking on information in warfare dating back to the 1990s, only recently has the structure and strategy for Chinese military cyber/information warfare forces started to be revealed.[39] Notably, the 2015 national defense white paper on "China's Military Strategy," called for the PLA to "expedite the development of a cyber force" and to enhance its capabilities in "cyberspace situation awareness" and "cyber defense," with the objective "to stem major cyber crises, ensure national network and information security, and maintain national security and social stability."[40] At a basic level, the PLA's approach to employing military cyber forces should be understood as another piece in China's strategy of 'active defense' (积极防御). In essence, that concept emerges from Mao's aphorism, "We will not attack unless we are attacked, but we will surely counter-attack if attacked."[41] When applied to the cyber domain, this logic implies that offensive operations at the tactical and operational levels would be consistent with a defensive orientation at the strategic level.[42] At the strategic level, the question of what constitutes an "attack" is likely to be decided according to political and ideological factors, particularly in cyberspace.

Inherently, the PLA's approach to cyber conflict is informed by Chinese strategic culture, which includes elements that may be better suited to an era of cyber conflict in some respects. For the U.S. and most Western militaries, there tends to be a clear legal and structural distinction between "peace" and "warfare."[43] In contrast, the PLA appears to place these along a spectrum, recognizing that peacetime preparations are essential to wartime operations in cyber or psychological operations. In the *Science of Military Strategy*, PLA thinkers discuss the dynamics of "military struggle" in the cyber domain, highlighting the functional "integration" of peacetime and wartime in cyberspace.[44] According to the PLA's official dictionary of military terminology "military struggle" (军事斗争) involves "the use of military methods in order to advance the struggle among nation states or political groups to achieve a definite political, economic or other objective; the highest form is warfare."[45] This concept emerges from certain Marxist and Maoist antecedents consistent with the CCP's tradition of combined political and military struggle.[46] Increasingly, the PLA considers cyber capabilities a critical component in its overall integrated strategic deterrence posture, alongside space and nuclear deterrence. PLA thinkers highlight that "blinding," "paralyzing," and "chaos-inducing" methods of deterrence in cyber space and other domains will "probably possess even more ideal deterrence outcomes."[47]

Traditionally, the PLA has emphasized seizing "information dominance" at the earliest feasible stage in a conflict. Its attempts to do so are projected to involve strikes against key nodes in an adversary's command and control systems using integrated information and firepower assaults, based on authoritative materials and commentary from PLA academics and strategists. Unsurprisingly given the perceived dominance of offensive attacks in this domain, the PLA is believed to be oriented towards seizing the initiative through a first strike (先发制人). To date, however, it does not appear that the PLA has a formal and updated doctrine, or rather operational regulations (作战条令) for cyber/information operations, such that its current approach, including to such issues as cyber deterrence, may be continuing to evolve.[48] In that regard, it will be important to continue to trace the manner in which American concepts and frameworks might be adopted and adapted or dismissed by PLA strategists going forward at a time when Chinese military force posture for information operations is continuing to evolve.

The notable conceptual asymmetries between American and Chinese thinking on cyber information and influence operations are clearly highlighted by the different definitions used by Chinese military thinkers. According to the official dictionary of PLA military terminology, published in 2011, the definition of information operations involves "integrating modes such as electronic warfare, cyber warfare, and psychological warfare to strike or counter an enemy," with the objective

> to interfere with and damage the enemy's information and information systems in cyberspace and electromagnetic space; to influence and weaken the enemy's information acquisition, transmission, processing, utilization and decision-making capabilities; and to ensure the stable operation of one's own information systems, information security, and correct decision making.[49]

Increasingly, Chinese strategists recognize that battlespaces are expanding from the tangible domains to new virtual domains. Looking at the lessons of recent conflicts, "Local wars under informatized conditions have shown that the influence of operations in 'intangible spaces' on the course and outcome of a war surpasses the influence of 'tangible spaces,'" according to one authoritative assessment.[50] Consistently, PLA thinking tends to emphasize the psychological dimensions of conflict in the information age.

For the PLA, psychological warfare is recognized as an imperative for offensive and defensive purposes. According to the PLA's official terminology, psychological warfare involves "operations using specific information and media to influence the target's psychology and behavior in order to advance the achievement of political and military combat objectives, based on strategic intent and operational tasks." According to a PLA textbook on the topic, the objectives involve "breaking down the enemy psychologically while stabilizing and inspiring one's own troops."[51] These "combat measures" are intended to advance the "goal of winning without a fight or emerging victorious from a fight." In practice, psychological warfare involves defensive and offensive activities that must be undertaken continuously. According to *Lectures on the Science of Information Operations*, "Because the execution of psychological warfare has no stringent time or space limitations, it runs throughout times of war and peace, and it permeates politics, economics, culture, religion, science and technology, society, and all other domains." Within the conduct of information operations, "The use of modes of information countermeasures such as electronic psychological warfare and network psychological warfare to influence, intimidate, strike, and subjugate the opponent psychologically, belongs to the category of the battle of wits."[52] Increasingly, this "battle of wits" seems to be playing out in real-time against Taiwan.

## The "three warfares" in action

The PLA has utilized techniques and methods associated with the three warfares to target Taiwan, particularly through the efforts of the former General Political Department's (GPD) Base 311 (Unit 61716), its "Public Opinion Warfare, Psychological Warfare, and Legal Warfare Base" (舆论战心理战法律战基地). Base 311, which has its headquarters in Fujian, within Fuzhou province, seemingly oversees at least six regiments that are responsible for engaging in the three warfares against Taiwan, including through multiple forms of propaganda.[53] In peacetime, Base 311's employment of the three warfares has included the utilization of a commercial front, the China Huayi Broadcasting Corporation (中国华艺广播公司, CHBC).[54] Typically, the commander of Base 311 is dual-hatted as the CEO (or chairman, 董事长) of CHBC.[55]

Base 311's position and function within the PLA has evolved notably as a result of the ongoing reforms. There are indications that Base 311, which was previously subordinated to the former GPD, may now be under the aegis of the PLA's new Strategic Support Force, potentially under its Political Work Department or Network Systems Department.[56] The potential transfer of Base 311 to the PLASSF is be consistent with the PLA's intensified emphasis on ensuring the operational relevance and strategic impact of the three warfares in a wartime context. In practice, the conceptual framework of the three warfares is closely linked to the PLA's thinking on information warfare, which incorporates cyber warfare, electronic warfare, and also psychological warfare. In this regard, this potential organizational shift could prelude an enhanced focus on integrating the three warfares into information operations on the battlefield. However, it is unclear how and to what extent Base 311's activities, including those of its front organizations, will continue to be coordinated with other key actors in the PLA's political work/warfare system in the future.[57] At present, there is also not evidence available regarding whether Base 311 would be commanded directly through the PLASSF or instead be either commanded from a higher echelon under the Central Military Commission or potentially through a theater command.

Going forward, it is likely that Base 311, which is now openly identified as subordinate to the PLA Strategic Support Force,[58] will be a critical player not only in peacetime operations targeting Taiwan and beyond but also in undertaking any wartime activities. During Taiwan's fall 2018 local elections, there were credible allegations of interference by China that involved attempts to manipulate media and public opinion.[59] There are also reasons for concern that Taiwan's media and information ecosystem may be particularly vulnerable to such efforts going forward.[60] Just as Russia initially targeted nations within its "near abroad" before turning to employ similar techniques against the United States, Taiwan may also become a critical bellwether for the techniques and relative sophistication of Chinese attempts to undertake electoral interference or psychological operations that could be turned against overseas Chinese populations and perhaps even against the United States in the future.[61]

Beyond these strategic principles, how might the PLA seek to employ aspects of the three warfares in an operational scenario, against Taiwan or another potential adversary? The second edition of the AMS *Science of Joint Campaigns Textbook* (联合战役学教程), published in 2012, indicates that the three warfares are conceptualized as critical aspects of the PLA's approach to joint campaign scenarios, which include the island blockade campaign (岛屿封锁战役) and island assault campaign (岛屿进攻战役), scenarios that would in all likelihood be directed against Taiwan.[62] In particular, during efforts to "create pre-war momentum" (战前造势), public opinion warfare and psychological warfare would be employed as the primary content of efforts to disintegrate enemy forces and "consolidate" (巩固) oneself.[63] Through these and related efforts—such as reconnaissance and counter-reconnaissance, as well as cyber offensives and defensives—the PLA would seek to seize the initiative and create a favorable situation for the joint offensive campaign.[64] In the midst of a joint offensive campaign, in order to "expand" upon combat success (战果) and further develop the assault, the campaign commander would seek to undermine the adversary's will to resist and intensify its chaos, including through the implementation of public opinion warfare, psychological warfare, and legal warfare, seeking through this combination of firepower strikes and psychological attacks (攻心) to "rapidly disintegrate the enemy forces' psychology and morale."[65]

## Potential emerging techniques and capabilities

In an era of big data and rapid advances in artificial intelligence, China, unsurprisingly, appears to be actively interested in new techniques to exploit these technologies to monitor and manipulate public opinion.[66] Whereas there is relative concern in the U.S. to the question of the impact of public opinion on AI, including regarding the societal impact of automation and military applications, there is greater attention in China about how AI will affect or could be leveraged to impact public opinion and propaganda going forward. In some cases, initial efforts to do so may be fairly clumsy, as in the case of an "AI news anchor" that was featured in state media.[67] Increasingly, there are active efforts under way to explore the intersection of big data and public opinion, by academics, Party researchers, and also military academics and officers. Notably, in 2018, the PLA's National Defense University convened a forum on big data and "national ideological security" that explored various dimensions of this challenge.[68]

As an initial example of how this thinking is starting to evolve, a paper authored by the director of the PLA Theoretical Propaganda and Editing Room for *PLA Daily*, the PLA's official media outlet, raised concerns about the risks and opportunities that these technologies could present, including the chance to attempt to seize "cyber public opinion dominance" (制网络舆论权) in order to achieve an advantage in "public opinion struggle."[69] Potentially, big data could play an essential function in: monitoring hotspots through massive information collection, intelligent semantic analysis, and machine learning technologies engaged in continuous surveillance of the Chinese information ecosystem; improved online monitoring of public opinion risks to ensure preparedness for any potential incidents; overall analysis of trends in public opinion in order to enable the development of more targeted action plans in response; organizing a targeted strike in the case of an incident to prevent any "malicious attack on the Party's leadership" and the active guidance of public attitudes to "strengthen online positive propaganda." In the aggregate, these functions could be applicable defensively and offensively, and domestically and internationally, in ways that bolster regime security or exploit vulnerabilities in other systems.

Going forward, current developments in the field of AI could contribute to new threats of propaganda and psychological operations in the future that may pose novel challenges. Concerningly, the highly precise targeting and manipulation of human emotions that AI technologies can already enable, as demonstrated in contexts that range from advertising to elections, could create new human vulnerabilities that are much harder flaws than those that are technical in nature to mitigate. Potentially, parallel advances in neuroscience could even allow the PLA to contest "brain control" or "cognitive dominance" (制脑权) for more sophisticated exploitation, as some thinkers have argued.[70] The advent of false images known as "deep fakes" suggest a future in which today's "truth decay" could accelerate, exacerbating mistrust in democratic societies that exacerbates vulnerabilities to authoritarian influence. Similarly, advances in national language processing could enable the generation of misinformation at high scale, lower cost, and with greater sophistication. Meanwhile, as militaries explore advances in autonomous systems and human machine teaming, new techniques for "hacking" AI, including data poisoning and exploitation via hardware or algorithmic vulnerabilities, may become a new frontier of psychological warfare. Of course, parallel technological advancements can provide useful countermeasures for these threats, including new options for detection of doctored or falsely generated, along with improved verification of AI systems.[71] However, it remains to be seen how this "offense-defense balance" may

## 50 Elsa B. Kania

evolve overall going forward as militaries experiment with and develop countermeasures for these capabilities.

## Notes

1 "Document 9: A ChinaFile Translation," November 8, 2013, www.chinafile.com/document-9-chinafile-translation.
2 For an English translation of this commentary in full, see: www.newamerica.org/cybersecurity-initiative/blog/chinas-strategic-thinking-building-power-cyberspace/.
3 This is consistent with a very expansive concept of national security, as Dr. Samantha Hoffman has discussed: http://nationalinterest.org/feature/dangerous-love-chinas-all-encompassing-security-vision-16239.
4 See the official English translation: http://eng.mod.gov.cn/publications/2017-03/03/content_4774229.htm.
5 Arguably, the "Great Cannon" attack on GreatFire.org was seen as a "defensive" response to an "attack" that violated China's cyber sovereignty by attempting to breach the Great Firewall.
6 For further context, see: www.tandfonline.com/doi/full/10.1080/10670564.2016.1206281, http://news.sohu.com/20161108/n472633628.shtml.
7 For excellent research on early indications of this shift towards automation, see: https://citizenlab.ca/2016/11/wechat-china-censorship-one-app-two-systems/.
8 Molly Roberts' research provides the best overview of issues of censorship. For a good example of adaptive countermeasures, see the use of emojis and blockchain by China's #MeToo movement to counter the removal of reports on incidents of sexual harassment.
9 For instance, the CAC's former and formative director, Lu Wei, was previously head of the Beijing Propaganda Department, and his successor, Xu Lin, and the current director, Xuang Rongwen, both have had a background in China's Central Propaganda Department. Their selection clearly signals the CAC's priorities in that direction.
10 For the authoritative research on these issues, see Anne-Marie Brady's *Marketing Dictatorship*, https://books.google.com/books/about/Marketing_Dictatorship.html?id=ClVo0rZvE6EC&printsec=frontcover&source=kp_read_button#v=onepage&q&f=false.
11 These views are reflected in this article: http://news.china.com/news100/11038989/20130917/18050830.html, www.cac.gov.cn/2017-09/16/c_1121674888.htm.
12 For an excellent analysis, see: "In Xi We Trust: How Propaganda Might Be Working in the New Era," *MacroPolo*, September 12, 2018, https://macropolo.org/committee-analysis/in-xi-we-trust/.
13 See: www.81.cn/jmywyl/2017-03/22/content_7534870_3.htm.
14 For an early and insightful analysis of these issues, see: Peter Mattis, "China's International Right to Speak," *China Brief*, October 19, 2012, https://jamestown.org/program/chinas-international-right-to-speak/.
15 I defer to the expertise of Dr. Samantha Hoffman on all matters involving social management, including the global implications of social credit. See, for instance: https://jamestown.org/program/managing-the-state-social-credit-surveillance-and-the-ccps-plan-for-china/.
16 Since 2007, when Hu Jintao initially emphasized the importance of Chinese culture to the nation's rejuvenation, China has embarked upon a global "charm offensive" to enhance its soft power, which has "emerged as the most potent weapon in Beijing's foreign policy arsenal" by some assessments. See: Hu Jintao, "Hold high the great banner of socialism with Chinese characteristics and strive for new victories in building a moderately prosperous society in all respects," *China Daily* (2007): 2007–10; and Joshua Kurlantzick, *Charm offensive: How China's soft power is transforming the world*. Yale University Press, 2007.
17 David Shambaugh, "China's Soft-Power Push: The Search for Respect," *Foreign Affairs*, July/August 2015, www.foreignaffairs.com/articles/china/2015-06-16/china-s-soft-power-push.
18 Joseph S. Nye, Jr., *Soft Power: The Means To Success In World Politics*. According to Nye, who first conceived of the concept, soft power "coopts people rather than coerces them," based on the "ability to shape the preferences of others" through attraction, such as that of culture.
19 In particular, this report from the National Endowment for Democracy highlighted ways in which such authoritarian influence can have an adverse impact on democratic governance. While noting

that CCP "united front work" has been an integral element of this agenda, I will not address that issue directly in this paper.

20  Given the scope of this paper, I will not address the question of Chinese Communist Party influence and interference as it manifests through the activities of the United Front Work Department, although this is also a critical dimension of understanding China's "sharp power." For a notable analysis of the concept, see: Peter Mattis, "U.S. Responses to China's Foreign Influence Operations" Testimony before the House Committee on Foreign Affairs, Subcommittee on Asia and the Pacific – March 21, 2018, https://docs.house.gov/meetings/FA/FA05/20180321/108056/HHRG-115-FA05-Wstate-MattisP-20180321.pdf.

21  "Sharp Power: Rising Authoritarian Influence," National Endowment for Democracy, December 5, 2017, www.ned.org/sharp-power-rising-authoritarian-influence-forum-report/.

22  In practice, the exercise of this power has extended to attempts to reshape the behavior of international companies, including on issues that would seem fairly trivial, such as how their websites refer to Taiwan. For a great analysis of the topic, see: Samantha R Hoffman, "Programming China: the Communist Party's autonomic approach to managing state security," PhD diss., University of Nottingham, 2017.

23  Of those, some are situated within Chinese social sciences: Gu Mengjie, "Some Thinking on the New Chinese Word "Huayuquan,"" http://en.cnki.com.cn/Article_en/CJFDTotal-SYBX200801008.htm. Paul S.N. Lee, "The Rise of China and Its Contest for Discursive Power," *Global Media and China* 1(1–2) (2016) 102–120, http://journals.sagepub.com/doi/pdf/10.1177/2059436416650549. Kejin Zhao, "China's Rise and its Discursive Power Strategy," *Chinese Political Science Review* 1(5) (September 2016) 39–564, https://link.springer.com/article/10.1007/s41111-016-0037-8.

24  Of relevance, in the existing social sciences literature, the notion of *discursive* power has a unique lineage and distinct but relevant meaning, involving the "mobilization" of particular discourses to generate certain effects. The phrase "discursive power" can also be an alternative translation of *huayuquan*, but I use the phrasing "discourse power" to refer to the Chinese conceptualization of the term.

25  In practice, the exercise of discursive power can involve the leveraging of history or salient narratives to achieve a desired outcome. Some of the literature has examined Chinese foreign policy and legitimizing techniques through this framework, including examining at the Chinese government's use of discourse on the history of the Sino-Japanese war, including to bolster domestic legitimacy, though with only limited success. Karl Gustafsson, "Is China's Discursive Power Increasing? The 'Power of the Past' in Sino-Japanese Relations," *Asian Perspective* 38 (2014), 411–433, https://s3.amazonaws.com/academia.edu.documents/37939825/107048.pdf?AWSAccessKeyId=AKIAIWOWYYGZ2Y53UL3A&Expires=1540749704&Signature=JfT02%2FwcjERcDCFORlTWaQEZJaU%3D&response-content-disposition=inline%3B%20filename%3DIs_China_s_Discursive_Power_Increasing_T.pdf.

26  Yiwei Wang, "China Model Is Breaking Through the Hegemony of Universal Values," *People's Daily*, January 10, 2013, http://theory.people.com.cn/n/2013/0111/c40531-20166235.html.

27  For discussion and context on these remarks, see "Grasp the International Discourse Power and Effectively Disseminating the Voice of China—Analysis of the Theories of Xi Jinping's External Propaganda Work" [把握国际话语权 有效传播中国声音——习近平外宣工作思路理念探析], Xinhua, April 06, 2016, http://webcache.googleusercontent.com/search?q=cache:nQlx6j3z3-4J:www.xinhuanet.com/politics/2016-04/06/c_1118542256.htm+&cd=1&hl=en&ct=clnk&gl=us.

28  David Murphy, "Huayuquan: Speak and Be Heard," in *Shared Destiny*. ANU Press, 2015.

29  Ibid.

30  For a recent discussion that frames these issues in the cyber age, see: 着眼过好网络关时代关 努力推动政治工作创新发展, 军队党的生活, October 30, 2018,

31  Wu Jieming [吴杰明] and Liu Zhifu [刘志富], *An Introduction to Public Opinion Warfare, Psychological Warfare, [and] Legal Warfare* [舆论战心理战法律战概论], National Defense University Press, 2014, p. 1.

32  These efforts have included the development of curricula for educating officers in public opinion warfare, psychological warfare, and legal warfare. This process resulted in the publication of numerous articles in *PLA Daily* and military region newspapers, as well as multiple books and textbooks, on the topic. In subsequent years, the PLA implemented institutional mechanisms that

entailed a series of supporting documents and regulations, efforts to deepen three warfares education and training, the construction of specialized forces, the guarantee of equipment and materials, and also research and drills on operational art theories and actual combat. Reportedly, there was also progress in the construction (建设) of "three warfares forces," while seeking to ensure that the concepts were conveyed and practiced with consistency throughout the PLA. See: http://news.xinhuanet.com/mil/2004-06/21/content_1538252.htm. In some cases, the progress towards the establishment of three warfare forces or psychological warfare forces, which also are often situated within the PLA's information operations forces, may have remained inconsistent. For instance, by one account, PLA's "experimental psychological warfare forces" were still in an "exploratory" (探索) stage as of 2010. Further commentary on the topic of "specialized three warfares forces" emphasizes the importance of enhancing their education and training.

33 Similarly, the Nanjing Political Institute has become an important center for training and research in political work, including the three warfares. Since 2003, the Nanjing Political Institute has established a "psychological warfare specialized research center," military political work informationization research and development center, and a military political work research institute. Notable scholars associated with the Nanjing Political Institute have published on topics such as the "new requirements of wartime political work in informationized warfare" and the impact of military press releases on public opinion.

34 Established in 1977, the Xi'an Political Institute has traditionally been the primary educational institution for training the PLA's political work cadre (政工干部), while also serving as a research institution.

35 Academy of Military Science Military Strategy Research Department [军事科学院军事战略研究部], eds., *The Science of Military Strategy* [战略学]. Military Science Press, 2013, p. 131.

36 Wu Jieming [吴杰明] and Liu Zhifu [刘志富], *An Introduction to Public Opinion Warfare, Psychological Warfare, [and] Legal Warfare* [舆论战心理战法律战概论], National Defense University Press, 2014, p. 1.

37 Wu Jieming [吴杰明] and Liu Zhifu [刘志富], *An Introduction to Public Opinion Warfare, Psychological Warfare, [and] Legal Warfare* [舆论战心理战法律战概论], National Defense University Press, 2014, p. 1.

38 There are many clichés that recur in the study of China. I believe that the concept of "winning without fighting" is one that merits the cliché and frequent invocation.

39 See James Mulvenon's early and influential research on these issues.

40 Ministry of National Defense of the People's Republic of China [中华人民共和国国防部], "China's Military Strategy" [中国的军事战略], State Council Information Office [国务院新闻办公室], May 26, 2015, www.mod.gov.cn/auth/2015-05/26/content_4586723.htm.

41 Ministry of National Defense of the People's Republic of China [中华人民共和国国防部], "China's Military Strategy" [中国的军事战略], State Council Information Office [国务院新闻办公室], May 26, 2015, www.mod.gov.cn/auth/2015-05/26/content_4586723.htm.

42 That is my interpretation, subject to debate.

43 Of course, I acknowledge that this distinction can become very blurred in the U.S. in light of recent history. Relative to the U.S., the PLA also lacks the same legal culture.

44 Academy of Military Science Military Strategy Research Department [军事科学院军事战略研究部] (ed.), *The Science of Military Strategy* [战略学], 2013, p. 320.

45 *Military Terminology of the Chinese People's Liberation Army*, Military Science Press, 2011.

46 Academy of Military Science Military Strategy Research Department [军事科学院军事战略研究部] (ed.), *The Science of Military Strategy* [战略学], 2013, p. 320.

47 Ibid.

48 As I've observed elsewhere, it appears that the PLA started to work on updating its doctrine (or what appears to be an analog thereof but has never been released publicly) around 2004, intended to formalize this fifth generation in 2008, and then ultimately decided not to do so for reasons that were unknown but may (speculatively) have reflected a lack of consensus on certain key issues. As of 2016, there were some indications that aspects of these doctrinal concepts were close to finalized, but no official announcement of their release has been made up to early 2019, and there continue to be exhortations for more effective integration of new concepts into official doctrine in PLA media commentary, indicating that there is still some obstruction in the process.

49 *Military Terminology of the Chinese People's Liberation Army*, Military Science Press, 2011.

50 Ye Zheng [叶证], *Lectures on the Science of Information Operations* [信息作战科学教程], Military Science Press [军事科学出版社], 2013.

51 Ye Zheng [叶证], *Lectures on the Science of Information Operations* [信息作战科学教程].

52 Ibid.

53 Mark Stokes and Russell Hsiao, "The People's Liberation Army General Political Department Political Warfare with Chinese Characteristics," October 14, 2013, www.project2049.net/documents/PLA_General_Political_Department_Liaison_Stokes_Hsiao.pdf.

54 Ibid.

55 Major General Wang Shu (王树 or 汪澍), who became the commander of Base 311 in 2010, was concurrently the chairman (董事长) of CHBC. Since Wang Shu was promoted to become the director of the Nanjing Political Institute in 2015, there has been no official announcement regarding who would take over his role as commander of Base 311. However, since mid-2015, Qiu Yu (邱雨) has since been identified as the chairman of CHBC, potentially an indicator that he is also the current commander of Base 311.

56 Full credit for this initial assessment goes to John Costello, who first determined that Base 311 had been resubordinated to the PLASSF on available indications of personnel affiliations that had shifted.

57 For instance, there are indications that Base 311 had previously collaborated with or otherwise provided support to the former GPD Liaison Department (总政治部联络部), the Chinese Communist Party's Taiwan Propaganda Leading Small Group, and also the Taiwan Affairs Leading Small Group, based on reports of interactions with figures from these organizations. Such collaborations will likely continue, but the coordination of these various political warfare activities could remain a challenge for the PLA.

58 Potentially, the fact that this affiliation is now openly named is a response to the public "attribution" of this change in structure in published writings by several analysts who leverage open sources, myself and John Costello. If this is the case, that raises the possibility that "forced transparency" may be an effective means of encouraging the PLA to confirm its force structure.

59 See Lauren Dickey's analysis at the time.

60 Jessica Drun, "Taiwan's Social Media Landscape: Ripe for Election Interference?", Center for Advanced China Research, November 13, 2018, www.ccpwatch.org/single-post/2018/11/13/Taiwans-Social-Media-Landscape-Ripe-for-Election-Interference.

61 Clearly, there is a long history to efforts by China to interfere in American politics, but the techniques used are often much simpler, involving.

62 Li Yousheng [李有升] (ed.), *The Science of Joint Campaigns Textbook* [联合战役学教程], Military Science Press [军事科学出版社], 2012, p. 203.

63 Ibid., p. 212.

64 Ibid.

65 Ibid., p. 231.

66 At the same time, militaries can start to leverage virtual reality for improved training and psychological conditioning in ways that may prove advantageous.

67 http://webcache.googleusercontent.com/search?q=cache:c8rfXuJ_jXkJ:news.cctv.com/2018/02/19/ARTI95D1AEAkhSr1NBCRrubf180219.shtml+&cd=13&hl=en&ct=clnk&gl=us.

68 黄昆仑, "关注大数据时代的国家舆论安全".

69 黄昆仑, "关注大数据时代的国家舆论安全".

70 朱雪玲 曾华锋, "军事对抗已从物理战场拓展到认知战场, 从有形战场扩展到无形战场, "制脑权"的较量正向我们走来——制脑作战: 未来战争竞争新模式".

71 Wang Ruifa, Tao Ningwei, Peng Xu, Luo Yuzhen, Liao Dongsheng, Application and prospect of virtual reality in psychological warfare[J].Defense Science and Technology, 2018, 39(6): At the same time, militaries can start to leverage virtual reality for improved training and psychological conditioning in ways that may prove advantageous.

# 5

# CYBER CONFLICT AT THE INTERSECTION OF INFORMATION OPERATIONS

## Cyber-enabled information operations, 2000–2016

*Colin Foote, Ryan C. Maness, Benjamin Jensen, and Brandon Valeriano*

While the rise of cyber security issues as a "tier one" national security threat war was predicted for decades and is now seen as common fact, many have missed the proliferation of Information Operations (IO) as a crucial coercive factor in international politics. From the election attacks in 2016 by Russia directed against the United States to the nearly continuous cycle of information operations between India versus Pakistan and North Korea versus South Korea, the modern age has witnessed a proliferation of cyber-enabled information operations.

This style of political contestation is more than social media warfare; cyber-enabled information operations are dangerous attacks on the foundations of trust and knowledge. They seek to damage the integrity of defensive systems and hobble command and control capabilities. They can strike at the homeland and create divisions that rupture the fault lines in society. Enabled by the rise of digital communication and fiber infrastructure, we seek to understand the foundations of the practice of cyber-enabled information operations.

In this study we empirically operationalize, define, and catalog cyber-enabled information operations between adversaries. Overall, we find strong evidence for a rise in cyber-enabled information operations, but with critical caveats. These operations are often attached to the more benign disruption activities. One country, Russia, dominates the use of cyber-enabled information operations in the international system. These are not the existential threats promised (Lin 2019), but opportunistic attacks that correspond with ongoing actions highlighting weaknesses in cyber defenses.

To meet the challenge of information operations, we must first understand the process and dynamics inherent in these forms of modern-day political warfare. Our study here provides an early attempt to empirically catalog these attacks and seeks to understand their impact. Only through the beginnings of this process can we come to handle the advent and evolution of information warfare.

## Defining cyber-enabled information operations

### Information warfare

The term "information warfare" has become rather broad, including all forms of information and communication. It can mean anything from attacks on information, simply stealing information, to managing the reception of information and the interpretation of signals. We want to focus on what might be considered informational power. Castells (2013: 10) articulates the concept quite well but first defining power as the ability to control or coerce. In this

> world of networks, the ability to exercise control over others depends on two basic mechanisms: (1) the ability to constitute network(s), and to program/reprogram the network(s) in terms of the goals assigned to the network, and (2) the ability to connection and ensure the cooperation of different networks by sharing common goals and combining resources.
>
> *(Castells 2013: 45)*

In this articulation, information power would be the ability to control the nodes and networks in order to control the message the masses or a target receives.

According to the U.S. Joint Chief of Staff's Joint Publication (JP) 3–13, information operations are defined as "the integrated employment, during military operations, of information-related capabilities (IRCs) in concert with other lines of operation to influence, disrupt, corrupt, or usurp the decision making of adversaries and potential adversaries while protecting our own" (JP 3–13 2014: ix). This narrow definition of information operations (IOs) separates the concept from cyber operations, which are considered separate from IOs, as the Joint Chief has a separate publication (JP 3–12 2018) on cyberspace operations.

For our purposes, we distinguish information operations from the more universal awareness of what the general public conceives as an attack on information. We also want to avoid the broad definition of information operations on a spectrum as defined by the U.S. military, which includes electronic warfare, psychological operations, cyber operations, and social network exploitation.

The more specific conceptualization of information operations as a function of gathering, providing, and denying information in order to improve decision-making is a useful starting point.[1] In this way information warfare is a tool of coercion, intended to deny benefits to the opposition and add benefits to the attacker. In the military parlance of the OODA (observe, orientate, decide, act) loop, information warfare introduces doubt in the enemy's loop and enhances the decision-making process of the attacker.

We dial down on information operations utilized during cyber incidents/campaigns; actions now termed cyber-enabled information operations (CIO).[2] The Senate Armed Services Subcommittee defined the domain as including "the gathering and dissemination of information in the cyber domain."[3] Jane's dissects modern cyber-enabled information operations never really defining the bounds of their investigation but the exercise operates under the general idea of using "information missions ... to undermine an adversary at all levels of leadership and to influence its decision making."[4] Lin and Kerr (2019) use the term cyber-enabled information operations frequently but never define what an action of this sort constitutes beyond linking the term with the cognitive dimensions of information warfare and information operations (IWIO).

Our focus for the term cyber-enabled information operations is on actions launched during ongoing cyber operations and allows us to examine how information and data is weaponized adjunct to cyber incidents and campaigns. Rather than documenting more broad attacks on truth and meaning, we seek to understand how data can be manipulated and/or used to message in a coercive operation against a rival state. We can make no claims about the broader tendency of states to use information operations against each other; rather we are concerned here only with information operations that occur during cyber operations. Information control is a form of power, and conceptualizing cyber-enabled information operations as a method of coercion is critical in understanding the functions and process of modern information warfare.

## The evolving understanding of cyber operations

Commander of U.S. Cyber Command, General Paul Nakasone, distinguishes between espionage and disruptive and destructive forms of cyber conflict (Nakasone 2019: 12). We have covered similar forms in our coding of cyber events with a typology of disruptive, espionage, and degrading attacks (destructive is too limiting since destruction is so rare in cyberspace) in order to delineate different types of cyber conflict and their probability of achieving coercive effect (Valeriano, Jensen, and Maness 2018). We have found in the past that the majority of the actions in the cyber domain are espionage while degrade attacks are rare, but also the most likely form to be coercive in terms of changing a target's behavior (Valeriano et al. 2018). Of the 192 cyber incidents between state rivals from the years 2000–2014, we find that 70 incidents are considered disruptions, 97 are espionage operations, and 25 are degradation incidents (Valeriano et al. 2018). Only 11 incidents (6 percent) have been able to change a target state's behavior.

It is important to note the evolution of cyber conflict and the utility of operations in the information space as they are aided by these information operations. Nakasone offers a new form, noting "now we're seeing what many call a corrosive threat, which is the ability to weaponize information in order to conduct influence campaigns, steal intellectual property, or leverage someone's personally identifiable information" (Nakasone 2019: 12). We focus here on influence campaigns (messaging) and leveraging information (manipulation), bringing a new addition to the cyber conflict literature by conceptualizing information attack as an adjunct or aid to cyber operations.

## Cyber-enabled information operations

Noting a need to consider the evolving methods of conflict in cyberspace, we now code cyber-enabled information operations as concentrated state level efforts to manipulate data for coercive purposes or those operations seeking to utilize compromised information to send specific messages to the adversary. The focus is really on the manipulation and messaging aspects of information operations during ongoing cyber operations.

A more encompassing definition seeking to count all instances where information was simply compromised or stolen would be needlessly broad and not helpful in understanding the coercive potential of information operations. Information operations do not merely steal data but seek to disseminate information when it might harm the adversary or alter that data to manipulate the sentiment in the opposition. Stealing information is espionage. To truly understand the coercive potential of information operations, we need to be more specific.

*Cyber-enabled information operations (CIO)* are therefore defined, for the purposes of this investigation and our dataset, as *state-based actions, in the context of an ongoing cyber action, seeking to communicate a message or manipulate the reception of digital information for malicious purposes among a targeted population.* The actions are intended to sow discontent, change policy direction, or serve as a warning to an adversary in the digital space (See Jensen, Valeriano, and Maness 2019).

## Research design

All variables extracted for analysis originate from the updated Dyadic Cyber Incident and Campaign Dataset (DCID) version 1.5 (Maness, Valeriano, and Jensen 2019). This improved version our state-based cyber events cover the years 2000–2016 with a focus on rival interactions. The primary variable under analysis for this chapter is the CIO variable described in the previous section. Which countries utilized these cyber-enabled information operations the most? Which methods of cyber operations are utilized to enable the following information operations against the target state? Which strategic objectives were targeted by corresponding information operations? In this chapter we start the investigation and seek to establish a baseline of knowledge about cyber-enabled information operations.

To uncover the dynamics of cyber-enabled information operations, we employ two methods: the first is simple crosstabulations (crosstabs) that compare two categorical variables and their subsequent expected versus observational counts to see if there are any countries, strategies, or methods that fall outside the normal distribution of expectations. The simple way to measure whether certain categorical variables' attributes, when compared to one another, fall out of the range of what is considered normal is to add Pearson residuals to the crosstabs analysis in order to get a tangible measure of the number of standard deviations between the expected value (mean) and the observed value for each case of cross-tabulated variables. Put simply, we want to know if certain countries, methods, and strategic objectives tend to use CIOs when compared to others.

The dependent variable for all three crosstabulations examined below is our cyber-enabled information operation (CIO) variable. The variable is a simple binary categorical variable that measures with the presence (1) or absence (0) of an information operation to manipulate or message the opposition launched either in tandem with the original cyber incident or as a result of the cyber incident's successful breach.

Each independent variable for the three crosstab analyses is a nominal categorical variable, with the first identifying each country in the DCID v1.5 dataset. However, because crosstabs require a minimum amount of cases for each country in order for results to have meaning, we only include states that have initiated a cyber incident at least five times in the 2000–2016 time period. Five cases are the standard minimum when conducting these categorical, chi-squared analyses. The first independent variable represents the countries that have engaged in cyber conflict with their rivals at least five times during the years covered in the DCID dataset.

The second independent variable under examination is the strategic objective of the initiating state against its target (Valeriano et al. 2018). This nominal variable has four values: the first being disruptive events, which are low-cost, low pain nuisance cyber operations intended to send an ambiguous signal to the target that has either a coercive intent or is used as a disinformation tool (Valeriano et al. 2018). These disruptive events mostly come in the form of defacements (vandalism) or denial of service (DDoS) attacks and can be easily eradicated from systems with no permanent damage.

Espionage, or manipulative cyber strategy, comes in two forms: short-term espionage is the theft of information and the immediate usage of that information for strategic gain. The Russian hacking of the Democratic National Committee (DNC) and the subsequent selective release of that information to Wikileaks in 2016 is an example of this type of espionage. The second form of manipulative strategy is what is called long-term espionage, which entails the stealing of strategic information from a target in order to leverage that information at a later point in time (Maness et al. 2019). These operations are forward-thinking and can be seen as altering the balance of information for strategic advantage. The Chinese intellectual property theft of the U.S. and Western private sector such as Lockheed Martin's F-35 plans, as well as Chinese hacks of the U.S. government such as the Office of Personnel Management (OPM) hacks are examples of this strategy.

Degradations are the final strategic objective code in the DCID data, which covers more high cost, high pain cyber operations that are usually intended to break networks by wiping data or causing a physical malfunction in critical systems (sabotage). The Stuxnet attack on Iranian centrifuges is an example of this more destructive form of cyber operations (Valeriano et al. 2018).

The third independent variable for the macro analysis of this chapter compares the cyber method utilized with the CIO dependent variable. There are four nominal variables for this category: vandalism, denial-of-service, network intrusions, and network infiltrations (Maness et al. 2019). Vandalism methods are usually always website defacements and these usually have a propagandist, disinformation, or psychological operative element to them. We therefore expect most of the CIO variables to be associated with this independent variable. The next variable is what is called the denial of service (DoS), which includes DoS, distributed denial of service (DDoS), and other botnet and bandwidth limiting cyber strategies. As these methods are very public and intend to send an ambiguous message to the adversary's government and general public, we expect some CIOs to be associated with these types of attacks. Network intrusions are mostly espionage campaigns and utilize social engineering as the primary intrusion method. Network infiltrations are more sinister and include malware (virus, worm, logic bombs, wiper malware, keystroke logs, etc.).

Following our statistical analysis, we develop two case studies that dig deeper into the attributes of cyber-enabled information operations in order to identify processes and mechanisms. The first case study is the Russian hacking group Pawn Storm's assault on the World Anti-Doping Agency (WADA) after the group found that many Russian Olympic athletes were taking banned substances in order to gain an edge in the Olympic Winter Games in Sochi, Russia in 2014, as well as the Rio Summer Olympics of 2016. As a result of this scandal, the Russian Olympic team was banned from the following Winter Games in 2018 in South Korea. WADA was heavily targeted by the Russian government with cyber intrusions and information operations. The second case study uncovers the very interesting and unique India–Pakistan cyber rivalry. While in the conventional realm the two countries are very aggressive with each other in the conventional domains, in the cyber realm the two countries engage in very low-level defacement and propaganda operations for psychological purposes. We now turn to the findings of these two methodologies employed to look at CIO from a macro and micro perspective.

## Findings and analysis

Table 5.1 shows the results of the crosstabs analysis of countries that engage with their rivals in the cyber domain and how they use information operations. The United States and China utilize information operations much less than expected; the results are statistically significant. This means that the U.S. and China use CIOs much less than expected according to our data sample. The United States uses cyber operations sparingly, and when it does it usually will attempt to degrade systems for coercive effect. Furthermore, the U.S. has yet to fully integrate its cyber operations with its information operations in terms of military strategy and doctrine. The Chinese are very well known for their long-term espionage operations, which do not usually have an immediate information operation following the cyber incident. When it does launch information operations it usually targets social media sites and does so with its immediate rivals surrounding the South China Sea. It seems the two most powerful countries in the world are not utilizing information operations as much as the top revisionist power in the world, Russia.

Russia utilizes CIOs more than expected at the 90 percent confidence level. This is not surprising as the hacking of private entities and political parties of the West has been on the rise since around 2014 (Maness et al. 2019). They hack these organizations with the purpose of releasing the information that may make status quo candidates or parties look unfavorable to the domestic audience. These types of information operations are not just cyber-enabled, however. Russia extensively uses social media platforms and state-owned media companies to

**TABLE 5.1** Crosstabulations of state actors who launch cyber-enabled information operations with Pearson residuals

| Initiating country | Cyber-incidents, no information operations (Expected frequency) Pearson residual | Cyber-incidents with information operations (Expected frequency) Pearson residual |
| --- | --- | --- |
| United States | 21 (15.4) | 0 (5.6) |
| | 1.43 | −2.37** |
| Russia | 41 (47.7) | 24 (17.3) |
| | −0.97 | 1.60* |
| Iran | 26 (24.2) | 7 (8.8) |
| | 0.37 | −0.61 |
| Israel | 8 (6.6) | 1 (2.4) |
| | 0.55 | −0.90 |
| China | 67 (54.3) | 7 (19.7) |
| | 1.73* | −2.87** |
| North Korea | 18 (19.1) | 8 (6.9) |
| | −0.24 | 0.41 |
| South Korea | 3 (5.1) | 4 (1.9) |
| | −0.94 | 1.56 |
| India | 1 (5.1) | 6 (1.9) |
| | −1.82* | 3.03*** |
| Pakistan | 2 (9.5) | 11 (3.5) |
| | −2.44** | 4.05*** |

*Notes*
Pearson chi-squared 62.31 (df=8)
***Likelihood-ratio chi-squared 64.87 (df=8)
***n=255, *p<0.10, **p<0.05, ***p<0.01

60 Colin Foote et al.

spread their misinformation and disinformation campaigns in an attempt to divide targeted populations over candidates, issues, and partisan platforms. The Russians have possibly weaponized this latter strategy more than any other country.

The India–Pakistan dyad also contains the two countries that utilize CIO more than what is expected at the 99 percent confidence level. What is surprising about these two countries is their use of website defacements, which are quite benign and low-level in the long term, and the number of militarized disputes the two countries have had over the 2000–2016 period in conjunction with these propagandist campaigns. The disputed region of Kashmir is where most of these violent actions happen, with subsequent propagandist content peppering each government's networks in conjunction with these very dangerous kinetic actions. More on Russian, Indian, and Pakistani CIOs will be discussed in the next section.

Table 5.2 contains the results of the crosstabs between CIOs and the strategic objective of the initiating state. Not surprisingly, disruptions are the only variable in this analysis to have positive statistical significance, which means more disruptions than what is expected at the 99 percent confidence level are observed. As disruptions contain vandalism and denial of service operations, these types of cyber incidents are usually the ones that will contain either an overt or ambiguous signal to the target government, and sometimes populations, launched through information operations.

Following the results of Table 5.2, Table 5.3 shows that Vandalism is the most extensively utilized method of cyber operation that has an information operation component. Denial of service, which can include botnets, DDoS, ransomware, and other network usage denial strategies, is also utilized more than what would be expected according to the null hypothesis at the 99 percent confidence level. According to these results, the utilization of propaganda, disinformation, and psy-ops is most associated with disruptions, specifically vandalism methods for strategic advantage against the targeted state.

With a simple grasp about which countries are utilizing CIOs more than others, which strategic objectives are most conducive to CIOs, and which cyber methods are most likely to contain CIOs, we now turn to two cases to get a better sense of what goes on during these

TABLE 5.2 Crosstabulations of cyber operation strategic objective and cyber-enabled information operations with Pearson residuals

| Strategic objective | Cyber-incidents, no information operations (Expected frequency) Pearson residual | Cyber-incidents with information operations (Expected frequency) Pearson residual |
| --- | --- | --- |
| Disruption | 30 (62.4) | 56 (23.6) |
|  | −4.10*** | 6.67*** |
| Short-term espionage | 67 (58.1) | 13 (22.0) |
|  | 1.18 | −1.91* |
| Long-term espionage | 65 (47.2) | 0 (17.8) |
|  | 2.60** | −4.22*** |
| Degradation | 31 (25.4) | 4 (9.6) |
|  | 1.11 | −1.81* |

Notes
Pearson chi-squared 95.42 (df=3)
***Likelihood-ratio chi-squared 105.49 (df=3)
***n=266, *p<0.10, **p<0.05, ***p<0.01

**TABLE 5.3** Crosstabulations of cyber method and cyber-enabled information operations with Pearson residuals

| Cyber method | Cyber-incidents, no information operations (Expected frequency) Pearson residual | Cyber-incidents with information operations (Expected frequency) Pearson residual |
| --- | --- | --- |
| Vandalism | 0 (20.3) | 28 (7.7) |
| | −4.51*** | 7.33*** |
| Denial of service | 24 (33.4) | 22 (12.6) |
| | −1.62* | 2.64** |
| Network intrusions | 125 (104.5) | 19 (39.5) |
| | 2.01** | −3.26*** |
| Network infiltrations | 44 (34.8) | 4 (13.2) |
| | 1.55 | −2.53** |

*Notes*
Pearson chi-squared 107.11 (df=3)
***Likelihood-ratio chi-squared 109.06 (df=3)
***n=266, *p<0.10, **p<0.05, ***p<0.01

cyber-enabled acts of malicious intent. The first is the Russian CIO against the World Anti-Doping Agency (WADA), and the second unpacks the dynamics of a very unique cyber-rival dyad: India and Pakistan.

## Russia versus the World Anti-Doping Agency

### *Narrative*

In the last decade Russia's brazen actions in cyberspace dramatically rose to the forefront of global attention with its cyber activities in Eastern Ukraine, Crimea, Georgia, Estonia, Western elections, and against WADA. While research is now showing that Russia is leaning towards leveraging internal governmental organizations as opposed to the crowd-sourced system of hacktivist organizations that it used in the past, it is still important to understand how crowd-sourced proxies were used to leverage data for influence.[5] The 2016 Rio Olympics and WADA provides a case study of how Russia operationalized hacktivist organizations to breech and subsequently dump critical data as influence operations to undermine WADA.

The motivation behind the Russian hacking of the WADA during the 2016 Rio Olympics originates with the 2014 Sochi Olympics when a Russian whistleblower alleged a national cheating scheme that supported the use of performance enhancing drugs.[6] The investigation by the *New York Times* with the help from a Russian whistleblower Grigory Rodchenkov, who was responsible for drug testing in Russia, stated that the performance enhancing drug abuse was being conducted at the state level. The international sports antidoping watchdog found evidence that 1,000 athletes were ultimately involved.[7]

The fallout from the 2014 Olympics doping scandal comes on the heels of Russia dominating the medal count, with 33 total medals consisting of 13 golds placing first overall with a seven-medal gap between first and second place.[8] Unquestionably, Russia took a blow on the international stage as a result of the WADA findings. Eventually the International Olympic Committee (IOC) disregarded the WADA call to ban Russia entirely from the 2016 Rio Olympics, but instead allowed 271 out of 389 athletes to compete.[9] The strain between the WADA and Russia widened as a result and the 2016 summer games with 118 Russian athletes banned from participating.

WADA's highly damaging report stated,

> The investigation has confirmed the existence of widespread cheating through the use of doping substances and methods to ensure, or enhance the likelihood of, victory for athletes and teams. The cheating was done by the athletes' entourages, officials and the athletes themselves.

The WADA report placed the organization firmly in the crosshairs of Russia's cyber capabilities.[10] Research points to Russia having a relatively low threshold when it comes to using cyber capabilities to attempt to exert influence.[11] This is further reinforced by the findings presented in Table 5.1, with Russia being the initiator in 28 percent of the global CIO actions. China follows far behind in second place initiating 7 percent of global cyber-enabled information actions.

While the hack occurred over a two-year span, primarily focusing on spear phishing, the Pawn Storm group, which is known to have ties to Russian military intelligence (GRU), utilized remote hacking of local networks and also mirrored organization websites to obtain passwords.[12] Allegations against these Kremlin-based hackers stated that agents in Russia centered their attention on the routers used by the hotel chains that were hosting Olympic officials in Rio.[13] Russian operatives were able to gain access to the WADA's medical files and doping results database when an official used the hotel chains router to log into his account, which allowed for a large amount of data to be pulled from the dataset on August 16, 2016 and September 6 2016.[14] On September 13, 2016, the anti-doping agency announced the hack:

> The World Anti-Doping Agency (WADA) confirms that a Russian cyber espionage group operator by the name of Tsar Team (APT28), also known as Fancy Bear, illegally gained access to WADA's Anti-Doping Administration and Management System (ADAMS) database via an International Olympic Committee (IOC)-created account for the Rio 2016 Games. The group accessed athlete data, including confidential medical data – such as Therapeutic Use Exemptions delivered by International Sports Federations (IFs) and National Anti-Doping Organizations (NADOs) – related to the Rio Games; and, subsequently released some of the data in the public domain, accompanied by the threat that they will release more.[15]

Upon obtaining access to WADA's files, the Russian group posted on their website (See Figure 5.1), "We are going to show the world how Olympic medals are won … We hacked the World Anti-Doping Agency databases and we were shocked what we saw. We do not forgive. We do not forget. Expect us."[16]

The statements serve to allege that Russia was not the only country with performance enhancing drugs being used by athletes.[18] #OpOlympics was the code name given to the hack by Russian proxies, a method that Anonymous typically coalesces crowd-sourced

FIGURE 5.1  Russian Hacking Group Fancy Bear propaganda[17]

hacking activities against an objective.[19] The acknowledgment of the first dump occurred on September 14, 2016 – only one day after the announcement of the hack by WADA:

> The World Anti-Doping Agency (WADA) confirms that the Russian cyber hackers, 'Fancy Bear' [aka Tsar Team (APT28)] have leaked another batch of confidential athlete data from WADA's Anti-Doping Administration and Management System (ADAMS). Similar to the leak that the Agency announced on 13 September, this time the group released the confidential athlete data of 25 athletes, from eight countries, into the public domain. The targeted athletes include ten from the United States, five from Germany, five from Great Britain, one from the Czech Republic, one from Denmark, one from Poland, one from Romania, and one from Russia.[20]

In the end, by October 5, the data dump eventually expanded to include 41 athletes from 13 countries.[21] Russia employed commonly used external and internal news sites to run stories about the hack, leaning heavily in RT (Russia Today) as well as social media, and web blogs run by the Fancy Bear team to reach global audiences.[22] On September 19, 2016 President Putin publicly lauded the Fancy Bear hacks, while simultaneously denying any Russian involvement,

> As you know, we do not welcome hackers and their actions, but it was thanks to them that we learned that people who took part in the Olympic Games and were outwardly perfectly healthy were actually taking prohibited substances that gave them and gives them clear advantages in sports competition.[23]

## Assessment

In the end, two distinct factors motivated the Russian IO operation: 1. Russian global credibility was on the line, 2. high impact, low-cost opportunity. Russia believes that it is constantly fighting both an internal and external existential threat, and any action deemed damaging to Russian credibility is seen as an attack on the state.[24] When the news broke about the Russian state-sponsored doping program, their state-run anti-doping agency was suspended internationally. On September 20, 2018 the Russian anti-doping agency was reinstated as a result of an internal vote within the executive board of WADA, but still marred in controversy.[25]

The hack, #OpOlympics, heavily alluded to the hypocrisy of the global community with regards to performance enhancing drugs. Numerous news sources and both unofficial and official tweets from Russian organizations demonstrated headlines that specifically stated this.[26] Russia likely viewed the hack as a reciprocation for their damaged global credibility.

Finally, the cost of the hack was relatively low as it employed unsophisticated levels of both physical and digital spy craft. Russian anti-doping credibility had already taken a hit as a result of the whistleblower, so blowback from anything damage of the hack would be minimal. The benefit of damaging the WADA and global anti-doping credibility in light of the Russian scandal far outweighed the cost of employing a handful of agents around the global and empowering a proxy hacker collective to release the data, while simultaneously capitalizing on it through both traditional and untraditional news outlets.

Ultimately, international sports teams and athletes were forced to defend themselves.[27] National tabloids quickly jumped on the bandwagon, amplifying the Russian narrative, "Drug storm hits football: Russian hackers claim nine players in Britain failed tests to leave sport's clean image in tatters."[28] While coercion is hard to prove, research does show the effects of the hacks were felt throughout the international sporting community when athletes had to respond to allegations, many of which painted a contradictory image of sports and doping, while lessoning the criticism of Russia.

## The India–Pakistan rivalry

### Narrative

The conflict over the territories of Jammu and Kashmir, often referred to as solely the Kashmir conflict, have raged since the British partition of India and Pakistan in 1947.[29] Highly contentious and highly political, both India and Pakistan routinely clash over the borders of Kashmir.[30] In the last half century the region has seen four wars, with the most recent being in 1999, but as technology has advanced the conflict has traversed across physical space into digital space.[31] Referring to Table 5.1, India has initiated 7 percent of known global CIO actions, while Pakistan has initiated 11 percent. The 2014 data breach of the Pakistani Peoples Party (PPP) by India and subsequent hack of the Press Club of India are primary examples of these types of low level, propagandist attacks.

The origin of the Pakistani breach of the Press Club of India (PCI) (Press Clubs are common worldwide as they are a society for journalists) involved a 16-year-old Indian hacker known as "Bl@ck Dr@gon" who defaced the PPP websites. While the hack was co-ordinated across multiple Indian hackers, Bl@ck Dr@gon acknowledged and claimed credit for the smear campaign on Bilawal Bhutto.[32] The Indian hacker stated that it was a retaliatory hack for Bilawal Bhutto's (Chairman of the PPP) controversial comments against India.[33] The hack and smear campaign on the PPP prompted Pakistani hackers to deface the PCI's website with strong anti-Modi statements.[34] In both data breaches, the perpetrators challenged the other state to try and trace their hacks, as all of these infiltrations were credited to "patriotic hackers."[35] While local media did not delve into the methods and means of these cyber incidents, the hackers on both sides touted that the security of the websites were subpar.[36] Research demonstrates that typically Indian and Pakistani hackers use Structured

Query Language (SQL) injections to change the appearance of a website or redirect to another website, which are more commonly known as defacements.[37]

## Assessment

Initial research into the hack showed minimal fallout, with the main action inciting a website defacement battle between the rivals. Internationally the hacks went largely unnoted as only regional and nation news reported on the hacks. Furthermore, the India and Pakistani CIO conflict demonstrates two of the original principles: 1. regional/global credibility and 2. high impact, low-cost. First, Indian and Pakistani hackers claimed that the hacks were retaliatory, not escalatory in nature. As the target of the smear campaigns was political officials on both ends, the target audience was likely localized, or internal to the state to demonstrate success against each other. The defacements likely did little besides create agitation on both ends but built credibility in the population by demonstrating the ease at which they accomplished the hacks.

Both of the cyber operations by Indian and Pakistani hackers were relatively unsophisticated, with no significant data dumps, or technical capabilities leveraged. These propaganda campaigns were simply website defacements and smear campaigns. These activities are very low cost, as both sides were lobbying virtual bullets back and forth. When a response is needed, CIOs provides a low-cost option, especially combined with an ongoing conflict, or moral high ground. Research shows that these CIO actions are often only annoyances with no lasting damage, while on the other hand there is a worry that these defacements could escalate and prompt a conventional conflict.[38] While this worry exists, no research exists demonstrating that this link has happened or occurred.

It is likely that the threshold to conduct CIO is lowered when states are in perpetual conflict with each other. India and Pakistan both hold a significant number of the global CIO actions, and a large part of this is likely because both states fully acknowledge they are primary rivals of each other, with militarized disputes being the norm over the years. Minimal attempts are made to hide or obscure the true origin of the hacks.

## Case study summaries

The findings from both the Russian versus WADA and India versus Pakistan CIO demonstrate similar characteristics. First, both CIOs were relatively unsophisticated and were able to be employed at low cost and low risk; this ensured that even if no coercion was evident from the operations, nothing was lost either. Furthermore, both operations were loosely obscured, but the true origin of the hacks is well known. Given the context of the disputes and the managed relations range for states engaged in a rivalry, there is was little chance of escalation.

Both CIO attacks were prompted by threats to state credibility at a regional and global stage. Research points to credibility being the main target of the operations, and the main reason CIO is employed as an option. When countries are in competition with each other, the threshold to conduct CIO is lowered significantly and becomes an expected norm. Cyber actions in this context are done out of the shadows and in the public because they are often meant to reassure a concerned public and demonstrate to the opposition that they have credible capabilities to strike back.

## Conclusions

Despite a clear awareness of the issue of information warfare and shifting doctrines of information operations, scholars have generally failed to empirically examine the shape and context of actual cyber-enabled information operations. In this research, we sort through an early conception of what an empirical examination of cyber-enabled information operations might look like if we ransack the cyber domain for all current known examples.

This effort in scoping the domain through a constricted examination can bear fruit. Our findings are clear, CIO is a rare condition that mostly proliferates between states engaged in direct contagious rivalries such as Indian and Pakistan. Otherwise, the clear outlier is Russia, the leader in the field of cyber-enabled information operations which fits well with their strategic vision of reflexive control. Whether or not these operations are successful in shaping the adversary is a different question. We have found in the past that compellent actions attempted through disruptive operations typically fail (Valeriano et al. 2018). If most cyber-enabled information operations launched by Russia are also disruptive operations, we would expect the findings to not shift. CIO is mainly a tool to react in an environment where a state has lost control and seeks to affect change from a position of weakness, not dominance.

Future examinations should move beyond the restriction on cyber-enabled information operations and explore the shape of information operations that do not necessarily have a cyber component. Cyber adjunct actions might be the most impactful, but they are surely the minority in the system since IO can be a low-tech operation used to influence an adversary.

We have tilled the ground with this investigation and hopefully enabled future scholars to come after us and shape the field of information operations more in the future. Work that follows on must be clear, empirical, and pay careful attention to the realities of the domain and not focus so much on the outliers that seem to shape the conversation. In fact, here Russia is the outlier but also likely an ineffective operator seeking to control a system that has long moved beyond its simple view of reflective control of the adversary. The adversary is much more nebulous and dispersed than in the past, bifurcating into more individual societies. Using IO against a collective society might work if there are stable views amongst the masses, but it surely will have limited impact against developed democracies with multiple constituencies.

## Notes

1 https://warontherocks.com/2019/06/the-united-states-needs-an-information-warfare-command-a-historical-examination/
2 Origins of the term are tough to place. On April 27, 2017, the Senate Armed Services Committee had a hearing on "Cyber-Enabled Information Operations," www.armed-services.senate.gov/imo/media/doc/17-37_04-27-17.pdf
3 www.armed-services.senate.gov/imo/media/doc/17-37_04-27-17.pdf
4 www.janes.com/images/assets/438/77438/Cyber-enabled_information_operations_The_battlefield_threat_without_a_face.pdf
5 Michael Connell and Sarah Vogler, "Russia's Approach to Cyber Warfare (1Rev)" (Center for Naval Analyses Arlington United States, March 1, 2017), https://apps.dtic.mil/docs/citations/AD1032208.

6 Rebecca R. Ruiz and Michael Schwirtz, "Russian Insider Says State-Run Doping Fueled Olympic Gold," *The New York Times*, January 19, 2018, sec. Sports, www.nytimes.com/2016/05/13/sports/russia-doping-sochi-olympics-2014.html.

7 Rebecca R. Ruiz, "Report Shows Vast Reach of Russian Doping: 1,000 Athletes, 30 Sports," *The New York Times*, December 22, 2017, sec. Sports, www.nytimes.com/2016/12/09/sports/russia-doping-mclaren-report.html.

8 Tony Manfred, "Here's a Full List of Medal Winners at the Sochi Olympics," *Business Insider*, accessed April 11, 2019, www.businessinsider.com/olympic-medal-count-2014-2.

9 "Rio Olympics 2016: Which Russian Athletes Have Been Cleared to Compete?," August 6, 2016, sec. Olympics, www.bbc.com/sport/olympics/36881326.

10 Jack Robertson, "Independent Commission Investigation." November 9, 2015, www.wada-ama.org/sites/default/files/resources/files/wada_independent_commission_report_1_en.pdf

11 Connell and Vogler, "Russia's Approach to Cyber Warfare (1 Rev)."

12 Rebecca R. Ruiz, "What U.S. Prosecutors Say 7 Russian Spies Did to Attack Antidoping Efforts," *The New York Times*, October 5, 2018, sec. Sports, www.nytimes.com/2018/10/04/sports/russia-cyberattacks-antidoping.html.

13 Ruiz.

14 Ruiz.

15 "WADA Confirms Attack by Russian Cyber Espionage Group (13 September 2016)," World Anti-Doping Agency, September 13, 2016, www.wada-ama.org/en/media/news/2016-09/wada-confirms-attack-by-russian-cyber-espionage-group.

16 Andy Greenberg, "Russian Hackers Get Bolder in Anti-Doping Agency Attack," *Wired*, September 14, 2016, www.wired.com/2016/09/anti-doping-agency-attack-shows-russian-hackers-getting-bolder/.

17 Greenberg.

18 Jason L. Jarvis, "Digital Image Politics: The Networked Rhetoric of Anonymous," *Global Discourse* 4, no. 2–3 (July 3, 2014): 326–49, https://doi.org/10.1080/23269995.2014.923633.

19 "Fancy Bears Release Data on Soccer Players' TUE Drug Use and Doping Cases," *Security Affairs*, August 24, 2017, https://securityaffairs.co/wordpress/62302/data-breach/fancy-bears-doping.html; Jarvis, "Digital Image Politics."

20 "WADA Confirms Another Batch of Athlete Data Leaked by Russian Cyber Hackers 'Fancy Bear' (14 September 2016)," World Anti-Doping Agency, September 14, 2016, www.wada-ama.org/en/media/news/2016-09/wada-confirms-another-batch-of-athlete-data-leaked-by-russian-cyber-hackers-fancy.

21 "Cyber Hack Update: Data Leak Concerning 41 Athletes from 13 Countries and 17 Sports (23 September 2016)," World Anti-Doping Agency, September 23, 2016, www.wada-ama.org/en/media/news/2016-09/cyber-hack-update-data-leak-concerning-41-athletes-from-13-countries-and-17.

22 @DFRLab, "#PutinAtWar: WADA Hack Shows Kremlin Full-Spectrum Approach," *Medium* (blog), October 14, 2018, https://medium.com/dfrlab/putinatwar-wada-hack-shows-kremlin-full-spectrum-approach-21dd495f2e91.

23 "President of Russia," accessed April 12, 2019, http://en.special.kremlin.ru/events/president/news/52915.

24 Connell and Vogler, "Russia's Approach to Cyber Warfare (1Rev)."

25 Ruiz, "What U.S. Prosecutors Say 7 Russian Spies Did to Attack Antidoping Efforts."

26 @DFRLab, "#PutinAtWar."

27 www.bbc.com/sport/football/41011854

28 www.dailymail.co.uk/sport/sportsnews/article-4812334/Fancy-Bears-hackers-leak-football-drug-use.html

29 Sumantra Bose, *Kashmir: Roots of Conflict, Paths to Peace* (Harvard University Press, 2009) p. 2.

30 Bose, p. 3.

31 Bose; Marie Baezner, "Regional Rivalry between India-Pakistan: Tit-for-Tat in Cyberspace," August 6, 2018.

32 "Press Club Of India | Press Club Of India," accessed April 18, 2019, www.pressclubofindia.org/; "16-Year-Old Indian Hacked Pakistan People's Party Site? – Latest News | Gadgets Now," Gadget Now, October 19, 2014, www.gadgetsnow.com/tech-news/16-year-old-Indian-hacked-Pakistan-Peoples-Party-site/articleshow/44872665.cms.

68 Colin Foote et al.

33 "16-Year-Old Indian Hacked Pakistan People's Party Site?"; *IndiaToday* in New Delhi, October 9, 2014. UPDATED: October 9, and 2014 22:10 Ist, "Indo-Pak Tension Enters Cyberspace, Press Club of India's Website Hacked," *India Today*, accessed April 17, 2019, www.indiatoday.in/india/story/hackers-post-anti-modi-comments-on-press-club-of-indias-website-209307-2014-10-09.

34 DelhiOctober 9, October 9, and Ist, "Indo-Pak Tension Enters Cyberspace, Press Club of India's Website Hacked."

35 "Hackers from India, Pakistan in Full-Blown Online War – Latest News | Gadgets Now," *Gadget Now*, October 10, 2014, www.gadgetsnow.com/tech-news/Hackers-from-India-Pakistan-in-full-blown-online-war/articleshow/44766898.cms; DelhiOctober 9, October 9, and Ist, "Indo-Pak Tension Enters Cyberspace, Press Club of India's Website Hacked."

36 "Hackers from India, Pakistan in Full-Blown Online War – Latest News | Gadgets Now."

37 Baezner, "Regional Rivalry between India-Pakistan."

38 Baezner.

# References

@DFRLab. "#PutinAtWar: WADA Hack Shows Kremlin Full-Spectrum Approach." *Medium (blog)*, October 14, 2018. https://medium.com/dfrlab/putinatwar-wada-hack-shows-kremlin-full-spectrum-approach-21dd495f2e91.

"16-Year-Old Indian Hacked Pakistan People's Party Site? – Latest News | Gadgets Now." *Gadget Now*, October 19, 2014. www.gadgetsnow.com/tech-news/16-year-old-Indian-hacked-Pakistan-Peoples-Party-site/articleshow/44872665.cms.

Baezner, Marie. *"Regional Rivalry between India-Pakistan: Tit-for-Tat in Cyberspace,"* August 6, 2018.

Bose, Sumantra. *Kashmir: Roots of Conflict, Paths to Peace.* Cambridge, MA: Harvard University Press, 2009.

Castells, Manuel. *Communication power.* Oxford: Oxford University Press, 2013.

Connell, Michael, and Sarah Vogler. "Russia's Approach to Cyber Warfare (1Rev)." Center for Naval Analyses Arlington United States, March 1, 2017. https://apps.dtic.mil/docs/citations/AD1032208.

"Cyber Hack Update: Data Leak Concerning 41 Athletes from 13 Countries and 17 Sports." World Anti-Doping Agency, September 23, 2016. www.wada-ama.org/en/media/news/2016-09/cyber-hack-update-data-leak-concerning-41-athletes-from-13-countries-and-17.

*DelhiOctober 9, IndiaToday* in New, 2014 UPDATED: October 9, and 2014 22:10 Ist. "Indo-Pak Tension Enters Cyberspace, Press Club of India's Website Hacked." *India Today.* Accessed April 17, 2019. www.indiatoday.in/india/story/hackers-post-anti-modi-comments-on-press-club-of-indias-website-209307-2014-10-09.

"Doping in Sport: What Is It and How Is It Being Tackled? – BBC Sport." Accessed April 12, 2019. www.bbc.com/sport/athletics/33997246.

"Fancy Bears Release Data on Soccer Players' TUE Drug Use and Doping Cases." *Security Affairs*, August 24, 2017. https://securityaffairs.co/wordpress/62302/data-breach/fancy-bears-doping.html.

Greenberg, Andy. "Russian Hackers Get Bolder in Anti-Doping Agency Attack." *Wired*, September 14, 2016. www.wired.com/2016/09/anti-doping-agency-attack-shows-russian-hackers-getting-bolder/.

"Hackers from India, Pakistan in Full-Blown Online War – Latest News | Gadgets Now." *Gadget Now*, October 10, 2014. www.gadgetsnow.com/tech-news/Hackers-from-India-Pakistan-in-full-blown-online-war/articleshow/44766898.cms.

Jarvis, Jason L. "Digital Image Politics: The Networked Rhetoric of Anonymous," *Global Discourse 4*, 2–3 (July 3, 2014): 326–349.

Jensen, Benjamin, Brandon Valeriano, and Ryan Maness. "Fancy Bears and Digital Trolls: Cyber Strategy with a Russian Twist," *Journal of Strategic Studies 42*, 2 (2019): 212–234.

Lin, Herbert and Kerr, Jaclyn, "On Cyber-Enabled Information Warfare and Information Operations" (May 2019), forthcoming, *Oxford Handbook of Cybersecurity*, 2019. Available at SSRN: https://ssrn.com/abstract=3015680.

Lin, Herbert, "The Existential Threat from Cyber-Enabled Information Warfare," *Bulletin of the Atomic Scientists 75*, 4 (2019): 187–196.

Manfred, Tony. "Here's A Full List Of Medal Winners At The Sochi Olympics." *Business Insider.* Accessed April 11, 2019. www.businessinsider.com/olympic-medal-count-2014-2.

Nakasone, Paul M. "A cyber force for persistent operations," *Jt. Force Q 92* (2019): 10–14.

"President of Russia." Accessed April 12, 2019. http://en.special.kremlin.ru/events/president/news/52915.

"Press Club Of India | Press Club Of India." Accessed April 18, 2019. http://www.pressclubofindia.org/.

"Rio Olympics 2016: Which Russian Athletes Have Been Cleared to Compete?," August 6, 2016, sec. Olympics. www.bbc.com/sport/olympics/36881326.

Robertson, Jack. "Independent Commission Investigation." November 9, 2015. www.wada-ama.org/sites/default/files/resources/files/wada_independent_commission_report_1_en.pdf.

Ruiz, Rebecca R. "Report Shows Vast Reach of Russian Doping: 1,000 Athletes, 30 Sports." *The New York Times*, December 22, 2017, sec. Sports. www.nytimes.com/2016/12/09/sports/russia-doping-mclaren-report.html.

Ruiz, Rebecca R. "What U.S. Prosecutors Say 7 Russian Spies Did to Attack Antidoping Efforts." *The New York Times*, October 5, 2018, sec. Sports. www.nytimes.com/2018/10/04/sports/russia-cyberattacks-antidoping.html.

Ruiz, Rebecca R., and Michael Schwirtz. "Russian Insider Says State-Run Doping Fueled Olympic Gold." *The New York Times*, January 19, 2018, sec. Sports. www.nytimes.com/2016/05/13/sports/russia-doping-sochi-olympics-2014.html.

STAFF, U.S. Joint Chief of. "Information Operations." (2014).

Valeriano, Brandon, Benjamin M. Jensen, and Ryan C. Maness. *Cyber Strategy: The Evolving Character of Power and Coercion* (Oxford: Oxford University Press, 2018).

"WADA Confirms Another Batch of Athlete Data Leaked by Russian Cyber Hackers 'Fancy Bear'." World Anti-Doping Agency, September 14, 2016. www.wada-ama.org/en/media/news/2016-09/wada-confirms-another-batch-of-athlete-data-leaked-by-russian-cyber-hackers-fancy.

"WADA Confirms Attack by Russian Cyber Espionage Group." World Anti-Doping Agency, September 13, 2016. www.wada-ama.org/en/media/news/2016-09/wada-confirms-attack-by-russian-cyber-espionage-group.

**PART II**

# (Cyber-enabled) Information at war

# 6

# BEAR MARKET? GRIZZLY STEPPE AND THE AMERICAN MARKETPLACE OF IDEAS

## A. Trevor Thrall and Andrew Armstrong

In the wake of the 2016 presidential election, American intelligence services unanimously concluded that Russia used social media and other means in an effort to polarize the American electorate and to help Donald Trump win the election (ICA 2017). While there is no question these actions violate international norms of state sovereignty and international law, considerable debate remains as to whether these actions had any meaningful impact on the election's outcome and what danger such efforts pose in the future. The Russian intention to influence the American marketplace of ideas—and public behavior—is certainly real. But in this chapter we ask the more essential question: does it *matter*? Was 2016 the first salvo in the ideational battlefield of the future? Does Russian meddling pose an existential threat to Western democracy? Or is it simply an inexpensive low-risk gambit from an adversary too weak to engage in traditional forms of mischief?

The conventional wisdom today is that this new era of digital propaganda poses a clear threat to American democracy. Analyses by Jamieson (2019), Mayer (2018), and Hunt (2018) for example, have argued Russian efforts probably tipped the election to Donald Trump, have the capacity to inflict widespread influence on American public attitudes, and will erode the effectiveness of the American marketplace of ideas as a whole. This concern has led political commentators to argue:

> Globally, the implications of Russia's social media active measures are dire. Social media has played a key role in controversial decisions such as Brexit, and in politics and elections around the world, including those of France, Estonia and Ukraine. In heated political contests such as Brexit and the U.S. presidential election, Russian social media active measures could tip the balance of an electoral outcome by influencing a small fraction of a voting public.
>
> *(Weisburd et al. 2016)*

Four main themes animate the alarmist arguments. First, there is the immediate challenge of vastly increased volume of information. Digital platforms facilitate the rapid and broad dissemination of misleading cues, and this deluge of debate makes it difficult to parse truth from falsehood. Second, social media, as the 2016 election underscored, allow political actors to mask their identity, making it difficult for citizens to use source and context cues to help resist persuasive messages (Tormala & Petty 2002; Pornpitakpan 2004). Third, new dynamics of information bypass quality safeguards like journalistic mediation and impartial fact-checking. Thus, at the very time when the presence of misinformation is greatest, traditional democratic institutions are least able to mediate debate. Finally, those concerned also worry about the vulnerability of historic safeguards to digitization. Traditional media outlets, long heralded as the watchdogs of democracy, are struggling to moderate debate on the digital frontier. For example, by the time mainstream media alerted the public to Russian misinformation much of its damage was already done. It was only *after* all the 2016 election that the public began to appreciate the full extent of foreign involvement and mobilize against it (ICA 2017). The public sphere may correct itself in time, but that is of little consolation if an adversary like Russia has already achieved its goals.

There is also evidence that the Russians were able to translate messaging into tangible behavior. While the full reach of the Russian campaign may never be known, it is clear that their messages appeared in the social media feeds of millions of Americans (Byers 2017; Mueller 2019). Russian-generated messages were viewed by millions of citizens, so it is reasonable to assume that at least some citizens were meaningfully influenced. What is more, the Russians were able to transcend messaging and to achieve actual political mobilization in targeted segments of the population. In one infamous case, Russian efforts were instrumental in organizing *both* sides in a protest/counter protest in Texas (Lister & Sebastian 2017). What further proof is needed, alarmists argue, that digital propaganda presents a clear and present danger to American society?

As compelling as the conventional wisdom sounds, most analyses of information warfare aimed at the American public have been based on faulty assumptions about how the American marketplace of ideas works. As a result, most of the discussion to date tends to downplay the marketplace's strengths and exaggerate its weaknesses.

In this chapter, we argue that the market's failure was not as significant as is often portrayed and that it is less vulnerable to foreign interference than many believe. In part, ironically, this is due to the fact that the American marketplace of ideas does not function nearly so well under normal circumstances as most people think. In reality it is expansive, noisy, full of propaganda and misinformation of domestic origins, and slow to correct itself at the best of times. The addition of a little more partisan propaganda and conspiracy theorizing in 2016 was unlikely to move the needle much.

Even more fundamentally, though the alarmists correctly note that Americans often had great difficulty identifying Russian trolls on social media, little of what we know about the dynamics of political communication suggests that those tweets and posts made much of an impact. For better or worse, the public is sturdily anchored in its biases, beliefs, and predispositions. Observers routinely bemoan the polarization of the American electorate and the tendency of American voters to dismiss inconvenient truths and cling blindly to their beliefs in the face of new information, but this tendency also provides an extremely tough defense against attempts by anyone, including anonymous Russian trolls, to influence public attitudes in a meaningful way.

In many ways, Russia seems to have become a convenient third party to blame for many of the United States' preexisting conditions. The social schisms at the heart of Russia's strategy were well entrenched before any foreign interference: hyper-partisanship, distrust and disdain of the media, personal vilification of opposing politicians (Abramowitz & Saunders 2005; Iyengar & Hahn 2009). These are scourges of America's own making. Nor was Russia responsible for the majority of crackpot conspiracy theories, media mistrust, and post-truth politicking that consumed the 2016 election. Even if all their efforts were systematically coordinated towards a particular outcome, it was unlikely to be enough to shift the overall tenor of sociopolitical debate. Russian efforts may have stoked partisan ire, but probably did little to fundamentally change the outcome of the election.

In this chapter we provide a new framework for thinking about the vulnerability and resilience of the American marketplace of ideas by correcting several of the most common misconceptions about how it really works. Our goal is not to prove that the Russian campaign had no influence or even to argue that it did not tip the scales in favor of Donald Trump. Instead, our aim is to move the debate forward by identifying the actual strengths and weaknesses of the American marketplace of ideas in order to help analysts collect the necessary data and make arguments that make sense.

To this end we begin with a critique of the traditional model of the marketplace of ideas and the introduction of a revised model that we call the marketplace of values. We then use our new model to critique the alarmist narrative about Russia's impact on the 2016 election, generating a more sanguine assessment of the vulnerability of the U.S. public sphere to outside influence. We conclude with some thoughts about the implications of our arguments for the future.

## The marketplace of ideas is really a marketplace of values

Assessments of the threat from information warfare require assumptions about the process by which information flows through society and then has an impact on public knowledge and opinions. The most common set of assumptions about this process, often made implicitly rather than explicitly, fit neatly within what scholars call the marketplace of ideas framework. In its idealized form, the marketplace of ideas (MOI) operates much like its traditional economic analog, embracing a "libertarian, laissez-faire approach to speech" where the "same 'invisible hand' that guides unregulated economic markets to maximum efficiency will guide unregulated markets in ideas to maximum discovery of truth" (Coplan 2015, 548). From this perspective, objective truth and time are the ultimate arbiters. After sufficient debate and deliberation, the public will eventually embrace good ideas and facts, by virtue of their inherent superiority, eschewing bad ideas and falsehoods. As John Stuart Mill (1991: 40) summarized the process: "Wrong opinions and practices gradually yield to fact and argument."[1] Or as his fellow Englishman John Milton (1644) famously wrote two hundred years before Mill, "who ever knew Truth put to the worse, in a free and open encounter?"

In this view, the invisible hand of the market guides the public toward truth and accurate assessments of the conditions of the day, with sound policy resulting from the interplay of ideas and argument. The health of an economic market reveals itself through competitive prices and healthy consumer demand and satisfaction with available products. The health of the marketplace of ideas, on the other hand, depends on the degree to which public debate reveals an accurate analysis of the situation and, more challengingly, on the degree to which public debate helps improve the proposals political leaders present to their publics. In theory, given enough time society's understanding should reflect an underlying reality, and society should be correspondingly better off.

As with economic markets, the smooth functioning of the marketplace of ideas relies on a series of important assumptions. The first is the assumption of unfettered competition among people with different ideas about the nature of the problem at hand and different proposals about solutions to the problem. The competitive process, as Mill argued, should help weed out poorly formed arguments and help separate truth from falsehood. Scholars of deliberative democracy have buttressed this argument in more recent times by arguing that extended deliberation from many perspectives increases the amount of information available for decision making, makes it more likely that the right answer has been revealed in discussion, and thus makes it more likely that good ideas will trump bad ideas (Habermas 1997; Gutman & Thompson 2009).

Many disciplines have leveraged the idea of the assiduity of the collective. Aristotle wrote of the "wisdom of crowds" in politics. In the early 20th century the British statistician Francis Galton was interested in the predictive aptitude of individuals and groups. At a country fair he asked individuals to guess the weight of an ox. While individual guesses varied widely, he noted that the median guess was within 1% of the actual weight of the beast (Galton 1907; Surowiecki 2005). This emergent wisdom is not constrained to contemplating beef. Pop-science has shown that large groups outperform individuals on a wide variety of tasks (Surowiecki 2005). In short, the result of group deliberation often appears more than the sum of its parts.

In turn, the knowledge that the truth will emerge should also deter politicians from lying or making foolish statements that will be exposed as such by public debate, and should thus prevent extreme or risky policies generating broad support. In the realm of foreign policy, for example, Kaufmann (2004) argues that, "The marketplace of ideas helps to weed out unfounded, mendacious, or self-serving foreign policy arguments because their proponents cannot avoid wide-ranging debate in which their reasoning and evidence are subject to public scrutiny." Similarly, Reiter and Stam (2002, 146) argue that an open market of ideas "undercut[s] fallacious claims made by leadership … reducing the ability of leaders to shape foreign policy" when they lose credibility in the market. Modern scholars of the marketplace have thus identified both access to the news media and the diversity of opinions expressed therein as an important measure of healthy market functioning.

Second, the MOI model assumes that time has a more or less unidirectional impact, with the public coalescing around the truth given enough time for debate and deliberation. Scholars from Mill onward have argued that healthy markets, all things being equal, should trend towards greater accuracy over time. More time gives the market time to correct, for good information to diffuse, and for arguments to be weighed and decisions to be made about the quality of competing perspectives. It is a useful tautology to stress that truth has the great advantage of being *true*; presumably this gives truth the opportunity to overcome falsehoods if given enough time.

Baum and Groeling (2009), for example, suggest that political reality is "elastic." Early on in policy debate elites are able to use their privileged position in society to set the baseline of social knowledge. In this stage public opinion—lacking firsthand knowledge or alternative perspectives—is generally deferential, mirroring the tenor of elite debate. Over time other voices will gain traction in public debate. Eventually, however, the intrinsic accuracy and value of good arguments triumphs and the public gravitates towards enlightened opinion regardless of source. Of course, *how* these countervailing arguments are able to enter the market is a critical issue in its own right.

The American marketplace of ideas **77**

For now, it is important to underscore that time is not simply a mechanism to uncover the truth, it is also a metric to assess the overall health of the public sphere. Sociopolitical analysis is *hard*, and even the best and brightest experts can take lifetimes to understand the most complex issues (Tetlock 2005). But expert assessment is only the first hurdle. Once experts achieve consensus within their field, there is often a lag period between their assessment and broader public opinion. The public sphere needs time—potentially years—to allow viewpoints to vie for acceptance. Even with this complexity in mind, all things being equal robust MOIs should be the fastest to coalesce around the truth.

Third, and most critically, the standard marketplace of ideas model depends on the assumption that people themselves seek the truth, prefer "good" policies to "bad" policies. This, in turn, gives political elites a strong incentive to adopt and promote the truth and policies rooted in honest and accurate assessments of the world. For those philosophers among us, the correspondence between "little t" social truth and "big T" universal Truth is compelling in its own right. In practice, the public sphere, as a happily heterogeneous collective, may need something more than epistemological appeal for Truth to triumph in everyday practice. What makes truth so compelling in this market-based perspective?

In a commercial context a superior product is expected to dominate over time. There are a host of measurable benchmarks which consumers and industry members can turn to: reliability, performance, cost, safety, etc. Presumably, products which consistently outperform the competition come to dominate commercial markets. Honda makes efficient, reliable cars and thrives. Yugo makes the fateful decision to build … Yugos. One manufacturer became a global player, the other an automotive dodo. Simple. Of course, tangible products are one thing; but what is the hallmark of a winning *idea*? What makes an idea competitive? This is not as straightforward a question as one might think.

The first instinct of many, and this is certainly reflected in much of the literature, is to turn to truth as the common denominator adjudicating between ideas. True statements are not simply desirable because they are epistemologically sound; the fact that they correspond to the world provides tangible benefit. Pragmatists argue that "truth" in the context of social debate "is not merely copying of reality, but consists of the 'cash value' to some human purpose or conception that brings ourselves within the neighborhood of reality for us" (Wonell 1985, 677). Truth, in short, is *useful*. Concepts which are true, or at least *truer* than alternatives, provide greater benefits compared to those which are less true.

At first blush, this connection between truth and benefit seems self-evident. There are many issues for which coming down on the right/wrong side of an objective question has clear and tangible implications. Is human activity contributing to climate change? Is an adversary working on building a nuclear bomb? Will this vaccine help prevent disease? There are a host of key social issues where coalescing around a true answer, presumably, would have clear social benefits.

As with economic theory, advocates of MOI theory acknowledge that the conditions for well-behaving markets do not always work as Mill described. Market "failures" can stem from many sources including government control of the media, manipulative political elites, poor news media performance, or the failure to expose the public to a full range of information and debate about a topic. Most analyses of the 2016 campaign rely on some mix of these sorts of failures to explain the Russians' success. From the MOI perspective, however, it is important to note that these challenges are typically seen as departures from the normal operation of a healthy marketplace of ideas in the modern Western democratic setting

(Snyder & Ballantine 1996; Kaufmann 2004). For advocates working from the MOI framework market failures are, at least in theory, preventable with the right sorts of reforms or improved defenses, as the recent deluge of policy recommendations for preventing future Russian attacks illustrates. Facebook and other networks have instituted a formal review process to identify and suspend suspect accounts. Similarly, politicians have proposed fact-checking legislation to monitor the truthfulness of social advertising (Stewart 2019). While such measures will not eliminate the problem, from the MOI perspective they will presumably reduce the impact of foreign misinformation campaigns.

### Except that it ain't so: the marketplace of values

The marketplace of ideas model is undeniably elegant and compelling, an Enlightenment-era cocktail of Bayesian opinion formation, free speech, and capitalism. Unfortunately, its most foundational premise is false. As Mark Twain (2014[1894]) once mused, "truth is mighty and will prevail. There is nothing wrong with this, except that it ain't so." The driving force behind public acceptance of information and arguments in the marketplace is not truth, but values. Most people prefer truth to lies, of course, but for the most important political issues, truth runs a distant second to people's beliefs, identities, and deeply-held values. Further, contrary to the assumption that all citizens share a passion for a single universal truth or the "best" solution to political problems, the marketplace of values is home to wildly varying attitudes and beliefs about fundamental questions including how society should look and how the government should operate. Crucially, these differences are not merely the result of inadequate deliberation or a lack of information. They are the result of conflicting values, worldviews, and emotional connections to ideas, people, symbols, and even gods. As a result, the natural equilibrium is not consensus but conflict, not a singular public truth but contending value judgments about the world and how it should be.

Shifting to a marketplace of values perspective has at least three important implications for the performance and outputs of the public sphere. First, though competition and debate can certainly reveal new information and increase public knowledge, more debate about deeply political issues tends to lead to polarization rather than consensus (Thrall 2007). For example, consider the hot-button issues of climate change and gun violence. In 2000 there was a fifteen-percent spread in public opinion across the two parties about the proper course of action. Rather than coalesce around a generally accepted approach, greater debate has instead doubled the opinion gap between Republicans and Democrats over the following two decades (Newport & Dugan 2017).

Second, while in the MOI model political elites have a powerful incentive to promote accurate assessments and "good" policies, the values-based perspective suggests that elites actually have incentives to promote ideas and information that resonate with the values of their own coalitions. Regardless of the facts about gun violence, for example, Republican candidates benefit from arguing that gun control is a bad idea because to Republican voters Second Amendment rights are more salient than gun-related deaths. Regardless of the facts about raising taxes on economic growth, Democratic candidates benefit from calling for higher taxes because their voters value equality over economic growth. Nationalists of both parties benefit from calling the United States the "greatest country" in the world, not because the statement is accurate, but because it strikes a deep emotional chord with most Americans.

The American marketplace of ideas  **79**

This disjuncture between truth and values also sheds light on the public's surprising response to Russia's election interference. If the public market was purely motivated by truth, all citizens should equally decry foreign election interference. This was clearly not the case. A 2017 poll found that Republicans were far more likely than Democrats—25% to 4%—to reject the *fact* (confirmed by the unanimous conclusion of American intelligence agencies) that Russia was involved in election interference (Taylor 2017). This disparity should not exist in a truth-driven market, particularly given the unanimous conclusion of the intelligence community. The marketplace of values perspective, on the other hand, easily explains the way in which partisan interests affect people's evaluations of the facts.

Third, thanks to the first two points, time does not always produce a wiser public, nor more accurate publicly shared assessments of the world, nor momentum for better public policies. In fact, social reality is far more elastic than most MOI advocates have argued. Society is quite capable of losing truth when false claims begin to resonate more strongly with the public. New bouts of misinformation, like false prophets, can challenge and undermine prevailing wisdom. Consider the emergence of the anti-vaccine movement. Before the use of immunization was widespread, many worried about both its efficacy and potential side effects. But after the eradication of smallpox, and the near-elimination of polio, measles, and other diseases demonstrated the value and safety of immunization, the benefit of its widespread use became generally accepted practice. In the past decade, however, a new movement relying on pseudo-science and rooted in a deep distrust of science, medicine, and government has begun to challenge the safety of time-tested immunization. Contrary to the predictions of the marketplace of ideas model, a growing number of Americans have embraced this position and the number of children not being immunized is steadily rising (Hotez 2017).

To accept that we live in a marketplace of values is to accept the fact that measuring its performance is a Quixotic proposition. For most important political issues, the most salient issues are not facts but beliefs, identities, and values. Given this, it is not clear why truth should enjoy the privileged position it tends to have in academic circles. After all, the Gordian knot of the debate over tax policy is not the facts about deficits and revenue generation, but the clash over what sort of tax policy is the fairest. Though clearly accurate information about the world matters, the most critical information are not facts but arguments that connect values, policies, and outcomes. From this perspective the current debate, or market position, is not so much right or wrong as it is closer or further from one's preferred state depending on what values one holds.

Attempts to retain a more "objective" approach to assessing market performance only serve to highlight the nature of the opinion formation process. Taking the level of public consensus around the truth as our yardstick, the market's performance appears to be steadfastly mediocre at best. The climate change debate illustrates this point. At first blush, climate change appears to be an easy test for a market-based model of communication. The issue at question—whether human action is related to global warming—is an objective question with a clear right/wrong answer. It has been studied exhaustively for decades, and at great cost. The scientific community has reached overwhelming consensus. One would think that this would be a home run for the MOI; the shining example of how open debate leads the public toward enlightened consensus. And yet it hasn't. In fact, according to survey data, after more than twenty years of vigorous debate the public remains heavily divided over the scientific basis of climate change (Newport & Dugan 2017). Likewise, the public also remains divided over the appropriate policy responses. In this case, neither the believers nor the skeptics can applaud the performance of the marketplace of values, because it has clearly produced division rather than consensus around whichever truth one believes to be true.

This polarization dynamic appears to be most powerful for issues that evoke deeply held beliefs and values, such as abortion, the death penalty, and other topics of partisan debate. One might, therefore, hold out some hope that for nonpolitical issues the marketplace might operate more in line with the ideal model. Unfortunately, the general public indifference to nonpolitical issues means that most people learn too little to do much useful updating of their opinions until they become important enough to pay attention to. At that point, unfortunately, issues often become politicized. Climate change followed this path, for example, with little polarization on the issue in the 1980s when it was primarily a concern among scientists, but increasing polarization following its entry into political debate in the 1990s.

## What happened in 2016

From the marketplace of ideas perspective, 2016 clearly represented a market failure. The standard narrative runs something like this: Russia's campaign illustrated the marketplace's vulnerability to malicious information, foiling the market's normal corrective mechanisms by using fake social media accounts and leveraging the social topography of the digital marketplace of ideas to help spread their messages. The Russian strategy took advantage of the fact that a healthy marketplace of ideas requires individuals to be exposed to free-wheeling debate and multiple perspectives. Russia also benefited from the fact that many Americans now inhabit informational echo chambers and social networks in which they receive only friendly partisan messages, increasing the likelihood that those individuals would trust Russian messages they got during the campaign. Russia's ability to use online advertising and social media tools to micro-target individuals based on demographics and partisanship in key battleground states allowed it to tailor its campaign for maximum impact. Finally, because the Russians used fake accounts and denied responsibility, the marketplace of ideas simply could not correct itself before the voting occurred, making it likely that Russia's efforts helped elect Donald Trump. Looking forward, given this recipe, there is little reason to believe that the Russians, the Chinese, and other adversaries will not be able to influence future political debates and elections.

## *The market is large and competition is fierce*

A less alarmist analysis of 2016, however, and one that accounts for the behavior of marketplace of values, produces a more sanguine assessment. The American marketplace is certainly quite defenseless in one sense; there is no way to prevent actors from introducing malicious messages into the public sphere. But while much has been made of how technological developments made it possible for Russia to meddle in the U.S. election, we must also account for the fact that technology has made it possible for *everyone* to take part in the conversation. Digital technologies and the new economics of communication have produced an open, defenseless, but also massive information environment, whose sprawling noisiness is itself a tremendous bulwark against external influence.

Logically, the larger the marketplace of ideas—the more voices, the more information, etc.—the greater the effort needed to get people's attention and to effect meaningful change in public attitudes (Thrall, Stecula, & Sweet 2014). Alarmists frequently repeat what sound like impressive statistics when they describe Russian's 2016 information campaign: thousands of advertisements and millions of tweets shared and viewed millions of times. Facebook's general counsel offered the public a glimpse into the extent of Russia's efforts (Byers 2017). Their data suggests that 11.4 million users saw ads purchased by Russia's Internet Research Agency (IRA), and 29 million users were served other forms of Russian content. All told, 126 million people may have seen Russia-generated information in some form. While it is impossible to know how many of those 126 million *possible* impressions were actually read, the numbers certainly appear staggering.

What alarmists tend not to mention is just how many tweets and ads were being generated by everyone other than the Russians. Russia's campaign looks far less impressive in that context, as Nate Silver (2018) pointed out:

> Platform-wide, there are something like 500,000,000 tweets posted each day. What fraction of overall social media impressions on the 2016 election were generated by Russian troll farms? 0.1%? I'm not sure what the answer is, but suspect it's low, and it says something that none of the reports that hype up the importance of them address that question.

Looking at campaign spending also helps put things in perspective. Within Facebook, for example, reports suggest that Russia's Internet Research Agency (IRA) spent approximately $46,000 during the 2016 elections. In contrast, the Clinton and Trump campaigns alone spent over $80 million (Wagner 2017), not counting the amount spent by the Republican and Democratic parties or their various allies. Russia's efforts may have garnered a lot of scrutiny, and the rightful outrage makes it easy to lose sight of the bigger picture.

Special investigator Robert Mueller's 2019 indictment of a cast of characters for 2016 election interference suggests that the Russia propaganda machine was run much like a commercial firm, with a set budget and targeted goals for exposure. Though the exact scope of the effort is unknown, estimates peg the monthly budget of the Russians at approximately 1.25 million dollars (Mueller 2019). At that rate, for the sake of discussion, let us assume that Russia's IRA would have spent a total of roughly $20 million to influence the U.S. election.

A Russian outlay of $20 million would place it as just the thirteenth largest Super PAC by expenditure 2016 (OpenSecrets 2020). Beyond that, $20 million is a rounding error in the context of the broader election environment. OpenSecrets estimates over a billion dollars was spend by Super PACs in the 2016, which itself was only a fraction of the estimated $6.5 billion spent during the election cycle by all sources. Of this, an estimated $2.4 billion was spent on the presidential race alone. Alternately, if one looks solely at online spending, it is estimated that over campaigns at all levels spent over $1.4 billion (Maguire 2016). These figures, by sheer volume, should offer some solace. Even if one assumes that Russia targeted all their spending to advance a preferred candidate, rather than the pursuit of general discord, their effort represented less than 1% of online spending on the presidential election.

Of course, overall spending is only part of the equation. Over the past several election cycles only a handful of states were genuinely competitive at the national level. Reflecting on the 2016 election, Philip Bump (2016) noted:

> The most important states, though, were Michigan, Pennsylvania and Wisconsin. Trump won those states by 0.2, 0.7 and 0.8 percentage points, respectively — and by 10,704, 46,765 and 22,177 votes. Those three wins gave him 46 electoral votes; if Clinton had done one point better in each state, she'd have won the electoral vote, too.

If one wanted to maximize ROI on a campaign to swing the national election, it makes sense to target a hundred thousand voters across a handful of states. Indeed, the Muller report makes it clear that the IRA focused their efforts on these critical regions.

But once again, it is important to remember that the Russians were not the only players. Just as outside forces may try to overemphasize certain states, so too do domestic interest groups and the candidates themselves. In 2012, for example, just three states—Florida, Virginia, and Ohio—represented 47% of all TV spending by the presidential campaigns (Peterson 2016). One might even argue that the universally acknowledged importance of swing states would work *against* concerted foreign efforts to swing an election. The fact that the vast resources of domestic campaigns saturate a handful of markets makes it even more difficult for propaganda campaigns to leave a meaningful footprint.

### The importance of elite cues and the limits of credibility laundering

As a great deal of research has documented, most Americans remain fairly indifferent to politics most of the time and do not follow most political news closely if at all (Carpini & Keeter 1996). Most don't even tune in seriously to presidential campaigns until Labor Day, polls indicate. An important consequence is that—in line with the marketplace of values model—most Americans rely heavily on trusted political and other elites to help them interpret new information and form opinions (Zaller 1994; Guisinger & Saunders 2017).

This fact helps explain why the Russians had to use fake social media accounts to promote their messages: had they identified themselves as working for the Russian government, few if any Americans would have shared their tweets and posts. Instead, the Russians used a series of "credibility laundering" strategies to overcome people's typical psychological defense against embracing foreign messages. The simplest form of credibility laundering was simply posting the sort of polarizing messages that might encourage American partisans to repost and retweet them, thus allowing the attackers to launder their messages via more reputable sources. The hope was that the sharer's credibility among his or her friends would help make the original source irrelevant and boost the impact of the Russian message.

The Russians also attempted to leverage the credibility of well-known organizations by creating social media accounts for fake organizations that sounded like real ones. For example, building on the ubiquity of the Black Lives Matter movement, the IRA created messages under the guise of like-sounding organizations that it invented such as "Black Matters" or "Woke Blacks." The bet was that the casual reader would not recognize the counterfeit nature of the fake accounts, consume them uncritically, and share them with others.

The ultimate form of Russian credibility laundering was to leverage social media to infiltrate mainstream debate via authoritative news organizations. For example, a Russian propaganda story on a fake news site, having been credibility laundered through a series of reposting efforts, ultimately found its way onto coverage of mainstream outlets such as Fox

News (MacFarquhar & Rossback 2017). Though this story was eventually debunked and removed from the website, it nonetheless underscores a key vulnerability in the public sphere. Once false stories are co-opted by the mainstream, the narrative can be difficult to shift.

As nefarious as these all seem, however, this strategy of credible laundering and anonymous subversion has significant limits, defined by the marketplace of values and elite cues theory. In fact, given the robust debate within academic circles about the impact of political campaigns on American voters, where the two main actors are highly trusted and credible within their own parties, the notion that fake Russian Twitter and Facebook accounts have somehow cracked the code seems farfetched for several reasons.

First, though the average American may not have been very good at distinguishing fake news online, mainstream media outlets are in fact quite good at it, despite a mistake here and there. Without the bully pulpit of the mass media enjoyed by legitimate political voices, Russian influence depended on shaping attitudes via individual social media accounts at the grassroots level, an extremely difficult prospect given the size of the electorate.

Second, though diehard partisans may well have been susceptible to Russian messages sharing their point of view—who doesn't like retweeting snide attacks on the opposition, after all? —the vast bulk of such messages are so partisan that they are unlikely to make much of an impact for several reasons. First, elite cues theory suggests that the impact of anonymous messages is likely to pale in comparison to those coming from identifiable and credible sources. Second, given how well anchored most people are by their predispositions, cursory views of bite-sized social media posts from dubious sources are especially unlikely to produce persuasive effects. Indeed, it appears the Russians recognized this and focused more on amplifying existing attitudes than on persuasion.

Third, the tendency for people to associate in social media networks with people they already agree with provides another fire break on the spread of such messages. Partisans may stoke their mutual fury in these networks, but their ire is inherently self-contained. And though perhaps regrettable, the fact that like-minded people in 2016 traded Russian messages back and forth would have done little to change the overall scorecard.

## *Polarization blunts the impact of political messages*

As pollsters have been documenting for some time, the United States has been getting slowly more politically polarized for at least twenty years (Pew 2017). Americans are now, as numerous historians have suggested, more divided now than at any point since Vietnam, or even possibly since the Civil War (Brownstein 2008; Taranto 2018). Hyper-partisanship. Media distrust. Racism. These issues were rooted long before the last election. The United States did not need any assistance to become a nation bitterly divided. To borrow the words of Walt Kelly, we have met the enemy, and he is us.

However, the interplay between hyper-partisanship and election vulnerability is not straightforward. At one level, as discussed previously, hyper-partisanship might make the public sphere more receptive to targeted misinformation. However, looking at the broader social context, the polarization of American society across a crisscrossing series of value fault lines represents another important *defense* against external influence.

The increasing "clarity of party differences" has reduced voter "indecision and ambivalence and increasing reliability in presidential voting" (Smidt 2015, 365). On most political issues, and in most presidential elections, there are relatively few undecided voters open to forming a new opinion and few partisans open to adopting the opposing point of view. Given this backdrop, it is difficult to imagine the Russian campaign, especially as small as it was, having much impact with respect to where Americans stood on Trump versus Clinton or on other major social and political issues.

If the Russians were less focused on trying to persuade voters to vote for Trump and more on simply aggravating existing divisions in American society, the bar for exerting influence would certainly be lower. Suggestive evidence that the Russians had some success on this score comes from the IRA's ability to use various identity-based Facebook pages and ads to convince Americans, even if in limited numbers, to participate in what they thought were legitimate public demonstrations. But even this "success" may simply be a reflection, rather than a cause, of American attitudes. With Donald Trump pushing hard in the same direction on most of those issues, it is not clear that the Russians had any independent impact whatsoever.

## Conclusion

Of course, no discussion of Russian meddling would be complete without acknowledging the elephant in the room: Donald Trump. It is hard to imagine any other candidate from 2016 or past elections expressing Trump's openness to outside forces. Even if there was no direct collusion with the Russian operation, his public statements and his campaign's behavior were far afield of traditional norms. From publicly inviting a hack of Hilary's emails, to his public embrace of Putin, Trump's messaging was remarkably pro-Russian. It is absurd to think that past nominees like McCain or Romney would have been so tolerant of outside interference, so quick to echo Russian rhetoric.

Trump's candidacy also speaks to the broader tension between the role of truth and values in the public sphere. Fact-check services—exemplified by Politifact, Factcheck.org, or the *Washington Post*'s fact-checker—provided a real-time gauge of candidate truthfulness over the course of the election. A March 2016 article by Lippman et al. from *Politico*, for example, analyzed hours of campaign speeches to suggest Trump averaged one misstatement every five minutes. But Lippman and colleagues are hardly alone. The ready availability of fact-checking services gave rise to a cottage industry of academics harping on Trump's seemingly troubled relationship with the truth.

Indeed, if the public sphere was founded on truthfulness, Trump would never have become president. However, not every citizen—as demonstrated by the election itself—had the same reaction to Trump's persona or rhetorical flourish. As one Trump supporter suggested in a June 2016 interview:

> So, I like to believe that a lot of that is just maybe, like, some political marketing. I see where he's coming from with it, but it's not like there's not already something like a wall there, and it's not like bills and such haven't been proposed previously. But I would take it more as political marketing — I think he's making a stand and wants to be a little bit more outrageous with it to draw attention to the ideology that he wants to stand for things that people aren't standing for. And, honestly, I think he's a marketing genius.
>
> *(Johnson 2016)*

Clearly it was the sentiment and confidence behind Trump's words—rather than any relationship to objective truth—which lay at the heart of his appeal. Trump often exaggerated or misrepresented crime statistics on the campaign trail. After his convention speech a journalist from CNN challenged Newt Gingrich, acting as a campaign surrogate, about Trump's apparent willingness to distort the fact that, in general, national crime had decreased dramatically. To which Gingrich replied "the average American, I will bet you this morning, does not think that crime is down, does not think that we are safer … People feel more threatened. As a political candidate, I'll go with what people feel." Gingrich, we suggest, was exactly right. A market driven by values, rather than truth, is better able to explain the contemporary political landscape.

In our view Trump himself helped produce the perfect storm. If the Russian campaign did tip the election to Trump, it did so in part thanks to Trump's unprecedented campaign. By emphasizing divisive issues, eschewing fact and data for vitriol and personal attacks, and by welcoming rather than condemning Russian meddling, Trump fostered favorable conditions for foreign impact. We can think of no previous campaign in American history in which a trusted figure like Trump provided so much political cover for malicious foreign messages. And indeed, since taking office Trump has continued to dismiss Russian responsibility for any wrongdoing during 2016. Without this kind of insider support, we find it hard to believe that future foreign interference campaigns will gain nearly so much traction.

## Note

1 John Gray and G. W. Smith, Eds. *John Stuart Mill On Liberty: In Focus* (London: Routledge 1991), p. 40. In arguing against British censorship laws some years earlier John Milton provided one of the most famous quotations for this view in his pamphlet, *Areopagitica* (1644): "And though all the winds of doctrine were let loose to play upon the earth, so Truth be in the field, we do injuriously by licensing and prohibiting to misdoubt her strength. Let her and Falsehood grapple; who ever knew Truth put to the worse in a free and open encounter?"

## References

Abramowitz, A., & Saunders, K. (2005, June). Why can't we all just get along? The reality of a polarized America. In *The Forum 3, 2*. De Gruyter.

Baum, M. A., & Groeling, T. J. (2009). *War stories: The causes and consequences of public views of war.* Princeton, NJ: Princeton University Press.

Brownstein, R. (2008). *The second civil war: How extreme partisanship has paralyzed. Washington and polarized America.* New York: Penguin.

Bump, P. (2016). Donald Trump will be president thanks to 80,000 people in three states. Retrieved April 28, 2020 from www.washingtonpost.com/news/the-fix/wp/2016/12/01/donald-trump-will-be-president-thanks-to-80000-people-in-three-states/.

Byers, D. (2017). Facebook says it sold ads to Russian 'troll farm' during 2016 campaign. Retrieved November 18, 2019, from https://money.cnn.com/2017/09/06/media/facebook-russia-ads-2016-election/index.html.

Carpini, M. X. D., & Keeter, S. (1996). *What Americans know about politics and why it matters.* New Haven, CT: Yale University Press.

Coplan, K. S. (2012). Climate change, political truth, and the marketplace of ideas. *Utah Law Review*, 545–601.

Galton, F. (1907). Vox populi (the wisdom of crowds). *Nature, 75*(7), 450–451.

Gray, J., & Smith, G. W. (Eds.). (1991). *J.S. Mill's On Liberty in focus.* New York: Routledge.

Guisinger, A., & Saunders, E. N. (2017). Mapping the boundaries of elite cues: How elites shape mass opinion across international issues. *International Studies Quarterly, 61*(2), 425–441.

Gutmann, A., & Thompson, D. F. (2009). *Why deliberative democracy?*. Princeton, NJ: Princeton University Press.

Habermas, J. (1989). The public sphere: an encyclopedia article. In: Bronner, E., Kellner, D. (eds), *Critical theory and society*. New York: Routledge, pp. 102–110.

Hotez, Peter J. (2017). *How the anti-vaxxers are winning*. New York Times. Retrieved November 25, 2019 from www.nytimes.com/2017/02/08/opinion/how-the-anti-vaxxers-are-winning.html.

Hunt, A. R. (2018). Yes, Russian election sabotage helped Trump win. Retrieved November 20, 2019, from www.bloomberg.com/opinion/articles/2018-07-24/russian-meddling-helped-trump-win-in-2016.

Intelligence Community Assessment. (2017). Assessing Russian activities and intentions in recent US elections. Retrieved November 1, 2019, from www.dni.gov/files/documents/ICA_2017_01.pdf.

Iyengar, S., & Hahn, K. S. (2009). Red media, blue media: Evidence of ideological selectivity in media use. *Journal of Communication, 59(1)*, 19–39.

Jamieson, K. H. (2018). *Cyberwar. How Russian hackers and trolls helped elect a president: What we don't, can't, and do know*. New York: Oxford University Press.

Johnson, J. (2016). Many Trump supporters don't believe his wildest promises—and they don't care. Retrieved November 2, 2019 from www.washingtonpost.com/politics/many-trump-supporters-dont-believe-his-wildest-promises--and-they-dont-care/2016/06/06/05005210-28c4-11e6-b989-4e5479715b54_story.html.

Kaufmann, C. (2004). Threat inflation and the failure of the marketplace of ideas. *International Security, 29(1)*, 5–48.

Lippman, D., Samuelsohn, D., & Arnsdorf, I. (2016). Trump's week of errors, exaggerations and flat-out falsehoods. Retrieved November 14, 2019 from www.politico.com/magazine/story/2016/03/trump-fact-check-errors-exaggerations-falsehoods-213730.

Lister, T., & Sebastian, C. (2017). Stoking Islamophobia and secession in Texas – from an office in Russia. Retrieved November 18, 2019 from www.cnn.com/2017/10/05/politics/heart-of-texas-russia-event/index.html.

MacFarquhar, N., & Rossback, A. (2017). How Russian propaganda spread from a parody website to Fox News. Retrieved November 3, 2019 from www.nytimes.com/interactive/2017/06/07/world/europe/anatomy-of-fake-news-russian-propaganda.html.

Maguire, R. (2016). $1.4 billion and counting in spending by super PACS, dark money groups. Retrieved April 28, 2020 from www.opensecrets.org/news/2016/11/1-4-billion-and-counting-in-spending-by-super-pacs-dark-money-groups/

Mayer, J. (2018). How Russia helped swing the election for Trump. Retrieved November 20, 2019 from www.newyorker.com/magazine/2018/10/01/how-russia-helped-to-swing-the-election-for-trump.

Milton, J. (1644), Areopagitica. Retrieved November 20, 2019 from www.gutenberg.org/ebooks/608.

Mueller, R. S. (2019). *The Mueller Report: Report on the investigation into Russian interference in the 2016 Presidential Election*. WSBLD.

Newport, F., & Dugan, A. (2017). Partisan differences growing on a number of issues. Retrieved November 14, 2019 from https://news.gallup.com/opinion/polling-matters/215210/partisan-differences-growing-number-issues.aspx.

OpenSecrets.org, retrieved April 28, 2020 from www.opensecrets.org/outsidespending/summ.php?cycle=2016&chrt=P&disp=O&type=U.

Peterson, N. (2016). The geography of campaign spending. Retrieved November 17, 2019 from https://liberal-arts.wright.edu/applied-policy-research-institute/article/the-geography-of-campaign-spending.

Pew Research Center (2017). Political polarization, 1994–2017. Retrieved April 28, 2020 from www.people-press.org/interactives/political-polarization-1994-2017/.

Pornpitakpan, C. (2004). The persuasiveness of source credibility: A critical review of five decades' evidence. *Journal of applied social psychology, 34(2)*, 243–281.

Reiter, D., & Stam, A. C. (2002). *Democracies at war*. Princeton, NJ: Princeton University Press.

Silver, N. (2018). How much did Russian interference affect the 2016 Election? Retrieved November 15, 2019 from https://fivethirtyeight.com/features/how-much-did-russian-interference-affect-the-2016-election/.

Smidt, C. (2017). Polarization and the decline of the American floating voter. *American Journal of Political Science, 61(2)*, 365–381.

Snyder, J., & Ballantine, K. (1996). Democracy and the marketplace of ideas. *International Security*, *21*(2), 5–40.

Stewart, E. (2019). Facebook's political ads policy is predictably turning out to be a disaster. Retrieved November 20, 2019, from www.vox.com/recode/2019/10/30/20939830/facebook-false-ads-california-adriel-hampton-elizabeth-warren-aoc.

Surowiecki, J. (2005). *The wisdom of crowds*. New York: Anchor.

Taranto, J. (2018). Moderate voters, polarized parties. Retrieved November 20, 2019 from www.wsj.com/articles/moderate-voters-polarized-parties-1515193066.

Taylor, J. (2017). Majority of Americans believe Trump acted either illegally or unethically with Russia. Retrieved November 14, 2019 from www.npr.org/2017/07/06/535626356/on-russia-republican-and-democratic-lenses-have-a-very-different-tint.

Tetlock, P. (2005). *Expert political judgment: How good is it? How can we know?* Princeton, NJ: Princeton University Press.

Thrall, A. T. (2007). A bear in the woods? Threat framing and the marketplace of values. *Security Studies*, *16*(3), 452–488.

Thrall, A. T., Stecula, D., & Sweet, D. (2014). May we have your attention please? Human rights NGOs and the problem of global communication. *International Journal of Press/Politics*, *19*(2), 135–159.

Tormala, Z. L., & Petty, R. E. (2002). What doesn't kill me makes me stronger: The effects of resisting persuasion on attitude certainty. *Journal of Personality and Social Psychology*, *83*(6), 1298.

Twain, M. (1894[2014]). *Mark Twain on common sense: Timeless advice and words of wisdom from America's most-revered humorist*. New York: Simon & Schuster.

Wagner, F. (2017). Donald Trump and Hillary Clinton spent $81 million on Facebook ads before last year's election. Retrieved April 28, 2020 from www.vox.com/2017/11/1/16593066/trump-clinton-facebook-advertising-money-election-president-russia

Weisburd, A., Watts, C., & Berger, J., (2016). Trolling for Trump: How Russia Is Trying to Destroy Our Democracy. Retrieved April 28, 2020, from https://warontherocks.com/2016/11/trolling-for-trump-how-russia-is-trying-to-destroy-our-democracy/.

Wonnell, C. T. (1985). Truth and the marketplace of ideas. *UC Davis Law Review, 19*, 669.

Zaller, J. (1994). Elite leadership of mass opinion. In: Bennett, W.L., Paletz, D.L., eds, *Taken by storm: The Media, public opinion, and foreign policy in the Gulf War*. Chicago, IL: University of Chicago Press, pp. 186–209.

# 7

# COMMANDING THE TREND

## Social media as information warfare

*Jarred Prier*

## Introduction

For years, analysts in the defense and intelligence communities have warned lawmakers and the American public of the risks of a cyber Pearl Harbor. The fear of a widespread cyber-based attack loomed over the country following intrusions against Yahoo! email accounts in 2012, Sony Studios in 2014, and even the United States government Office of Personnel Management (OPM) in 2015. The average American likely did not understand exactly how, or for what purposes, US adversaries were operating within the cyber domain, but the implications of future attacks were not difficult to imagine. Enemies of the United States could target vulnerable power grids, stock markets, train switches, academic institutions, banks, and communications systems in the opening salvos of this new type of warfare.[1]

In contrast to more traditional forms of cyberattack, cyber operations today target people within a society, influencing their beliefs as well as behaviors, and diminishing trust in the government. US adversaries now seek to control and exploit the trend mechanism on social media to harm US interests, discredit public and private institutions, and sow domestic strife. "Commanding the trend" represents a relatively novel and increasingly dangerous means of persuasion within social media. Instead of attacking the military or economic infrastructure, state and nonstate actors outside the United States can access regular streams of online information via social media to influence networked groups within the United States.

This chapter analyzes how two US adversaries hijacked social media using four factors associated with command of the trend. First it provides a basis for commanding the trend in social media by analyzing social media as a tool for obtaining and spreading information. It then looks more specifically at how US adversaries use social media to command the trend and target US citizens with malicious propaganda. Next, the two most prominent, recent case studies provide evidence of how nonstate and state actors use social media to counter the United States. The first case study covers the Islamic State (IS) from 2014 to 2016 by examining the group's use of social media for recruiting, spreading propaganda, and proliferating terror threats. The second case describes the pattern of Russian hacking, espionage, disinformation, and manipulation of social media with a particular focus on the United States presidential election of 2016. Evidence for this second case study comes from nearly two years of research on Twitter accounts believed to be part of a Russian information warfare network. The chapter concludes with implications and predictions of how social media will continue to develop, what can be expected in the future, and how the United States can respond to the growing threat of adversaries commanding the trend.

## Commanding the trend in social media

The adaptation of social media as a tool of modern warfare should not be surprising. Internet technology evolved to meet the needs of information–age warfare around 2006 with the dawn of Web 2.0, which allowed internet users to create content instead of just consuming online material. Instead, the individual could decide what was important and only read what was important, on demand. Not only could users select what news they want to see, but they could also use the medium to create news based on their opinions.[2] The social nature of humans ultimately led to virtual networking. As such, traditional forms of media were bound to give way to a more tailorable form of communication. US adversaries were quick to find ways to exploit the openness of the internet, eventually developing techniques to employ social media networks as a tool to spread propaganda. Social media creates a point of injection for propaganda and has become the nexus of information operations and cyber warfare. To understand this, we must examine the important concept of the social media trend and look briefly into the fundamentals of propaganda. Also important is the spread of news on social media, specifically, the spread of "fake news" and how propaganda penetrates mainstream media outlets.

## Trending social media

Social media sites like Twitter and Facebook employ an algorithm to analyze words, phrases, or hashtags to create a list of topics sorted in order of popularity. This "trend list" is a quick way to review the most discussed topics at a given time. According to a 2011 study on social media, a trending topic "will capture the attention of a large audience for a short time" and thus "contributes to agenda setting mechanisms."[3] Using existing online networks in conjunction with automatic "bot" accounts, foreign agents can insert propaganda into a social media platform, create a trend, and rapidly disseminate a message faster and cheaper than through any other medium. Social media facilitates the spread of a narrative outside a particular social cluster of true believers by commanding the trend. It hinges on four factors: (1) a message that fits an existing, even if obscure, narrative; (2) a group of true believers predisposed to the message; (3) a relatively small team of agents or cyber warriors; and (4) a network of automated "bot" accounts.

The existing narrative and the true believers who subscribe to it are endogenous, so any propaganda must fit that narrative to penetrate the network of true believers. Usually, the cyber team is responsible for crafting the specific message for dissemination. The cyber team then generates videos, memes, or fake news, often in collusion with the true believers. To achieve the effective spread of propaganda, the true believers, the cyber team, and the bot network combine efforts to take command of the trend. Thus, an adversary in the information age can influence the population using a variety of propaganda techniques, primarily through social media combined with online news sources and traditional forms of media.

A trending topic transcends networks and becomes the mechanism for the spread of information across social clusters. Here the focus is primarily on Twitter, a "microblogging" site where each post is limited to 140 characters.[4] Facebook also has a trends list, but it is less visible than the Twitter trends list, and the two applications serve different purposes. Facebook maintains a function of bringing friends and families together. On Facebook, your connections are typically more intimate connections than you would expect on Twitter, which focuses less on bringing people together and more on bringing ideas together. As a microblog, Twitter's core notion is to share your thoughts and feelings about the world around you with a group of people who share similar interests. The individuals who follow each other may not be friends but could be a team of like-minded academics, journalists, sports fans, or politicos. When a person tweets, that tweet can be viewed by anyone who follows that person, or anyone who searches for that topic using Twitter's search tool. Additionally, anyone can "retweet" someone else's tweet, which broadcasts the original to a new audience. Twitter makes real-time idea and event sharing possible on a global scale.[5] Another method for quick referencing on Twitter is using a "hashtag." The tweet would then be visible to anyone who clicked on the link along with all of the other tweets using the same hashtag.

A trend can spread a message to a wide group outside of a person's typical social network. Moreover, malicious actors can use trends to spread a message using multiple forms of media on multiple platforms, with the ultimate goal of garnering coverage in the mainstream media. Command of the trend is a powerful method of spreading information whereby, according to an article in *The Guardian*, "you can take an existing trending topic, such as fake news, and then weaponise it. You can turn it against the very media that uncovered it."[6]

Because Twitter is an idea-sharing platform, it is very popular for rapidly spreading information, especially among journalists and academics; however, malicious users have also taken to Twitter for the same benefits in recent years. At one time, groups like al-Qaeda preferred creating websites, but now, "Twitter has emerged as the internet application most preferred by terrorists, even more popular than self-designed websites or Facebook."[7] Twitter makes it easy to spread a message to both supporters and foes outside of a particular network. Groups trying to disseminate a message as widely as possible can rely on the trend function to reach across multiple networks.

Three methods help control what is trending on social media: trend distribution, trend hijacking, and trend creation. The first method is relatively easy and requires the least amount of resources. Trend distribution is simply applying a message to every trending topic. Using the example above, someone could tweet a picture of the president with a message in the form of a meme—a stylistic device that applies culturally relevant humor to a photo or video—along with the unrelated hashtag #SuperBowl. Anyone who clicks on that trend list expecting to see something about football will see that meme of the president. Trend hijacking requires more resources in the form of either more followers spreading the message or a network of "bots" (autonomous programs that can interact with computer systems or users) designed to spread the message automatically. Of the three methods to gain command of the trend, trend creation requires the most effort. It necessitates either money to promote a trend or knowledge of the social media environment around the topic, and most likely, a network of several automatic bot accounts.

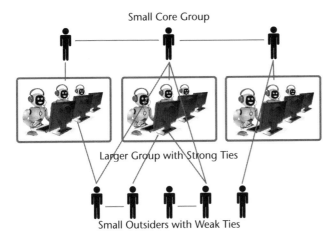

**FIGURE 7.1** Illustration of a bot network

Bot accounts are non-human accounts that automatically tweet and retweet based on a set of programmed rules. In 2014, Twitter estimated that only 5 percent of accounts were bots; that number has grown along with the total users and now tops 15 percent.[8] Some of the accounts are "news bots," which just retweet the trending topics. Some of the accounts are for advertising purposes, which try to dominate conversations to generate revenue through clicks on links. Some bots are trolls, which, like a human version of an online troll, tweet to disrupt the civil conversation.

For malicious actors seeking to influence a population through trends on social media, the best way to establish trends is to build a network of bot accounts programmed to tweet at various intervals, respond to certain words, or retweet when directed by a master account. Figure 7.1 illustrates the basics of a bot network. The top of the chain is a small core group. That team is comprised of human-controlled accounts with a large number of followers. The accounts are typically adversary cyber warriors or true believers with a large following. Under the core group is the bot network. Bots tend to follow each other and the core group. Below the bot network is a group consisting of the true believers without a large following. These human-controlled accounts are a part of the network, but they appear to be outsiders because of the weaker links between the accounts. The bottom group lacks a large following, but they do follow the core group, sometimes follow bot accounts, and seldom follow each other.

Enough bots working together can quickly start a trend or take over a trend, but bot accounts themselves can only bridge the structural hole between networks, not completely change a narrative. To change a narrative, to conduct an effective influence operation, requires a group to combine a well-coordinated bot campaign with essential elements of propaganda.

## Propaganda primer

Messaging designed to influence behavior has been around for centuries but became easier as methods of mass communication enabled wider dissemination of propaganda. Observing the rise of mass media and its presence in daily life, French philosopher Jacques Ellul noted the simplicity of propaganda in 1965. According to Ellul, "Propaganda ceases where simple dialogue begins."[9] That said, it is worth noting Eric Hoffer's comments that "propaganda on its own cannot force its way into unwilling minds, neither can it inculcate something wholly new."[10] For propaganda to function, it needs a previously existing narrative to build upon, as well as a network of true believers who already buy into the underlying theme. Social media helps the propagandist spread the message through an established network.

A person is inclined to believe information on social media because the people he chooses to follow share things that fit his existing beliefs. That person, in turn, is likely to share the information with others in his network, to others who are like-minded, and those predisposed to the message. With enough shares, a particular social network accepts the propaganda storyline as fact. But up to this point, the effects are relatively localized. The most effective propaganda campaigns are not confined just to those predisposed to the message. Essentially, propaganda permeates everyday experiences, and the individual targeted with a massive media blitz will never fully understand that the ideas he has are not entirely his own.

A modern example of this phenomenon was observable during the Arab Spring as propaganda spread on Facebook "helped middle-class Egyptians understand that they were not alone in their frustration."[11] In short, propaganda is simpler to grasp if everyone around a person seems to share the same emotions on a particular subject. Even a general discussion among the crowd can provide the illusion that propaganda is information.[12] In other words, propaganda creates heuristics, which is a way the mind simplifies problem solving by relying on quickly accessible data. The availability heuristic weighs the amount and frequency of information received, as well as recentness of the information as more informative than the source or accuracy of the information.[13] Essentially, the mind creates a shortcut based on the most—or most recent—information available, simply because it can be remembered easily. Often, the availability heuristic manifests itself in information received through media coverage.

The availability heuristic is important to understanding individual opinion formation and how propaganda can exploit the shortcuts our minds make to form opinions. The lines in Figure 7.2 show formation of opinions temporally, with double arrows influencing a final opinion more than single arrows. The circled containers indicate a penetration point for propaganda exploitation. As previously described, mass media enables rapid spread of propaganda, which feeds the availability heuristic. The internet makes it possible to flood the average person's daily intake of information, which aids the spread of propaganda.

One of the primary principles of propaganda is that the message must resonate with the target. Therefore, when presented with information that is within your belief structure, your bias is confirmed and you accept the propaganda. If it is outside of your network, you may initially reject the story, but the volume of information may create an availability heuristic in your mind. Over time, the propaganda becomes normalized—and even believable. It is confirmed when a fake news story is reported by the mainstream media, which has become reliant on social media for spreading and receiving news.

Figure 7.3 maps the process of how propaganda can penetrate a network that is not predisposed to the message. This outside network is a group that is ideologically opposed to the group of true believers. The outside network is likely aware of the existing narrative but does not necessarily subscribe to the underlying beliefs that support the narrative.

Command of the trend enables the contemporary propaganda model, to create a "firehose of information" that permits the insertion of false narratives over time and at all times.[14] Trending items produce the illusion of reality, in some cases even being reported by journalists. Because untruths can spread so quickly now, the internet has created "both deliberate

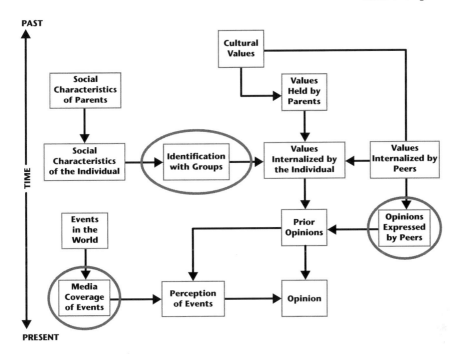

FIGURE 7.2  Model of individual opinion formation
*Source:* Reproduced by permission from Alan D. Monroe, Public Opinion in America (New York: Dodd, Mead, & Co., 1975), 147.

and unwitting propaganda" since the early 1990s through the proliferation of rumors passed as legitimate news.[15] The normalization of these types of rumors over time, combined with the rapidity and volume of new false narratives over social media, opened the door for "fake news."

The availability heuristic and the firehose of disinformation can slowly alter opinions as propaganda crosses networks by way of the trend, but the amount of influence will likely be minimal unless it comes from a source that a nonbeliever finds trustworthy. An individual may see the propaganda and believe the message is popular because it is trending but still not buy into the message itself. Instead, the individual will likely turn to a trusted source of news to test the validity of the propaganda. Therefore, we must now analyze modern journalism to determine how command of the trend can transform propaganda from fake news to real news.

## Social networks and social media

Currently, 72 percent of Americans get digital news primarily from a mobile device, and people now prefer online news sources to print sources by a two-to-one ratio.[16] The news consumer now selects from an abundance of options besides a local newspaper, based on how the consumer perceives the credibility of the resource. As social media usage has become more widespread, users have become ensconced within specific, self-selected groups, which means that news and views are shared nearly exclusively with like-minded

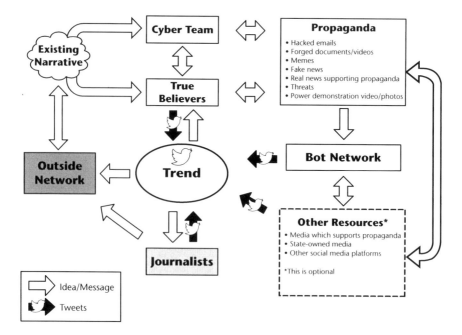

**FIGURE 7.3** Process map of how propaganda spreads via the trend

users. In network terminology, this group phenomenon is called homophily. More colloquially, it reflects the concept that "birds of a feather flock together." Homophily within social media creates an aura of expertise and trustworthiness where those factors would not normally exist.

Along the lines of social networking and propaganda, people are more willing to believe things that fit into their worldview. Once source credibility is established, there is a tendency to accept that source as an expert on other issues as well, even if the issue is unrelated to the area of originally perceived expertise.[17] Ultimately, this "echo chamber" can promote the scenario in which your friend is "just as much a source of insightful analysis on the nuances of U.S. foreign policy towards Iran as regional scholars, arms control experts, or journalists covering the State Department."[18]

If social media facilitates self-reinforcing networks of like-minded users, how can a propaganda message traverse networks where there are no overlapping nodes? This link between networks is only based on that single topic and can be easily severed. Thus, to employ social media effectively as a tool of propaganda, an adversary cannot rely on individual weak links between networks. Instead, an adversary must exploit a feature within the social media platform that enables cross-network data sharing on a massive scale: the trending topics list. Trends are visible to everyone. Regardless of who follows whom on a given social media platform, all users see the topics algorithmically generated by the platform as being the most popular topics at that particular moment. Given this universal and unavoidable visibility, "popular topics contribute to the collective awareness of what is trending and at times can also affect the public agenda of the community."[19] In this manner, a trending topic can bridge the gap between clusters of social networks. A malicious actor can quickly spread propaganda by injecting a narrative onto the trend list.

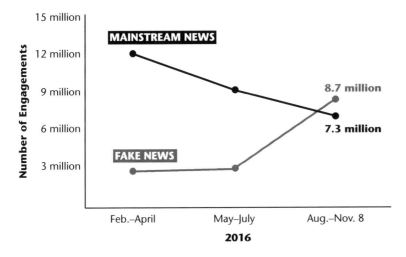

**FIGURE 7.4** Total Facebook engagements for top 20 election stories

The combination of networking on social media, propaganda, and reliance on unverifiable online news sources introduces the possibility of completely falsified news stories entering the mainstream of public consciousness. This phenomenon, commonly called fake news, has generated significant criticism from both sides of the American political spectrum, with some labeling any contrary viewpoints fake. In reality, fake news consists of more than just bad headlines, buried ledes, or poorly sourced stories.[20] Fake news is a particular form of propaganda composed of a false story disguised as news. On social media, this becomes particularly dangerous because of the viral spread of sensationalized fake news stories.

A prime example of fake news and social media came from the most shared news stories on Facebook during the 2016 US presidential election. The source of the fake news was a supposedly patriotic American news blog called "End the Fed," a website run by Romanian businessperson Ovidiu Drobota. One story stating that the pope endorsed Donald Trump for president received over one million shares on Facebook alone, not to mention shares on Twitter.[21] Other fake news stories from that site and others received more shares in late 2016 than traditional mainstream news sources (see Figure 7.4).[22]

It is important to recognize that more people were exposed to those fake news stories than what is reflected in the "shares" data. In some cases, people would just see the story in a Facebook or Twitter feed; in many cases, people actively sought out news from those sources, which are fiction at best and foreign propaganda at worst. Over time, those fake news sources become trusted sources for some people. As people learn to trust those sources, legitimate news outlets become less trustworthy. A 2016 poll by Gallup showed American trust in mass media is at an all-time low.[23]

When news is tailorable to one's taste and new stories are popping up around the world every second, mainstream journalists have to change their methods to compete with other sources of news. Therefore, if social media is becoming a source for spreading news and information, journalists will try to keep up by using social media to spread their stories and to acquire information first. According to an Indiana University School of Journalism study, the most common use of social media for journalists is to check for breaking news.[24] As a result, mainstream journalists tend to use tweets as a legitimate source, especially when there is a lack of more valid or confirmed sources.[25] Overreliance on social media for breaking news can become problematic in the midst of an ongoing information operation. If an adversary takes control of a trend on Twitter, the trend is likely to be noticed by mainstream media journalists who may provide legitimacy to a false story—essentially turning fake news into real news. This is the initial setup for how social media became extremely influential via an adversary's propaganda. IS and Russia successfully manipulated social media, particularly Twitter. Although they had different objectives, the tools and techniques were similar. Both foreign actors used command of the trend to spread propaganda that influenced the emotions, opinions, and behavior of US citizens in a manner antithetical to US interests. In essence, IS and Russia hijacked social media through propaganda narratives, true believers, cyber warriors, and a bot network.

## Hijacking social media: the case of IS

IS could have been considered either a large terrorist organization or a very fragile state with a weak army. However, the perception of IS varies. To believers, IS is a religious caliphate, but much of the rest of the world assumes it is a terrorist group that represents a perversion of faith. IS managed to master the art of manipulation because a single message simultaneously targeted potential allies and foes alike. Its use of social media is a case study in effective propaganda techniques that bolstered recruiting, increased brand recognition, and spread terror with minimal effort. It quickly became the first organization to use social media effectively to achieve its goals.

Although IS may use terrorism as a tactic, the organization behaves differently than any other terrorist organization in the world.[26] The differences are apparent in every aspect, from operations to recruiting to governing. The last factor is the key discriminator. As a descendant of al-Qaeda in Iraq, the group struggled to find its way after the death of leader Abu Musab al-Zarqawi in 2006; under the leadership of Abu Bakr al-Baghdadi the group has established clear lines of authority, taxation and educational systems, trade markets, even policing and a judiciary (covering civil, criminal, and religious complaints).[27] Gaining and holding land is just a part of what IS believes is the destiny of the organization and its followers. Certainly, the desire is to create a caliphate,[28] but its ultimate purpose is more apocalyptic in nature: IS seeks to usher in the end of the world.[29] Its members believe that their actions will bring the forces of the world to attack their caliphate and result in the imminent defeat of the infidel army in the Syrian town of Dabiq, thus triggering the end of the world and the final purge of evil.[30] IS is a revolutionary force with doomsday cult beliefs.[31]

To advance the organization's objectives, IS used messages that served to spread its propaganda on social media to a broad audience that fit within a narrative of strength for the supporter and a narrative of terror for the adversary. In other words, IS cyber warriors combined propaganda with command of the trend to accomplish three things with one message. First, they demonstrated the weakness and incompetence of the international community to fight them online and on the battlefield. Second, they injected terror into the mainstream media. Finally, and most importantly, they recruited new fighters to join them on the battlefield in Iraq and Syria—and online.

## IS commanding the trend

Through a combination of ingenious marketing and cyber mastery, IS bolstered its message around the world. First, the group refined IS branding. The organization projects a very specific image to the world that affects the viewer differently based on beliefs. To a follower, the images that are shared via social media demonstrate strength and power. To the nonfollower, the images are grotesque and horrifying. In other words, no matter what IS puts out in social media the result is a win for the organization because the same message successfully targets two different groups. The amplification of those messages by creating trends on Twitter is guaranteed to get further attention once the tweet falls into the mainstream media. Thus, IS is capable of using relatively small numbers of Twitter users (see Table 7.1) to project an aura of strength.

The method for expanding the reach of a single IS tweet or hashtag involves a network of legitimate retweets combined with bots and unwitting Twitter users. While IS does maintain a strong network of true believers, the numbers are relatively small and spread thinly across the Middle East. Therefore, IS must game the system and rig Twitter for a message to go viral. One high-tech method for creating a bot network was a mobile app called "Dawn of Glad Tidings." The app, designed by IS cyber warriors, provides updates on IS activities and spiritual guidance to the user. When users download the app, they create an account that links to their Twitter account, which then gives the app generous permissions, allowing the app to tweet using that user's account.[32] The app then retweets on behalf of the user when a master account sends an IS-branded tweet.

Over time, the hashtag generates enough tweets to start localized trends. Once the trend surfaces, it is broadcast over trend-monitoring networks, like the Arabic Twitter account @ActiveHashtags.[33] That causes the hashtag to gather more attention across the region and then be retweeted by real followers and other bot accounts. The final step in the process is when the trend goes global.

Worldwide trends on Twitter have been a boon for IS. Creating and hijacking trends garnered attention for the group that would otherwise have gone unnoticed on social media. The peak of IS trend hijacking was during the World Cup in 2014. As one of the world's

**TABLE 7.1** Snapshot of IS Twitter activity

| Twitter-related activity studied | Related statistics |
| --- | --- |
| Estimated number of overt IS Twitter accounts | 46,000 |
| Number of "bot" accounts | 6,216 |
| Average number of tweets per day per user | 7.3 |
| Average number of followers | 1,004 |
| Most common year accounts created | 2014 |
| Top languages | Arabic (73%), English (18%), French (6%) |
| Top locations | "Islamic State," Syria, Iraq, Saudi Arabia[a] |

*Source*: J. M. Berger and Jonathon Morgan, "The ISIS Twitter Census," Brookings Institute, accessed 20 March 2015, www.brookings.edu/research/the-isis-twitter-census-defining-and-describing-the-population-of-isis-supporters-on-twitter/.

*Notes*
a  Based on location-enabled users and self-defined account locations.

most popular sporting events, it was no surprise that the hashtag #WorldCup2014 trended globally on Twitter nonstop during the tournament. At one point though, nearly every tweet under this hashtag had something to do with IS instead of soccer. The network of IS supporters and bot accounts hijacked the trend. Because people were using the hashtag to discuss the matches and advertisers were using the trend for marketing, Twitter struggled to stop the trend and the subsequent IS propaganda effort.

In fact, IS cyber warriors and true believers foiled most of the early attempts by Twitter to stop IS from using their platform to spread propaganda. Twitter's initial reaction was to suspend accounts that violated the user terms of the agreement. The result was creative user names by IS supporters; for example, a user named @jihadISIS42 was created after @jihadISIS41 was suspended, which was set up after @jihadISIS40 was suspended.[34] Each new account demonstrated a deep dedication to the cause that, when combined with the seemingly significant presence on social media, presented the group as dominating social media.

In the case of #WorldCup2014, IS took command of the trend by hijacking, using the opportunity to push recruiting messages, and making terror threats against the tournament venues in Brazil. Additionally, the co-opted hashtag often directed users to other hashtags in what was ultimately a successful attempt to generate worldwide trends of other IS-related themes. One successful hashtag-creation effort was #StevensHeadinObamasHands, which included memes of President Barack Obama and IS-held American journalist Steven Sotloff. The implication was that the president of the United States did not care to or was powerless to stop the murder of an American citizen. Once again, IS appeared to be disproportionately powerful because of the command of the trend.

Due to the organization's aggressive communications strategy and branding, the IS social media presence consistently outperforms similar jihadist groups in the region that have the same number of, or more, followers.[35] Unlike al-Qaeda, which largely limited its online activity to websites, IS wanted to communicate with a broader audience—it wants to communicate directly to the whole world. In addition to spreading terror threats, the appearance of the group as a powerful state appealed to a group of true believers who turned to IS as new recruits to fight in Iraq and Syria. IS used social media from 2014 to 2016 to demonstrate power, sow fear in the international audience, and recruit the true believers. All the while, they used the true believers following on social media to boost their trends on social media. However, the group currently finds itself altering its modus operandi due to the recent loss of territories in Iraq and Syria, combined with a spate of successful terrorist-style attacks in Europe. The ongoing worry for counterterrorism experts is finally beginning to come to fruition: the recruit staying home to fight instead of joining IS overseas.

After years of maintaining a significant presence on social media, IS is using Twitter less now for official communication. The reasoning is likely twofold. First, the group has lost territory in Iraq and Syria and is adjusting its strategies. Second, Twitter has removed over 600,000 IS-related accounts consisting of bots, cyber warriors, and true believers.[36] Additionally, Twitter has adjusted the program to find terror-related videos, memes, and photos soon after an account from the IS network posts the propaganda. The reasons IS seemed so powerful is that, when viewed through the lens of terrorist groups, it advertised using weaponized social media campaigns. Its intense social media presence, ghastly videos, massive recruiting, and victories against Iraqi security forces made IS seem disproportionately stronger than it was.

**TABLE 7.2** IS case study analysis

| Requirement | Example |
| --- | --- |
| Propaganda narratives | 1. IS is strong; everyone else is weak. |
| | 2. True believers should join the cause. |
| True believers | Muslims believing in the caliphate of al-Baghdadi |
| Cyber warriors | Propaganda makers, video editors, app programmers, recruiters, spiritual leaders using low- and high-tech tools to advertise IS on social media |
| Bot network | Unwitting victims of spiritual-guidance app "Dawn of Glad Tidings" |

In summation, IS serves as a model for any nonstate group attempting to use social media for cyber coercion. Table 7.2 summarizes its use of the four requirements to gain command of the trend based on the analysis within this case study.

At the same time IS was weaponizing Twitter, Russia was using it to simultaneously cause confusion and garner support for its invasion of Crimea. Soon, Russia's command of the trend would be used to target the United States 2016 presidential election.

## Russia: masters of manipulation

Russia is no stranger to information warfare. The original technique of Soviet actors was through *aktivnyye meropriyatiya* (active measures) and *dezinformatsiya* (disinformation). According to a 1987 State Department report on Soviet information warfare, "active measures are distinct both from espionage and counterintelligence and from traditional diplomatic and informational activities. The goal of active measures is to influence opinions and/or actions of individuals, governments, and/or publics."[37]

In other words, Soviet agents would try to weave propaganda into an existing narrative to smear countries or individual candidates. Active measures are designed, as retired KGB General Oleg Kalugin once explained,

> to drive wedges in the Western community alliances of all sorts, particularly NATO, to sow discord among allies, to weaken the United States in the eyes of the people in Europe, Asia, Africa, Latin America, and thus to prepare ground in case the war really occurs.

Editor, translator, and analyst of Russian Federation trends Michael Weiss says, "The most common subcategory of active measures is *dezinformatsiya*, or disinformation: feverish, if believable lies cooked up by Moscow Centre and planted in friendly media outlets to make democratic nations look sinister."[38]

The techniques Russia uses today are similar to those they used during the Cold War, but dissemination is more widespread through social media. Recently, the Russian minister of defense acknowledged the existence of their cyber warriors in a speech to the Russian parliament, announcing that Russia formed a new branch of the military consisting of information warfare troops.[39] The Internet Research Agency, as it was called in 2015, now seems to be the information warfare branch he openly admitted to. This army of professional trolls' mission is to fight online. The Russian trolls have a variety of state resources at their disposal, including a vast intelligence network to assist their cyber warriors.

The additional tools available to Russia also include RT (Russia Today) and Sputnik, the Kremlin-financed television news networks broadcasting in multiple languages around the world. Before the trolls begin their activities on social media, the cyber warrior hackers first provide hacked information to Wikileaks, which, according to CIA director Mike Pompeo, is a "non-state hostile intelligence service abetted by state actors like Russia."[40] In intelligence terms, WikiLeaks operates as a "cutout" for Russian intelligence operations—a place to spread intelligence information through an outside organization—similar to the Soviets' use of universities to publish propaganda studies in the 1980s.[41] The trolls then take command of the trend to spread the hacked information on Twitter, referencing WikiLeaks and links to RT news within their tweets. These Russian efforts would be impossible without an existing network of American true believers willing to spread the message. The Russian trolls and the bot accounts amplified the voices of the true believers in addition to inserting propaganda into that network. Then, the combined effects of Russian and American Twitter accounts took command of the trend to spread disinformation across networks.

The cyber trolls produced several hoaxes in the United States and Europe, like the Louisiana hoax, according to Adrian Chen in his article "The Agency" in *The New York Times Magazine*.[42] Protests of police departments throughout the United States during the summer of 2015 provided several opportunities to manipulate narratives via social media, and it is likely Russian trolls hijacked some of the Black Lives Matter-related trends to spread disinformation and accuse journalists of failing to cover important issues.[43] The Russian trolls said the idea was to spread fear, discrediting institutions—especially American media—while making President Obama look powerless and Russian president Vladimir Putin more favorable.[44]

Several hijacked hashtags in 2015 attempted to discredit the Obama administration while spreading racist memes and hoaxes aimed at the African American community. In other words, the Russian trolls seemed to target multiple groups to generate anger and create chaos. One particularly effective Twitter hoax occurred as racial unrest fell on the University of Missouri campus that fall.

### #PrayforMizzou

On the night of 11 November 2015, #PrayforMizzou began trending on Twitter.[45] The trend was a result of protests at the University of Missouri campus over racial issues; however, "news" slowly started developing within the hashtag that altered the meaning and soon shot the hashtag to the top of the trend list. The news was that the KKK was marching through Columbia and the Mizzou campus. One user, display name "Jermaine" (@Fanfan1911), warned residents, "The cops are marching with the KKK! They beat up my little brother! Watch out!" Jermaine's tweet included a picture of a black child with a severely bruised face; it was retweeted hundreds of times. Additionally, Jermaine and a handful of other users continued tweeting and retweeting images and stories of KKK and neo-Nazis in Columbia, chastising the media for not covering the racists creating havoc on campus.

Looking at Jermaine's followers, and the followers of his followers, one could observe that the original tweeters all followed and retweeted each other. Those users also seemed to be retweeted automatically by approximately 70 bots. These bots also used the trend-distribution technique, which used all of the trending hashtags at that time within their tweets, not just #PrayforMizzou. Spaced evenly, and with retweets of real people who were observing the Mizzou hashtag, the numbers quickly escalated to thousands of tweets within a few minutes. The plot was smoothly executed and evaded the algorithms Twitter designed to catch bot tweeting, mainly because the Mizzou hashtag was being used outside of that attack. The narrative was set as the trend was hijacked, and the hoax was underway.

The rapidly spreading image of a bruised little boy was generating legitimate outrage across the country and around the world. However, a quick Google image search for "bruised black child" revealed the picture that "Jermaine" attached to the tweet was a picture of an African American child who was beaten by police in Ohio over one year earlier. The image and the narrative were part of a larger plot to spread fear and distrust. It worked.

The University of Missouri student body president tweeted a warning to stay off the streets and lock doors because "KKK members were confirmed on campus." National news networks broke their coverage to get a local feed from camera crews roaming Columbia and the campus looking for signs of violence. As journalists continued to search for signs of Klan members, anchors read tweets describing shootings, stabbings, and cross burnings. In the end, the stories were all false.

Shortly after the disinformation campaign at Mizzou, @Fanfan1911 changed his display name from Jermaine to "FanFan" and the profile picture of a young black male changed to the image of a German iron cross. The next few months, FanFan's tweets were all in German and consisted of spreading rumors about Syrian refugees. Russian active measures in Europe around this time were widely reported, and the account that previously tweeted disinformation regarding Mizzou now focused on messages that were anti-Islamic, anti-European Union, and anti-German Chancellor Angela Merkel. His tweets reached a crescendo after reports of women being raped on New Year's Eve 2016. Some of the reports were false, including a high-profile case of a 13-year-old ethnic-Russian girl living in Berlin who falsely claimed that she was abducted and raped by refugees.[46] Once again, Russian propaganda dominated the narrative.[47] Similar to previous disinformation campaigns on Twitter, the Russians trolls were able to spread the information because of an underlying fear and an existing narrative that they were able to exploit. The trolls used trend-hijacking techniques in concurrence with reporting by Russian state-funded television network Russia Today. To attempt to generate more attention to the Russian anti-Merkel narrative in European media, Russian foreign minister Sergey Lavrov accused German authorities of a "politically correct cover-up" in the case of the Russian teen.[48] Because of the Russian propaganda push, the anti-immigration narrative began spreading across traditional European media.[49] In fact, a magazine in Poland devoted an entire issue to the topic of Muslim immigration with a disturbing cover photo entitled "Islamic Rape of Europe."[50]

In addition to the German tweets, FanFan began tweeting in English again in the spring of 2016. His tweets and the tweets of other Russian trolls were spreading in America. The narrative they spread was developing a symbiotic relationship with American right-wing news organizations like Breitbart and its followers on social media—a group of true believers in the Russian propaganda narrative.

Additionally, the troll network already seeded various social media platforms with pages designed for spreading disinformation.[51] Seemingly patriotic American Facebook pages linked articles to RT, legitimate American news sources advocating a right-leaning

**102** Jarred Prier

perspective, Breitbart, right-wing conspiracy sites like InfoWars, and non-factual "news" sites like The Conservative Tribune and Gateway Pundit. The Facebook pages also linked to Russia-run sites with nothing but false news stories. Based on anti-Obama sentiment, the Facebook pages were popular among conservative users but not getting broad exposure.

Before 2016, Russian active measures were also used in European elections, most notably the "Brexit" campaign. One European expert on Russia quoted in the *Atlantic* article "War Goes Viral" summarized Putin's intent as "not to make you love Putin"; instead "the aim is to make you disbelieve anything. A disbelieving, fragile, unconscious audience is much easier to manipulate."[52] Active measures enable manipulation. Smearing political candidates, hacking, the spread of disinformation, and hoaxes all contribute to a breakdown of public trust in institutions.

As the 2016 US presidential campaign began in earnest, much of the online animosity was now directed at Obama's potential successor: Hillary Clinton. She became a rallying cry for Trump supporters and a force-multiplying tool for the Russian trolls.

## *Influencing the 2016 Presidential Election*

According to the Office of Director of National Intelligence (ODNI) Report on Russian Influence during the 2016 presidential election, "Moscow's influence campaign followed a messaging strategy that blends covert intelligence operations—such as cyber activity—with overt efforts by Russian Government agencies, state funded media, third-party inter-mediaries, and paid social media users, or 'trolls.'"[53] In the case of the 2016 election, Russian propaganda easily meshed with right-wing networks known as the "alt-right" and also with supporters of Senator Bernie Sanders in the left wing of the Democratic Party. Hillary Clinton had been a target of conservative groups since she first came into the national spotlight as first lady in the 1990s.[54] Thus, groups on the left and right presented strong opposition to her candidacy in 2016, which meant Russian trolls already had a narrative to build upon and a network of true believers on social media to spread their propaganda.

In a September 2016 speech, Clinton described half of candidate Trump's supporters as "deplorables." She went on to say that the other half of Trump's supporters were just people who felt the system had left them behind, who needed support and empathy. Clearly, she was not referring to all of Trump's supporters as deplorable, but the narrative quickly changed after social media users began referring to themselves as "Deplorable" in their screen names.

Before the "basket of deplorables" comment, the trolls primarily used an algorithm to rapidly respond to a tweet from Donald Trump. Those tweets were prominently displayed directly under Trump's tweet if a user clicked on the original. Those users became powerful voices with large followings; Trump himself frequently retweeted many of those users.[55] However, after the Clinton speech, a "people search" on Twitter for "deplorable" was all one needed to suddenly gain a network of followers numbering between 3,000 and 70,000.

Once again, FanFan's name changed—this time to "Deplorable Lucy"—and the profile picture became a white, middle-aged female with a Trump logo at the bottom of the picture. The FanFan follower count went from just over 1,000 to 11,000 within a few days. His original network from the Mizzou and European campaigns changed as well: tracing his follower trail again led to the same groups of people in the same network, and they were all now defined by the "Deplorable" brand. In short, they were now completely in unison with a vast network of other Russian trolls, actual American citizens, and bot accounts from both countries on Twitter. With a large network consisting of Russian trolls, true believers, and bots, it suddenly became easier to get topics trending with a barrage of tweets. The Russian trolls could employ the previously used tactics of bot tweets and hashtag hijacking, but now they had the capability to create trends.

Besides creating trends, the trolls could relay strategy under the radar using Twitter. That is to say, a message could be delivered in the form of a picture that did not include any words. The lack of words would spread the message to the followers in a timeline, but retweets would not develop any trends—only that network of followers or someone actively observing the network saw the messages. Often, anonymous users discussed the tactics behind the trend creation on the social media site 4Chan or on the bulletin board called "/pol/" and subsequently coordinated the trend within the Deplorable Network on Twitter.

The most effective trends derived from this strategy came in the days following the release of the "Access Hollywood" tape from 2005 in which Trump had made vulgar remarks.[56] The Deplorable Network distributed the corresponding strategy throughout the network to drown out negative attention to Trump on Twitter. Coinciding with the implementation of the strategy to mask anti-Trump comments on Twitter, WikiLeaks began releasing Clinton campaign chairman John Podesta's stolen emails.[57] The emails themselves revealed nothing truly controversial, but the narrative that the trending hashtag created was powerful. First, the issue of hacked emails developed into a narrative conflating Podesta's emails to the issue of Clinton's use of a private email server while she was secretary of state. The Clinton server was likely never hacked, but the problem of email loomed over her candidacy.

Secondly, the Podesta email narrative took routine issues and made them seem scandalous. The most common theme: bring discredit to the mainstream media. Podesta, like any campaign manager in modern politics, communicated with members of the press. Emails communicating with reporters were distributed via trending tweets with links to fake news websites. The fake news distorted the stolen emails into conspiracies of media "rigging" of the election to support Hillary Clinton. The corruption narrative also plagued the Democratic National Committee (DNC), which experienced a hack earlier in the year by Russian sources and revealed by WikiLeaks.[58]

A month after the election, a man drove from his home in North Carolina to Washington, DC, to uncover the truth behind another news story he read online. He arrived at Comet Ping-Pong, a pizza restaurant, with an AR-15, prepared to free children from an underground child sex trafficking ring in the restaurant. After searching the store, he found no children. The story was a hoax. One of the emails stolen from John Podesta was an invitation to a party at the home of a friend that promised good pizza from Comet Ping Pong and a pool to entertain the kids. Fake news sites reported the email as code for a pedophilic sex party; it was widely distributed via the trending #PodestaEmail hashtag and an associated new hashtag, #PizzaGate.

The #PizzaGate hoax, along with all of the other false and quasi-false narratives, became common within right-wing media as another indication of the immorality of Clinton and her staff. Often, the mainstream media would latch onto a story with unsavory backgrounds and false pretenses, thus giving more credibility to all of the fake news; however, the narrative from the #PizzaGate hoax followed the common propaganda narrative that the media was trying to cover up the truth, and the government failed to investigate the crimes. Ultimately, that is what drove the man to inquire into the fake news for himself.[59]

Finally, the stolen emails went beyond sharing on social media. The trend became so sensational that traditional media outlets chose to cover the Podesta email story, which gave credibility to the fake news and the associated online conspiracy theories promulgated by the Deplorable Network. The WikiLeaks release of the Podesta emails was the peak of Russian command of the trend during the 2016 election. Nearly every day #PodestaEmail trended as a new batch of supposedly scandalous hacked emails made their way into the mainstream press.

By analyzing the followers of a suspected Russian troll, a picture emerges regarding the structure of the network that was active during the 2016 election. The core group in the Deplorable Network consisted of Russian trolls and popular American right-wing accounts like Jack Posobiec, Mike Cernovich, and InfoWars editor Paul Joseph Watson. The Network also consisted of two bot accounts while the remaining nodes are individual accounts likely consisting of human-managed accounts. In total, the Deplorable Network was approximately 200,000 Twitter accounts consisting of Russian trolls, true believers, and bots.

Based on my analysis, the bot network appeared to be between 16,000 and 34,000 accounts.[60] The cohesiveness of the group indicates how a coordinated effort can create a trend in a way that a less cohesive network could not accomplish. To conduct cyberattacks using social media as information warfare, an organization must have a vast network of bot accounts to take command of the trend. With unknown factors like the impact of fake news, the true results of the Russian influence operation will likely never be known.

As Ellul said, experiments undertaken to gauge the effectiveness of propaganda will never work because the tests "cannot reproduce the real propaganda situation."[61] The concept itself is marred by the fact that much of the social media support Trump received was through real American true believers tweeting. However, two numbers will stand out from the 2016 election: 2.8 million and 80,000. Hillary Clinton won the popular vote by 2.8 million votes, and Donald Trump won the electoral vote via a combination of just over 80,000 votes in three key states. One could easily make the case—as many on the left have done—that Clinton lost because of the Russian influence.[62] Conversely, one could also argue she was destined to lose because of a botched campaign combined with a growing sense of disenchantment with the American political system. However, one cannot dispute the fact that Russia launched a massive cyber warfare campaign to influence the 2016 presidential election.[63]

For the most part, the Russian trolls became savvier with their techniques as they adapted to the influence operation in the United States. However, some users, like FanFan, were sloppy with their tradecraft and were obvious to anyone monitoring. The trolls were occasionally sloppy with their IP address locations as well. Following the first presidential debate, the #TrumpWon hashtag quickly became the number one trend globally. Using the TrendMap application, one quickly noticed that the worldwide hashtag seemed to originate in St. Petersburg, Russia. Russian trolls gave obvious support to Donald Trump and proved that using social media could create chaos on a massive scale, discredit any politician, and divide American society.

Adrian Chen, the *New York Times* reporter who originally uncovered the troll network in Saint Petersburg in 2015, went back to Russia in the summer of 2016. Russian activists he interviewed claimed that the purpose of the trolls "was not to brainwash readers, but to overwhelm social media with a flood of fake content, seeding doubt and paranoia, and destroying the possibility of using the Internet as a democratic space."[64] The troll farm used similar techniques to drown out anti-Putin trends on Russian social media in addition to pumping out disinformation to the United States.

A Congressional Research Service Study summarized the Russian troll operation succinctly in a January 2017 report:

> Cyber tools were also used [by Russia] to create psychological effects in the American population. The likely collateral effects of these activities include compromising the fidelity of information, sowing discord and doubt in the American public about the validity of intelligence community reports, and prompting questions about the democratic process itself.[65]

For Russia, information warfare is a specialized type of war, and modern tools make social media the weapon. According to a former Obama administration senior official, Russians regard the information sphere as a domain of warfare on a sliding scale of conflict that always exists between the US and Russia.[66] This perspective was on display during a Russian national security conference "Infoforum 2016." Andrey Krutskih, a senior Kremlin advisor, compared Russia's information warfare to a nuclear bomb, which would "allow Russia to talk to Americans as equals," in the same way that Soviet testing of the atomic bomb did in 1949.[67]

From 2015 to 2016, Russian trolling modus operandi took a logical path from small stories designed to create panic and sow seeds of doubt to a social media machine that IS could only imagine. In warfare strategy, narrative manipulation through social media cyber operations is the current embodiment of taking the fight directly to the people. The 2016 election proved that using social media to influence political outcomes, as opposed to violence or Cold War-like posturing, is a highly effective strategy in modern information warfare—a strategy that will likely continue as technology continues to develop and adapt to the ever-growing social media landscape as more actors gain the ability to take command of the trend.

## The future of weaponized social media

Smear campaigns have been around since the beginning of politics, but this article illustrated novel techniques recently employed by a terrorist group and foreign state actor, with each attack gaining popularity and credibility after trending on Twitter. The attacks, often under the guise of a "whistleblower" campaign, make routine political actions seem scandalous. Additionally, WikiLeaks advertises that it has never published anything requiring retraction because everything it posts is supposedly authentic stolen material. Just like the Podesta email releases, several politicians and business leaders around the world have fallen victim to this type of attack.

Recall the 2015 North Korean hacking of Sony Studios. Lost in the explosive nature of the hacking story is that the fallout at the company was not because of the hacking itself but from the release of embarrassing emails from Sony senior management, as well as the salaries of every employee at Sony. The uproar over the content of the emails dominated social media, often fed by salacious stories like the RT headline: "Leaked Sony emails exhibit wealthy elite's maneuvering to get child into Ivy League school." Ultimately, Sony fired a senior executive because of the content of her emails.[68]

In another example from May 2017, nine gigabytes of email stolen from French presidential candidate Emmanuel Macron's campaign were released online and verified by WikiLeaks. Subsequently, the hashtag #MacronLeaks trended to number one worldwide. It was an influence operation resembling the #PodestaEmail campaign with a supporting cast of

**TABLE 7.3** Russia case study analysis in 2016 election

| Types | Examples |
| --- | --- |
| Propaganda narratives | <ul><li>Anything discrediting to Hillary Clinton</li><li>News media hides information</li><li>Politicians are rigging the system</li><li>Global elite trying to destroy the world</li><li>Globalism is taking jobs and destroying cultures</li><li>Refugees are terrorists</li><li>Russian foreign policy is strong on antiterrorism</li><li>Democrats and some Republicans want WWIII with Russia</li></ul> |
| True believers | Alt-right, some Bernie Sanders supporters, followers of InfoWars and Breitbart, 4Chan /pol/ users. |
| Cyber warriors | Hackers and professional trolls |
| Bot network | Large, sophisticated network that leveraged cyber warriors and true believer accounts to create the "Deplorable Network." |

some of the same actors. During the weeks preceding the French election, many accounts within the Deplorable Network changed their names to support Macron's opponent, Marine Le Pen. These accounts mostly tweet in English and still engage in American political topics as well as French issues.[69] Some of the accounts also tweet in French, and a new network of French-tweeting bot accounts uses the same methods as the Deplorable Network to take command of the trend.

In his book *Out of the Mountains*, David Kilcullen describes a future comprising large, coastal urban areas filled with potential threats, all connected.[70] The implications of his prediction are twofold. First, networks of malicious nonstate actors can band together to hijack social media using a template similar to IS. Although these groups may not have the power to create global trends, they can certainly create chaos with smaller numbers by hijacking trends and creating local trends. With minimal resources, a small group can create a bot network to amplify its message. Second, scores of people with exposure to social media are vulnerable to online propaganda efforts. In this regard, state actors can use the Russian playbook.

Russia will likely continue to dominate this new battlespace. It has intelligence assets, hackers, cyber warrior trolls, massive bot networks, state-owned news networks with global reach, and established networks within the countries Russia seeks to attack via social media. Most importantly, the Russians have a history of spreading propaganda. After the 2016 elections in the United States, Russian trolls again worked toward influencing European elections. Currently, Russian trolls are active in France, the Balkans, and the Czech Republic using active measures and coercive social media messages.[71] It is clear that other countries are attempting to build capabilities to match the Russian cyber troll influence.

Already, Turkey, Iran, and Venezuela are noted as having bot networks and cyber warriors similar to Russian trolls.[72] With these other states, a popular use for the trolls in the social media battlespace is to stoke nationalism and control the narrative within their own borders. For example, the fake Twitter followers of Venezuelan president Nicolás Maduro number so many that he is now the "third-most-retweeted public figure in the world, behind only the king of Saudi Arabia and the pope."[73]

With a large enough bot network, states can also control messages outside of social media using similar techniques. Manipulating search engines is called "search engine optimization," which uses bot accounts to increase the number of clicks to a particular web page after performing a search. The search engine algorithm then prioritizes that page in response to subsequent searches using the same keyword. A Google search for "ODNI Report" is illustrative: in March 2017, the top Google results were RT articles lambasting the intelligence assessment that named the Russian government as the perpetrators behind the 2016 election interference.

Techniques like search engine optimization and command of the trend will become common in future wars to sow discord and spread false information, with the aim of causing the other side to change its course of action. These online weapons should frighten every leader in a democracy. Perhaps most frightening is the Oxford Internet Institute Unit for Propaganda discovery that "hundreds of thousands of 'sleeper bots' exist on Twitter."[74] These bots are accounts that are active but have not yet started tweeting. Researchers do not know who owns the accounts or what will trigger them. The ease of use and large numbers of active bots and sleeper bots indicate a high likelihood of social media continuing to be used for propaganda, especially as more and more state and nonstate organizations realize the impact they can make on an adversary.

Thus far, the United States response has been relatively weak. For one, the US government does not prioritize information operations the way it once did during the Cold War. When Eisenhower started the United States Information Agency (USIA), the objective was to compete with Soviet propaganda around the world. The mission statement of USIA clarified its role:

> The purpose of the United States Information Agency shall be to submit evidence to peoples of other nations by means of communication techniques that the objectives and policies of the United States are in harmony with and will advance their legitimate aspirations for freedom, progress, and peace.[75]

Knowing what we know now about Russian disinformation active measures, USIA was never truly equipped to fight an information war. The agency became a public diplomacy platform with a positive message rather than a Soviet style campaign of negative smear tactics. Accordingly, several questions arose: should USIA spread propaganda? Should it seek out and attempt to remove negative publicity about the US? Should it slander opponents? Most importantly: should it do any or all of these things when the American public could be influenced by a message intended for an international audience?[76]

Those problems persist today because the government lacks a centralized information authority since the mission of USIA was relegated to the Department of State. Several failed attempts to counter IS on Twitter show the US government's weakness when trying to use social media as a weapon. One example is the Center for Strategic Counterterrorism Communications, created in 2010, which started the program "Think Again, Turn Away." The State department awarded a $575,046 contract to a Virginia-based consulting firm to manage the project.[77] The intent was to curb the appeal of IS by creating a counternarrative to the IS message on social media. Unfortunately, the Twitter campaign had undesirable consequences after the account sent tweets arguing the finer points of the Islamic faith with IS sympathizers. Rita Katz best summarized the failure:

In order to counter a problem, one must first study it before adopting a solution. Had the people behind "Think Again, Turn Away" understood jihadists' mindsets and reasons for their behavior, they would have known that their project of counter-messaging would not only be a waste of taxpayer money but ultimately be counterproductive.[78]

In the end, the "Think Again, Turn Away" campaign was almost comical as it could not communicate effectively with any audience and severely discounted the importance of its message. Jacques Ellul noted that democracies were prone to having problems with outward communication through propaganda. Because democracies rely on presenting an image of fairness and truth, "propaganda made by democracies is ineffective, paralyzed, mediocre."[79] The United States was ill equipped to combat Soviet active measures during the Cold War, and it remains unable to compete using social media as an influence operation.

Unfortunately, countering Russian influence operations has taken a partisan slant within the United States. Many downplay the Russian role in the 2016 election while others appear to be so blinded by the Russian operation that they cannot see the underlying conditions that allowed for the spread of that narrative in the first place.[80] With the two parties unable to reach a consensus on what happened or the impact of the operation, they fail to realize that as technology improves and proliferates around the world, disinformation campaigns and influence operations will become the norm. The attack in a future information war could be toward either political party and come from any of the several countries attempting to build an online army in the mold of Russia's trolls and bot network.

## Conclusion

In the 1987 book *Truth Twisters*, Richard Deacon laments the future of independent thinking, as computers "could become the most dangerous hypnotic influence in the future. Allowing oneself to be manipulated and controlled by it."[81] He believed that such technology could lead one to commit treason without realizing any manipulation. Propaganda is a powerful tool, and, used effectively, it has been proven to manipulate populations on a massive scale. Using social media to take command of the trend makes the spread of propaganda easier than ever before for both state and nonstate actors.

Fortunately, social media companies are taking steps to combat malicious use. Facebook has been at the forefront of tech companies taking action to increase awareness of fake news and provide a process for removing the links from the website.[82] Also, although Facebook trends are less important to information warfare than Twitter trends, the website has taken measures to ensure that humans are involved in making the trends list. Furthermore, Twitter has started discreetly removing unsavory trends within minutes of their rise in popularity. However, adversaries adapt, and Twitter trolls have attempted to regain command of the trend by misspelling a previous trend once it is taken out of circulation. Still, even if the misspelled word regains a spot on the trend list, the message is diminished.

The measures enacted by Facebook and Twitter are important for preventing future wars in the information domain. However, Twitter will also continue to have problems with trend hijacking and bot networks. As demonstrated by #PrayforMizzou and #WorldCup2014, real events happening around the world will maintain popularity as well-intending users want to talk about the issues. In reality, removing the trends function could end the use of social media as a weapon, but doing so could also devalue the usability of Twitter. Rooting out bot accounts would have an equal effect since that would nearly eliminate the possibility of trend creation. Unfortunately, that would have an adverse impact on advertising firms that rely on Twitter to generate revenue for their products.

With social media companies balancing the interests of their businesses and the betterment of society, other institutions must respond to the malicious use of social media. In particular, the credibility of our press has been put into question by social media influence campaigns—those groups should respond accordingly. For instance, news outlets should adopt social media policies for their employees that encourage the use of social media but discourage them from relying on Twitter as a source. This will require a culture shift within the press and fortunately has gathered significant attention at universities researching the media's role in the influence operation. It is worth noting that the French press did not cover the content of the Macron leaks; instead, the journalists covered the hacking and influence operation without giving any credibility to the leaked information.

Finally, our elected officials must move past the partisan divide of Russian influence in the 2016 election. This involves two things: first, both parties must recognize what happened—neither minimizing nor overplaying Russian active measures. Second, and most importantly, politicians must commit to not using active measures to their benefit. Certainly, the appeal of free negative advertising will make any politician think twice about using disinformation, but the reality of a foreign influence operation damages more than just the other party, it damages our democratic ideals. Senator John McCain summarized this sentiment well at a CNN Town Hall: "Have no doubt, what the Russians tried to do to our election could have destroyed democracy. That's why we've got to pay … a lot more attention to the Russians."[83]

This was not the cyber war we were promised. Predictions of a catastrophic cyberattack dominated policy discussion, but few realized that social media could be used as a weapon against the minds of the population. IS and Russia are models for this future war that uses social media to directly influence people. As technology improves, techniques are refined, and internet connectivity continues to proliferate around the world, this saying will ring true: He who controls the trend will control the narrative—and, ultimately, the narrative controls the will of the people.

## Notes

1 Elisabeth Bumiller and Thom Shanker, "Panetta Warns of Dire Threat of Cyberattack on U.S.," *New York Times*, 11 October 2012, www.nytimes.com/2012/10/12/world/panetta-warns-of-dire-threat-of-cyberattack.html?mcubz=0/.
2 Jeremy Scott-Joynt, "What Myspace Means to Murdoch," BBC News Analysis, 19 July 2005, http://news.bbc.co.uk/2/hi/business/4697671.stm.
3 Sitaram Asur, Bernardo A. Huberman, Gabor Szabo, and Chunyan Wang, "Trends in Social Media: Persistence and Decay" (unpublished manuscript, submitted to Cornell University Library arXiv 7 February 2011), 1, https://arxiv.org/abs/1102.1402?context=physics.
4 "Blog" is short for "web log." A blog is a way to share your thoughts via the internet. A microblog is a blog with a character limit to the text.
5 Rani Molla, "Social Studies: Twitter vs. Facebook," *Bloomberg Gadfly*, 12 February 2016, www.bloomberg.com/gadfly/articles/2016-02-12/social-studies-comparing-twitter-with-facebook-in-charts.

6 Carole Cadwalladr, "Robert Mercer: The Big Data Billionaire Waging War on the Mainstream Media," *Guardian*, 26 February 2017, www.theguardian.com/politics/2017/feb/26/robert-mercer-breitbart-war-on-media-steve-bannon-donald-trump-nigel-farage.

7 Gabriel Weimann, *Terrorism in Cyberspace: The Next Generation* (Washington, DC: Woodrow Wilson Center Press, 2015), 138.

8 Alex Lubben, "Twitter's Users Are 15 Percent Robot, but That's Not Necessarily a Bad Thing," VICE News, 12 March 2017, https://news.vice.com/story/twitters-users-are-15-percent-robot-but-thats-not-necessarily-a-bad-thing.

9 Jacques Ellul, *Propaganda: The Formation of Men's Attitudes* (New York: Knopf, 1965), 6.

10 Eric Hoffer, *The True Believer: Thoughts on the Nature of Mass Movements* (New York: Harper & Row, 1951), 105.

11 Thomas Rid, *Cyber War Will Not Take Place* (New York: Oxford University Press, 2013), 132.

12 Ellul, 85.

13 Daniel Kahneman, *Thinking, Fast and Slow* (New York: Farrar, Straus & Giroux, 2011), 87.

14 Christopher Paul and Miriam Matthews, *The Russian "Firehose of Falsehood" Propaganda Model*, RAND Report PE-198-OSD (Santa Monica, CA: RAND, 2016), 4, www.rand.org/pubs/perspectives/PE198.html.

15 Garth Jowett and Victoria O'Donnell, *Propaganda & Persuasion*, 5th ed. (Thousand Oaks, CA: SAGE, 2012), 159.

16 Katerina Eva Matsa and Kristine Lu, "10 Facts about the Changing Digital News Landscape," Pew Research Center, 14 September 2016, www.pewresearch.org/fact-tank/2016/09/14/facts-about-the-changing-digital-news-landscape/.

17 Jowett and O'Donnell, *Propaganda & Persuasion*, 300.

18 Tom Hashemi, "The Business of Ideas Is in Trouble: Re-injecting Facts into a Post-truth World," *War on the Rocks*, 9 December 2016, https://warontherocks.com/2016/12/the-business-of-ideas-is-in-trouble-re-injecting-facts-into-a-post-truth-world/.

19 Asur, Huberman, Szabo, and Wang, "Trends in Social Media," 1.

20 *Merriam-Webster Dictionary Online*, s.v. "lede," accessed 10 October 2017, www.merriam-webster.com/dictionary/lede. "The introductory section of a news story that is intended to entice the reader to read the full story."

21 Tess Townsend, "The Bizarre Truth behind the Biggest Pro-Trump Facebook Hoaxes," Inc.com, 21 November 2016, www.inc.com/tess-townsend/ending-fed-trump-facebook.html.

22 Craig Silverman, "This Analysis Shows How Viral Fake Election News Stories Outperformed Real News on Facebook," Buzzfeed News, 16 November 2016, www.buzzfeed.com/craigsilverman/viral-fake-election-news-outperformed-real-news-on-facebook?utm_term=.qwWdA0G8G#.fcEv1Qono.

23 Art Swift, "Americans' Trust in Mass Media Sinks to New Low," Gallup, 14 September 2016, http://news.gallup.com/poll/195542/americans-trust-mass-media-sinks-new-low.aspx.

24 Andrea Peterson, "Three Charts that Explain how U.S. Journalists Use Social Media," *Washington Post*, 6 May 2014, www.washingtonpost.com/news/the-switch/wp/2014/05/06/three-charts-that-explain-how-u-s-journalists-use-social-media/?utm_term=.9cdd82cb8fa7.

25 Weimann, *Terrorism in Cyberspace*, 138.

26 Audrey Kurth Cronin, "ISIS Is Not a Terrorist Group," *Foreign Policy* (March/April 2015), www.foreignaffairs.com/articles/middle-east/isis-not-terrorist-group.

27 Stephen M. Walt, "ISIS as Revolutionary State," *Foreign Policy* (November/December 2015): 42, www.belfercenter.org/publication/isis-revolutionary-state.

28 Caliphate is defined as "a form of Islamic government led by a person considered a political and religious successor to the Islamic prophet, Muhammad, and a leader of the entire Muslim community. Source: Wadad Kadi and Aram A. Shahin, "Caliph, caliphate," in *The Princeton Encyclopedia of Islamic Political Thought*, ed. Gerhard Bowering, Patricia Crone, Wadad Kadi, Devin J. Stewart, Muhammad Qasim Zaman, and Mahan Mirza (Princeton, NJ: Princeton University Press, 2013), 81–86, www.jstor.org/stable/j.ctt1r2g6m.8.

29 Graeme Wood, "What ISIS Really Wants," *Atlantic*, March 2015, 3, www.theatlantic.com/magazine/archive/2015/03/what-isis-really-wants/384980/.

30 Dabiq is also the name of the ISIS magazine, which is available electronically and spread via social media.

31 Walt, "ISIS as Revolutionary State," 43.

32 J. M. Berger, "How ISIS Games Twitter," *Atlantic*, 16 June 2014, www.theatlantic.com/international/archive/2014/06/isis-iraq-twitter-social-media-strategy/372856/.

33 Ibid.

34 "Terrorist Use of Social Media: Policy and Legal Challenges," roundtable forum (Washington, DC: Council on Foreign Relations, 14 October 2015).

35 Berger, "How ISIS Games Twitter."

36 Carleton English, "Twitter Continues to Wage its Own War against ISIS," *New York Post*, 21 March 2017, http://nypost.com/2017/03/21/twitter-continues-to-wage-its-own-war-against-isis/.

37 United States Department of State, report, *Soviet Influence Activities: A Report on Active Measures and Propaganda, 1986–87* (Washington, DC: Bureau of Public Affairs, 1987), viii.

38 Natasha Bertrand, "It Looks Like Russia Hired Internet Trolls to Pose as Pro-Trump Americans," *Business Insider*, 27 July 2016, www.businessinsider.com/russia-internet-trolls-and-donald-trump-2016-7.

39 Vladimir Isachenkov, "Russia Military Acknowledges New Branch: Info Warfare Troops," AP News, 22 February 2017, www.apnews.com/8b7532462dd0495d9f756c9ae7d2ff3c.

40 Richard Gonzalez, "CIA Director Pompeo Denounces WikiLeaks as 'Hostile Intelligence Service,'" NPR, 23 April 2017, www.npr.org/sections/thetwo-way/2017/04/13/523849965/cia-director-pompeo-denounces-wikileaks-as-hostile-intelligence-service.

41 Malcolm Nance, *The Plot to Hack America: How Putin's Cyberspies and WikiLeaks Tried to Steal the 2016 Election* (New York: Skyhorse Publishing, 2016), Kindle edition, 1,839.

42 Adrian Chen, "The Agency," *New York Times Magazine*, 2 June 2015, www.nytimes.com/2015/06/07/magazine/the-agency.html. On 11 September 2014, the small town of St. Mary Parish, Louisiana, was thrown briefly into a panic when residents began hearing reports through text, social media, and on local television stations that a nearby chemical plant fire was spreading toxic fumes that would soon endanger the whole town. The entire narrative was based on falsified—but very real looking—online news stories, hashtag manipulation, and mass texts (SMS) to various numbers with the local area code and dialing prefix. The actual source for the news was not the chemical factory; it was a nondescript building in St. Petersburg, Russia, where an army of online cyber-warrior trolls seeks to distribute false information.

43 Statement of Clint Watts, Foreign Policy Research Institute fellow, in "Disinformation: A Primer in Russian Active Measures and Influence Campaigns," testimony before the Senate Intelligence Committee, 115th Cong., 1st sess., 30 March 2017, www.intelligence.senate.gov/sites/default/files/documents/os-cwatts-033017.pdf.

44 Chen, "The Agency."

45 Because of the Adrian Chen article, I observed particular tweeting patterns of certain individuals involved in a hoax on the campus of the University of Missouri that seemed to match the methods of the Russian trolls interviewed by Chen. I mention only one particular user in this article, but I also monitored a dozen or so accounts that contributed to that hoax. Each account followed a pattern that also happened to align with noted Russian influence operations in Europe and eventually in the US presidential election. I describe that transition in the article. From those accounts, I built a database of suspected Russian bot accounts to build a network map. The Mizzou hoax was a trend hijacking effort launched by actors who later proved to match the Russian modus operandi of using cyber trolls originally observed by Adrian Chen and confirmed by the Office of the Director of National Intelligence (ODNI) report and Foreign Policy Research Institute fellow Clint Watts in his testimony before the Senate Intelligence Committee (note 43).

46 Nadine Schmidt and Tim Hume, "Berlin Teen Admits Fabricating Migrant Gang-Rape Story, Official Says," CNN, 1 February 2016, www.cnn.com/2016/02/01/europe/germany-teen-migrant-rape-false/index.html.

47 Judy Dempsey, "Russia's Manipulation of Germany's Refugee Problems," Carnegie Europe, 28 January 2016, http://carnegieeurope.eu/strategiceurope/?fa=62611.

48 Schmidt and Hume, "Berlin Teen Admits Fabricating Migrant Gang-Rape Story."

49 Barbara Tasch, "'The Aim Is to Weaken the West': The Inside Story of How Russian Propagandists Are Waging War on Europe," *Business Insider*, 2 February 2017, www.businessinsider.com/russia-propaganda-campaign-weakening-europe-2017-1?r=UK&IR=T.

50 Harriet Sherwood, "Polish Magazine's 'Islamic Rape of Europe' Cover Sparks Outrage," 18

February 2016, www.theguardian.com/world/2016/feb/18/polish-magazines-islamic-of-europe-cover-sparks-outrage.

51  Chen, "The Agency."

52  Robinson Meyer, "War Goes Viral: How Social Media Is Being Weaponized across the World," *Atlantic*, 18 October 2016, www.theatlantic.com/magazine/archive/2016/11/war-goes-viral/501125/.

53  Office of the Director of National Intelligence (ODNI), Intelligence Community Assessment Report, *Assessing Russian Activities and Intentions in Recent US Elections*, 6 January 2017, ii, www.dni.gov/files/documents/ICA_2017_01.pdf.

54  Hanna Rosin, "Among the Hillary Haters," *Atlantic*, 1 March 2015, 63, www.theatlantic.com/magazine/archive/2015/03/among-the-hillary-haters/384976/.

55  K. Thor Jensen, "Inside Donald Trump's Twitter-Bot Fan Club," *New York Magazine*, 15 June 2016, http://nymag.com/selectall/2016/06/inside-donald-trumps-twitter-bot-fan-club.html.

56  David A. Farenthold, "Trump Recorded Having Extremely Lewd Conversation about Women in 2005," *Washington Post*, 8 October 2016, www.washingtonpost.com/politics/trump-recorded-having-extremely-lewd-conversation-about-women-in-2005/2016/10/07/3b9ce776-8cb4-11e6-bf8a-3d26847eeed4_story.html.

57  "The Podesta Emails," Politico LiveBlog, accessed 6 December 2016, www.politico.com/live-blog-updates/2016/10/john-podesta-hillary-clinton-emails-wikileaks-000011.

58  ODNI Report, 2.

59  Faiz Siddiqui and Susan Svrluga, "N.C. Man Told Police He Went to D.C. Pizzeria with Gun to Investigate Conspiracy Theory," *Washington Post*, 5 December 2017, www.washingtonpost.com/news/local/wp/2016/12/04/d-c-police-respond-to-report-of-a-man-with-a-gun-at-comet-ping-pong-restaurant/?utm_term=.c33057f66007.

60  This count is based on analysis of the followers of followers of suspected troll accounts and bots. The study was conducted 15 March 2016. The number of accounts appears to have reduced dramatically since May, following the French election, implying that Twitter suspended some of the accounts. Unfortunately, software limitations prevent this analysis from being more accurate. Additionally, it is nearly impossible to derive the exact number of Russian accounts from that network using my available resources.

61  Ellul, *Propaganda*, 6.

62  Many on the left have mischaracterized the attack as "Russian hacking of the election," which has in turn conflated the issue of the John Podesta email theft with a hacking of the actual election systems. To be clear: there is no evidence of any sort of hack on any ballot-counting systems, only evidence outlined in this paper of two hacks (Democratic National Committee and Podesta) combined with an influence/information operation.

63  ODNI Report, 1.

64  Adrian Chen, "The Real Paranoia-Inducing Purpose of Russian Hacks," *New Yorker*, 27 July 2016, www.newyorker.com/news/news-desk/the-real-paranoia-inducing-purpose-of-russian-hacks.

65  Catherine Theohary and Cory Welt, "Russia and the U.S. Presidential Election," CRS Report no. IN10635 (Washington, DC: Congressional Research Service, 2017).

66  David Ignatius, "Russia's Radical New Strategy for Information Warfare," *Washington Post*, 18 January 2017, www.washingtonpost.com/blogs/post-partisan/wp/2017/01/18/russias-radical-new-strategy-for-information-warfare/?utm_term=.da53e31d7aaa.

67  Ibid.

68  "Ex-Sony Chief Amy Pascal Acknowledges She Was Fired," NBCNews.com, 12 February 2015, www.nbcnews.com/storyline/sony-hack/ex-sony-chief-amy-pascal-acknowledges-she-was-fired-n305281.

69  The political left in the United States seems to have a large group of bot accounts forming around the "Resist" movement. It is unclear whether those accounts are foreign cyber warriors or bots, but external actors can certainly feed off the underlying narratives and tap into existing networks of true believers.

70  David Kilcullen, *Out of the Mountains: The Coming Age of the Urban Guerrilla* (New York: Oxford University Press, 2013), 231.

71  Anthony Faiola, "As Cold War Turns to Information War, a New Fake News Police Combats Disinformation," *Washington Post*, 22 January 2017, www.washingtonpost.com/world/europe/as-cold-war-turns-to-information-war-a-new-fake-news-police/2017/01/18/9bf49ff6-d80e-11e6-a0e6-d502d6751bc8_story.html?utm_term=.7c99cc2fadd5.

72 Meyer, "War Goes Viral."
73 Ibid.
74 Cadwalladr, "Robert Mercer: The Big Data," 1.8.
75 Malcolm Mitchell, *Propaganda, Polls, and Public Opinion: Are the People Manipulated?* (Englewood Cliffs, NJ: Prentice-Hall, 1977), 12.
76 Ibid., 13.
77 Rebecca Carroll, "The State Department Is Fighting with ISIL on Twitter." Defense One, 25 June 2014, www.defenseone.com/technology/2014/06/state-department-fighting-isil-twitter/87286/.
78 Rita Katz, "The State Department's Twitter War with ISIS Is Embarrassing," *Time*, 16 September 2014, http://time.com/3387065/isis-twitter-war-state-department/.
79 Ellul, *Propaganda*, 241.
80 Adrian Chen, "The Propaganda about Russian Propaganda," *New Yorker*, 1 December 2016, www.newyorker.com/news/news-desk/the-propaganda-about-russian-propaganda.
81 Richard Deacon, *The Truth Twisters* (London: Macdonald, 1987), 95.
82 Michelle Castillo, "Facebook Found Fake Accounts Leaking Stolen Info to Sway Presidential Election," CNBC.com, 27 April 2017, www.cnbc.com/2017/04/27/facebook-found-efforts-to-sway-presidential-election-elect-trump.html.
83 Eric Bradner, "At CNN Town Hall, McCain and Graham Give Their View of Trump's Presidency so Far," CNN, 2 March 2017, www.cnn.com/2017/03/01/politics/john-mccain-lindsey-graham-town-hall/index.html.

# 8

## CYBER BY A DIFFERENT LOGIC

### Using an information warfare kill chain to understand cyber-enabled influence operations

*Christopher Whyte and Ugochukwu Etudo*

Despite the relative commonality of cyber conflict as a feature of world politics in the 21st century, few threats to national and international security have so completely captured the attention of practitioners, policymakers and scholars as has the specter of cyber-enabled influence operations targeting Western societies. Since at least 2014, significant operations undertaken by agents of the Russian Federation, Iran, China and North Korea have utilized a range of digital methods in efforts to interfere with the domestic political processes of European, North American and Asian democracies. In paradigm cases in Britain, Germany and the United States, actors either encouraged or directly sponsored by the Russian government have coupled the use of cyber instruments with attempts to manipulate democratic discourse using social media, conspiratorial communities – that act as hubs for the dissemination of sensationalist narratives – and conventional methods of interference, such as dark money and blackmail.

There is some irony in the emphasis on cyber operations as a significant part of recent experiences with anti-democratic information warfare (IW). On the one hand, it seems likely the case that such activities have enhanced the practice of political warfare seen over the past several years. On the other hand, as experts elsewhere in this volume have alluded to, major interference campaigns in Europe and North America have most clearly benefited from digital developments pertaining to the design and use of modern Internet-enabled media platforms. Specifically, the ability of meddling foreign threat actors to covertly enter domestic conversations via use of fake accounts, to spread false narratives and facts in a manner that is generally hard-to-track for the average citizen, and to strategically inject information that counters the moderating effects of time and diverse debate on national deliberations creates numerous challenges for democratic process. At the same time, lacking oversight of the platforms that now so critically underwrite much democratic conversation – including services offered by companies like Twitter, Facebook, Apple and Google – has meant that the threat of foreign influence via such vectors is an underrealized one, or at least was until comparatively recently. Simply put, it seems most likely that a confluence of circumstances brought about by new environmental conditions in the age of the Internet and social media is responsible for the uptick in foreign efforts to digitally interfere in Western societies over the past decade. Given this, there is some degree of irony in the fact that cyber elements of the thing are so often emphasized as impactful while more recognizable cyber threats to national security, such as theft of intellectual property or malicious infection of industrial control systems, are often given second billing.

This chapter aims to contextualize the role of cyber intrusion as a component element of information warfare in the age of the Internet. To date, much work on this topic has either relegated the discussion of cyber operations' impact to case analysis or described their impact in terms of broad characteristics (e.g. that, generically speaking, the relative anonymity and low barriers to operation associated with engagement in cyberspace reduce the costs of political warfare that might have traditionally required a human intelligence corollary to be successful). Such work is valuable, to be sure, and constitutes much of the intellectual fodder upon which policymaking and further research in this topic area now critically relies. Nevertheless, there remain few efforts to discuss the role of cyber actions taken in support of IW campaigns as a tactical proposition useful to practitioners who want to employ cyber defensive techniques to disrupt malicious attack in the context of influence operations.

The sections below present an information warfare kill chain as a means of considering the potential role of cyber operations in effectively supporting influence operations. The kill chain is a threat model that is often used by security managers and operators to better understand the imperatives and likely approaches taken by attackers. Traditionally utilized as a framework for analyzing military operations, variations of the kill chain have been adopted as the most popular threat model for cybersecurity practitioners. The cyber kill chain, made popular by companies like Lockheed Martin and Mandiant, describes the actions a dedicated attacker might take in scouting a target, developing relevant cyber assets, breaching target security and moving laterally until the primary objective can be achieved. Though the model is extremely linear, it effectively mirrors the logic of computer network attack. Moreover, the model is somewhat flexible insofar as it can be employed alongside other threat frameworks – such as the diamond model – that allow defenders to think of cyber operations as multi-pronged, cross-domain intelligence operations.

Here, we suggest that a kill chain for information warfare campaigns must mirror the logic of such operations even where the purpose may be to better understand the role of cyber activities therein. This point is not particularly controversial. As a substantial emerging body in political science holds, cyber capabilities are most often best thought of as adjunct modifiers of other conflict processes more than they are singularly meaningful for coercion or the conduct of war. As such, cyber conflict is best understood in the context of other logics of political engagement. We argue in this chapter that digital age influence operations prosecuted by non-domestic actors are defined by four operational realities that must be addressed in order for success in interference efforts. First, foreign IW operators are not organically, publicly aligned to an entrenched domestic constituency, unlike traditional political entities. Second, such actors are unable to operate transparently in pursuit of their advocacy. Third, attempts to spread influence in the age of the Internet are subject to the unique dynamics of virtual community social engagement, particularly issue transience and the algorithmic determinants of significant content. And finally, the infrastructure of attack is normatively-oriented and – much as is the case with much organized cyber crime – platform- and service-defined, which limits the opportunities for cyber operations to enhance IW. Due to the need to address these realities, IW campaigns emphasize the cyclical employment of rhetoric designed to (1) piggyback onto (rather than create) divisive triggering events, (2) "capture" audiences and (3) leverage audience growth towards greater outreach. Within this structure of approach, cyber operations offer enhanced abilities to magnify the effects of triggering events and artificially inflate the visibility of fabricated IW content along several lines.

The remainder of the chapter proceeds in five parts. First, we offer background on cyber-enabled influence operations employed against national targets in Europe, North America and Asia over the past decade. Second, overview work done on the kill chain and the need to build better threat models of information warfare. Then, based on the need of IW operators to address the several key operational realities outlined above, we describe an influence operations kill chain based on a popular theoretical understanding of audience engagement from communications studies scholarship – fear appeals. Fourth, use the model to discuss Russian-backed activities in the United States since 2014 and in several European cases over the same time period to illustrate the utility of the approach for thinking about IW. Finally, we conclude and offer suggestions for those interested in disrupting and deterring cyber-enabled interference campaigns.

## The rise of cyber-enabled information warfare

During the course of the 2010s, Western democratic polities have increasingly encountered broad-scoped efforts to use digital methods and to manipulate the trappings of today's digital society by foreign adversaries. These adversaries are varied in their constitution and approach to disinformation and interference. On the less sophisticated end of the spectrum, there is substantial evidence that the so-called Islamic State and al Qaeda have both sponsored efforts to spread fabricated news content and social impressions online towards specific disruptive ends.[1] On the other end, nation states like China and Iran have quickly moved from exploratory interference in Western political processes to more highly-structured efforts to mislead publics and skew the outcomes of discourse. Iran has rapidly learned from the example of others active since at least 2014 and has been accused in 2018 and 2019 of funding large-scale organized trolling and fake news dissemination. China, arguably starting from a more domestically well-informed position vis-à-vis the tactics and coordination of misdirection and astroturfing, targeted neighboring countries in East Asia consistently across the 2010s, particularly the Republic of China (Taiwan).[2]

Many cases of information warfare targeting democratic states involve the employment of cyber instruments of state power to support manipulative or disruptive activities achieved via use of, among other things, social media platforms. Much of the time, cyber actions in this vein involve simple harassment of domestic targets. The Chinese government, for instance, has been accused several times of being behind denial of service attacks on Taiwan-based lobbying organizations notable for their support of a strong declaration of independence from the mainland. In other cases, cyber actions have been used either to furnish IW efforts with richer informational content with which to pursue disinformation and misinformation tactics or to hijack the devices and service of individual citizens. Few cases demonstrate these latter tactics as fully as do the extensive operations undertaken by the Russian Federation in the past decade.

Since about late 2014, the Russian Federation has employed information operations against almost two dozen countries, mostly located in Europe and North America.[3] Cyber techniques were employed by the Russians in more than a third of all cases. In most situations, Russian interference in Western societies has come to orient on particular moments of discursive significance, including national elections and referenda. In virtually all cases, Russian interference has occurred in clear support of those domestic factions least hostile to the Russian Federation's interests. In almost no cases have such factions actively espoused support of Russian policy, however; rather, supported factions are simply notably not *anti-Russian* (i.e. not vocally supportive but unwilling to criticize in line with mainstream perspectives) or otherwise represent some alignment with Russian interests, such as euroskepticism.[4]

In more than half of all cases of Russian interference since 2014, an outcome favorable to Russian interests occurred.[5] In almost all cases, Russian-backed activity revolved around the use of social media and the development of supporting information ecosystems that allowed for the spread of contextual disinformation. This is, as most experts agree, merely a digital age continuation of the tactics preferred by the Soviet Union during the Cold War that emphasized two forms of action as necessary for domestic turmoil. The first is action taken to support favored issue positions or political candidates; the second is active efforts to induce malaise, demoralization and mistrust of process broadly in target countries. In the paradigm example of recent information warfare that was Russia's interference in the 2016 presidential election season in the United States, these actions were facilitated by broad-scoped infiltration and use of popular social media platforms like Twitter, Facebook and Instagram. Together, these platforms featured more than 82 million distinct pieces of misleading content viewed by as many as 126 million users published by the Internet Research Agency (IRA), Russia's anointed arm in the operational conduct of foreign interference.[6]

Russia's efforts between 2014 and 2016 are among the most well-studied cyber-enabled information operations to date. Scholars of cyber conflict have pointed to incidence of cyber activity aiding Russia's efforts on at least two primary fronts. First, as Jensen et al. describe, at least two well-known threat actors linked with the Kremlin – the Fancy Bear and Cozy Bear threat groups – were active in targeting political party targets in the spring and summer of 2016.[7] One such attack, an intrusion of the Democratic Congressional Campaign Committee (DCCC) that provided stolen credentials leading to a compromise of Democratic National Committee (DNC) servers, has received a great amount of attention as an obvious source of internal information of a potentially scandalous nature that may have allowed the Russians to better target their disinformation efforts (despite there being no evidence that stolen data was reused or leaked from that particular attack).[8] Second, as several information systems and cybersecurity researchers have noted, the IRA itself deployed several pieces of malware in the form of compromised applications available direct-from-website and from both Apple's App Store and Google Play. A limited cross-section of audiences targeted in the broader disinformation effort were exposed to messaging that encouraged downloading of these applications, most of which were designed to clandestinely direct bystander traffic towards other examples of IRA content for purposes of "liking" or "upvoting" to artificially boost the visibility thereof.[9]

With regards to the broader strategy of information operations enabled by various web technologies, most research has thus far discussed the IRA approach as an attempt to agenda set. The IRA's operations during the 2016 election season were, according to most commentators, ultimately quite sophisticated in nature, though there was a clear learning curve as operators tested different approaches and attempted to engage an almost-bizarrely diverse cross section of issue communities through 2014 and 2015. In one 2018 paper, authors Boatwright, Linvill and Warren show bot personas linked with Russian efforts on Twitter would regularly adopt diverse narrative roles in line with well-defined sectors of civil society, from left vs. right political perspectives to distinct activist positions and entertainment commentary.[10] Within these different role elements of the IRA's campaign, operators directed their bot assets to behave radically differently from one another.[11] For instance, some accounts would react with highly-tailored outrage to accusations of being fake. Likewise, with regards to content being pushed by bot accounts, some would rarely engage political issues and associated fake information directly, while others would do nothing but spam sensationalist links and messaging. All told, while Russia's efforts both in the United States and elsewhere was clearly targeted at scale and involved mass production of altered or fabricated content, research has already demonstrated some real nuance in the manner of how assets were employed by the IRA. In other words, while it is tempting to assume that disruption writ large has been the focus of sophisticated, well-resourced information operators over the past decade, most research suggests to some greater or lesser degree that cyber-enabled IW campaigns have been shaped by a logic of engagement.

## The need to threat model information operations

Conceptualizing digitally-enabled interference by foreign state actors in Western societal and political processes has not been an easy task for scholars to date. Despite a breadth of efforts to contextualize such campaigns so that they might be included in discussions of digital age deterrence and resilience, almost no work effectively captures the normative corollaries of cyber conflict practiced in aid of influence operations. The same is true in reverse. Such conceptualization is needed if researchers are to clarify the strategic nature of cyber-enabled information warfare and elucidate the possibilities for better defense.

### Defining interference in the digital age

In recent years, what has been called "cyber-enabled information warfare" (or "information operations") in this chapter so far has been given numerous other labels in both popular and policymaker settings. Nevertheless, from "influence activities" and "political warfare" to "election hacking," "electoral interference" and "foreign meddling" in the political processes of democratic states, what is being described is really – either entirely or in part, depending on the use of such terms – the application of what has traditionally been labeled "hybrid warfare"[12] efforts by adversaries of the United States and partner nations. Quite simply, "hybrid warfare" refers to the blend of nontraditional – usually non-military – instruments of statecraft with more conventional tools in order to further a state's national interests. In particular, hybrid warfare involves the use of various elements of a state's arsenal of foreign interference and influence in service of strategic objectives, including the employment of limited military force, utilization of intelligence assets and disruption of both social and political processes via propaganda.

To simply say that hybrid warfare involves a blended effort to manipulate state competitors is analytically insufficient here, however, because the statement doesn't intrinsically describe the particular scenario or the tactics of "hacking" democratic processes that are so much of the substance of cyber-enabled IW in recent years. As a label broadly employed by scholars and practitioners of international security, "hybrid warfare" – or even "political warfare" or "information warfare" – does little to impart understanding of what within democracies is being hacked and how. When pundits, scholars and laymen invoke the concept of "hacking" Western democracy, they are clearly referring to something more than network-centric warfare and the broad-scoped intrusions into military, industrial and other national security systems that have come to constitute the scope of cyber conflict over the past quarter century. Rather, this hacking is clearly linked to the manner in which information technologies have transformed the ideational landscape of European and North American political systems in recent years. "Election hacking" – a phrase often used to proxy for democratic interference more broadly – inherently and obviously deals with something less well parameterized than cyber conflict, where digital instruments of harm and emergent new media products intersect with the traditional operation of Western societies. At the same time, it also deals with something more particular in its manifestation than those national efforts to use media to influence foreign citizenry that are the common focus of scholarly study, such as Japanese propagandizing during the Pacific War. And yet, a survey of popular and policymaker discussions of such threats would likely show that understanding of the thing remains anchored to assessments of cybersecurity challenges. Given the degree to which the effects of recent IW campaigns have emerged from foreign action beyond the scope of cyber operations, it's not clear why this should be the case. In other words, it's not immediately clear from existing definitions either what is being "hacked" or how cyber conflict ends up as a critical element of what makes modern cyber-enabled IW so apparently potent.

## Threat modeling the attack surface of democracies: current scope and shortcomings

Perhaps the most notable attempts to surface a logic of information operations in the current era of Internet-aided "democracy hacking" have been those of tech luminary Bruce Schneier and his colleagues. Schneier's writings on what happened in 2016 in the United States and what might be under way in numerous other Western countries emphasize the notion that democratic systems of governance are information systems.[13] This is not a particularly novel point in some ways, as entire fields of political science and communications studies hold that societal mechanisms of democratic participation and contestation rely on the assurance of informational conditions along the same lines a secure cyber system might (i.e. effective democratic governance requires a degree of ability to authenticate the source of public information, means for gauging the quality thereof, etc.). Nevertheless, the point is an extremely salient one. In all political systems, Schneier and his co-author argue, there are such things as common and contested categories of societal knowledge. Common knowledge is that which everyone agrees on, such as how the nuts and bolts of the system function or who/what within the system is legitimate.[14] Contested knowledge is the opposite and tends, at least in relatively stable political systems, to be the stuff of "low" politics, such as how much taxes should be paid or how much government should dictate monetary policy.[15] Today, information operations aim to degrade the integrity of these bodies of knowledge, Schneier argues, with democracies being specifically vulnerable to efforts that dilute certitude among the general population as to what persons, institutions and symbols represent.

Though the framework likely yet stands to benefit from some years of further scholarly and practitioner development, Schneier's suggestion that democracies are best understood as information production, presentation, dissemination and consumption machines is a compelling one. It also lends itself to some early efforts to model information warfare in the digital age via reference to a logic of vulnerability of the underlying systems – in this case not networked computer systems, but rather entire polities. In 2018, the New York Times suggested a set of "laws" or "commandments" of disinformation operations by referencing the work of Anthony Soules, a former National Security Agency (NSA) operative who now works in cybersecurity.[16] Soules, who worked for the NSA during a critical pre-digital age episode of disinformation by a foreign power, observed that information operations were a naturally blended exercise in human intelligence, signals disinformation and sociological analysis of trends in a target nation's sociopolitical discourse. His own observations of Operation Infektion, a Russian effort to spread the rumor that the government of the United States created the HIV virus as a part of a special weapons development program, amounted to the realization that almost any lie can be sold effectively – no matter how ridiculous and outlandish – with the right combination of actions.[17]

In 2019, Schneier summarized and (minimally) adapted Soules' earlier suggested steps of successful disinformation (see Figure 8.1).[18] All successful disinformation campaigns, they argue, start with intelligence gathering and analysis to discover the fault lines that exist to be taken advantage of within a target nation's contemporary sociopolitical discourse. This closely mirrors the expected first step outlined in the cyber kill chain model of threat analysis.[19] There, effective reconnaissance of a target is the necessary first step in discovering what attack vectors stand to be most profitable to a malicious intruder. Thereafter, an attack gears up, weaponizing their available assets and tailoring their approach to achieve an initial intrusion of target systems. Once engaged, an attacker delivers further exploitation designed to escalate access privileges, cover tracks, achieve control of needed processes and complete a given mission. With information campaigns, the jump-off point is no different than that envisioned by the cyber kill chain except perhaps in the implied scope. Prosecutors of IW efforts must understand the nature of division and the state of political knowledge so that they effectively weaponize their available assets for interference.

After reconnaissance, Soules and Schneier suggest that disinformation campaigns proceed through several distinct – often contemporaneous – phases. Having identified sources of division, IW operators must then create the narratives that can disrupt the ideational status quo. In Operation Infektion, that was a single big lie that was intended to single-handedly skew discourse on America's actions in pursuit of Cold War victory. In more recent incidence of information warfare, such narratives are rarely so singular or cohesive. Rather, as much research referenced earlier in the chapter has shown,[20] disinformation and misinformation targeted all parts of the political spectrum, included appeals to members of diverse societal occupations and did not consistently uphold the integrity of lies being peddled.

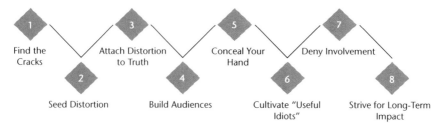

**FIGURE 8.1** Anthony Soules' "Commandments" of disinformation (updated by Bruce Schneier)

Following the "weaponization" of the toolkit of digital interference, execution of disinformation campaigns proceed through several different stages. Distortion narratives are targeted to the general population in both direct and indirect formats. Directly, steps are taken to build the infrastructure of outreach and to, if possible, build audience loyalty so that messaging can be echoed over time. Indirectly, IW operators seek out kernels of truth and tie them to fabricated or sensationalized information so as to enhance credibility and odds of acceptance by one or more elements of the populace. This approach follows what numerous communications scholars have observed over recent decades as an approach to the subversion of opinion that considers preferences as clustered points of view on different topics that together amount to a worldview. Altering an individual's worldview rarely occurs via the sale of a major alternative perspective. More often, contrasting perspectives are distilled to their palatable component elements, which are then held in proximity to robust pillars of an individual's current worldview. Over time, that set of symbols becomes more considerable to the target and the legitimacy of the status quo worldview becomes more susceptible to degradation.

In the latter stages of an information operation, IW operators attempt to enhance their effort along two distinct lines. The first is denial of involvement, first via direct actions taken to conceal any interference and then by direct rejection of accusations made against the attacking force. The second is adaptation that allows time-limited efforts at interference to translate into long-term propositions for subversion and the degradation of foreign power. At this stage, targets of opportunity become particularly valuable as potential "force" multipliers. Soules cites the presence of "useful idiots," local symbols or personalities whose personal social or political interests align with those of the IW campaign to such a degree that they can be prompted to aid the interference effort without knowing that they are doing so.

## An information warfare kill chain: assumptions and tactical realities

Taken together, the "commandments" Soules suggests and that Schneier augments amount to the overarching tasks prosecutors of information warfare must undertake if their campaign is to succeed. These steps are mirrored in other attempts to model information operations, such as the Malign Foreign Influence Campaign Cycle promulgated by the Department of Justice[21] or misinformation frameworks suggested by the Alliance for Securing Democracy and the Credibility Coalition.[22] And yet, there are distinct shortcomings to the manner in which both analysts generalize about information warfare efforts by applying broad principles of approach to a kill chain format. One obvious flaw is that the steps outlined in Figure 8.1 suggest linearity but actually don't demand it. Aside from initial steps to reconnoiter and assess opportunities for ideational attack, IW operators may undertake some or all of the described actions contemporaneously. From an analytic perspective, this is clearly problematic as it merely suggests types of activities to be looked for without imparting useful framing about the relationship between actions. Another shortcoming lies in the level of analysis being suggested. Strategic analysis of IW campaigns is clearly beneficial for some policy-relevant and scholarly tasks. Practically, there are few opportunities to look to specific techniques or to hypothesize about where to look for foreign interference, given the broad trappings of the model. In fairness, this is a problem that exists with the cyber kill chains various iterations as well – analysts must often look to other threat models in order to move investigation past the limitations of a perspective that trades specificity for parsimony.

For the purposes of this chapter's remit of better conceptualizing and contextualizing the role of cyber operations in recent information warfare episodes, clearly a more nuanced threat model is required. The model we suggest varies from Soules' framework significantly in terms of where it looks for inspiration. The information kill chain of the previous section largely builds its stages from assessment of particular cases, including Operation Infektion and Russian interference in the president election season in 2016. While case-specific construction of guiding logic of conflict processes is sometimes desirable, often unavoidable and occasionally critical for extending understanding of a given type of political activity, we instead base our alternative framework on common constraints and characteristics of operation that apply broadly to all foreign purveyors of informational interference in the digital age. This approach brings with it the benefit of a more organic focus on operational approaches to disinformation than is typically the case with attempts to broadly categorize the phenomenon. Moreover, it provides an external basis for operationalizing approaches to distortion and interference that link temporal elements (i.e. the steps of the chain of events under investigation) of the proposed model.

## *Underlying assumptions*

The first major assumption underlying our proposed model emerges from the most obvious implication of foreign-based attempts at interference being inherently about persuasion and mobilization beyond the traditional context of domestic politics. If the distortions and skewness of informational processes in Western societies in recent years were solely the work of dissidents or countercultural forces, current efforts to explore the nuance of such efforts would exist more substantially in the journals of the communications studies field and in the forums of political science dedicated solely to the function of domestic polities. Instead, interference has been foreign in nature. Here, the primary difference between foreign and domestic sources of such interference is the presence or lack thereof of an extant constituency within a target nation that might be courted directly. Foreign operators of IW campaigns must start without either an established constituency or a clear sector of the general population that can be reached via traditional means of political messaging. Over the course of their effort, they must reach relevant audiences without such initial advantages and, if possible, construct the equivalents of the legitimate means of tying sociopolitical causes to societal groups available to domestic players.

Secondly, and also obviously to some degree, foreign IW operators must keep their involvement in any attempt to persuade and activate populations within a targeted state secret. While it is true that some level of positive attribution is permissible in the age of the Internet so long as enough distortion of common knowledge occurs, foreign involvement generally needs to remain hidden. This is most particularly true at the "on the ground" points of interference where foreign operators interact directly with a targeted population. During the 2016 election season, Russian backing of organizations engaged on Twitter and perceived Russian ownership of a troll systematically resulted in negative pushback from legitimate users across the social and political spectrums.[23] Even where bot accounts were seen to be peddling content in support of users' stated interests or agenda, obvious or suggested foreign backing was almost universally met with hostility.

Foreign prosecutors of information warfare campaigns must also contend with dynamics of community discourse and formation unique to the age of the Internet. A further shortcoming of the model suggested by Soules and supported by Schneier is that it is based on pre-digital age attempts at interference in a Western democracy. In stating that foreign powers must build audiences in order to peddle disinformation, the researchers' reference the basic assumption outlined above that there is no domestic constituency to which IW operators might naturally speak. Those lines of communication must be built before messaging can occur.

In the digital age, however, developing mechanisms of community engagement is not as simple a task as it was in eras past. While there is certainly an argument that speaking to elements of the population of a targeted democracy is easier in the age of the Internet due to the wonders of social media and the natural capacities for anonymity and information manipulation that come with it, significant changes in the global information environment itself pose additional challenges for IW operators. Specifically, advocacy communities that might be activated on a given issue are no longer anchored to specific geographic, ideological or publication-specific characteristics.[24] A great deal of research into the organization of virtual communities has emphasized the manner in which interested elements of the population of a given social media platform only temporarily band together in common engagement when activated by a triggering event.[25] Whereas in eras past voter groups defined by their geographic location or by their party affiliation could be reliably activated on a host of interrelated issues, today most sociopolitical engagement – at least online – involves only limited core communities of cross-issue interested individuals and substantial satellite communities that form temporarily based on a number of factors. For IW operators, this portends a twofold challenge of (1) determining what factors are most likely to prompt large-scale engagement with peddled content at a given point in time and (2) determining what kinds of action can grow the core community susceptible to their messaging.

Finally, when it comes to designing the digital means of approach to interference, IW operators must naturally recognize that the infrastructure of attack is defined in both normative and platform – meaning the design and operation of service mediums like Instagram, Twitter, RenRen or Facebook – terms within the target country. Here, the operational requirements of information operations (which may include cyber operations as adjunct tools of information weaponization) differ from those of more conventional computer network intrusion activities in that the infrastructure is not a static set of networks, devices and corresponding human users. To some degree, the requirements of operation placed on IW operators are similar to those of organized cyber criminals wherein the underlying business model to be taken advantage of is based around services and common platforms rather than a host of underlying technologies to be addressed in turn. With cyber crime, much of the global industry from criminal products has adapted to mimic and build from the focus on platform capitalism that dominates legitimate business sectors.[26] Criminals build tools and offer services specifically moded to take advantage of the common platforms consumers use to shop, bank, interact and more. Criminals also design the infrastructure of illicit enterprise – such as that needed to facilitate the trading of stolen data – around the user-oriented features and other design characteristics of legitimate commercial ventures that are the primary determinants of the value of criminal operation. With information warfare, prosecutors must undertake the same task, relying not on a relatively static view of what attack infrastructure looks like but rather shifting tools and strategies to fit (1) usership trends and (2) the prominence of certain algorithmic features of popular platforms.

## *Operationalizing distortion*

In the digital age, foreign prosecutors of information warfare campaigns must not only identify potential injection points for distortion of the social and political processes of a target state; they must work to build the mechanisms of outreach to engage with relevant constituencies with (typically) no prior in-roads that might be typically of domestic advocacy operations. They must do so whilst not appearing to be involved in interference efforts, which may involve the use of "useful idiots," parallel employment of dark monies or the parceling of disinformation with nuggets of fact. At the same time, they must adopt strategies and lay foundations that allow for repeated activation and attraction of relevant domestic audiences. Because community activity in social Internet platforms of all stripes is inherently less centralized and permanent than might have been the case in pre-digital eras, IW operators must build tools that allow for episodic distortion rather than rely on the longevity of overarching sales pitches. These tools and techniques, however, cannot be static and by the very nature of the enterprise must involve blended semantic and syntactic methods for cyclical injection of content.

The model we suggest pivots on this final point – that effective tools for ensuring cyclical opportunities for distortion must center on the information being conveyed and the platform infrastructure over which that occurs. In the communications studies and political science, numerous research programs analyze and conceptualize the manner in which societal actors tailor and communicate messaging designed to adaptively compel different forms of citizen engagement. One such program, that focused on fear appeals made to citizens in political messaging, seems particularly appropriate for informing a microfoundational threat model of information operations.

Fear appeals are messaging that is designed to arouse anxiety in an individual sufficient to prompt them to action.[27] The logic of fear appeals is straightforward – scared people change their behavior to address whatever it is that scares them. That said, fear appeals theory effectively adds nuance to this basic premise in describing some nuance in the construction and application of such messaging.[28] Individuals feel fear based on the varying characteristics of a message as being more of less objectively worrisome. At the same time, proximity to an individual can heighten the impact of a given fear appeal, with proximity being prospectively defined in a number of different ways. An individual may feel anxiety related to fear messaging more acutely when the threat involved is urgent or physically proximate. At the same time, fear may be felt when the issue in question is more significant to a person's moral code, emotional priorities or ideological inclinations.

Fear appeals also work to greater or lesser degrees given the efficacy sales pitch bound up in messaging. Simply put, individuals faced with a threat must determine the degree to which they might be capable of taking action before they decide how to react. This occurs on two different levels. First, individuals must determine whether or not they are capable of addressing a given worrisome issue. Second, they must then determine whether or not their action is likely to result in an amelioration of the situation. Given the result of this calculation, a decision can then be made to act or not.

For information warfare operators, this set of distinctions made about persuasive messaging – when combined with techniques unique to operation on Internet engagement platforms – provides a baseline set of assumptions useful for constructing approaches to cyclical engagement of audience, the capture of audiences. The ideal outcome for IW operators is that targeted populations will take predictable action to decisively address new information – i.e. distorted information – being fed to them. This results in the greatest disturbance of natural social and political processes. Secondarily, action that does not address new information decisively but rather leads to mere changes in perspective can be useful. In communications, these responses are differentiated as "danger control" and "fear control" actions. The latter type of actions occurs when individuals are not convinced that they are capable of affecting what threatens them and differs from the former in that only the feeling of fear itself is controlled for (via, for instance, opting to watch more Fox News or MSNBC).

## The information warfare kill chain

Information operations in the digital age involve cyclical measures taken to accomplish the semantic engagement, audience capture and furthering of messaging described above. The lynchpin of much of this effort is efficacy messaging achieved via direct audience engagement by bots, trolls, useful idiots and an array of altered or fabricated content spreading distortion narratives. Efficacy messaging without pre-existing threat messaging and a bona fide issue upon which to build narrative is destined to be ultimately ineffectual, however. Thus, the parallel initial stages of our suggested kill chain (see Figure 8.2) are a distinct triggering event and messaging that emphasizes a threat as more or less severe.

The kill chain we suggest in this section is informed by much recent research and original analysis of events surrounding Russian and Iranian interference in Western political processes between 2014 and 2019. Recent research suggests that IRA operations in the United States through 2017 included content drops timed to carefully coincide with "polarizing" domestic events.[29] In the United States, these included rallies held in support of and in opposition to then-candidate Donald Trump and incidence of violence tied to the black community. One research paper, in particular, demonstrated a clear link between the actions of IRA operators in pushing out fabricated narrative and sensational messaging based on Black Lives Matters (BLM) protest events, incidents that themselves proxy directly for divisive outrage stemming from, among other things, the killing of black individuals by police officers.[30]

Following such events, there are two ways in which an IW campaign can produce opportunities to focus audiences on an issue such that subsequent messaging can be used to mobilize or demobilize sentiment. The first is the fabrication of narratives or events sufficient to capture audience attention. The second is the opportunistic use of naturally-occurring events as the basis for attempts to persuade, mobilize and build narrative. The first method is difficult to affect given the issues of purchase faced by foreign prosecutors of IW without natural roles in the target nation's information environment. Nevertheless, if successful, fabricated information can start the process desired by IW operators, given the subsequent provision of messaging about the severity of the issue at hand. By far, more reliable starting points for the information operations cycle are discrete triggering events that occur naturally, such as a political rally, geopolitical incident or the death of a citizen at the hands of law enforcement. The advantage of strategic focus on such events is threefold. First, the potential for compromise of the campaign is essentially nil at point $t$-minus zero, since there is no direct involvement of the foreign force. Second, relying on exogenous events to cyclically attempt to distort domestic discourse provides better quality triggers for exploitation than an IW effort to fabricate the same might be capable of. Finally, such events will typically produce their own surge of commentary and community engagement – as opposed to

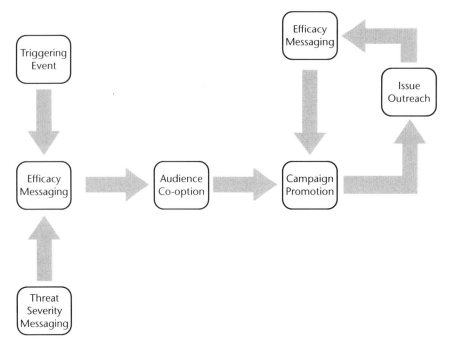

FIGURE 8.2  An information operations kill chain

activity that is entirely urged by interfering elements – that can then be assessed and exploited as needed.

Research that links the timing of Russian – and, to a lesser degree, Iranian – IW actions with domestic events has also highlighted the surge of content that follows in terms of both volume and emotive language.[31] In periods between major triggering incidents, bot and troll activity on social media sites fall into a sort of station-keeping mode characterized by efforts on the parts of different accounts to seed diverse narratives into regular virtual community discourse and to build persona bona fides to increase the credibility of an account. Following a relevant trigger, these accounts then adopt strong emotive overtones that seek to build up divisive sentiment. Significantly, Russian efforts in the United States and Western Europe have notably taken to fabricating debate between communities, often starkly characterized by competing ideological perspectives.[32] Doing so ostensibly allows IW operators to diversify opportunities for audience capture, strengthen the case that a vibrant civil society argument is emerging and produce chances to link otherwise disparate virtual communities.

At this juncture, the core active element of IW messaging occurs. Efficacy messaging – i.e. attempts to sell the audience on the need to take action – is tied directly to threat messaging that seems to have some degree of audience relevance. In IRA efforts through at least 2016 in the United States, research shows a clear shift in topical messaging from broad issues like anti-black community discrimination or immigration to functional versions of the same, including advertisements for self-defense classes and explicit advocacy for organizations like BLM.[33] Through this shift, IW operators pivot their target audience from issue grievances towards actionable concepts, a move which both maximizes division sparked by foreign effort and increases the likelihood of future triggering events for IW operators to work in reference to.

Following an appropriate triggering issue/event and subsequent media coverage, IW operators seek to build a foothold within the targeted population. Following the bid to move audiences from issues grievance to divisive action, the aim of IW operators in a given attack lifecycle is simply to enhance future lifecycles. The most significant of the tasks at this stage – audience capture and growth – can occur in a number of different formats. At the broadest level, IW operators might hope that narrative development around crises might be significant enough to carry certain proposed positions and fabricated or modified ideas forward as self-invoking elements of discourse either in the mainstream or among significant elements of the population. At the level of those who converse with elements of an IW campaign, such as bot or troll accounts on social media sites, foreign operators might take actions that reference the algorithmic possibilities of the platforms via which interference occurs to "capture" an audience. This might include messaging designed to invite citizens to "like," "follow" or otherwise revisit the active engagement of IW sources of information.[34] And IW operators might also take the opportunity of engagement with an activated cross-section of a target nation's population to inject lateral opportunities for audience capture, such as via the use of malware.

Analysis of content peddled by Internet Research Agency in the United States across a number of formats between 2014 and 2016 shows clear attention paid to efforts to capture audiences via platform features. Ugochukwu et al. (2019) demonstrate not only that efficacy messaging administered in social media content clearly followed broader alarmist threat messaging, but that it also had clear capture corollaries in the proceeding periods. Specifically, Facebook ad content in the days following initial threat references and efficacy bids would increasingly feature stock language aimed at linking audience members with elements of the IRA effort.[35] For instance, advertisements in that phase of a given event-defined period of activity would feature "click here to join" or click to "like" wordage not found in closer proximity to triggering incidents.

These phases of IW engagement also included inducements to download seemingly unrelated software that was actually infected. Via the medium of Facebook advertisements, the IRA during 2015 and 2016 particularly attempted to push the download of an application called FaceMusic, a program that ostensibly offered users the chance to listen to free music. In reality, the application was malware designed to take hold on a host computer, open a browser in the background and navigate to predetermined content published by the IRA in one of a number of formats. FaceMusic was a sociopolitical manifestation of click fraud, an effort to artificially inflate the perceived popularity (and thus visibility) of content by using compromised computers to spoof administrators into seeing activity – including page visits or more active "upvoting" actions – from independent IP addresses. Though evidence suggests an extremely limited foothold on the broader population of social media platforms in the case of FaceMusic, the potential of such an action is obvious. Given enough compromise, IW operators might be able to manipulate the visibility-setting algorithms underlying mainstream media platforms without appearing in any way to be doing so (as might be the case, for instance, with the use of hordes of bot accounts).

Finally, once IW operators have engaged some cross-section of the target population in a given episode and taken steps to ensure audience growth in future stages of the campaign, the focus of a given information operations incident shifts to broader advocacy of narrative positions espoused by the campaign beyond the scope of the triggering incident. In the final stages of the IW attack lifecycle, operators simply seek to stretch out the term of their prospective impact for as long as possible. As Ugochukwu et al. (2019) report, IRA advocacy in social media content out beyond a couple of days from triggering events shifted focus from incident-relevant topics to broader themes. Here, a microcosm of the event–tied sequence of messaging as about threat severity and audience efficacy plays out in a repeating fashion until, without the benefit of an anchoring incident, patterns of audience engagement fall back to pre-episode norms.

## Cyber operations and information operations in the 2010s

Scholarly work on the nexus of cyber and information operations has come to numerous initial conclusions about the role of digital intrusion as a force multiplier for Internet-enabled efforts to propagandize. Much commentary has focused on the prospective role of espionage enabled by cyber operations – operations that need not be particularly sophisticated – for upgrading influence efforts. Though there is no evidence that information stolen from the DNC in 2016 made its way into Russia's broader influence campaign, the precedent is clear – stolen information might enrich information warfare by providing that kernel of truth so important for the successful sale of fabricated narratives. Indeed, even the fact of cyber intrusions itself might affect the provenance of information efforts, as knowledge of compromise may convince some domestic elements that nuggets of truth might exist even where the links between digital attack and media manipulation are not obvious. At the very least, cyber intrusions might distract from the other excesses of foreign influence operators attempting to manipulate domestic political processes via use of Internet media platforms. These issues lie at the fore of research for social scientists attempting to unpack the contours of democratic vulnerabilities to information warfare in the digital age. It might be hoped that at least some of what is so often expounded as uniquely threatening about cyber-enabled information warfare has been the result of under-realization of the space and so might be remediable simply taking common sense steps.

As this chapter has described, however, the opportunities for cyber operations to play a role in information warfare beyond the paradigm case of high-profile espionage giving way to enriched propaganda exist. By outlining a more tactical version of an information operations kill chain than has been promulgated to this point, we point out several junctures at which cyber operations – as naturally multiform and multi-purpose instruments of interaction – might be employed to augment IW efforts. Perhaps the most obvious opportunity therefore is in actions taken to grow the reach and audience of a given campaign. Given that modern IW campaigns are not one-and-done efforts to promote singular concepts or ideas as might have been true in eras past, it makes significant sense to think about them in the same vein as traditional political campaigns, just with unique operating requirements placed upon them. With the imperative to capture an audience and reach as many people as possible, cyber instruments might be used to artificially enhance the visibility of content as described above. Taken to a more elaborate setting, malware spread via social media interactions might also offer opportunities for widespread data collection on engaged persons. Particularly where such persons hail from critical voting jurisdictions, such information could be a critical asset for IW campaigns seeking to tailor content to local circumstances or to launch parallel efforts to degrade the nature of discourse at critical junctures.

## Implications for defense and deterrence

Defense against cyber-enabled information operations is virtually destined to be a complicated affair requiring persistent action against would-be foreign interferers. In particular, effective deterrence of the worst excesses of such interference inevitably requires more than passive defensive efforts that revolve around the hardening of cyber-physical systems, greater regulation of information platforms (which is a difficult sell and, often, a logistical impossibility in democratic nations) and improved efforts to educate citizenry. Defense means active efforts to deconstruct adversary interference, attribute inappropriate intrusion and punish overt manipulation, even – and perhaps most specifically – where such manipulation remains largely hidden from public view.

This sentiment mirrors the recent shift in strategic thinking by the American defense establishment that effectively deterring foreign aggression is more a task of constantly molding foreign behavior through persistent engagement than it is about setting big, clear red lines. And yet, there remain significant additional challenges to deterrence of cyber-*enabled* threats to national security above and beyond the more traditional counter-command/control operations that are the bread and butter of operators within the Pentagon. To what degree might counter-offensive cyber action be effective in shaping foreign behavior if many of the primary vectors of foreign interference – such as social media platforms or civil society network systems – remain beyond the purview of the government to defend? At the same time, how can signals be clearly sent and credibility established if extended elements of information operations efforts are detached from central decision-making by some significant organizational divide? One might even consider a scenario in which hacking back or taking other punitive action to shape foreign propensities to interfere might provide the narrative fodder needed for threat actors like the IRA to galvanize fringe narratives about rigged democratic systems.

Without a doubt, one promising approach to reducing the impact of foreign influence operations might be to focus exclusively on the cyber corollaries thereof. By treating cyber operations as a distinct threat, Western governments may be able to reduce the use of digital intrusion to upgrade information warfare threats. In truth, of course, even that is unlikely to succeed in entirely removing the role of malicious code in such episodes because, as we demonstrate in our outlining of a more tactically-minded kill chain in this chapter, the opportunities for lateral injection thereof to augment the influence operations lifecycle exist beyond the case of splashy cyber espionage attempts. Nevertheless, such actions stand to reduce the role of cyber instruments to the level of platform features and the dynamics of virtual communities found thereon. At such a juncture, the value of threat models like the one proposed herein rises dramatically, with such alternative kill chains based on the logic of parallel conflict processes prospectively providing a basis for cyber threat mitigation beyond the purview of those traditional network intrusion-centric frameworks that continue to dominate perspective not only on cyber conflict, but also on so much conflict that is increasingly just cyber-*enabled* in the 21st century.

## Notes

1 For instance, Farkas, Johan, Jannick Schou, and Christina Neumayer. "Cloaked Facebook pages: Exploring fake Islamist propaganda in social media." *New Media & Society* 20, no. 5 (2018): 1850–1867.

2 Bradshaw, Samantha, and Philip N. Howard. "The Global Organization of Social Media Disinformation Campaigns." *Journal of International Affairs* 71, no. 1.5 (2018): 23–32.

3 Way, Lucan Ahmad, and Adam E. Casey. "How Can We Know if Russia is a Threat to Western Democracy? Understanding the Impact of Russia's Second Wave of Election Interference." (2019).

4 Ibid.

5 Ibid.

6 See Fiegerman, S., & D. Byers (2017). Facebook, Twitter, Google defend their role in election. CNN. Retrieved from http://money.cnn.com/2017/10/31/media/facebook-twitter-googlecongress/index.html; and Isaac, M. and Wakabayashi, D. (2017). Russian Influence Reached 126 Million Through Facebook Alone. *The New York Times*.

7 Jensen, Benjamin, Brandon Valeriano, and Ryan Maness. "Fancy bears and digital trolls: Cyber strategy with a Russian twist." *Journal of Strategic Studies* 42, no. 2 (2019): 212–234.

8 Ibid.

9 Lapowsky, Issie, "Russia-Linked Facebook Ads Targeted a Sketchy Chrome Extension at Teen Girls," *WIRED*, May 12, 2018.

10 Boatwright, Brandon C., Darren L. Linvill, and Patrick L. Warren. "Troll factories: The internet research agency and state-sponsored agenda building." *Resource Centre on Media Freedom in Europe* (2018).

11 Ibid.

12 It would not do here to proceed without recognizing that "hybrid warfare" is a term often used interchangeably and with a degree of conceptual confusion alongside others such as political warfare, irregular warfare, more recently as a description of hybrid force employed in network-dense environments, and information warfare.

13 For instance, Farrell, Henry, and Bruce Schneier. "Common-Knowledge Attacks on Democracy." *Berkman Klein Center Research Publication* 2018–7 (2018).

14 Ibid.

15 Ibid.

16 "Russian Disinformation: From Cold War to Kanye," *New York Times*, November 12, 2018.

17 Also see Bates, Stephen. "Disinforming the world: Operation INFEKTION." *The Wilson Quarterly* 34, no. 2 (2010): 13–15; and Boghardt, T. "Operation INFEKTION." *Soviet Bloc Intelligence and Its AIDS Disinformation Campaign. Stud Intell* 53 (2009): 1–24.

18 Schenier, Bruce, "Toward an Information Operations Kill Chain," *Lawfare*, April 24, 2019.

19 For more information on the kill chain in cyber threat analyses, see "Applying Security Awareness to the Cyber Kill Chain," SANS, May 31 2019.

20 Boatwright et al., for instance.

21 See "Report of the Attorney General's Cyber Digital Task Force," United States Department of Justice, July 2, 2018.

22 See "Misinformation has stages," Misinfosec Working Group, Credibility Coalition, May 13 2018.

23 See, for instance, Sanovich, Sergey. "Computational propaganda in Russia: the origins of digital misinformation." *Computational Propaganda Research Project. Working paper* 3 (2017).

24 For work on this topic, see *inter alia* Stefanidis, Anthony, Amy Cotnoir, Arie Croitoru, Andrew Crooks, Matthew Rice, and Jacek Radzikowski. "Demarcating new boundaries: mapping virtual polycentric communities through social media content." *Cartography and Geographic Information Science* 40, no. 2 (2013): 116–129; Shelton, Taylor, Ate Poorthuis, and Matthew Zook. "Social media and the city: Rethinking urban socio-spatial inequality using user-generated geographic information." *Landscape and Urban Planning* 142 (2015): 198–211; and Anselin, Luc, and Sarah Williams. "Digital neighborhoods." *Journal of Urbanism: International Research on Placemaking and Urban Sustainability* 9, no. 4 (2016): 305–328.

25 What Stefanidis et al. (2013) call "satellite" communities.

26 See McGuire, Mike, "The Web of Profit: A look at the cybercrime economy," *Venture Beat*, April 21, 2018.

27 Tannenbaum, Melanie B., Justin Hepler, Rick S. Zimmerman, Lindsey Saul, Samantha Jacobs, Kristina Wilson, and Dolores Albarracín. "Appealing to fear: A meta-analysis of fear appeal effectiveness and theories." *Psychological bulletin* 141, no. 6 (2015): 1178.

28 See, specifically, Witte, Kim. "Putting the fear back into fear appeals: The extended parallel process model." *Communications Monographs* 59, no. 4 (1992): 329–349; Rogers, Ronald W. "Attitude change and information integration in fear appeals." *Psychological Reports* 56, no. 1 (1985): 179–182;

and Leventhal, Howard. "Fear appeals and persuasion: the differentiation of a motivational construct." *American Journal of Public Health* 61, no. 6 (1971): 1208–1224.
29 Etudo, Ugochukwu, Victoria Yoon and Niam Yaraghi, "From Facebook to the Streets: Russian Troll Ads and Black Lives Matter Protests," HICSS 2019.
30 Ibid.
31 Such as Im, Jane, Eshwar Chandrasekharan, Jackson Sargent, Paige Lighthammer, Taylor Denby, Ankit Bhargava, Libby Hemphill, David Jurgens, and Eric Gilbert. "Still out there: Modeling and Identifying Russian Troll Accounts on Twitter." *arXiv preprint arXiv:1901.11162* (2019); Ghanem, Bilal, Davide Buscaldi, and Paolo Rosso. "TexTrolls: Identifying Russian Trolls on Twitter from a Textual Perspective." *arXiv preprint arXiv:1910.01340* (2019); and Xia, Yiping, Josephine Lukito, Yini Zhang, Chris Wells, Sang Jung Kim, and Chau Tong. "Disinformation, performed: self-presentation of a Russian IRA account on Twitter." *Information, Communication & Society* (2019): 1–19.
32 Boatwright et al. (2019).
33 Etudo, Ugochukwu, Christopher Whyte, Victoria Yoon and Naim Yaraghi, "Fear Appeals Model of Non-Anarchic Online Trolling: The Case of Russian Active Measures," Working Paper 2019.
34 Ibid.
35 Ibid.

# 9

# CYBER-ENABLED INFORMATION WARFARE AND INFLUENCE OPERATIONS

## A revolution in technique?

*Miguel Alberto Gomez*

Positive feelings towards cyber operations that date back to the 1990s are often associated with the increasing societal dependence on cyberspace, relatively low entry requirements and its perceived attribution problem. While regional disparities exist regarding the extent to which these technologies are progressively integrated into modern society, one cannot deny the fact that our day-to-day lives are enabled by advancements in Information Communication Technologies (ICT). Yet despite the level of integration and inter-dependency, actions within this domain remain strategically limited.

Regardless of the predictable logic that continued usage of susceptible technologies increases overall vulnerability, the opposite may instead be the case. The past decade saw greater initiatives to both educate and secure otherwise vulnerable infrastructure. While not perfect, these efforts have reduced the amount of exploitable low-level flaws. This casts doubt on the idea of cyberspace operations requiring fewer material and organizational resources. From a strategic perspective, activities in cyberspace are less of a revolution in military affairs and more a case of old wine in a new bottle. Interactions are framed within existing strategic relationships and are determined by pre-existing constraints. Moreover, the technological capabilities required to effectively operate in cyberspace limits the number of actors and thus partially address concerns of attribution (Lindsay, 2013; Slayton, 2017).

Interestingly, other related operations within the domain appear to be achieving significant gains in comparison to the former. Information Warfare/Information[1] Operations (IWIO) that sees the use of information by one party to deliberately confuse, mislead, and influence the choices of an adversary appear to be more effective than its more offense-oriented counterpart in realizing outcomes when employed.

IWIO is by no means a novel development. As noted by Rid (2012), its emergence demonstrates the case of shifting established behavior onto a new domain. This argument is extended by Jensen, Maness, and Valeriano (2016) who argue that interactions within this domain reflect existing strategic rivalries found in the physical domain. Yet with IWIO seemingly more effective than cyber operations patterned after convention interstate interactions, it begs the question as to whether or not something unique exists within cyberspace that allows the more effective use of these well-established tactics that date back to strategic thinkers such as Sun Tzu.

This chapter asserts that while tactics such as the use of propaganda have a long and storied history, psychological traits and processes that enable these tactics are more pronounced in this man-made space. Consequently, it is not that cyberspace brings about a revolution in IWIO, rather, it more effectively exploits elements of the human psyche that render audiences vulnerable to misinformation and malinfluence. With this in mind, the remainder of the chapter is organized as follows. The succeeding section provides a brief overview of human cognition that is crucial in explaining why IWIO are effective under the right circumstances. Given space constraints, however, it does not aspire to provide a complete account of the field of social and cognitive psychology that serves as the cornerstone for explaining the perceived success of IWIO. Following this, the chapter proceeds to present the underlying structure of cyberspace. The structure of cyberspace serves to amplify cognitive and affective processes that enable IWIO. The chapter then moves forward and attempts to surface the underlying mechanisms that explain how these individual processes are exploited and what makes cyberspace a particularly effective medium in this regard. While not necessarily explaining specific cases in detail, it dissects the different forms of IWIO and provides an account of how these interact with human cognition to meet its objectives. Finally, the chapter concludes by presenting current attempts to mitigate these threats and the extent to which these may be effective.

## Human cognition: hot and cold approaches

Individuals operate in a complex and highly uncertain environment. Our minds are constantly exposed to a variety of stimuli for which we have developed evolutionary mechanisms to deal with the deluge of information that results in (in)accurate judgements that eventually inform individual decisions. While we may wish to view ourselves as rational beings, how we process information often departs from the normative prescriptions of Rational Choice Theory. Of interest in this chapter specifically is the notion of hot and cold cognition. Hot cognition is characterized by affect-driven judgements and manifests as the need to maintain existing beliefs and other related structures. Cold cognition, in contrast, is thought to occur independent of affect and is associated with individual cognitive limitations and the need to preserve resources (Chong, 2013).

### Hot cognition

The assumption of rationality requires the identification of a solution once all possible alternatives have been assessed resulting in the selection of an optimal strategy that maximizes gains and minimizes potential losses. Through this normative approach, supporting and contradictory information serve to update pre-existing beliefs[2] to better much reality. Yet in opposition to the prescriptions of Rational Choice Theory, evidence shows that the availability of new information serves to either re-affirm pre-existing beliefs if congruent or ignore them if contradictory (Holmes, 2015; Jervis, 1976, 2009; Roach, 2016).

Relatedly, research also surfaces that motivated reasoning is rooted in past affect-laden experiences. When an individual is exposed to new information, they depend on affect-laden information stored in long-term memory. Once accessed, a specific affect is triggered along with the associated information. A heuristic mechanism evaluates these feelings with respect to the information triggered and reinforces the existing affect irrespective of dis-confirmatory information (Cassino, Taber, & Lodge, 2007; Lodge & Taber, 2000). Mercer (2010) furthers this argument and notes that emotions function as an assimilative mechanism for beliefs. In direct contrast to rationalists who argue that new information updates beliefs resulting in a convergence with reality, Mercer postulates that emotions assimilate new information into beliefs.

The pervasiveness of this reinforcement mechanism is made even more pronounced, given that pre-existing beliefs and new information need not be thematically aligned. In other words, new information does not have to be directly related to what is stored in memory. Instead, these need only be affectively or attitudinally congruent with one another in order for this reinforcement mechanism to manifest itself (Lord, Ross, & Lepper, 1979; Taber & Lodge, 2006).

This predisposition to maintain beliefs is associated directly with the means with which humans understand and operate within an uncertain and complex environment. Using simplification tools such as beliefs and related structures such as schemas, individuals ignore unnecessary details and focus instead on those that are crucial to beliefs that serve as the reference point (Crocker et al., 1984; Larson, 1994). Consequently, this suggests that changing these structures is a difficult but not impossible process as altering beliefs require significant shocks that forces a reassessment.

With respect to IWIO, its content often exploits emotionally charged issues linked to beliefs valued by the target audience. Consequently, operations aimed at manipulating behavior are often structured to reinforce these preferences as a means of mobilizing audiences into a particular course of action desired by the adversary. However, operations that rely solely on motivated reasoning for success are predicated on the existence of exploitable beliefs. Barring these, intended consumers may engage in a more balanced assessment of the available information, thus allowing them to dismiss inaccurate claims.

## Cold cognition

While motivated reasoning facilitates susceptibility to IWIO, the success of these operations is also subject to inherent cognitive limitations. Aside from beliefs, human beings have also developed cognitive shortcuts that allow us to process our information environment while simultaneously preserving valuable cognitive resources. Commonly referred to as heuristics, these are subconsciously invoked in response to a given stimulus and may also work in conjunction with more deliberate forms of reasoning. This mechanism is best explained through the Dual Process Theory (DPT).

Although variations exist that account for how the DPT manifests itself, it is basically divided into two stages: a heuristic (automatic) stage and an analytic (deliberate) stage (Evans, 1984). Initially, individuals subconsciously utilize cognitive shortcuts in order to efficiently identify relevant details in the information environment. This is an adaptive mechanism that functions to preserve valuable cognitive resources such as short-term memory. In contrast, the analytic stage is characterized by deliberate and resource-intensive reasoning that is more closely aligned with the normative expectations of Rational Choice Theory. Because of this, the latter tends to be slower and more laborious than the former.

More recently, Kahneman presented DPT as being composed of System 1 and System 2 processes (Kahneman, 2003). System 1 processes occur frequently and unconsciously while

System 2 are relatively infrequent and conscious acts. For the purpose of this chapter, two heuristics identified by Kahneman and other researchers provide crucial insight as to the perceived success of IWIO. Specifically, the accessibility of information, accurate or otherwise, prompts heuristics such as anchoring and availability.[3] Recurrent exposure promotes the formation of anchors or reference points particularly when individuals lack expertise on a given subject matter. This results in individuals assessing information relative to this reference rather than engaging in thorough and effortful analysis. Similarly, repeated exposure skews probabilities with respect to certain events when individuals threat these to be more frequent than they truly are, given the ease with which these are recalled. Although these mechanisms serve a positive function of conserving precious cognitive resources in an information rich environment, they negatively contribute to the rise of biased thinking that potentially results in more effective IWIO.

## Interaction of hot and cold cognition

While the previous section gives the impression that cold and hot cognition are mutually exclusive, research suggests that this may not necessarily be the case. Further investigation into this relationship feeds into the question of when do individuals decide to rely on intuition or heuristics and when do they commit to more effortful deliberation?

Several scholars propose (Thompson & Morsanyi, 2012; Thompson, Turner, & Pennycook, 2011) that the transition between the automatic and deliberate cognition hinges on a metacognitive experience they dub as the Feeling of Rightness (FOR). Their argument rests on the notion that the degree to which deliberate cognition occurs is determined by the outputs produced by the automatic and subconscious processes. Heuristic usage consists not only of the initial assessment of the information but also includes an accompanying sense of "correctness." The more "correct" this is thought to be, the less likely that more effort is exerted for additional processing. The authors draw parallels between this process and that of memory retrieval where the validity of information is contingent not only on the retrieved content, but on its associated affect as well.

This affective component is crucial if we consider the nature of the issues invoked by IWIO. Those wishing to influence audiences by exploiting their beliefs often frame their content in an attitudinally congruent manner. In so doing, the (mis)information appears to reaffirm their preconceived notions regarding a particular issue. And with affect thought to precede cognition, this alignment generates the required FOR that suppresses further deliberation and analysis (Markus & Zajonc, 1985). Phrased simply, because the information feels right, there is no need to question it further. The ability to quickly formulate judgements in an information rich environment allows us to remain ahead of the deluge but increases our susceptibility to IWIO. Although this phenomenon is not an outcome unique to cyber-enabled IWIO, the distinctive characteristics of cyberspace increase the susceptibility of specific groups to these operations.

## Cascading structures of cyberspace: from technology to information

Cyberspace, and its most readily accessible manifestation, the Internet; is often characterized as a monolithic construct. While this serves to simplify usage and stimulate further development; its underlying structure generates no small amount of uncertainty for lay individuals and serves to frame the manner in which it is exploited to meet strategic ends. With that in mind, any endeavor that strives to understand why actions in cyberspace succeed or fail must start with an analysis of how the domain is constructed.

While there exists no consensus on how best to characterize the structure of cyberspace, it is broadly thought to be composed of three (3) general levels: Physical, Syntactic, and Semantic (Libicki, 2009). Each of these levels is defined based on its role in the reception, transmission, and transformation of data. As the name suggests, the Physical level oversees the physical transformation and transmission of data. This includes the medium on which it exists (e.g. electro-magnetic) and the specific hardware required (e.g. cables, servers, etc.). Above this is the Syntactic level that dictates specific protocols that govern the transmission and processing of data. This layer implements previously agreed upon standards that allow for the interoperability of technologies between different manufacturers (e.g. TCP/IP). Finally, the Semantic level transforms the data into a form suited for human consumption such as individual texts of graphical representations. Other researchers, along with policy makers, argue that a fourth level exists. That of the cognitive/emotional level. Unlike the previous levels, this exists exclusively within the minds of individuals exposed to information obtained via cyberspace (Lin & Kerr, 2018). This hierarchical structure of cyberspace, while serving as both a useful pedagogical tool and a design mechanism that enables interoperability, carries significant technological and psychological implications that partially explain how states view and utilize the domain to meet their strategic aims.

Although the above hierarchy greatly simplifies our understanding of the inner workings of cyberspace, it also obscures the underlying complexity of the domain. Though this abstraction is of help, it masks the inherent unpredictability of the domain. As noted by Perrow (1984), complex and interdependent systems do not easily open themselves up for evaluation. This increases the risk of failures that cannot be pre-empted on the part of the designers. Furthermore, the interdependent nature of the domain suggests the possibility of a cascading of effects across levels (Saltzman, 2013). For instance, a disruption in the Physical level inhibits communication between other components of the system. Similarly, disruption of protocols at the Syntactic level limits the interaction between disparate systems or even the processing of information in a single system. Actors that depend on the technological functionality of the domain in support of strategic goals (e.g. economic success) tend to view cyberspace as an enabler and perceive threats in the context of actions that disrupt these processes. This is apparent in how certain actors such as the United States define cyberspace and the manner in which power is exercised (USA, 2018).

In our attempt to understand why cyber-enabled IWIO appear to be more effective, it is crucial to note that this potential for cascading effects extends into the cognitive/emotional level. If we simplify cyberspace as merely a medium through which information is transmitted between individuals, then both form and content could have a direct bearing on those that consume it. For example, a tweet in August 2013 that an explosion occurred in the White House prompted stocks to plummet for a brief period (Greenfield, 2013). More recently, unsubstantiated news triggered a wave of far-right riots in the German city of Chemnitz in 2018 (Welle, 2018). These and other related incidents demonstrate that the cascading effect of malicious behavior in cyberspace is not limited solely to physical or digital effects but directly impacts an audience's perceptions and judgements. This ability to exert influence shapes how actors such as Russia and China define cyberspace (Valeriano, Jensen, & Maness, 2018).

This, however, is not a novel concept. The idea of manipulating an adversary's thinking through information presents itself as far back as the writings of Sun Tzu who notes that "*the supreme art of war is to subdue the enemy without fighting*". For those versed in the growing field of cybersecurity, this goes against the Clausewitzian notion of compelling an adversary to act by overpowering or disrupting their ability to exercise power within cyberspace (Borghard & Lonergan, 2017; Liff, 2012). Truth be told, advancements in cyber capabilities coupled with the institution of offense-centric strategies suggests that actions in cyberspace more akin to armed conflict take precedence in the minds of strategists and political elites. However, with growing awareness of the organizational and technological resources required to effectively execute these operations, adversaries are more likely to resort to the weaponization of information as a low-cost alternative to influence target audiences in support of their strategic objectives.

## Information warfare/influence operation typologies

IWIO can be broadly categorized into three (3) forms based on intent: propaganda operations, leak operations, and chaos-producing operations (Lin & Kerr, 2018). Although these are treated as separate categories, they are not necessarily mutually exclusive. Leak operations can, as a secondary effect, produce chaos with respect to the target audience. Similarly, propaganda operations may involve the use of leaked documents or information, with the contents supporting the preferred or espoused narrative.

Propaganda operations are defined as "organized attempts through communication to affect belief or action or inculcate attitudes in a large audience in ways that circumvent or suppress an individual's adequately informed, rational, and reflective judgement" (Marlin, 2013, 22). This definition is instrumental in highlighting the advantages offered by cyberspace when executing these operations. The emphasis on the operation's goal of affecting belief while suppressing rational choice signals an inherent tendency of individuals to value information aligned with their beliefs over others' irrespective of its validity. While this is not a particularly novel claim, later sections demonstrate how the nature of cyberspace makes it difficult to counteract such processes.

Chaos producing operations are those that seek to confuse and disrupt through misinformation. Although some scholars believe that these serve no other purpose than to engineer chaos without a corresponding behavioral outcome, real-world cases demonstrate that the affective consequences of such prompt specific patterns in judgement that manifest themselves as specific real-world actions (Blum, Silver, & Poulin, 2014; Reinhardt, 2017). Apart from its affective component, the uncertainty introduced by misinformation also promotes the emergence of specific cognitive biases as a means of countering the lack of readily available information (Kahneman, Slovic, & Tversky, 1982; Norman & Delfin, 2012). Consequently, it is difficult to claim that these operations are unlikely to result in observable behavioral changes. Although both propaganda and chaos producing operations function regardless of the truth value of the communicated information, the former is usually associated with a particular political objective. The latter, in contrast, may be exercised without such association, though having a specific political alignment does not necessarily diminish its overall effectiveness if carried out correctly.

Finally, leak operations endeavor to present audiences with information that would otherwise be out of bounds due (e.g. classification). Disclosure, when conducted under the appropriate context, generates notoriety and attention that may be disproportionate to its actual value. Unlike the previous operations, the disclosure of information depends on the careful balance between true and false claims. If properly conducted, leak operations serve to reduce the trust between audiences and an adversary (Lin & Kerr, 2018).

## Cognitive effects of information warfare/influence operations

As the preceding section suggests, biased judgements may emerge despite our best efforts to meet the normative requirements of rational choice. With this in mind, we are left to address the question of what makes IWIO particularly well suited to exploiting these all too common human traits? Although the operations we term as IWIO are not by any means novel, the characteristics of this new operational space increases our reliance on a handful of cognitive processes to manage the voluminous amount of information available to us. While useful, these increase the likelihood of biased judgements that further the aims of adversaries by facilitating decisions and actions that serve the interests of adversaries.

In their book chapter, Lin and Kerr (2018) highlight a number of characteristics that enable IWIO. While these permit IWIO to be carried out more efficiently compared to conventional domains, a handful enable the efficient exploitation of bias-inducing cognitive process. These characteristics include high connectivity and low cost, low latency, multiple distribution points, and disintermediation. The remainder of this section elaborates on how each of these characteristics contributes to the impact of cyber-enabled IWIO.

### *High connectivity and low cost*

Internet usage measured as the percentage of the global population with access more than doubled between 2007 and 2017. Similarly, fixed broadband subscriptions have nearly tripled within the same period (World Bank, 2019). This massive growth with respect to information access coupled with the relatively low costs associated with its conveyance suggests that barriers for producing and consuming (mis)information is much lower than at any other point in human history. Such a degree of interconnection allows an individual with a relatively small interpersonal network to disproportionately disseminate information by exploiting the interconnected nature of individuals within this space.

Though this vast access to information may be employed as a means to better the human condition, for malicious actors it serves to enable the manipulation of information to influence behavior. The recent surge in fake news and propagandistic material has prompted research focused on how the environment enables and magnifies the effects of these operations. To this end, two accounts stand out as competing explanations. On the one hand, some argue that motivated reasoning (i.e. hot cognition) with respect to ideologically congruent information motivates individuals to believe and share such information. On the other, individuals may simply be cognitive misers (i.e. cold cognition) who are unwilling to invest additional cognitive resources, given the deluge of information presented to them.

When faced with contradictory information, individuals tend to either reject contradictory information outright or to reframe it to maintain congruence with existing belief structures. In the context of IWIO, and specifically propaganda and leak operations, researchers observe a link between ideological alignment and information preferences. In his study of electoral behavior, Redlawsk (2002) notes that individuals take longer to process incongruent information and are motivated to search for (congruent) information pertaining to their desired candidates. Similarly, other studies highlight attitudinal congruence with respect to information. This is observed when, given the ability to freely search for information, individuals tend to gravitate towards attitudinally congruent information (Gaines & Kuklinski, 2011; Taber & Lodge, 2006). With information freely available through platforms such as social media and the ease with which content is constructed and disseminated, it is easy to see how an explanation based on motivated reasoning can account for the success of IWIO.

Challenging this notion of a motivated reasoning favoring attitudinally congruent information, an emerging body of research has advanced the possibility that inherent cognitive limitations result in cold, heuristically driven information processing. Owing to the volume of information an individual is exposed to, the decision to favor a given subset may have less to do with pre-existing beliefs and more with the need to limit the amount of cognitive resources invested. In their large-scale experimental study, Pennycook and Rand (2019) convincingly demonstrate that the ability to discern misinformation is grounded in the predisposition to critically assess information instead of adherence to a specific belief. This is despite the existence of warnings that question the accuracy of the information provided. Relatedly, Rapp and Salovich (2018) argue that an individual's level of confidence with respect to their subject matter expertise leads non-experts to believe in falsehoods given the absence of alternatives accessible to them while experts, confident in their knowledge, believe themselves immune to misinformation.

## Low information latency and multiple distribution points

Along with the reach and accessibility offered by cyberspace, information spreads at a rate incomparable to previous forms such as print media. With mobile devices constantly connected to the global information network, (mis)information is easily pushed to audiences. With this in mind, concerns over the effects of emotionally charged information and persistent exposure come to the fore.

The ability to quickly disseminate emotionally charged misinformation as a component of chaos producing operations or leaks triggers a host of affect-influenced biases with the potential to sway an audience's behavior. Reinhardt (2017) argues that despite not having directly experienced it, individuals exposed to accounts disasters develop significantly stronger reactions to it than those experiencing it first-hand. He notes that the interaction between fear, uncertainty, and media exposure, untampered by experience, skews risk assessments beyond that projected by experts. With respect to IWIO, content describing the disastrous outcomes of certain policies, the ineptitude of certain leaders, or even the "danger" posed by certain groups may result in similar outcomes.

This is unsurprising as fear has been shown to constrain cognitive process in favor of a fight-or-flight response (Dolan, 2016). Fear, for the purpose of clarity, is distinct from anxiety as the latter prompts greater introspection compared to the former (Gray, 1990; Whalen, 1998). Consequently, it is unsurprising that simply being informed of a possible threat or threat actor without additional context or expertise results in biased judgement. Complicating matters further, the speed and breadth with which misinformation is shared through this domain allows a misrepresentation of the scope and severity of the a given situation – if it had occurred at all.

Real world cases of misinformation producing chaos as a result of the above process are disturbingly becoming commonplace. In Germany cases of sexual assault by immigrants fueled protests and riots in a number of cities (Welle, 2018). While in India fears concerning a rise in kidnappings encouraged mob violence that prompted the popular messaging service WhatsApp to limit the number of messages shared among users in India (McLaughlin, 2018).

Apart from the unsubstantiated increase in one's threat sensitivity, the ease with which this is shared and propagated may also trigger recollection bias "whereby people who observe a highly unexpected event hold current risk beliefs about a similar event that are no higher than their recollection of their prior beliefs" (Viscusi & Zeckhauser, 2017, 969). Although one can claim that simply passing information to individuals within one's network does not guarantee that others will perceive the information to be accurate, it has been shown that prior exposure increases fluency[4] that, over time, leads to the acceptance of (mis)information (Pennycook, Cannon, & Rand, 2018).

## *Disintermediation of information*

While computing technologies make it easier to disseminate (mis)information through tools such as social media, the disappearance of intermediaries (e.g. editors) further enables the manipulation and misrepresentation of facts. Furthermore, this increased dependence on computerized tools gives rise to a "machine heuristic" in which individuals exercising this heuristic believe news available through these platforms is free from subjective human judgements (Sundar, Knobloch-Westerwick, & Hastall, 2007). Though it cannot be denied that traditional media has, on occasion, promoted specific ideologies, discounting human agency is naïve as the underlying mechanisms that generate content for these new platforms are defined by human beings and are equally vulnerable to bias. The surge in the number of bots prior to the 2016 presidential elections in the United States demonstrates the problems associated with liberalizing the production and dissemination of information (Guilbeault & Woolley, 2016).

Although skeptics may argue that a growth in volume does not necessarily lead to an increase in consumption, the rate at which information spreads and its relationship with other pieces of information buoys its perceived credibility. Sundar et al. (2007) demonstrate through a cross-national study that news cues in terms of a headline's recency and suggested relevance represented by the number of related articles is enough for individuals to positively value its content. Granted that the source of the information remains significant for individuals, in cases where information is perceived to be recent (i.e. breaking news) and is widely reported on (i.e. viral), reputation is discounted in favor of these other two attributes. This finding is even more significant when viewed alongside others that observe that ideological orientation may not play as significant a role as initially believed (Pennycook et al., 2018; Pennycook & Rand, 2019). Consequently, the pace with which (mis)information is shared prompts readers to disproportionately value its veracity while inflating its perceived urgency. Taken together, these processes result in the activation of a number of biases that increases the efficacy of cyber-enabled IWIO.

The above, however, should not be understood as a confirmation that IWIO works best in the cyber domain and poorly in the real-world. Instead, readers should interpret these arguments as an attempt to surface that cyberspace simply allows IWIO to be exercised more effectively since its characteristics more easily enable the activation of hot and/or cold cognitive processes that result in biased judgements. Furthermore, it should be pointed out that because of increasing dependence on this domain in conjunction with the relatively low cost associated with IWIO, cyber-capable actors are likely to continue engaging in such actions in pursuit of their respective interests.

## Containing the effects of information warfare/influence operations

The prevalence of IWIO calls for the development of countermeasures to blunt the worst of its effects. In keeping with the objectives of this chapter, this subsection does not discuss specific initiatives aimed at achieving this goal. It instead sheds light on the underlying concepts that limit the ability of misinformation to influence the perceptions and behavior of audiences. While human cognitive and affective processes facilitate the success of IWIO, these processes also serve to curtail the objectives of malicious actors. As a caveat, however, readers should be informed that while research demonstrates that some of these processes succeed under controlled (i.e. experimental) conditions, applying these may not necessarily be a straightforward process.

### *Disrupting information encoding*

As the name suggests, certain solutions attempt to address the issue by focusing on how information is processed by the target audience. For the most part, these efforts are aimed at disrupting information encoding. A number of studies demonstrate that prior knowledge serves as a cornerstone for judgement (Lau & Redlawsk, 2001; Saunders, 2017). While experts and non-experts exhibit noticeable differences on how knowledge is utilized, both still employ new (mis)information even when prior accurate knowledge is available. For non-experts this may simply result from a lack of trust in the quality of information they possess or an over-reliance on heuristic mechanisms that result in a sub-optimal judgement. Experts, on the other hand, may believe themselves immune to such effects and may fail to conduct a thorough evaluation (Rapp & Salovich, 2018). To demonstrate this phenomenon, a group of students were given text to read about the first president of the United States, George Washington. A subset of the students read text that clearly stated his election as the first president. The remaining students, in contrast, read a more stylized version of the same text that introduces a degree of uncertainty on whether or not he would be elected as the first president. Although both groups correctly identified George Washington as the first president of the United States, those that read the stylized version took longer to answer. This delayed response suggests that these students may have entertained the possibility that the inaccurate information (i.e. he did not become president) could actually be true (Gerrig, 2018).

An explanation for this reliance on misinformation is associated with the process of comprehension that activates prior knowledge. The characteristics of the information presented results in either the strengthening or weakening of associations between new episodic information and those stored in long-term memory. Given the limited availability of cognitive resources and the motivations of an individual, either the episodic or stored information is utilized (Van den Broek, Rapp, & Kendeou, 2005). Experimentally, attempts

**142** Miguel Alberto Gomez

to exploit this mechanism to counter misinformation have been tested. Broadly speaking, these have involved motivating participants to think more critically of the information provided them either through explicit directions within the experimental instrument or by disrupting them at key points during the encoding process, such as when critical assertions are made (Donovan, Theodosis, & Rapp, 2018). While the designs vary, the overarching goal is to motivate individuals to critically assess the information provided. The results of these studies are, however, inconsistent with some showing increased ability to discern and reject misinformation while others showing no difference at all.

The shortcomings of this approach may be traced to the nature of the task at hand. Although participants are explicitly instructed to dedicate more resources to the task, the inconsequential nature of these experiments may force them to revert to possibly incorrect information stored in short-term memory (Holland, 2008). This problem may even be compounded if the solution is attempted in a real-world setting. Reliance on readily available information in short-term memory is a coping mechanism, given the amount of information available to an individual. With most of the content in news feeds and social media being of little direct interest and the distance between the consumer and potential consequences of this information, there would be little motivation to invest precious cognitive resources for critical assessment.

### *Exploiting affective states*

Emotions feature heavily in how we process information. When processing new (mis)information, associations are formed with affect-laden information stored in long-term memory. This specific affect, along with its associated information, is triggered in response to a stimuli (e.g. new information): a heuristic mechanism that evaluates an individual's feelings with respect to the association and reinforces a particular affect regardless of the nature of whether or not the stimuli is aligned with the information stored in memory (Dreyer, 2010; Slovic, Finucane, Peters, & MacGregor, 2007). This broad mechanism provides an account for the effects of partisanship and perceptions involving political communication and electoral behavior (Redlawsk, 2002; Rudolph, 2006). While these studies are numerous and account for why IWIO effectively exploits existing preferences, they provide much needed insight as to who would most likely engage in the critical analysis of available information.

Weeks (2015) argues that an individual's emotional state when processing information influences the extent to which partisan biases come into play. This is particularly salient given the emotive nature of issues in which IWIO comes into being. Specifically, Weeks notes that anger and anxiety, along with other factors such as the availability of corrective information either aggravate or mitigate susceptibility to misinformation. While both reflect negative valences, these are distinct emotions with unique implications for information assessment.

Anger is a negatively valanced emotion that emerges when goals are unmet, when one is offended, or a perceived violation to oneself or standards is experienced (Carver & Harmon-Jones, 2009). This emotion is associated with a feeling of certainty and control. With respect to cognition, anger inhibits information seeking, learning, and deliberation (Redlawsk, Civettini, & Emmerson, 2010). Anxiety, in contrast, promotes a sense of uncertainty and a lack of control resulting in elevated levels of arousal. This results in individuals seeking more information and other activities as a means of reducing these feelings (Eysenck, Derakshan, Santos, & Calvo, 2007). In his study, Weeks notes that anxious individuals when presented with misinformation along with a corrective mechanism are more likely to develop a critical mindset and thus move away from incorrect beliefs. In contrast, angry individuals become intransigent and maintain existing beliefs despite attempts at correction.

These findings surface a pattern necessary in developing countermeasures to IWIO; that of a multidimensional approach. On its own, emotional states do not appear to have a significant impact on altering beliefs. Similarly, corrective mechanisms such as fact checking and warnings do not critically alter utilization of misinformation (Sundar et al., 2007; Weeks, 2015). A successful approach must not only correctly assess the veracity of the information provided; it must also be presented in a manner that does not result in greater intransigence on the part of the audience.

## Moving forward

As the chapter illustrates, the efficacy of cyber-enabled Information Warfare/Influence Operations is not solely the result of the environment in which these are conducted. Although the continued utilization of cyberspace enables faster and cheaper communication that allows these operations to reach a wider audience, success is furthered by the underlying cognitive and affective mechanisms common to human beings regardless of the domain through which information is disseminated and consumed.

Because of our need to maintain pre-existing beliefs and constraints with respect to cognitive resources, human beings readily resort to heuristic mechanisms when forming judgements. While efficient, these mechanisms promote a host of biases that enable IWIO. This situation is aggravated within the cyber domain where such biases are amplified due to the incentivization of maintaining beliefs with the availability of attitudinally congruent information and with the overreliance on heuristics due to the sheer volume of information in this space.

While this paints a bleak picture, mechanisms that empower IWIO may also be employed to counter these. If information is simply too abundant that critical thinking is impaired, then improving how information is presented or managing the volume of information presented at any given time may prompt a more deliberative assessment on the part of audience members. Similarly, if affect along with corrective mechanisms are crucial in debiasing individuals, then these should be constructed in a manner to evoke the desired emotion while still providing correct information. Finally, no single solution provides a panacea for this phenomenon. Existing solutions need to be exercised conjunctively to obtain the desired effects.

It is unlikely that IWIO will fall by the wayside. Its limited material and organizational requirements relative to offensive cyber operations suggest its continued use alongside more conventional means of exerting influence. However, by understanding what enables these operations and why they appear to be so effective in cyberspace is a necessary first step in blunting their degenerative effects.

## Notes

1 Also called "Influence" Operations.
2 For the purpose of this chapter, the related concepts of beliefs and schemas are used interchangeably and are defined a "cognitive structure that represents knowledge about a concept or type of stimulus, including its attributes and relations among those attributes" (Crocker, Fiske, & Taylor, 1984).

3 Although a number of heuristics may be triggered due to exposure to IWIO, these two are of interest for this chapter given the unique characteristics of cyberspace.
4 A heuristic mechanism in which constant exposure to a particular object (e.g. a type of information) results in its overvaluation in comparison to other objects.

## References

Blum, S. C., Silver, R. C., & Poulin, M. J. (2014). Perceiving risk in a dangerous world: Associations between life experiences and risk perceptions. *Social Cognition, 32*(3), 297–314.

Borghard, E. D., & Lonergan, S. W. (2017). The logic of coercion in cyberspace. *Security Studies, 26*(3), 452–481.

Carver, C. S., & Harmon-Jones, E. (2009). Anger is an approach-related affect: Evidence and implications. *Psychological Bulletin, 135*(2), 183.

Cassino, D., Taber, C. S., & Lodge, M. (2007). Information processing and public opinion. *Politische Vierteljahresschrift, 48*(2), 205.

Chong, D. (2013). Degree of rationality in politics. In L. Huddy (Ed.), *The Oxford handbook of political psychology* (Second ed., pp. 96–129). Oxford: Oxford University Press.

Crocker, J., Fiske, S. T., & Taylor, S. E. (1984). Schematic bases of belief change. In R. Eiser (Ed.), *Attitudinal judgment* (pp. 197–226). New York: Springer.

Dolan, T. M. (2016). Emotion and strategic learning in war. *Foreign Policy Analysis, 12*(4), 571–590.

Donovan, A. M., Theodosis, E., & Rapp, D. N. (2018). Reader, interrupted: Do disruptions during encoding influence the use of inaccurate information? *Applied Cognitive Psychology, 32*(6), 775–786.

Dreyer, D. R. (2010). Issue conflict accumulation and the dynamics of strategic rivalry. *International Studies Quarterly, 54*(3), 779–795.

Evans, J. (1984). Heuristic and analytic processes in reasoning. *British Journal of Psychology, 75*(4), 451–468.

Eysenck, M. W., Derakshan, N., Santos, R., & Calvo, M. G. (2007). Anxiety and cognitive performance: Attentional control theory. *Emotion, 7*(2), 336.

Gaines, B. J., & Kuklinski, J. H. (2011). Experimental estimation of heterogeneous treatment effects related to self-selection. *American Journal of Political Science, 55*(3), 724–736.

Gerrig, R. (2018). *Experiencing narrative worlds*. London: Routledge.

Gray, J. A. (1990). Brain systems that mediate both emotion and cognition. *Cognition & emotion, 4*(3), 269–288.

Greenfield, R. (2013, May 23). Look what the hacked AP Tweet about White House bombs did to the market. *The Atlantic*. Retrieved from www.theatlantic.com/technology/archive/2013/04/hacked-ap-tweet-white-house-bombs-stock-market/315992/.

Guilbeault, D., & Woolley, S. (2016). How Twitter bots are shaping the election. *Technology*. Retrieved from www.theatlantic.com/technology/archive/2016/11/election-bots/506072/.

Holland, N. N. (2008). Spider-Man? Sure! The neuroscience of suspending disbelief. *Interdisciplinary science reviews, 33*(4), 312–320.

Holmes, M. (2015). Believing this and alieving that: Theorizing affect and intuitions in international politics. *International Studies Quarterly, 59*(4), 706–720.

Jensen, B., Maness, R. C., & Valeriano, B. (2016). Cyber victory: The efficacy of cyber coercion. Paper presented at the Paper presented at the Annual Meeting of the International Studies Association.

Jervis, R. (1976). *Perception and misperception in international politics* (New ed.). Princeton, NJ: Princeton University Press.

Jervis, R. (2009). Understanding beliefs and threat inflation. *American Foreign Policy and the Politics of Fear: Threat Inflation since, 9*(11), 16–39.

Kahneman, D. (2003). A perspective on judgment and choice: Mapping bounded rationality. *American psychologist, 58*(9), 697–720.

Kahneman, D., Slovic, P., & Tversky, A. (1982). *Judgment under uncertainty: heuristics and biases*. Cambridge; New York: Cambridge University Press.

Larson, D. W. (1994). The role of belief systems and schemas in foreign policy decision-making. *Political Psychology, 15*(1), 17–33.

Lau, R. R., & Redlawsk, D. P. (2001). Advantages and disadvantages of cognitive heuristics in political decision making. *American Journal of Political Science, 45*(4), 951–971.

Libicki, M. C. (2009). *Cyberdeterrence and cyberwar*. Santa Monica, CA: Rand Corporation.

Liff, A. P. (2012). Cyberwar: a new "absolute weapon"? The proliferation of cyberwarfare capabilities and interstate war. *Journal of Strategic Studies*, *35*(3), 401–428.

Lin, H., & Kerr, J. (2018). On cyber-enabled information/influence warfare and manipulation. In *Oxford Handbook of Cybersecurity*. Oxford: Oxford University Press.

Lindsay, J. (2013). Stuxnet and the limits of cyber warfare. *Security Studies*, *22*(3), 365–404.

Lodge, M., & Taber, C. (2000). Three steps toward a theory of motivated political reasoning. In A. Lupia, M. D. McCubbins, & S. Popkin L. (Eds.), *Elements of reason: Cognition, choice, and the bounds of rationality* (Vol. *183*, pp. 183–213). Cambridge, UK: Cambridge University Press.

Lord, C. G., Ross, L., & Lepper, M. R. (1979). Biased assimilation and attitude polarization: The effects of prior theories on subsequently considered evidence. *Journal of Personality and Social Psychology*, *37*(11), 2098.

Markus, H., & Zajonc, R. B. (1985). The cognitive perspective in social psychology. *Handbook of social psychology*, *1*, 137–230.

Marlin, R. (2013). *Propaganda and the ethics of persuasion*. Peterborough, Ontario: Broadview Press.

McLaughlin, T. (2018). How WhatsApp fuels fake news and violence in India. Retrieved from www.wired.com/story/how-whatsapp-fuels-fake-news-and-violence-in-india/.

Mercer, J. (2010). Emotional beliefs. *International Organization*, *64*(1), 1–31.

Norman, E. R., & Delfin, R. (2012). Wizards under uncertainty: Cognitive biases, threat assessment, and misjudgments in policy making. *Politics & Policy*, *40*(3), 369–402.

Pennycook, G., Cannon, T. D., & Rand, D. G. (2018). Prior exposure increases perceived accuracy of fake news. *Journal of Experimental Psychology: General*, *147*(12), 1865.

Pennycook, G., & Rand, D. G. (2019). Lazy, not biased: Susceptibility to partisan fake news is better explained by lack of reasoning than by motivated reasoning. *Cognition*, *188*, 39–50.

Perrow, C. (1984). *Normal accidents: living with high-risk technologies*. Princeton, NJ: Princeton University Press.

Rapp, D. N., & Salovich, N. A. (2018). Can't we just disregard fake news? The consequences of exposure to inaccurate information. *Policy Insights from the Behavioral and Brain Sciences*, *5*(2), 232–239.

Redlawsk, D. P. (2002). Hot cognition or cool consideration? Testing the effects of motivated reasoning on political decision making. *Journal of Politics*, *64*(4), 1021–1044.

Redlawsk, D. P., Civettini, A., & Emmerson, K. M. (2010). The affective tipping point: Do motivated reasoners ever "get it"? *Political Psychology*, *31*(4), 563–593.

Reinhardt, G. Y. (2017). Imagining worse than reality: comparing beliefs and intentions between disaster evacuees and survey respondents. *Journal of Risk Research*, *20*(2), 169–194.

Rid, T. (2012). Cyber war will not take place. *Journal of Strategic Studies*, *35*(1), 5–32.

Roach, S. C. (2016). Affective values in international relations: Theorizing emotional actions and the value of resilience. *Politics*, *36*(4), 400–412.

Rudolph, T. J. (2006). Triangulating political responsibility: The motivated formation of responsibility judgments. *Political Psychology*, *27*(1), 99–122.

Saltzman, I. (2013). Cyber posturing and the offense-defense balance. *Contemporary Security Policy*, *34*(1), 40–63.

Saunders, E. N. (2017). No substitute for experience: Presidents, advisers, and information in group decision making. *International organization*, *71*, S219–S247.

Slayton, R. (2017). What Is the cyber offense-defense balance? Conceptions, causes, and assessment. *International Security*, *41*(3), 72–109.

Slovic, P., Finucane, M. L., Peters, E., & MacGregor, D. G. (2007). The affect heuristic. *European Journal of Operational Research*, *177*(3), 1333–1352.

Sundar, S. S., Knobloch-Westerwick, S., & Hastall, M. R. (2007). News cues: Information scent and cognitive heuristics. *Journal of the American Society for Information Science and Technology*, *58*(3), 366–378.

Taber, C. S., & Lodge, M. (2006). Motivated skepticism in the evaluation of political beliefs. *American Journal of Political Science*, *50*(3), 755–769.

Thompson, V., & Morsanyi, K. (2012). Analytic thinking: do you feel like it? *Mind & Society*, *11*(1), 93–105.

Thompson, V., Turner, J. A., & Pennycook, G. (2011). Intuition, reason, and metacognition. *Cognitive Psychology*, *63*(3), 107–140.

USA. (2018). *National Cyber Security Strategy of the United States of America*. Washington D.C.

Valeriano, B., Jensen, B., & Maness, R. C. (2018). *Cyber Strategy: The Evolving Character of Power and Coercion*. New York: Oxford University Press.

Van den Broek, P., Rapp, D. N., & Kendeou, P. (2005). Integrating memory-based and constructionist processes in accounts of reading comprehension. *Discourse Processes, 39(2–3)*, 299–316.

Viscusi, K., & Zeckhauser, R. J. (2017). Recollection Bias and Its Underpinnings: Lessons from Terrorism Risk Assessments. *Risk Analysis, 37(5)*, 969–981.

Weeks, B. E. (2015). Emotions, partisanship, and misperceptions: How anger and anxiety moderate the effect of partisan bias on susceptibility to political misinformation. *Journal of Communication, 65(4)*, 699–719.

Welle, D. (2018). German state official: Fake news fueled Chemnitz riots. Retrieved from www.dw.com/en/german-state-official-fake-news-fueled-chemnitz-riots/a-45263589.

Whalen, P. J. (1998). Fear, vigilance, and ambiguity: Initial neuroimaging studies of the human amygdala. *Current Directions in Psychological Science, 7(6)*, 177–188.

World Bank (2019). World Bank Open Data. Retrieved from https://data.worldbank.org/.

# PART III

# Building resilience: Questions of legality, diplomacy and society

# 10

## MIGHT OR BYTE(S)

### On the safeguarding of democracy in the digital age

*Christopher Colligan*

### Introduction

In conversation with pundits and national security practitioners, it is not uncommon to hear the opinion that the information revolution centered on digital computers, the Internet and web technologies constitutes a revolution in military affairs (RMA).[1] Just as with the advent of iron weaponry, gunpowder or the airplane, the argument goes, this most recent information revolution has changed the character of warfighting enough that entire new paradigms of contestation must be adopted. Among scholars, whether or not the Internet itself constitutes an RMA is a hotly contested question, with many arguing that cyberspace simply opens up new adjunct possibilities for the conduct of war and doesn't change its form entirely. Regardless of which side one aligns with, however, there is no escaping the fact that the information age is forcing governments and militaries to reconceptualize the manner in which conflict is *organized*. With so much coercive power nested beyond the traditional centers of state capability and with an expansive societal attack surface to consider, national authorities face the daunting task of building formal structures and strategic cultures that can accommodate – indeed, *must* accommodate by necessity – collaboration between governmental, military and private civilian actors.

This chapter takes up the question of how the need to conduct and defend from information operations in the age of cyber conflict is affecting – and might affect in the future – existing civil–military regimes in different countries. Since little work to date has taken up this remit, it does so by initially considering the literature on relations between civilian governments and military forces. Traditionally, the study of civil–military relations pursues two primary research questions. First, how do civilians ensure control over an institution (i.e. the military or paramilitary forces) within which they have centralized most of the coercive power of the state? It is important to note here that although scholarship on the topic generally assumes – at least when Western countries are under consideration – that effective control of the military *intrinsically* involves democratic conditions, this is not the same as understanding what is involved with effective *democratic* control of the military (Cottey, Edmunds and Forster 2002). In other words, answering this question is critical because the existence of democratic process is not synonymous with democratic authority over the coercive arms of the state. As such, civil–military scholarship necessarily aims to answer a second question: just how do civilians ensure military effectiveness? After all, political agents, government institutions and citizenry all have a vested interest in ensuring that the ability of their state to effectively defend territory and national interests is as well-developed as possible, and thus are rarely likely to tolerate military autonomy.

It is important to note that civil–military affairs is a subfield of political science and national security studies ridden with contradictory assumptions about the intersection of these competing imperatives. A defining feature of the subfield is that researchers typically present the above questions in tandem – and thus in tension – leading to civil–military relations scholarship that considers the benefits of relatively greater or lesser civilian oversight (or "intrusion" in military affairs) vis-à-vis military efficacy most often in *normative* terms. The result of this natural tendency is that scholarship on civil–military relations has often been defined by the cultural and methodological inclinations of scholars spread across different national circumstances. During the Cold War, for instance, civil–military scholarship beyond the United States tended to conceptualize the first question above as implying that, in essence, healthy and democratic forms of government translate to coup prevention in some form or another. A problem therein, of course, is that this framing of the question includes an in-built assumption that military organizations by themselves have no compunction regarding coups. Logically, this is not always the case and scholarship *within* the United States has frequently acknowledged that coups are an extraordinarily remote concern at worst. Rather, American scholarship asserts that what sits at the heart of questions of civil–military relations is not some intrinsic threat of military overthrow but rather the complex nature of efforts to maximize military effectiveness via the organization, provision and administration of the military bureaucracy. The tensions for scholars in this vein emerge from process and the political interests of relevant stakeholders. Here too, however, there are problems. As will be discussed below, this emphasis on the day-to-day management of civil–military relations has produced an unfortunately narrow focus on institutional variables among scholars interested in Western national security apparatuses.

Given that this chapter attempts to consider civil–military relations in the context of an emergent threat, I adopt a broader sociological approach than is common in scholarship focused on the context of the United States. Specifically, I suggest that the context of cyber conflict and digital age information operations requires a fundamental rethinking of the research program on civil–military relations to incorporate consideration of *both* private actors and uncertainty that is both technologically and societally exogenous to the government–military apparatus. To be clear, the question asked in this chapter – i.e. how does the nature of an emergent security issue affect states' existing civil–military relationships? – is not one that civil–military relations scholars ever ask. However, it is one asked far too infrequently. Emergent threats – what Huntington calls "external imperatives" (Huntington 1957) – have only been the subject of civil–military scholarship in a handful of cases over the past two decades, with notable entries pertaining to changes in the overall threat environment (Desch 2008) and to norm formation around novel weapons systems (Tannenwald 2005; Mazanec 2015). As noted above, given that cyber-enabled information operations inherently affect civilian actors – whether by targeting them directly or by using civilian ICT infrastructure to facilitate the operation against civilian or military targets – it is clear that information operations *will* challenge existing civil–military arrangements. As such, anything short of a threat-driven – rather than theory-driven – assessment of the applicability of civil–military relations work seems impractical.

This chapter argues that the Internet adds a secondary paradox nested within the broad paradox that lies at the heart of civil–military relations theory – that the agent empowered by the principal to protect said principal must rely on actors subject to, yet outside of, the control of the principal in order to pursue missions in cyberspace. Briefly, this secondary paradox emerges from the significant condition of both (1) private ownership and operation of Internet infrastructure and (2) exogenous (to the state) design of the preponderance of those technologies that determine digital conflict potentialities. This digital age dynamic does little to alter the core feature of civil–military relations wherein, given some assumed ability to exercise oversight over the military, civilian government is incentivized to best enable the coercive capabilities thereof. Whereas in the past this might have largely involved direct augmentation of the technologies and resources directly employed by the military, however, today such actions inevitably imply action that runs counter to the economic, moral and civic conditions of democratic process, such as the regulation of Internet social media services or the direct legal mandating of systemic backdoors built into cryptosystems. And yet, this does not automatically imply some constraint on government incentives to empower the military, since *not* acting to diminish the significance of private ownership of Internet functions constitutes a dilution of the military's coercive power within a given state and a condition of compromised sovereignty at least where the Internet is concerned. How, then, might civilians in government enable the military if doing so not only risks an overly powerful agent, but also directly harms the civil society government represents?

The remainder of the chapter proceeds in several parts. First, I define the core civil–military problematique. Then, I discuss how the Internet alters the traditional civil–military problematique and consider the rich theoretical traditions of civil–military relations scholarship, asking what elements, if any, might be applied to research aimed at answering the above question. I suggest a series of initial lines of inquiry and address some of the unique challenges posed by cyber and information operations. I conclude by addressing the significance of the information revolution for civil–military studies as a whole, arguing that the thing is significant over and above perceived impact on national security because of the scope of the global transformation of socio-technical and cognitive processes it has set in motion.

## The civil–military problematique

Before broaching the question of how information operations in the digital age challenge extant civil–military regimes, it is necessary to first further define the problem of civil–military relations itself. Scholarly interest in the problem inherent within civil–military relations is best understood as a second-order principal–agent problem.[2] The first principal–agent relationship originates between civil society and the government it subsequently creates in order to better manage and govern an expanding community. Here, civil society is the principal (i.e. the "actor" with interests) and government is the agent of those interests. However, this first agent (the civilian government) must itself create other agents that are capable of carrying out specialized tasks. These other agents are usually sub-units of the government, such as a department of law enforcement or an environmental protection entity, and are not true independent agents insofar as the government has ultimate power of existence over them. This situation does not apply to the military, which is the secondary agent tasked with securing the polity from external threats. The situation does not apply simply because the government cannot perfectly exercise existential control over the military, since the military is vested with much of the state's coercive power.

Principal–agent problems arise when the principal fears or observes that its agent is failing to complete its assigned task. The civil–military principal–agent problem thus arises from a fear of an agent to whom the civilian government has abdicated all coercive means in the name of increased protection from external threats. On a crude individual level, one could portray this particular relationship between civilian and military parts of government as giving an acquaintance your handgun – because they are a better shot – and then asking them to protect you from individuals that may be interested in robbing, injuring or killing you. At this point, however, you have detached from your direct control the most potent coercive capability you originally possessed – the handgun – and are at the mercy of your acquaintance for protection. What is stopping that individual from subsequently robbing you, attacking someone else with a gun registered in your name or otherwise imposing demands that are not in your best interest?

Thus, in constructing a relationship between civilian and military authorities, the state traditionally attempts to reconcile two possibly conflicting interests. First, the military must be powerful enough to defeat likely adversaries. Second, the civilian government must effectively maintain control over an organization to whom it has abdicated coercive means. Efforts to fulfill one of these interests may correspondingly decrease the likelihood of fulfilling the other interest. For example, heavy institutional or budgetary controls may undermine the military to the point that it is unable to protect the state from likely adversaries. Such an arrangement is particularly dangerous when opaque institutional controls aimed at maintaining internal security decrease an otherwise powerful military's effectiveness, as these states may appear threatening to external actors, while simultaneously being unable to adequately protect themselves (e.g. Stalin's Soviet Union following the Great Purge, Iraq in the early-1990s, etc.) (Talmadge 2013; Stoecker 2018). Alternatively, civilian elites ill-versed in their state's military affairs may pursue aggressive foreign policies whose requirements the military is ill-equipped to meet. This second potentiality may be particularly acute in states with a notable civil–military gap (i.e. a divergence in the views and interests of both parties). These undesirable outcomes ostensibly lead to the conclusion that states should simply empower their agents, whether through the removal of institutional controls or an increase in budgetary allotments.

However, empowering one's military likely increases the civilian government's vulnerability to the military's wishes. Traditionally, civil–military scholars have operationalized this vulnerability in the easily observable occurrence of a coup. However, limiting observable dysfunctional civil–military relations to coups overlooks the vast majority of civil–military relationships and the myriad ways in which militaries seek to exert influence over civilian governments. For example, a policy-oriented military may independently pursue or pressure civilian governments into certain foreign policies. Although less overt than a coup, such actions are no less insidious and are indeed particularly problematic for democracies, as they undermine the governing logics of democratic process. In democracies, military leaders may provide civilian leaders with threat assessments and the cost–benefit analyses pertaining to possible strategies, but civilian leaders must be the ones to ultimately decide on a course of action. By contrast, a military that actively advocates policy can produce *political* outcomes outside of their institutional purview that are at odds with desired citizen and civilian government policy preferences. For example, during American military action in Kosovo, the American military leaked its opposition to the use of ground forces to the *New York Times*, subsequently undermining the Clinton administration's ability to use the threat of ground forces as a coercive tool (Feaver 2003, 279). More banal forms of civil–military dysfunction might involve, for instance, a military campaigning for ever-increasing resources disproportionate to external threats (e.g. the purchase of strategic bomber fleets at a time where a state's main adversary has employed sophisticated air defenses and where ballistic missile alternatives are available), effectively bleeding a state dry. These forms of military-originated dysfunction thus represent a question of obedience: how does the state empower its military whilst ensuring that the agent does not become overly vulnerable?

In truth of course, it seems uncontroversial to say that this statement of the problematique of civil–military relations is overly broad. Indeed, as much is admitted by numerous researchers who work in the area. The picture of prospective imbalance between civilian and military authorities above is nested at the strategic level of analysis, and even institution-oriented assessments of civil–military relationships tend to emphasize the overarching context of high-level domestic politics and foreign policymaking. In reality, there is much that is not perfectly captured in descriptions of civil–military affairs that nest analysis in such a fashion, including the day-to-day operation of civil–military relationships in which innumerable personnel from both arms of government perform in complementary roles under singular mission sets. Given such a dynamic, overarching maximalist questions regarding the potential for military intervention in civilian affairs – essentially questions of military obedience to civilian will – make less sense than might questions about what kinds of strategic cultures lend themselves to mutually agreeable operating conditions. As is discussed below, of course, not all civil–military scholarship makes such broad overgeneralizations (often borne of methodological necessities surrounding operationalization of military "influence," "obedience," or civilian "control"). Nevertheless, it is worthwhile noting that while overarching challenge of civil–military coordination is as described above, much of what scholars ultimately examine is a deliberative process amongst representatives of the principal and the agent that consider themselves relative equals. This is a particularly significant point to bear in mind as the discussion of cyber conflict and information operations inevitably prompts us to consider necessary coordination with a host of parties beyond the state itself, including technology vendors, Internet Service Providers (ISPs) and digital services firms.

## Altering the civil–military problematique in the digital age

Though cyber conflict has manifested time and again in the national security experiences of powerful states in the international system for at least three decades, the rapidly increasing tempo of interstate engagement in the fifth domain over just the past ten years has succeeded in placing the issue at the head of government security agendas in most developed countries. Today, dozens of states across North America, Europe, the Middle East and Asia are spending significant sums in efforts to both flesh out operational capabilities and then nest those new abilities in appropriate institutional frameworks. The exact same observation might be made of national experiences with information warfare (IW). As other chapters in this volume have described, IW is an age-old set of strategies and techniques practiced by states in an effort to degrade and derail the power of peer competitors. In just the past decade, however, IW has likewise risen to the top of Western security agendas as encounters with novel influence campaigns augmented by a series of digital conditions have targeted dozens of countries. In many cases, of course, efforts to adapt to new IW and cyber conflict threats are hard to separate as governments see the two-threat phenomenon as two sides of a dice whose shape is characterized by broad-scoped changes to the function of global society by the Internet.

## Bringing in private actors: a digital age problematique and theory of civil–military relations

The paradox that lies at the heart of civil–military relations theory – that the agent empowered by the principal to protect it must necessarily be powerful enough to threaten the principal itself – might be extended to *democracies* in the digital age in three parts. First, as has always been true, civilian government (the principal) is incentivized to enable the function of the agent (i.e. the military) that has been empowered so as to provide societal protection. However, second, effectively doing so in the context of cyber conflict and broad-scoped digital insecurity would run counter to many of the civic and economic imperatives of the civil society that the principal represents. That said, third, *not* acting to ensure the effectiveness of the agent risks – perhaps even dictates – the dilution of the agent's coercive power and empowers other societal actors to some greater or lesser degree. Under such circumstances, there exist direct threats to the sovereign position of the principal. In essence, the trappings of national security in the digital age act to complicate the second question presented at the outset of this chapter surrounding the need for civilians to ensure military effectiveness, given some appropriate degree of oversight. How might civilians in government enable the military if doing so not only risks an overly powerful agent, but also directly harms the civil society government represents?

Some further explication is required here of how digital insecurity challenges traditional civil–military regimes. Given the focus of this volume, it is perhaps best to consider the context of cyber conflict processes and digital age information operations separately to emphasize the manner in which such challenges apply broadly, before discussing the intersection of both below. In both instances, the problematic emerges in considering both the offensive and defensive imperatives of the state.

Broadly, cyber conflict involves the use of networked computer systems to achieve disruptive, espionage and (rarely) destructive effects via operations against foreign adversaries.[3] Over the past several decades, advanced industrial states have increasingly conducted offensive cyber operations (OCO) aimed at broad-scoped societal interference and the degradation of adversaries' power (Whyte & Mazanec 2018). Cyber conflict takes varied forms. In just the past several years, state actors have been responsible for the disruption of electricity infrastructure, the physical sabotage of centrifuges used for uranium enrichment and the disruption of military command/control systems. State actors also – indeed, predominantly – employ cyber instruments to gather intelligence and better map the battlefield of international contestation.

If prompted, scholars and practitioners who specialize in cyber issues might acknowledge that a core functional characteristic of conflict in the digital age is the complex, fragmented nature of Internet infrastructure. Such infrastructure is the terrain over which states must operate for national security purposes and upon which the services and technologies – from programming languages to full stack software environments – that determine cyber conflict potentialities are built. The most notable feature of this terrain is its ownership and governance. The Internet is not owned fully or in large part by any one entity, even within a state (at least, a *democratic* state); rather, the backbone infrastructure of the thing – including fiber optic and submarine cables, satellites, etc. – is owned by thousands upon thousands of different private and civil entities, primarily commercial firms. When militaries engage in cyber conflict actions – say, in offensive operations designed to coerce a foreign power without resorting to higher levels of force – they primarily, often almost exclusively, operate over private third-party networks, the operators of which could disrupt the ability of the military to act by simply denying network usage. And defensively, of course, the privately-owned nature of Internet infrastructure is the principal detail responsible for what has been a massive expansion and diversification of the attack surface of nations. Critical elements of national infrastructure, from banking services to the grid, are more directly accessible via cyberspace for purposes of attack or espionage than was the case in the pre-Internet age. More to the point vis-à-vis the functionality of states' coercive power as vested in military and intelligence forces, vectors for disruptive, destructive and espionage operations from foreign sources are not only defined by the strategic posture of such forces. Rather, militaries are vulnerable to compromise, prospectively, via a wide array of affiliated civil society entities and a host of information technologies that undergird military functions.

With information warfare – here taken to mean the broad-scoped disinformation and psychological warfare campaigns seen prosecuting by actors like the Russian Federation in recent years[4] more so than the counter-command/control (C2) operations implied by early scholars studying "network-centric warfare" (Cebrowski & Garstka 1998; Moffat 2010) – a parallel set of unique operational dynamics exist vis-à-vis private ownership of the terrain of both societal and security functions in a given state. Offensively, IW operators like the Russian government-affiliated Internet Research Agency (IRA) built efficacy in their influence efforts by manipulating key features of commercial Internet services. The functionality of social media platforms like Twitter and Facebook, as well as the algorithmic predictability of aggregator sites like Reddit, have recently allowed foreign powers the ability to build sophisticated agenda-setting apparatuses entirely via manipulation of new digital systems embedded within democratic civil societies. Such manipulation, as was discussed in a previous chapter, even extends to cyber operations in aid of influence campaigns, with malware introduced in some instances to a susceptible civilian demographic for the purposes of yet further malicious alteration of organic discursive process. Defensively, of course, the strong implication herein suggested by numerous experts is that resilience to cyber-augmented IW must be nested at least on some level in the private sector where the technology and management that constitutes the clear vulnerability to broad-scoped societal manipulation resides.

In short, the very development that constitutes the most recent information revolution – i.e. the construction and expansion of the Internet around the world as a complex physical and logical system with no centralized control features – introduces a new paradox nested within the traditional paradox that sits at the heart of civil–military relations theory and research. Civilian governments, acting on behalf of civil society, empower militaries to protect the state and are incentivized, given some appropriate degree of oversight, to best enable the function thereof. Pathways to enabling the most effective version of military capabilities to conduct cyber conflict and combat IW threats, however, invariably suggest the curtailing of free market practices and accompanying sociopolitical freedoms now associated

**156** Christopher Colligan

with an open Internet. Certainly, at some level, government actions impose only limited restraints on civil society in aid of national security objectives, such as when states' mandate national encryption schemes. However, *effective* action to combat digital insecurity invariably implies, among other things, questionable limitations of free speech bound up in attempts to secure private commercial platforms and government regulation of industrial sectors where no need for active network management exists to legally justify such a move. Such potential moves to empower the coercive agent are largely unpalatable in Western democracies. And yet, without such actions, the power of the agent remains diluted, as dictated by exogenous technological and corresponding societal conditions. Private actors in civil society possess some of the capacity traditionally held by the military in partnership with civilian government authorities, some formation of whom might reasonably be able to challenge the military's coercive power. This dynamic constitutes a direct challenge to state sovereignty, tempered only by the degree to which digital security concerns are weakly linked to hard power. How, then, might civilians in government enable the military if doing so not only risks an overly powerful agent, but also directly harms the civil society government represents?

## *Empirics*

Though this chapter is not a fully-fledged empirical exploration of the dynamic described in this section, it is worthwhile noting a robust spectrum of case evidence that – at the very least – validates this notion of civil–military relations imbued with a secondary paradox borne of exogenous socio-technological conditions vis-à-vis the Internet. Regarding the challenges facing civilian government in democratic states constrained by exogenous conditions in their quest to empower the coercive agent, for instance, Shane and Hunker (2013) note that, in the United States, the federal government's attempts to form effective public–private partnerships with Internet service providers and technology companies have been consistently rebuffed on several fronts since at least the late 1990s. Given the redundancy of Internet functionality that emerges from the underlying packet switching technology involved, there is limited need for active network management to ensure that disruptions of one kind or another do not affect the nation as a whole. This same dynamic has enabled the continued existence of thousands of service providers even in a marketplace where several giants own and operate much of the domestic backbone, thus providing the government with an extremely fragmented landscape of numerous stakeholders that would need to be addressed in any effective oversight arrangement. At the same time, commercial firms have regularly turned to civic and moral arguments to underwrite their case against government involvement in the running of Internet services of any kind. Technology companies were notably vocal in 2011 following the publishing of a strategic document by the Obama administration outlining a goal for standardization of authentication techniques in new technologies, criticizing the move as being semi-authoritarian in its implications. Likewise, Apple, Inc. received broad support for its pushback and legal reproach of the federal government surrounding the case of the San Bernadino terrorist attacks in 2015, where the Federal Bureau of Investigation attempted to compel cooperation with cracking iPhones owned by the attackers involved. Since Apple's security software utilizes public key encryption to give only users the ability to access devices and accounts, cooperation would have meant the installation of a backdoor that would have systematically existed across all versions of the operating system involved. Apple felt so strongly that the move would have constituted unnecessary government oversight that the company took the extraordinary step of refusing to cooperate and engaging in litigation on the matter.

## Theories of military effectiveness in democracies

A series of theoretic traditions dot the landscape of civil–military relations scholarship, some of which, it is quite likely, have direct relevance to the nuanced challenge of national security in the digital age. Early studies of civil–military relationships, like that conducted in Samuel Huntington's famous book The Soldier and the State (1981), tended to construct a view of the balance between civilian and military interests in a way that included some assumption of the "right" of government to regulate its agent in some fashion. For Huntington, who predicted a series of societal variables as the cause of different civil–military regimes, effective military capabilities were achieved via regimes of "objective control" where the civilian government retained only high-level political control of policy and where a highly-professional military was given autonomy to perform its task. This contrasts with "subjective control" wherein civilians intrude into military affairs in extensive fashion, exerting control such that military effectiveness is hampered. Though the theory is arguably the most po-pularly salient even at time of writing this chapter, its implicit assumption of some organic right to unquestioned professionalism and its subjugation of political culture to security imperatives hampers its applicability to the challenges of the digital age. Moreover, as was noted at the outset of this chapter, it does little to predict the day-to-day realities of national security operation by blended civilian–military workforces.

By contrast, the assumptions of Morris Janowitz (2017), despite being arguably only a half-step removed from institutionalists like Huntington, suggest some applicability to the chal-lenges of the digital age. Janowitz suggested that militaries are naturally conservative and resistant to change and that civilian intervention was actually beneficial for cultivating the coercive capacity thereof. While it is almost inevitable that clashes of perspective would cause oscillation in the degree to which either civilian government or the military made inroads in controlling the other, advanced democracies are characterized by such vibrant civic structures and process that military forces will always remain distinct from the civic body. The goal of leaders should, thus, simply be to ensure a degree of convergence between the values of civilian government and military process such that innovation might be cultivated. The way to approach this task was to maintain the professionalism held up by Huntington as necessary to ensuring military effectiveness, but to augment the strategic culture of the military via educational programming, officer training in civilian setting and more. Doing so would allow civilian values to seep into the military without violating the professional autonomy of the military at the point of operation.

Not dissimilar in the broadest of strokes to convergence theory, concordance theory (Schiff 2008) argues that military effectiveness is best assured by the civilian government when the two, alongside the citizenry at large, come to agreement across four main issue areas – (1) what the social composition of the officer corps should look like, (2) what political decision-making processes are legitimate, (3) how military personnel should be recruited and (4) what style or form the military should take. Concordance theory is remarkably flexible by comparison with the theoretical traditions that Huntington and Janowitz stand as the poster-children of insofar as there is no assumption that the civilian government and military need

**158** Christopher Colligan

exist as separate worlds. It recognizes that national security in democracies is a blended affair. Moreover, it suggests four overarching areas within which coordinating processes might be assessed to have an effect on the broader civil–military regime, thus allowing for a clearer ability to predict the effects of day-to-day developments on military effectiveness writ large.

Finally, Peter Feaver (1998, 1999; Coletta and Feaver 2006), in the late 1990s, laid out the theory of civil–military relations that perhaps most clearly addresses the day-to-day operation of the national security establishment as opposed to the strategic perspective that many prior scholars have taken as given that both government and military possess. Feaver suggests that the military, as the agent of the principal (the civilian government) can repeatedly choose to either "work" or "shirk" its responsibilities – i.e. to do what it's told or to avoid obeying the principal. In order to ensure effectiveness, government needs to maintain a situation where the costs of monitoring the military are low and the likelihood of military "shirking" being caught is high. Regardless of some overarching ability to maintain a given strategic posture, the theory predicts the conditions that might allow a state's security apparatus to operate at peak efficiency at a given moment in time, thus ceding reasonable explanatory power to researchers that might wish to account for perceived discrepancies over time.

### Explaining civil–military–society relations in the digital age with "civ–mil" theory

The challenge of applying existing civil–military relations theory to the context of the digital age is, at least in part, clear in the need to control for a third actor – a private sector whose natural formation is determined by market forces rather than institutional trappings. Secondarily, of course, the challenge of applying existing theory can also be found in the need to consider the effects of uncertainty about the operational capabilities of the military that is directly determined by that third actor, the fragmented private sector.

Naturally, existing theory is most clearly suited to addressing the dual challenges of cyber conflict and digital age IW where there are clear cases of military jurisdiction. Where targeted systems are substantially operated under military, intelligence or government auspices, it is likely quite possible to develop effective civil–military regimes for rapid response, resilience and counter-offense. The same is likewise true where cyber operations are employed within a conventional military mission structure. And indeed, there is significant evidence of this in the – admittedly unusual – development of national cyber command institutions in the United States and Europe over the past two decades. In the U.S., a decade of experience, assessment and internal deliberation following the introduction of Joint Task Force Computer Network Defense (JTF-CND) in late 1998 resulted in the formation of Cyber Command (USCYBERCOM), an entity that blends elements of civilian, intelligence and military capacities so as to best address clear issues of national cyber insecurity. The challenges faced by American civilian and military practitioners in defining the objectives of USCY-BERCOM and the approaches to be taken in service thereof only further support the point insofar as doctrine and practice has so often involved vagaries even where institutional development has been firmly asserted. In other words, the need for a command like USCY-BERCOM is clear even where the exact intricacies of the extent of its mission are sometimes shrouded in legal and strategic questions.

By contrast, civil–military theorization as it currently exists is likely weakly suited to addressing those situations where the nature of a threat and related threat features is either distinctly or substantially non-military, including incidence of broad-scoped information operations in the digital age. This is in no small part due to the emphasis that is placed to this day on the assumptions of Huntington's institutionalist model of military effectiveness in democracies. As Feaver criticizes, civil–military relations literature that follows in the vein of Huntington's seminal study – which is most of the extant literature – is not deductive; rather, it is based on historical analysis of conditions, particularly from the early 20th century and the Cold War. As such, prevailing thought on civil–military conduct carries with it numerous in-built assumptions about the priorities of the state vis-à-vis national security and the character of threats facing democratic polities as somewhat monolithic in their constitution. The result of this – both for the case of information operations where military context is not the norm and for cyber conflict that is characterized by vagaries around attribution and the role of non-state actors – is a general under-specification of research questions that apply to the digital age and a broad lack of focus on the types of causal mechanisms that are likely to be relevant in the age of the Internet.

And yet, the expanded view of civil–military relations in theoretical traditions beyond Huntington's dominating school of thought do contain some promise for effective scholarly and practitioner work on addressing the dual paradoxes described above. In particular, fu-sionist approaches – meaning those that consider the line between civilian and military auspices to be increasingly blurred – overcome a fundamental flaw obvious in the prospect of applying these theories to the digital age: that any form of effective state engagement on digital security issues will require persistent engagement with foes and habitual interaction with prospective civilian and industrial targets of cyber aggression. The former assertion, found at the heart of the most recent strategic planning documents in the United States, holds that cyberspace is a domain defined by persistent contact with enemy forces. The implication thereof is that constant coordination with third-party enablers of cyber conflict is also ne-cessary for the effective conduct of digital operations, even in a purely military context. The latter assertion simply reflects the expanded attack surface of democracies faced with digital insecurity. In order to combat threats like cyber-enabled information operations, direct in-teraction with private actors and the systems they maintain is paramount to enabling the state in its defensive mission.

Overall, the elements emphasized in civil–military relations scholarship that are best-suited to foregoing explorations of how democratic states' might address the dual paradoxes are those that focus on strategic culture and convergence (or concordance) between disparate forces whose action is needed to best assure both political integrity and national security capabilities. Useful concepts to be explored in the context of digital age insecurity most assuredly include Janowitz' notion of professionalism as a modifiable construct that not only allows one actor to stave off the interference of others at the point of operation, but can also be tailored over time via education and other programming to ensure that specialist national security operators gain value from societal norms and context. Likewise, the drivers of concordance that Rebecca Schiff and others have explored in the context of conventional civil–military relationships have clear utility to the present day insofar as decision-making processes, recruitment format and the tone of national security operations all likely apply in some substantial form to the environment of national defense in the digital age. The chal-lenge, of course, remains in the adaptation of extant knowledge of the difficulties of ensuring security effectiveness in democracies to the new context of an environment dominated by private actor interests and coercive potential.

**160** Christopher Colligan

## Constructing civil–military research agendas for cyber conflict and information warfare

In this final section of the chapter, I suggest initial areas of inquiry that have yet to be taken up by scholars of international relations (IR) and civil–military relations more specifically.

### *Determining patterns of civil–military–society engagement*

In order to specify particular research questions that should shape a civil–military research agenda focused on insecurities in the digital age, it is first necessary to consider the broad-scoped nature of threats enabled by or delivered via cyberspace. This is a step not often taken by researchers aimed narrowly at the implications of the Internet for, say, intelligence gathering or interstate warfighting. Such analyses are most often driven by logical arguments about the characteristics of the domain that incline security actors towards particular modes of operation. For instance, one prominent argument goes that, because cyber instruments have a necessarily short shelf life – i.e. because code developed or tailored towards some specific intrusion purpose is susceptible to neutralization where defenders update their systems or apply patches – conflict in the domain is characterized by use-or-lose logics and subsequent first strike doctrines. For the purposes of civil–military(–society) relations scholars, the issue with such a focus is that such lines of inquiry tell us little about patterns of effect at the national level, which is a prerequisite to understanding how the state might move to engage civil society and empower the military.

As some work (Bayuk et al. 2012, for instance) has noted, the oft-cited assumption that digital insecurity affects nations in a form analogous to what one might see with punctuated terrorist attack or sophisticated, disruptive warfighting actions lacks on several fronts. The landscape of cyber incidents that pertain to national security or political integrity – from theft of military intellectual property to disruption of power systems and influence operations – often involves targets, delivery mechanisms and effects that look remarkably little like either of those things. This is significant because the nature of a threat determines not only these things, but also who the most relevant responders might be and what factors (e.g. techno-logical, institutional, sociological, etc.) must be addressed in order to build resilience. These are critical elements in need of identification by scholars if civil–military relations are to be properly studied in this context. Stating that cyber threats are substantially similar to terrorist or warfighting threats is akin to arguing that the greatest digital threats are those calamitous disruptions that are actually the rare occurrence in the short history of cyber conflict. These might include incidents like the blockade of Estonia in 2007, the disruption of uranium enrichment during Operation Olympic Games in 2009–2011 or the attack on Ukrainian energy providers in late 2015, events that affected national systems so critical to societal function that the jurisdiction of the military and government in response was unquestionable.

By contrast, the reality is that much digital disruption is more easily likened to irregular warfare, pandemic disease or even climate pollution in terms of how it impacts society and puts pressure on non-state stakeholders. As even the U.S. military now recognizes, en-gagement in cyberspace is best characterized as persistent contact between national and non-state adversaries across an immensely expansive societal attack surface. Human use of the domain for a variety of security purposes is, in short, incredibly noisy. Just as military doctrine has turned to the challenge of generating deterrent signal from noise, so too is the cybersecurity industry writ large characterized by a consistent need to address the digital "pollution" that interferes with our experience of the Internet's positive externalities. This has meant the rise to prominence of (1) those actors, such as cybersecurity insurance or incident response firms, that can generically handle diverse cyber challenges and (2) those actors, policies or practices that can incentivize better digital security hygiene via market mechanisms (much as how government may incentivize anti-polluting practices by taxing emissions). At the same time, the landscape of private actors significant to national cyber-security has yet further been shaped by the manner in which some of the most damaging attacks (financially, at least) are increasingly presenting in unpredictable fashion. Ransomware attacks enabled by worms that self-propagate – such as WannaCry or NotPetya – prevent responders from using traditional models of quarantine and threat mitigation, as the malware proliferates to information systems via hard-to-predict lateral connections in much the same fashion a pathogen might. Such patterns might also be said to characterize digital age in-fluence operations, where manipulated narratives, fake accounts and even cyber attacks often spread according to social networking dynamics rather than some underlying feature of singular networked-computer systems.

## Driving research questions

The shape of digital insecurity *must* sit at the heart of efforts to better assess patterns of civil–military–society engagement in the age of the Internet. This is particularly the case given that the problematique of digital age relations between the disparate elements described in sections above contains significant vagaries and no small degree of fluidity in terms of threat prioritization, threat evolution and nation-specific societal attributes. Understanding how and when governments will act to empower their coercive counterparts depends on narrow understanding of emergent conditions rather than some overarching, static image – the likes of which characterizes the dominating work of Huntington and other in-stitutionalists – of what national security involves.

The most obvious area of initial inquiry for scholars interested in developing under-standing of such actions is the broad set of sociological issues that must be addressed in bringing a third category of actors – private actors – so significantly into frameworks of national security in democratic polities. Two questions seem particularly fertile as ground for explorations. First, is there a "gap" in relations between civilian, military and private actors? In other words, are there clear differences in perspective on the roles that should be assumed and actions that must necessarily be taken to best secure digital democracy? If so, what is the nature of this gap? These questions are traditionally of civil–military interest and have driven much of American civil–military scholarship in the post-Cold War era (Feaver and Kohn 2001). As suggested at various points in previous sections, the civil–military relations lit-erature suggests a number of potential sources of such differentiation that can lead to friction in such coordinative relationships. One is disagreement on the nature of the threat. Scholars would do well to consider, across cyber conflict and adjacent issues (such as cyber-enabled information warfare threats), what structures or cultural impediments exist to concordance between relevant stakeholders in state and private settings. A related source of differentiation lies with the manner in which different stakeholders rank threats, even where general agreement on the source thereof exists. Here, the imperative for researchers is only partly to do a better job of adjudicating on what is most significant in terms of the function of the

**162** Christopher Colligan

"terrain" of cyberspace (i.e. what makes one element of critical infrastructure more "critical" than others); it is also to account for the competition of economic, political, moral and civic interests with regards to threat mitigation among the expansive set of relevant stakeholders in the private sector, from ISPs and technology vendor firms to civilian emergency response centers, universities and insurance companies.

Answering this first question, of course, by addressing these points then lends analytical capacity to exploring a subsequent prompt: where might "control" of private elements of the digital domain and its correlates actually matter for national security. This chapter has, so far, necessarily framed the problematique of civil–military relations in the digital age in broad terms. But it is incumbent upon researchers to add nuance to this initial articulation of a challenge. If it is possible to more clearly adjudicate on where military or government "control" or oversight will actually lead to security benefits, the driving question posed at the outset of this chapter can be clarified.

Naturally, other areas of inquiry stand to also help clarify the problematique outlined in this chapter beyond the sociological. Though there is a clear argument being made in this chapter that the addition of private actors to the equation of civil–military affairs demands greater focus on sociological features of the diverse state–society relationships, there is clear opportunity for narrower research on the core institutions of national security. How, for instance, might significant state institutions conceive of their interest and compete, both with one another and with civil-society counterparts. How might such arrangements of en-gagement and competition be affected by existing civil–military regimes across national circumstances over and above, for instance, the driving force of national experiences with digital insecurity? Such research trajectories are a natural segue for scholars interested in the fertile ground that is acquiring better understanding of the cross-national development of unique doctrines, institutions and norms related to cyber conflict and information warfare in the age of the Internet.

## Back to the future: remembering the role of information in civil–military regimes

This chapter has argued that the Internet adds a secondary paradox nested within the broad paradox that lies at the heart of civil–military relations theory – that the agent empowered by the principal to protect it must necessarily be powerful enough to threaten the principal itself. This secondary paradox comes from two primary factors: first, private ownership and operation of Internet infrastructure and, second, exogenous (to the state) design of the preponderance of those technologies that determine digital conflict potentialities. The result of this is that, today, state actions to empower its coercive agent will likely at the higher levels run counter to the economic, moral and civic conditions of democratic process. Far from simply constraining the state in such actions, however, this dynamic creates a singular tension for government stakeholders insofar as *not* acting to diminish the significance of private ownership of Internet functions constitutes a dilution of the mili-tary's coercive power within a given state and a condition of compromised sovereignty, at least where the Internet is concerned. The question of civil–military–*society* relations in the digital age is one of how civilians in government might enable the military if doing so not only risks an overly powerful agent, but also directly harms the civil society that govern-ment represents.

In conclusion, it is worthwhile addressing the broader context of the information revolution based on computers, the Internet and web technologies so that the significance of what has been broached in this chapter is properly understood. Regardless of whether one thinks of new information technologies as an RMA in the traditional sense, there is unquestionably some fact to the assertion that the Internet has fundamentally altered the informational substrates of world politics in ways that have clear implications for civil–military relations, even beyond the shape of specific cyber threats. The late Paul Virilio argued (1995) that information technologies tend to "speed up" societies across the landscape of human history, accelerating the tempo of political and economic interactions and complexifying the outputs of social engagement without necessarily altering the baseline correlates of human activity. The result is often a dramatic shortening of the shadow of the future, an injection of new uncertainty into society that produces a significant disruption to social identities and political worldviews. Such disruption, of course, often ends up being remedied through emergent conflict of one form or another.

This most recent information revolution is often said to be more dynamic than those seen across human history, in part because of the scope of its impact on societal functions and in part because the Internet has done more than create yet another new medium for interactivity; rather, it has itself become a new dimension for the expression of societal consciousness. Digital insecurity is not just concerning because it emerges from an unprecedentedly complex landscape of possible attack modes and vectors; it is concerning because the implications thereof for society are not static. There are ghosts in the code and rats in the wires that virtually ensure the evolution of what is meant by digital insecurity over time. The Internet is not an exogenous shock like those others that Virilio describes, but a broad-scoped transformation – a repeating series of mini-shocks – that brings with it a general condition of "future shock" for those stakeholders in national societies must try to reconcile current conditions with punctuated uncertainty about the future. For civil–military relations in the digital age, this implies a perpetual challenge insofar as significant stakeholders may only compromise on short-term issues. The question for scholars, as a result, must be on the fundamental compatibility of democracy with the national security imperatives of the Internet age – can democratic process be preserved in such a way that maintains the power of democratic protectors and insulates society from the prospective negative externalities of connectivity run amok?

## Notes

1 See, among others, Cooper 1994, Metz 1995, Sloan 2002, and Adamsky 2010.
2 Indeed, civil–military relations scholarship is in many forums virtually synonymous with the study of principal–agent problems in diverse settings. See *inter alia* Avant 1998, Sowers 2005, Sarigil 2014, etc.
3 For introductory work on the area, see *inter alia* Liff 2012, Rid 2012, Lindsay 2013, Gartzke 2013, Valeriano & Maness 2015, Buchanan 2016.
4 See, among others, Giles 2016, Way & Casey 2019, Jensen, Valeriano and Maness 2019.

## References

Adamsky, Dima. *The culture of military innovation: The impact of cultural factors on the revolution in military affairs in Russia, the US, and Israel.* Stanford, CA: Stanford University Press, 2010.

Avant, Deborah. "Conflicting indicators of 'crisis' in American civil–military relations." *Armed Forces & Society 24*, no. 3 (1998): 375–387.

Bayuk, Jennifer L., Jason Healey, Paul Rohmeyer, Marcus H. Sachs, Jeffrey Schmidt, and Joseph Weiss. *Cyber security policy guidebook*. Vol. 1. Hoboken: Wiley, 2012.

Buchanan, Ben. *The cybersecurity dilemma: Hacking, trust, and fear between nations*. New York: Oxford University Press, 2016.

Cebrowski, Arthur K., and John J. Garstka. "Network-centric warfare: Its origin and future." In *US Naval Institute Proceedings*, vol. 124, no. 1, pp. 28–35. 1998.

Cooper, Jeffrey R. *Another view of the revolution in military affairs*. Darby, PA: DIANE Publishing, 1994.

Cottey, Andrew, Timothy Edmunds, and Anthony Forster, eds. *Democratic control of the military in postcommunist Europe: Guarding the guards*. New York: Springer, 2001.

Coletta, Damon, and Peter D. Feaver. "Civilian monitoring of US military operations in the information age." *Armed Forces & Society 33*, no. 1 (2006): 106–126.

Desch, Michael C. *Civilian control of the military: The changing security environment*. Baltimore, MD: JHU Press, 2008.

Feaver, Peter D. "Crisis as shirking: An agency theory explanation of the souring of American civil–military relations." *Armed Forces & Society 24*, no. 3 (1998): 407–434.

Feaver, Peter D. "Civil–Military Relations" *Annual Review of Political Science* vol. 2 (1999): 211–241.

Feaver, Peter. "The civil–military gap in comparative perspective." *Journal of Strategic Studies 26*, no. 2 (2003): 1–5.

Feaver, Peter D., and Richard H. Kohn. *Soldiers and civilians: The civil–military gap and American national security*. Boston, MA: MIT Press, 2001.

Gartzke, Erik. "The myth of cyberwar: bringing war in cyberspace back down to earth." *International Security 38*, no. 2 (2013): 41–73.

Giles, Keir. *The next phase of Russian information warfare*. Vol. 20. Riga: NATO Strategic Communications Centre of Excellence, 2016.

Huntington, Samuel P. "Conservatism as an ideology." *American Political Science Review 51*, no. 2 (1957): 454–473.

Huntington, Samuel P. *The soldier and the state*. Cambridge, MA: Harvard University Press, 1981.

Janowitz, Morris. *The professional soldier: A social and political portrait*. New York: Simon & Schuster, 2017.

Jensen, Benjamin, Brandon Valeriano, and Ryan Maness. "Fancy bears and digital trolls: Cyber strategy with a Russian twist." *Journal of Strategic Studies 42*, no. 2 (2019): 212–234.

Liff, Adam P. "Cyberwar: a new 'absolute weapon'? The proliferation of cyberwarfare capabilities and interstate war." *Journal of Strategic Studies 35*, no. 3 (2012): 401–428.

Lindsay, Jon R. "Stuxnet and the limits of cyber warfare." *Security Studies 22*, no. 3 (2013): 365–404.

Mazanec, Brian M. *The evolution of cyber war: International norms for emerging-technology weapons*. Lincoln, NE: University of Nebraska Press, 2015.

Metz, Steven. *Strategy and the revolution in military affairs: From theory to policy*. Darby, PA: DIANE Publishing, 1995.

Moffat, James. *Complexity theory and network centric warfare*. Darby, PA: DIANE Publishing, 2010.

Rid, Thomas. "Cyber war will not take place." *Journal of Strategic Studies 35*, no. 1 (2012): 5–32.

Sarigil, Zeki. "The Turkish military: Principal or agent?." *Armed Forces & Society 40*, no. 1 (2014): 168–190.

Schiff, Rebecca L. *The military and domestic politics: A concordance theory of civil–military relations*. London: Routledge, 2008.

Shane, Peter M., and Jeffrey Allen Hunker, eds. *Cybersecurity: Shared risks, shared responsibilities*. Durham, NC: Carolina Academic Press, 2013.

Sloan, Elinor C. *Revolution in military affairs*. Vol. 5. Montreal, Quebec: McGill-Queen's Press-MQUP, 2002.

Sowers, Thomas S. "Beyond the soldier and the state: Contemporary operations and variance in principal–agent relationships." *Armed Forces & Society 31*, no. 3 (2005): 385–409.

Stoecker, Sally W. *Forging Stalin's army: Marshal Tukhachevsky and the politics of military innovation*. London: Routledge, 2018.

Talmadge, Caitlin. "The puzzle of personalist performance: Iraqi battlefield effectiveness in the Iran-Iraq war." *Security Studies 22*, no. 2 (2013): 180–221.

Tannenwald, Nina. "Stigmatizing the bomb: Origins of the nuclear taboo." *International Security 29*, no. 4 (2005): 5–49.

Valeriano, Brandon, and Ryan C. Maness. *Cyber war versus cyber realities: Cyber conflict in the international system.* Oxford, UK: Oxford University Press, 2015.

Virilio, Paul. *"Speed and information: Cyberspace alarm!."* Ctheory (1995): 8–27.

Way, Lucan Ahmad, and Adam E. Casey. *"How can we know if Russia is a threat to western democracy? Understanding the impact of Russia's second wave of election interference."* (2019).

Whyte, Christopher, and Brian Mazanec. *Understanding cyber warfare: Politics, policy and strategy.* London: Routledge, 2018.

# 11

# ON THE ORGANIZATION OF THE U.S. GOVERNMENT FOR RESPONDING TO ADVERSARIAL INFORMATION WARFARE AND INFLUENCE OPERATIONS

*Herbert Lin[1]*

## On the importance of information warfare and influence operations

Russian interference in the U.S. presidential election of 2016 impressed upon many Americans the significance and potential impact of information warfare and influence operations on the political fate of a nation. This paper defines information warfare and information[2] operations (IW/IO) as the deliberate use of information (whether true or false) by one party on an adversary to confuse, mislead, and ultimately to influence the choices and decisions that the adversary makes.[3] IW/IO is a hostile non-kinetic activity, or at least an activity that is conducted between two parties whose interests are not well-aligned. At the same time, IW/IO is not warfare in the Clausewitzian sense (nor in any sense presently recognized under the laws of war or armed conflict); it is better characterized as hostile or adversarial psychological manipulation. IW/IO has connotations of soft power (more properly, a mix of soft power and sharp power[4]): propaganda, persuasion, culture, social forces, confusion, deception. The patron saint of IW/IO is Sun Tzu, who wrote that "The supreme art of war is to subdue the enemy without fighting."

Regarding Russian activities in the 2016 election the Office of the Director of National Intelligence (ODNI) released a report in January 2017 stating that:[5]

> Moscow's influence campaign followed a Russian messaging strategy that blends covert intelligence operations—such as cyber activity—with overt efforts by Russian Government agencies, state-funded media, third-party intermediaries, and paid social media users or "trolls."

The ODNI report further concluded that Russian cyber activity regarding the U.S. election involved compromises of entities important to the Democratic Party, including email accounts of Democratic National Committee (DNC) and senior Clinton campaign personnel and probes of the election infrastructure of a number of states. It is also rumored that Russia also undertook hostile cyber activities against the Republican Party,[6] but no evidence or fruits of such alleged labors have as of yet come to light.

The full extent of Russia's overt efforts as described by the ODNI are still unknown at this writing (and may never be fully known).[7] However, a number of aspects are known with high confidence. For example:

- The Internet Research Agency (a Russian "troll factory") exposed 126 million people to troll content through Facebook.[8]
- Twitter identified 36,746 Russian automated accounts tweeting election-related content as Russian-linked, generating 1.4 million election-related tweets, many amplified through liking and retweeting.[9]
- Google identified about 1,100 videos with 43 hours of YouTube content tied to the Russian campaign, of which a few dozen had in excess of 5,000 views each.[10]
- Prior to the 2016 U.S. election, Cambridge Analytica improperly received the Facebook information of up to 87 million Facebook users, mostly in the United States.[11] According to Reuters, the former chief executive of Cambridge Analytica claimed that this firm had played a decisive role in U.S. President Donald Trump's 2016 election victory.[12]

Whether these effects had an impact on the outcome of the election is not known; although one study suggests that they may have been sufficient to flip the outcome from an expected Clinton victory to an unexpected Trump victory,[13] these findings have not been replicated in any other study to the best of this author's knowledge.

## Cyber war, information warfare, and influence operations

Many political commentators, Democrat and Republican alike, have pointed to the Russian interference with the 2016 election as cyber warfare. For example, Senator Dianne Feinstein has said "What we're talking about is a cataclysmic change. What we're talking about is the beginning of cyber warfare."[14] Similarly, former Vice President Dick Cheney stated that

> Putin's conduct … has to do with cyber warfare, cyberattack on the United States—the fact that he used his capabilities in the cyber area to try to influence our election …. Putin and his government, his organization, interfere[d] in major ways with our basic fundamental democratic processes. In some quarters, that would be considered an act of war.[15]

The conclusion that Russian interference in the 2016 election is an act of cyberwar is understandable but it is deeply misleading and even dangerous.[16]

To the extent that Russian meddling in the 2016 election involved malicious cyber activities, strengthening the electoral infrastructure of the United States would be part of a plausible response strategy. Indeed, a bipartisan group of six senators introduced on March 22, 2018 the "Secure Elections Act," which is intended to "streamline cybersecurity information-sharing between federal intelligence entities and state election agencies; provide security clearances to state election officials; and provide support for state election cybersecurity infrastructure." (See, for example, Sen. James Lankford's press release on the bill.[17]) The authors of this legislation, and press stories around it, characterize it as a bill to improve the cybersecurity of the U.S. election infrastructure.

168   Herbert Lin

The Secure Elections Act does address the covert Russian cyber activity to which the ODNI report referred, and it falls within the general scope of what the U.S. government defines as cybersecurity, an official definition of which is contained in NSPD-54:[18]

> Prevention of damage to, protection of, and restoration of computers, electronic communications systems, electronic communications services, wire communication, and electronic communication, including information contained therein, to ensure its availability, integrity, authentication, confidentiality, and nonrepudiation.

But the ODNI report also referred to overt Russian activities—messaging activities that can fairly be characterized as information warfare and influence operations directed against the United States. Even if the DNC and John Podesta (and others) had maintained perfect cybersecurity against intrusions, the overt Russian activities to affect political discourse during the election would have proceeded unimpeded (though the absence of the email releases might have diminished their effectiveness).

It is for this reason that a focus on election cybersecurity as it is defined by the U.S. government (and used to define responsibilities, authorities, budgets, and the like) is misleading and dangerous—it does not speak to the toxic nature of political discourse in an Internet-enabled information environment that Russia can manipulate in ways that may be entirely legal.

When adversaries wage cyberwar, they take advantage of design, implementation, or configuration flaws in the information technology systems and networks they target. For example, they exploit zero-day vulnerabilities in a system[19] or they successfully guess weak passwords or they enter an Internet-connected system through a port that was inadvertently left open. Better cybersecurity would help to reduce an adversary's ability to wage cyberwar.

By contrast, when adversaries wage cyber-enabled information warfare or conduct influence operations, they take advantage of the features that information technology systems and networks are designed to offer. The Russians used Facebook, Twitter, YouTube, and other social media exactly as they were designed to be used—to direct selected advertisements and other content to very narrowly defined audiences. They used Twitter exactly as it was designed to be used—to exploit automated accounts to amplify selected messages.

Recalling the definition of information warfare and influence operations above (i.e., the deliberate use of information to confuse, mislead, and affect the choices and decisions that the adversary makes), it is clear that better cybersecurity would not help to reduce an adversary's ability to wage information warfare or conduct influence operations.

This chapter provides an overview of the U.S. government's efforts to organize itself to deal with information warfare and influence operations. The following section reviews the nature of the threat, while subsequent sections detail the legal and bureaucratic obstacles to an effective public sector response.

### *Future cyber-enabled capabilities for IW/IO*

As innovative as the Russians' use of them may have seemed, the mechanisms of cyber-enabled IW/IO have been relatively simple. The future is likely to bring a new level of technological sophistication to the instruments of cyber-enabled IW/IO. Some of the possibilities include the following.

## Faked documents

To date, leaked documents have for the most part been authentic. But it does not take much imagination to consider artfully forged emails that are released along with purloined emails, with content in these forged emails intended to mislead and/or create artificial scandal. These forged emails will be difficult to distinguish from authentic emails that are released simultaneously.

Indeed, there is today at least one documented instance of such machinations. In May 2017, the Citizen's Lab at the University of Toronto released a report about documents stolen from a prominent journalist and critic of the Russian government that were manipulated and then released as a "leak" to discredit domestic and foreign critics of that government.[20]

## Name-matched use of personal information obtained from multiple sources

In 2018, the improper access of Facebook data by Cambridge Analytica made front-page headlines around the world. Although this incident involved the data from tens of millions of American Facebook users, it involved only one data source—Facebook. But there have been many data breaches over the past several years (e.g., Equifax, Anthem, the U.S. government Office of Personnel Management) that have resulted in the compromise of personal information. As capacious and detailed as Facebook is as a repository of personal information, adding even more information from other sources to the Facebook data trove can only be more worrisome. Combining information from multiple sources (multiple social media sources and multiple data brokers, for example) can result in profiles of individuals that are even more detailed than what was possible with Facebook data alone, and one can easily imagine that in the future specific individuals would be the recipients of specially targeted political messaging, a term that includes both explicit advocacy of candidates and hot-button issues that may affect a campaign.

## Exploitation of emotional state

Near-real time use of social media and other clues can help to pinpoint the moments in time when specific individuals are most susceptible to particular kinds of messaging. Demonstrating the feasibility of such targeting, a Facebook document leaked in May 2017 suggested that Facebook was capable of identifying teenagers at moments when they needed a boost in confidence, such as when they were feeling "stressed, "a failure", "worthless," "insecure," "defeated," "anxious," "silly," "useless," "stupid," or "overwhelmed."[21] Responding to stories about this leaked document, Facebook only stated that it was not offering tools to advertisers to target teenagers in such a manner.[22]

Given this backdrop, it is interesting to speculate on the possibility that an adversary might be able to target specific individuals with highly tailored messages at specific times of maximum emotional vulnerability or stress.

## AI-driven chatbots indistinguishable from human beings

AI-driven chatbots will be capable of engaging in realistic text-based conversation about hot-button issues that work to intensify anger and resentment on a one-on-one basis. Although these chatbots will not be able to successfully emulate all aspects of human communication, within the domain of a one-sided and biased political conversation it will be difficult or

**170** Herbert Lin

impossible to distinguish them from the persons they are trying to emulate. These chatbots are likely to work most effectively against audiences who do not expect to be talking to automated agents and who welcome the messages spreading.

### Realistic video and audio forgeries

From rudimentary scam robocalls that collect people's voices saying the word "yes" in order to confirm fraudulent purchases to sophisticated video editing programs, technology is enabling highly realistic forgery of speech and video (also known as deepfakes).[23]

For example, Adobe's Voco program (at this writing, still in beta testing and not yet on the market) has been described by one of its developers as Photoshop for Voice.[24] Where previous audio editing technologies that are limited to audio cutting, copying, and pasting, Voco allows editors to add words that don't appear in the original audio file in the same voice as the original narration with only about 20 minutes of recorded speech for analysis. Voco was demonstrated at Adobe's MAX Conference in 2016. Using a voice sample from the comedian Keegan-Michael Key to change a sample audio of him saying "I kissed my dogs and my wife" to a realistic sample of him saying "I kissed Jordan three times."[25] Today, Voco's capabilities are limited in that it can only be used to manipulate a word or short phrase rather than a longer sample, which for Voco tend to sound less natural.

Researchers have also been able to create digital replicas of faces that defeat relatively sophisticated facial recognition software. At a security conference in 2016, computer vision specialists from the University of North Carolina constructed 3D facial models based on publicly available Facebook photos and displayed them with mobile VR technology to defeat five out of five popular facial recognition systems tested (KeyLemon, Mobius, TrueKey, BioID, and 1D).[26]

These advances have been combined to create realistic video forgeries. Researchers at Washington University used footage and corresponding audio of President Obama to synthesize high-quality video of him speaking things he never actually said with realistic lip and head movements.[27] Researchers from the University of Erlangen-Nuremberg, the Max-Planck Institute for Informatics, and Stanford University improved on these methods to create a program that allows an individual to "control" the expressions of the target actor being mimicked (the researchers used footage of a variety of politicians/actors) with realistic facial transfer, in real time, and with smooth transition between expressions.[28]

Today, film makers have a wide variety of tools at their disposal to practice their craft, including compelling screenplays, powerful music, appropriate lighting and scene editing, close-ups, and so on, but their cinematic choices are made intuitively. Neurocinematics offers the possibility that decisions made to induce specific emotions in the viewer could be made on a much more reliable and repeatable basis—quite a boon for future IW/IO operators. Coupling neurocinematically informed film making with falsified video and audio footage suggests that future deepfake videos will make today's propaganda seem quite amateurish by comparison.

## Organizing the U.S. government to deal with information warfare and influence operations

The preceding section is profoundly important in understanding how the U.S. government is (or as will be seen, is not) organized to defend against cyber-enabled information warfare and influence operations. In particular, the concerns raised all relate to different kinds of speech, a term that is quite broad in the context of U.S. law, the Constitution, and the structure of U.S governmental institutions.

## On the First Amendment: some constitutional constraints on government action

Under current First Amendment jurisprudence and decades of precedent,[29] it is virtually certain that any government regulation directed at intentionally false, misleading, or polarizing speech would have to be drafted quite narrowly and with exceptional precision to avoid running afoul of the First Amendment. The Supreme Court will uphold content-based speech restrictions only if narrowly tailored to combat what the Court deems to be a compelling government interest. The relevant legal hurdles are likely all the more insuperable because much of the communication that forms the basis of cyber-enabled information warfare and influence operations is political speech—a form of expression that elicits the Supreme Court's greatest solicitude.

From this point on, the remainder of this section elaborates on this claim for the benefit of those unfamiliar with First Amendment jurisprudence.

Given that the concerns raised above relate to different kinds of speech, they necessarily implicate the U.S. Constitution, and especially the First Amendment, which places strong restrictions on the authority of government to restrict the content of speech; any content-based government restrictions on speech are subject to a standard of strict scrutiny and are allowable only in cases of compelling governmental interests and then only with the narrowest means possible so that only "bad" speech is restricted and "bad" is narrowly defined. Furthermore, a long history of Supreme Court decisions has held that political speech is among the most protected of all categories of speech.

One metaphor frequently used to describe the operation of the First Amendment is the marketplace of ideas. This metaphor posits that the value of a specific idea is determined in competition with other ideas rather than by the judgment of an external authority (such as government), and the judgments that people make in weighing these various ideas against each other determine which ones survive. Truth emerges through public debate and discourse of ideas, uninhibited by governmental interference.

In the marketplace of ideas, good ideas push out bad ideas. The philosophy underlying the First Amendment was developed by John Stuart Mill[30] at a time in human history when information available to the public was sparser by many orders of magnitude than it is today. The metaphor also implicitly assumes that information consumers have access to all of the ideas and information that must be compared, although it stretches the imagination to believe that is true in today's marketplace of ideas.

But—continuing the metaphor—markets sometimes experience market failure for various reasons, at which point governments often step in to remediate those failures. Furthermore, the discussion above suggests that the metaphor does not apply in today's information environment and in the presence of cyber-enabled IW/IO.[31] Thus, the important question that arises is this: to the extent that there is market failure today in the marketplace of ideas, how should the U.S. government respond?

A fundamental question of today is whether the cyber-enabled proliferation of false, misleading, and inauthentic statements designed to manipulate and distort the political process is so pervasive and so destructive that the nation should consider ways to prohibit such speech—while at the same time minimizing the dangers of either government abuse or undue restrictions on the marketplace of ideas. Even more problematic from a First Amendment standpoint are statements that are literally true but nevertheless misleading.[32]

And what of divisive ideas and opinions? To the extent that the political ideas and thoughts spread through cyber-enabled IW/IO are regarded as speech (and how could they not be?), any governmental restraints on that speech would be even more inherently suspect.

The First Amendment has also been used to ensure the rights of Americans to receive information from a diversity of sources, and in particular from foreign sources. For example, in considering the Postal Service and Federal Employees Salary Act of 1962 (which required that the Postmaster General detain and deliver only upon the addressee's request unsealed foreign mailings of "communist political propaganda"), the U.S. Supreme Court held unanimously that "The regime of this Act is at war with the 'uninhibited, robust, and wide-open' debate and discussion that are contemplated by the First Amendment."[33] Of particular note is the concurring opinion of Justice Brennan in this case in which he writes that "The dissemination of ideas can accomplish nothing if otherwise willing addressees are not free to receive and consider them. It would be a barren marketplace of ideas that had only sellers and no buyers." The U.S. Supreme Court has also held (again unanimously) that "The Constitution protects the right to receive information and ideas, regardless of their social worth, and to be generally free from governmental intrusions into one's privacy and control of one's thoughts."[34]

In light of these precedents, it is interesting to contemplate its applicability to U.S. government efforts to suppress foreign actors from introducing information in American public discourse. For example, if a substantial number of American citizens want to receive ads and videos from Russian troll farms, could the U.S. government constitutionally take action to prevent those citizens from receiving materials originating with those troll farms? Even today, Defense Department planners are required to take extra care in operations that might result in misinforming the American public.

The preceding discussion suggests strongly that cyber-enabled IW/IO as it has been practiced recently against the United States is specifically intended to cause market failure in the U.S. marketplace of ideas. At the same time, it is also clear that the First Amendment places significant limitations on direct U.S. government action to impede the flow of information from practitioners of cyber-enabled IW/IO to the United States.

Therefore, for the sake of analysis, this paper hypothesizes that there exist some indirect and thus constitutionally permissible strategies for combating IW/IO—strategies focusing, for example, on preventing unlawful foreign intervention in U.S. elections or in equipping U.S. audiences to be more cognizant of IW strategies and resistant to their influence. Assuming such strategies exist, it remains to be considered whether government has the expertise, knowledge, technical capabilities, and resources to act effectively and wisely in designing and implementing those strategies.

## U.S. government departments and agencies with some possible role in addressing adversary information warfare and influence operations

Given a host of other precedents regarding government regulation on the content of political speech, it is highly unlikely (arguably near-impossible) that any governmental restrictions on the content of political speech would stand up to scrutiny. Nevertheless, for the sake of argument, imagine that constitutional objections could be addressed successfully. In this hypothetical world, the government would be free to act—but would it have the expertise, knowledge, technical capabilities, and resources to act effectively and wisely?

The U.S. government consists of 15 departments (i.e., the executive departments of the executive branch) and a large number of agencies not affiliated with any department, each of which has different authorities for action and different expertise to support the exercise of those authorities.[35] What follows below is a listing of U.S. government departments and agencies whose mission and roles, in this author's assessment, have some possible relevance to addressing information warfare and/or influence operations conducted against the United States. (*Italicized material below refers to the part of the department or agency's authorities/mission/ expertise that may be relevant.*)

- The Department of Defense. The DOD has a well-articulated doctrine and framework for psychological operations—*how to use psychological operations against adversaries and how to respond to psychological operations conducted by adversaries.*[36] (The DOD has flipped repeatedly between "psychological operations" and "military information support operations" as the appropriate title for activities covered under this rubric.)

- The Department of Education. Under the rubric of the ED's mission to promote student achievement and preparation for global competitiveness by fostering educational excellence, *ED has from time to time supported efforts to promote critical thinking in schools.*[37]

- The Department of Justice. The DOJ prosecutes criminal activity. In February 2018, the DOJ indicted 13 Russian nationals and three Russian companies in connection with alleged interference with the 2016 campaign.[38] Specifically, *the indictment charged the defendants with one count of conspiracy "to defraud the United States by impairing, obstructing, and defeating the lawful functions of the Federal Election Commission, the U.S. Department of Justice, and the U.S. Department of State in administering federal requirements for disclosure of foreign involvement in certain domestic activities"* and one count of conspiracy to commit wire fraud and bank fraud by violating 18 USC Sections 1343 and 1344.

- The Department of State. Within the Department of State, the Under Secretary for Public Diplomacy and Public Affairs has the mission of supporting the achievement of U.S. foreign policy goals and objectives, advance national interests, and enhance national security by informing and influencing foreign publics and by expanding and strengthening the relationship between the people and Government of the United States and citizens of the rest of the world. The Under Secretary for Public Diplomacy and Public Affairs oversees the Bureau of Public Affairs (PA), the Bureau of International Information Programs (IIP), and the Global Engagement Center (GEC),[39] each of which with some expertise in some aspect of information warfare or influence operations.

  o The IIP supports people-to-people conversations with foreign publics on U.S. policy priorities, *developing multimedia communications products for both traditional communications and new media channels* and managing an overseas network of bricks-and-mortar American Spaces.[40]

o PA engages in strategic and tactical communications planning to advance America's foreign policy interests, uses social media and other modern technologies to engage the public, and oversees the State Department's six international Regional Media Hubs, which are overseas platforms for engagement of foreign audiences via the internet and broadcast and print media.[41]

o The GEC's role is to "lead, synchronize, and coordinate efforts of the Federal Government to recognize, understand, expose, and counter foreign state and non-state propaganda and disinformation efforts aimed at undermining United States national security interests."[42] In this role, it seeks to increase the reach and effectiveness of U.S. government communications; to identify efficiencies and opportunities in the messaging and partnership space, to drive a wedge between audiences that are most vulnerable to harmful propaganda and hostile nations, groups, and terrorists seeking to influence them; and to inject factual content about terrorist organizations into the information space to counter recruitment and radicalization to violence.

- The Broadcasting Board of Governors (BBG). The BBG's mission is *to inform, engage, and connect people around the world in support of freedom and democracy.*[43] The BBG oversees a number of international broadcast networks, including Voice of America; Radio Free Europe/Radio Liberty; Office of Cuba Broadcasting (including Radio and Television Martí and martinoticias.com); Radio Free Asia; Middle East Broadcasting Networks (including Alhurra Television, Radio Sawa and MBN Digital). These networks strive to provide programming that provides accurate, objective, and comprehensive news, especially in regions in which freedom of the press is limited, nonexistent, or not fully established.

- The Central Intelligence Agency (CIA). In 1976, the Senate Select Committee to Study Governmental Operations With Respect To Intelligence Activities reported that "The CIA currently maintains *a network of several hundred foreign individuals around the world who provide intelligence for the CIA and at times attempt to influence opinion through the use of covert propaganda.* These individuals provide the CIA with direct access to a large number of newspapers and periodicals, scores of press services and news agencies, radio and television stations, commercial book publishers, and other foreign media outlets."[44] If similar activities continue today, they are likely performed under authorities granted to the President under 50 USC § 3093 (Presidential approval and reporting of covert actions).

- The Federal Communications Commission. The role of the FCC is to promote connectivity and ensure a robust and competitive market in communications services such as cable, radio, television, satellite, and wire. The FCC is not permitted to promulgate regulations that infringe upon constitutionally protected free speech, even if such speech may be offensive to some parts of the public. On the other hand, *when certain kinds of speech are not fully protected (e.g., when speech can constitutionally be restricted or banned, as in the cases of indecent/profane or obscene material respectively), the FCC can and does enforce regulations to implement such restrictions or prohibitions.*[45]

- The Federal Election Commission (FEC). The FEC enforces federal campaign finance laws, which cover public disclosure of funds raised and spent to influence federal elections and restrictions on contributions and expenditures made to influence federal elections.[46] *For example, 52 USC 30121 makes it illegal for a foreign national, directly or indirectly, to make a contribution or donation of money or other thing of value in connection with a Federal election.*

- The Federal Trade Commission (FTC). The FTC works to prevent fraudulent, deceptive, and unfair business practices, and provide information to help consumers spot, stop, and avoid scams and fraud.[47]
- The Agency for International Development (USAID). USAID *promotes and demonstrates democratic values abroad*, and advances a free, peaceful, and prosperous world by providing international development and disaster assistance through partnerships and investments that save lives, reduce poverty, *strengthen democratic governance*, and help people emerge from humanitarian crises and progress beyond assistance.
- The Election Assistance Commission (EAC).[48] The Help America Vote Act of 2002 requires states to implement procedures for provisional voting, for providing voting information, for updating and upgrading voting equipment, implementing and maintaining statewide voter registration databases, for implementing voter identification procedures, and for managing procedures for administrative complaint. The EAC assists states in meeting these requirements, and under this rubric, it *maintains guidelines for electronic voting systems, operates the federal government's voting system certification program,* and administers a national clearinghouse on elections that includes shared practices, information for voters and other resources to improve elections.
- The National Science Foundation (NSF).[49] NSF is a federal agency created "to promote the progress of science; to advance the national health, prosperity, and welfare; *to secure the national defense* ..." Through grants and contracts, NSF supports basic research in all fields of fundamental science and engineering, except for medical sciences.[50]
- The National Endowment for the Humanities (NEH).[51] NEH promotes excellence in the humanities and *conveying the lessons of history to all Americans by awarding grants in the humanities*, which include but are not limited to the study and interpretation of "language, both modern and classical; linguistics; literature; history; jurisprudence; philosophy; archaeology; comparative religion; ethics; the history, criticism and theory of the arts; those aspects of social sciences which have humanistic content and employ humanistic methods; and the study and application of the humanities to the human environment with particular attention to reflecting our diverse heritage, traditions, and history and to the relevance of the humanities to the current conditions of national life."
- The Institute of Museum and Library Services (IMLS).[52] The IMLS mission supports America's museums, libraries, and related organizations through grantmaking, research, and policy development; these activities *promote literacy* and lifelong learning and increase access to information, ideas, and networks through libraries and museums.

### The bad fit of U.S. government authorities for addressing adversary information warfare and influence operations

The brief survey of Executive Branch departments and agencies suggests that a variety of U.S. government entities have some expertise that could be relevant to some aspects of the cyber-enabled information warfare/influence operations problem. But in most cases, the fit between the italicized authorities/mission/expertise and the cyber-enabled IW/IO conducted by adversaries in the United States is not quite right.

- The entity within the DOD responsible for homeland defense is the U.S. Northern Command (USNORTHCOM), which provides command and control for DOD homeland defense efforts and coordinates defense support of civil authorities. According to USNORTHCOM's web page,[53] USNORTHCOM is responsible for aerospace warning, aerospace control, and maritime warning for the continental United States (and Alaska and Canada as well). Its civil support mission includes domestic disaster relief operations that occur during fires, hurricanes, floods, and earthquakes, as well as counter-drug operations and managing the consequences of a terrorist event using weapons of mass destruction. Note the absence of any mention of combatting adversary propaganda—Northcom's military mission is to protect the homeland against physical attack, and its civil support mission is limited to responding to domestic disasters. More generally, 18 USC 1385 (also known as the Posse Comitatus Act) restricts the circumstances under which the Department of Defense can take action and the activities it can conduct within the United States.[54]
- Although the Department of Education has supported efforts to promote critical thinking in schools, education In the United States is primarily a state and local responsibility, and the federal government is not responsible for developing required curricula or determining requirements for enrollment and graduation. Thus, to the extent that instilling critical thinking habits enable citizens to better identify disinformation and fake news,[55] imparting those skills broadly to citizens in the course of their formal educational programs will not be a federal responsibility. Also, calls for the improvement of critical thinking in citizens have been common for at least a half-century,[56] and the same laments about the lack of critical thinking are seen today—a reality suggesting that the promotion of critical thinking skills in the population is at best a problem solved over a time scale measured in decades if not centuries.
- The DOJ indictments of February 2018 focused on conspiracy related to the nondisclosure of foreign involvement in certain domestic activities regarding U.S. elections in 2016.[57] But under U.S. law, both individuals and corporations and unions are allow to spend unlimited amounts of money on political messaging, as long as they operate independently of specific political campaigns.[58] Thus, it appears that if the activities alleged in the DOJ indictment had been undertaken by U.S. citizens properly registered as agents of foreign principals—and funded through mechanisms allowed by U.S. law—no U.S. laws would have been violated.
- The State Department's activities to advance U.S. foreign policy interests through people-to-people interactions and various strategic and tactical communications activities target foreign audiences and are not a defense against cyber-enabled IW/IO carried out against U.S. citizens.[59] The activities of the GEC have only recently turned to disinformation efforts conducted by nation states, and most of these activities focus on audiences outside the United States, relying on "fact-based narratives and analyses to counter adversarial foreign propaganda and disinformation directed at the United States and United States allies and partner nations."[60] However, one important focus of GEC activities calls for proposals to "identify, catalogue and, where feasible, quantify current and emerging trends in adversarial foreign propaganda and disinformation in order to

coordinate and shape the development of tactics, techniques, and procedures to expose and refute foreign disinformation." This last focus is directly on point but assumes the consumers of foreign disinformation actually care about being properly informed.

- As with the State Department, the Broadcasting Board of Governors operates outside U.S. territory, and thus their programming activities do not focus on U.S. citizens and cannot be a defense against cyber-enabled IW/IO carried out against U.S. citizens.
- The CIA has substantial expertise in propaganda and psychological operations, and could provide advice to other U.S. government agencies, but it is not permitted to conduct operations in the United States. Moreover, according to 50 USC 3093, covert action undertaken by the U.S. government must not involve any action that would violate the U.S. Constitution.[61] Additionally, it appears that Russian efforts to interfere with the U.S. political system, including the 2016 election, started at least as early as 2014.[62] If so, it suggests a possible intelligence failure—that the CIA (and the U.S. intelligence community more broadly) either did not know about the election threat posed by the Russians until two years after they had started or it did know and failed to disseminate information about that threat throughout the U.S. government.
- The ability of the FCC to restrict certain kinds of speech is limited today to "broadcast media." The Communications Act of 1934 establishes the authority of the FCC to manage the use of the relevant portion of the electromagnetic spectrum, which broadcast media—by definition—use. But the FCC lacks authority to interfere with speech—constitutionally protected or not—in any other kind of media, and in particular, today lacks the authority to do so on the Internet. As noted above, political speech receives the highest levels of constitutional protection.
- Federal campaign finance laws, enforced by the FEC, are for the most part intended to increase the transparency of political advertising. On March 26, 2018, the FEC issued a notice of proposed rule-making that would require political advertising on internet-enabled devices and applications to disclose the sources that funded such advertising.[63] The notice also noted the opinion of the U.S. Supreme Court in Citizens' United that "identification of the source of advertising may be required as a means of disclosure, so that the people will be able to evaluate the arguments to which they are being subjected."[64] However, the proposed rule does rest on several assumptions: that issue advertising (i.e., advertising that is not explicitly tied to a specific political campaign or party) is comparatively less important than political advertising, that citizens actually do care about who is funding a political ad, and that the identity disclosure requirements cannot easily be circumvented.
- The FTC's authority prevents fraudulent, deceptive, and unfair business practices, and provides information to help consumers spot, stop, and avoid scams and fraud have been limited to transactions in which consumers exchange money with a real or alleged goods or service provider, and almost certainly does not extend to election practices in which citizens lose no money.
- USAID only acts abroad, and thus has no authority or responsibility for domestic action.
- The Election Assistance Commission has provides assistance to the states for election administration, an activity that includes building and securing HAVA-mandated state voter registration databases and certifying the security of computer-based electronic voting machines. But as noted in Section 2, cybersecurity threats (such as these) are distinct from cyber-enabled IW/IO threats.

**178** Herbert Lin

- The National Science Foundation, the National Endowment for the Humanities, and the Institute of Museum and Library Services carry out their missions primarily through grant-making activities, and they do not have significant operational responsibilities regardless of the expertise that any of their staff may have as a result of those activities.

More broadly, this brief survey of departmental and agency authorities also suggests two high-level observations. First, the legal authorities of U.S. government departments and agencies have yet to catch up to the problem of cyber-enabled IW/IO conducted against the United States. Indeed, U.S. government authorities that might possibly be useful continue to be premised on the existence of a marketplace of ideas that works well to inform a public that routinely and systematically engages in critical thinking and reflection on political matters, even in an Internet-enabled information environment manipulated by sophisticated nation-state adversaries.

Second and perhaps more importantly, given the diffuse nature of the cyber-enabled IW/IO problem, it is not at all clear how the U.S. government could draw a "bubble chart"—that is, a chart depicting the organizational units sharing a common objective—with unambiguous lines of responsibility and authority. Who or what existing entity could be put "in charge" of responding to cyber-enabled IW/IO? If, as seems likely, no existing entity could do the job, what charge should be given to a new entity to address the problem?

To appreciate the complexity of the problem posed by cyber-enabled IW/IO, it is helpful to consider two other examples. One example is provided in Figure 11.1, which presents what is colloquially known in U.S. government cybersecurity circles as the "bubble chart"—it outlines the residence within the U.S. government of responsibility for different aspects of cybersecurity. Officials from the Obama Administration say that the chart was revised between 50 and 100 times before a consensus on its content was achieved.

The key feature of the cyber bubble chart is the spaces between the three bubbles, which refer to the Departments of Defense, Homeland Security, and Justice (FBI). With anything more than one bubble, there are necessarily gray areas in between them—gray areas in which responsibilities are unclear and information flows will be impeded in many possible operational scenarios. Put differently, the bubble chart clearly shows three distinct bubbles, with zero overlap between them. A footnote to the bubble chart explains why: "Nothing in this chart alters existing DHS, DOJ, and DOD roles, responsibilities, or authorities." And deliberations over the bubble chart for cybersecurity were conducted in the context of an accepted U.S. government definition of cybersecurity articulated in NSPD-54.

If it was so difficult to reach consensus on an issue area as well specified as cybersecurity, imagine the difficulties in determining responsibilities for a threat as diffuse as that posed by information warfare and influence operations.

A second example is from the early 1950s, when the U.S. government became aware of a national security threat from electromagnetic warfare, which was "the contest through preclusive use, jamming, interference and related measures for the control of all or parts of the radio spectrum or the denial of its use by others" and having a "direct bearing on diplomacy, limited or total military operations, economic warfare, psychological warfare and telecommunications policy."[65] According to an archive-based study by Jonathan Winkler,[66]

> Attempts to address these problems [i.e., the problems posed by electromagnetic warfare] required a level of interaction between the military, diplomatic, and

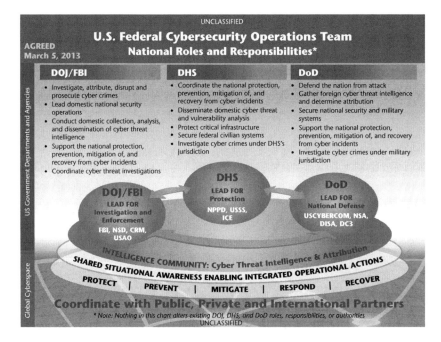

**FIGURE 11.1** Bubble chart for U.S. government cybersecurity roles and responsibilities

intelligence communities for which they were not prepared and that only the NSC could oversee. Even then, the matter was so complex that even the senior officials themselves acknowledged that it required presidential intervention and the emplacement of a technical advisor at the president's side.

Although the Eisenhower administration was able to address the problem in the short run by building additional communications facilities for the Department of Defense,

> the complex interconnected issues identified at the time by the participants about synthesizing federal defense requirements with civilian capabilities, making more efficient use of the radio spectrum, and balancing the desire for efficiency against the traditions of antimonopoly and plurality proved insurmountable.

Moreover,

> It was not possible to agree on whether there should be someone in the cabinet who would handle the problem of electromagnetic warfare and who that person should be .... Neither the Truman nor Eisenhower administrations could figure out how best to balance these weights in the absence of clear authority for dealing with the dual-use technology in war, peace, or somewhere in between such as the Cold War.

Winkler further writes that

> in 1953, NSC officials lamented that "the relative importance of this whole field of

activity" was not clear. They were unsure "whether a new agency is required, a new PSB-type Board, a new bureau in an old-line department like Commerce, or a staff in the Executive Office of the President. The Bureau [of the Budget] apparently needs guidance as to whether it might be raising a technical function too high, or not raising an extremely important function high enough."

To this author, the organizational parallels between the U.S. government trying to respond to the threat of electromagnetic warfare and trying to respond to cyber-enabled IW/IO are striking.

## Conclusion

In 1927, Supreme Court Justice Louis Brandeis' concurring opinion in *Whitney v. California* stated that:

> no danger flowing from speech can be deemed clear and present unless the incidence of the evil apprehended is so imminent that it may befall before there is opportunity for full discussion. If there be time to expose through discussion the falsehood and fallacies, to avert the evil by the processes of education, the remedy to be applied is more speech, not enforced silence. Only an emergency can justify repression.[67]

This extended passage is often summarized as "the cure for bad speech is more speech." But the information environment has changed greatly since 1927. Justice Brandeis' conclusion relies on citizens having the "opportunity for full discussion" and time to "avert the evil by the processes of education." Given the vastly increased volume and velocity of information today and cyber-enabled information warfare and influence operations exploiting these characteristics of the environment, both opportunity and time are in short supply.

As argued above, the likelihood of government action against the cyber-enabled proliferation of false, misleading, or inauthentic statements designed to manipulate and distort the political process is exceedingly low under current interpretations of the First Amendment. But constitutional interpretations do sometimes change in response to changes in circumstance and environment, although slowly. This author will not go further than to note that the advent of cyber-enabled speech of various kinds poses a significant and qualitatively different environment that may warrant such change in the future.

It is clearly good that some degree of public attention has been focused on the problems posed by cyber-enabled IW/IO conducted against the United States. But as serious as foreign election interference is to the nation's future, the real threat to the republic is the tribal and toxic nature of political discourse of today. Such tensions have been rising for some time, and yet their enormous amplification through cyber-enabled IW/IO has been shocking to many observers. Moreover, U.S. law today does not forbid any of the activities that might themselves be characterized as cyber-enabled IW/IO—in fact, First Amendment jurisprudence protects many of them explicitly.

Given the limitations on government action described above, action to ameliorate the problem by the private sector is a possible alternative. Indeed, the private sector in the United States owns and operates much of the technological infrastructure that provides the cyber-enabling part of cyber-enabled IW/IO. And the First Amendment places no constraints on private sector action, a point misunderstood by many citizens.

This paper does not address possible private sector actions, except to make the following point. The First Amendment would severely limit the influence that the U.S. government could exercise with respect to entities in the private sector. That is, government law, regulation, or policy to influence private sector actions would also be subject to court challenge if those actions impeded the free expression of ideas and opinions. However, if private sector entities were themselves willing to take such actions on their own (e.g., because they decided to do so as part of a different business model or as a matter of corporate ethics or, possibly, as a part of incentives that the U.S. government might offer), they would be entirely free to do so.[68]

In this new environment, perhaps a new social contract is needed between citizens and government regarding the extent and nature of the rights afforded by the First Amendment, which was adopted more than two centuries before the invention of the World Wide Web. Perhaps the private sector will find a business model that enables them to profit from more civil and reasoned discourse. Perhaps researchers will find effective ways to depolarize political dialogue. These elements may—or may not—have a place in a serious strategy for how to deal with the problems posed by cyber-enabled IW/IO, but whatever that strategy entails, the design of such a strategy is a necessary pre-requisite for any serious discussion of how the U.S. government should be structured to address these problems.

It may be possible to find a national consensus about awareness of the dangers of the problem posed by cyber-enabled information warfare and influence operations—obviously a necessary first step. But even with good leadership addressing the issue—focused on the problem; consistent in its approach (whatever it may be); committed to the idea of reality-based policy discourse—organizing the various assets of the U.S. government and the private sector—a whole-of-nation response rather than a whole-of-government response—to handle such a diverse threat would be a difficult if not daunting task. If national leaders deny the existence of the problem or benefit from it, making meaningful progress will be much, much more difficult.

I have argued that the information marketplace metaphor fails in the information environment and in the face of a foreign cyber-enabled information IW/IO threat that further undermines the operation of that market. Thus, we will need to examine what kind of coordinated national response is possible that would not threaten the values that underlie the First Amendment. We have our work cut out for us.

## Notes

1 I am grateful to Sonja Swanbeck for research assistance on the section in this chapter entitled "Future cyber-enabled capabilities for IW/IO." In addition, an early draft was helpfully critiqued by Matthew Waxman, Kurt Sanger, Jack Goldsmith, Jon Hermann, Anne Applebaum, Braden Allenby, Robert Jervis, Rosanna Guandango, and Peter Shane.
2 Also known as "influence operations."
3 This description of information warfare and influence operations is taken from Herbert Lin and Jaclyn Kerr, "On Cyber-Enabled Information/Influence Warfare and Manipulation", August 8, 2017, forthcoming *Oxford Handbook of Cybersecurity*, 2018. Available at SSRN: https://ssrn.com/abstract=3015680.
4 On soft power, see Joseph Nye, *Soft Power: The Means to Success in World Politics*, 2004. On sharp power, see Christopher Walker and Jessica Ludwig, "The Meaning of Sharp Power: How

Authoritarian States Project Influence," *Foreign Affairs*, November 16, 2017, www.foreignaffairs.com/articles/china/2017-11-16/meaning-sharp-power.

5 Office of the Director of National Intelligence, *Assessing Russian Activities and Intentions in Recent US Elections*, ICA 2017–01D, January 2017, www.dni.gov/files/documents/ICA_2017_01.pdf.

6 Statement of James R. Clapper, Former Director of National Intelligence, Before the Committee on the Judiciary, Subcommittee on Crime and Terrorism, United States Senate, Concerning Russian Interference in the 2016 United States Election, May 8, 2017, www.judiciary.senate.gov/imo/media/doc/05-08-17%20Clapper%20Testimony.pdf "The Russians used cyber operations against both political parties, including hacking into servers used by the Democratic National Committee and releasing stolen data to WikiLeaks and other media outlets. Russia also collected on certain Republican party-affiliated targets, but did not release any Republican-related data."

7 It should be recognized that these "overt" efforts were covert in at least one sense—the Russian actors concealed their identities in conducting their activities on social media.

8 Written Testimony of Colin Stretch, General Counsel, Facebook, to the Senate Judiciary Subcommittee on Crime and Terrorism, Hearing on "Extremist Content and Russian Information Online: Working with Tech to Find Solutions," October 31, 2017, www.judiciary.senate.gov/imo/media/doc/10-31-17%20Stretch%20Testimony.pdf.

9 Written Testimony of Sean J. Edgett, Acting General Counsel, Twitter, to the Senate Judiciary Subcommittee on Crime and Terrorism, Hearing on "Extremist Content and Russian Information Online: Working with Tech to Find Solutions," October 31, 2017, www.judiciary.senate.gov/imo/media/doc/10-31-17%20Edgett%20Testimony.pdf.

10 Written Testimony of Richard Salgado Senior Counsel, Law Enforcement and Information Security, Google, to the Senate Judiciary Subcommittee on Crime and Terrorism, Hearing on "Extremist Content and Russian Information Online: Working with Tech to Find Solutions," October 31, 2017, www.judiciary.senate.gov/imo/media/doc/10-31-17%20Salgado%20Testimony.pdf.

11 https://newsroom.fb.com/news/2018/04/restricting-data-access/.

12 www.reuters.com/article/us-facebook-cambridge-analytica/cambridge-analytica-ceo-claims-influence-on-u-s-election-facebook-questioned-idUSKBN1GW1SG.

13 Richard Gunther, Paul A. Beck, and Erik C. Nisbet, "Fake News May Have Contributed to Trump's 2016 Victory," March 8, 2018, https://assets.documentcloud.org/documents/4429952/Fake-News-May-Have-Contributed-to-Trump-s-2016.pdf. An earlier version of this report was published in *The Conversation*, February 15, 2018, http://theconversation.com/study-suggests-trump-may-owe-his-2016-victory-to-fake-news-91538.

14 Senate intelligence committee hearing in November 2017 on Social Media Influence in the 2016 U.S. Elections. www.intelligence.senate.gov/hearings/open-hearing-social-media-influence-2016-us-elections.

15 www.youtube.com/watch?v=Zjavv6DepKs&feature=youtu.be&t=16m.

16 The very term "act of war", let alone "act of cyberwar," is problematic from an international legal standpoint, as the term "act of war" has been replaced by terms used in the UN Charter, namely "armed attack" and "use of force." The Charter does not define these terms with any specificity, and since the Charter was written in 1945, long before cyber conflict was ever imagined as an issue of international relations, it is most unclear how "armed attack" and "use of force" apply to cyber war. Perhaps more importantly, how any nation under any particular circumstances interpret "armed attack" or "use of force" is first and foremost a political decision. Different governments in different nations under different circumstances will interpret it differently.

17 www.lankford.senate.gov/news/press-releases/senators-introduce-revised-secure-elections-act-with-burr-warners-support.

18 White House, *Cybersecurity Policy*, National Security Presidential Directive 54, January 8, 2008, https://fas.org/irp/offdocs/nspd/nspd-54.pdf.

19 A vulnerability is a design or implementation flaw in a system that may have been introduced accidentally (in which case it is usually called a "bug") or deliberately (e.g., by an untrustworthy insider). A system with a vulnerability can be penetrated by an adversary who knows of it. When an adversary uses a vulnerability that is unknown to others to effect penetration, it is termed a "zero-day" vulnerability, since the victim will have had zero days to repair it.

20 Adam Hulcoop et al., *TAINTED LEAKS: Disinformation and Phishing with a Russian Nexus*, Citizen's Lab, University of Toronto, May 25, 2017, https://citizenlab.ca/2017/05/tainted-leaks-disinformation-phish.

21 https://arstechnica.com/information-technology/2017/05/facebook-helped-advertisers-target-teens-who-feel-worthless/

22 https://arstechnica.com/information-technology/2017/05/facebook-helped-advertisers-target-teens-who-feel-worthless/

23 Annalyn Kurtz (Mar. 2017), "Regulators are Warning People not to fall for this sneaky phone scam," *Fortune Magazine*. Accessed at: http://fortune.com/2017/03/28/yes-scam-phone-call/

24 Matthew Gault (Nov 2016), " After 20 minutes of listening, new Adobe tool can make you say anything," Motherboard, https://motherboard.vice.com/en_us/article/jpgkxp/after-20-minutes-of-listening-new-adobe-tool-can-make-you-say-anything

25 Peter Dockrill, "Adobe's New 'Photoshop For Voice' App Lets You Put Words in People's Mouths", *Science Alert*, 11 November 2016, www.sciencealert.com/adobe-s-new-photoshop-for-voice-app-lets-you-put-words-in-people-s-mouths.

26 Initial experiments demonstrated a success against these facial recognition systems at a rate between 55 and 85% (see Lily Hay Newman (Aug. 2016) "Hackers trick facial-recognition logins with photos from Facebook (What else?)," *Wired*. Accessed at: www.wired.com/2016/08/hackers-trick-facial-recognition-logins-photos-facebook-thanks-zuck/). Using headshots of each individual taken under ideal lighting conditions (rather than the publicly available pictures from Facebook), the researchers were able to fool all five of the face recognition systems (see Yi Xu, True Price, Jan Michael Frahm, Fabian Monrose (2016) "Virtual U: Defeating Face Liveness Detection by Building Virtual Models from your Public Photos," *Proceedings of the 25th USENIX Security Symposium*. Accessed at: www.usenix.org/system/files/conference/usenixsecurity16/sec16_paper_xu.pdf).

27 Supasorn Suwajanakorn, Steven Seitz, and Ira Kemelmacher-Schilzerman (2017) "Synthesizing Obama: Learning Lip Sync from Audio," *ACM Transactions on Graphics* 36(4). Accessed at: http://grail.cs.washington.edu/projects/AudioToObama/siggraph17_obama.pdf

28 Justus Thies et al. (2016) "Face2Face: Real-time Face Capture and Reenactment of RGB Videos" Proceedings of Computer Vision and Pattern Recognition. Accessed at: www.graphics.stanford.edu/~niessner/papers/2016/1facetoface/thies2016face.pdf

29 In addition to the cases described in notes 51 and 52, see also *Meese v. Keene, 481 U.S. 465* (1987), https://supreme.justia.com/cases/federal/us/481/465/ (the Court was critical of a "paternalistic assumption that the public will misunderstand" the use of the term "political propaganda" and therefore will "misuse [that] information") and *United States v. Alvarez, 567 U.S. 709* (2012) ("the Court has never endorsed the categorical rule … that false statements receive no First Amendment protection").

30 Mill, John Stuart. *On Liberty*. London: Longman, Roberts & Green, 1869; Bartleby.com, 1999.

31 Tim Wu has also explored this issue, arguing that "it is no longer speech itself that is scarce, but the attention of listeners," an assertion that, if true, undercuts the basis on which the First Amendment was originally written and adopted. See Tim Wu, *Is the First Amendment Obsolete?*, Knight First Amendment Institute, Columbia University, September 2017, https://knightcolumbia.org/content/tim-wu-first-amendment-obsolete.

32 The following old story illustrates that sometimes the best way to lie is to tell the truth. A merchant ship docks in a new harbor. First night, the first mate goes ashore and returns drunk. The next morning, the captain enters into the ship's log: "The first mate returned drunk last night." The first mate pleads with the captain: "Captain, please don't let that stay in the log", the mate said. "This could keep me from getting a promotion." The captain says: "It is true that you returned drunk last night, and if it is true it has to go in the log. That's the rule." Next night, captain goes ashore and returns sober. The first mate enters into the log: "The captain returned sober last night."

33 *Lamont v. Postmaster General, 381 U.S. 301* (1965).

34 *Stanley v. Georgia, 394 U.S. 557* (1969).

35 The names and missions of U.S. government executive branch departments can be found at www.usa.gov/executive-departments; as of this writing, 15 departments are listed. As for U.S. government agencies not affiliated with any department, the term "independent agency" is not sufficiently well-defined for analytical purposes. The Administrative Conference of the United States (www.acus.gov/sites/default/files/documents/Sourcebook%202012%20FINAL_May%202013.pdf) notes

that there is no widely accepted definition of that term, noting that some scholars use the term to mean "any agency created outside the EOP [Executive Office of the President] or executive departments," while other scholars use the term to denote agencies whose leaders can only be removed "for cause," "inefficiency, neglect of duty, or malfeasance in office," or similar language. As the ACUS notes, "independence in this context means independence from political interference, particularly removal by the President." This paper has used an operational definition of the universe of agencies to be considered—the entities listed in the 2012 ACUS report as "independent agencies" as well as those listed on www.usa.gov/independent-agencies as "independent agencies."

36 Joint Chiefs of Staff, *Joint Publication 3–13.2, Psychological Operations*, Department of Defense, 2010, https://fas.org/irp/doddir/dod/jp3-13-2.pdf

37 See, for example, https://ies.ed.gov/funding/grantsearch/details.asp?ID=1397.

38 UNITED STATES OF AMERICA v. INTERNET RESEARCH AGENCY LLC et al., February 16, 2018, www.justice.gov/file/1035477/download.

39 www.state.gov/r/index.htm.

40 www.state.gov/r/iip/

41 www.state.gov/r/pa/

42 www.state.gov/r/gec/index.htm

43 www.bbg.gov/who-we-are/mission/

44 Final Report of the Select Committee to Study Governmental Operations With Respect To Intelligence Activities, United States Senate (the report is also known as the Church Committee report), www.intelligence.senate.gov/sites/default/files/94755_I.pdf, page 455.

45 www.fcc.gov/consumers/guides/fcc-and-freedom-speech.

46 www.fec.gov/about/mission-and-history/

47 www.usa.gov/federal-agencies/federal-trade-commission

48 www.eac.gov/about/help-america-vote-act.

49 www.nsf.gov/about.

50 www.nsf.gov/about.

51 www.neh.gov/about.

52 www.imls.gov/about-us.

53 www.northcom.mil/About-USNORTHCOM/

54 For the view of the Department of Defense on the restrictions imposed by the Posse Comitatus Act, see www.esd.whs.mil/Portals/54/Documents/DD/issuances/dodm/302501_vol03.pdf. According to this document, DOD can provide support to civilian law enforcement agencies, to the U.S. Secret Service, and for counter-drug operations.

55 See, for example, www.chronicle.com/paid-article/In-fake-news-climate-critical/36.

56 Raymond B. Fox, "Difficulties in Developing Skill in Critical Thinking", *The Journal of Educational Research* 55(7):335–337, April 1962, www.jstor.org/stable/27531140.

57 U.S. Department of Justice, indictment of Internet Research Agency, UNITED STATES OF AMERICA v. INTERNET RESEARCH AGENCY, February 26, 2018, page 3, www.justice.gov/file/1035477/download.

58 On individuals, see *Buckley v. Valeo, 424 U.S. 1* (1976), "The First Amendment requires the invalidation of the Act's independent expenditure ceiling, its limitation on a candidate's expenditures from his own personal funds, and its ceilings on over-all campaign expenditures, since those provisions place substantial and direct restrictions on the ability of candidates, citizens, and associations to engage in protected political expression, restrictions that the First Amendment cannot tolerate." The Act referred to above is the Federal Election Campaign Act of 1971, as amended in 1974, which limited expenditures by individuals or groups "relative to a clearly identified candidate" to $1,000 per candidate per election. On corporations, see *Citizens United v. Federal Election Commission, 558 U.S. 310* (2010), majority opinion by Justice Kennedy: "wealthy individuals and unincorporated associations can spend unlimited amounts on independent expenditures. Yet certain disfavored associations of citizens—those that have taken on the corporate form—are penalized for engaging in the same political speech … When Government seeks to use its full power, including the criminal law, to command where a person may get his or her information or what distrusted source he or she may not hear, it uses censorship to control thought. This is unlawful. The First Amendment confirms the freedom to think for ourselves."

59 I note without further comment that as positive and enlightened as these Department activities are from a U.S. perspective, one has to wonder how the governments of those audiences targeted by these activities feel about such communications.

60 www.grants.gov/web/grants/view-opportunity.html?oppId=301460.

61 In practice, this requirement shapes the scope and nature of U.S. propaganda because of concerns that such propaganda might reach and thus improperly influence U.S. persons.

62 U.S. Department of Justice, indictment of Internet Research Agency, *UNITED STATES OF AMERICA v. INTERNET RESEARCH AGENCY*, February 26, 2018, page 3, www.justice. gov/file/1035477/download.

63 FEDERAL ELECTION COMMISSION, 11 CFR Parts 100 and 110, Notice 2018–06, "Internet Communication Disclaimers and Definition of "Public Communication,"" *Federal Register* 83(58): 12864–12880, March 26, 2018. The notice covered "public communications on the internet that contain express advocacy, solicit contributions, or are made by political committees," colloquially referred to as "political advertising," and proposed a disclaimer (i.e., a notice to the public regarding the identity of the payor or sponsor of such public communications."

64 https://supreme.justia.com/cases/federal/us/558/310/opinion.html

65 Briefing notes, "Soviet Capability for Waging Electromagnetic Warfare," February 11, 1953, CIA-RDP80R01443R000100220012–5, CIA CREST database (hereafter CIA CREST), National Archives and Records Administration (hereafter USNA); Appendix 2, NSC 137, cited in Appendix II, Jackson Report (Report of President's Committee on International Information Activities), June 30, 1953, Special Collection, "Intelligence, Policy and Politics: The DCI, the White House, and Congress," doc. 5166d49399326091c6a60500, CIA FOIA Electronic Reading Room, 111–13. [Citation found in the Winkler paper of Footnote 94.]

66 Jonathan Winkler, The Forgotten Menace of Electro-Magnetic Warfare in the Early Cold War *Diplomatic History*, 42(2):254–280, April 2018, https://academic.oup.com/dh/article-abstract/42/ 2/254/3896229.

67 *Whitney v. California, 274 U.S. 357* (1927). https://supreme.justia.com/cases/federal/us/274/357/ case.html.

68 In August 2018, Apple, YouTube (owner and operated by Alphabet), Facebook, and Spotify took down podcasts and channels associated with Alex Jones, asserting that the Infowars author and founder had violated community standards for content posting. See Rich McKay, "Apple, YouTube, and others drop conspiracy theorist Alex Jones," *Reuters*, August 6, 2018, www. reuters.com/article/us-apple-infowars/apple-youtube-and-others-drop-conspiracy-theorist-alex-jones-idUSKBN1KR0MZ.

# 12

# VIRTUAL DISENFRANCHISEMENT

## Cyber election meddling in the grey zones of international law

*Michael Schmitt*

## Introduction

In the aftermath of the 2016 presidential election, outgoing administration officials, including President Barack Obama and senior leaders of the intelligence community, accused the Russian government of meddling in U.S. elections.[1] European leaders raised similar concerns regarding Russian interference in European elections.[2] In contrast, President Donald Trump labeled the claims a hoax, announced that he believed Russian President Vladimir Putin's denials of meddling, and called the intelligence agency directors political hacks.[3] Now, more than a year after his inauguration, President Trump continues to claim that the Russians had no impact on our votes whatsoever.[4]

The possibility that one State might interfere in the political processes of another is hardly shocking. Indeed, the U.S. has a long history of involving itself covertly and overtly in foreign elections.[5] But targeting a super power with an influence campaign that exploited social media and remotely conducting active intrusions into its cyber infrastructure marked a significant escalation in election meddling.[6] Various aspects of the Russian campaign almost certainly violated U.S. law, as suggested by the U.S. Department of Justice's February 2018 indictment under U.S. law of numerous Russians and Russian entities with close ties to the government.[7] Far less certain is the character of the operations under international law.

This article addresses the legality of both the Russian influence campaign and, since it is a growing phenomenon, cyber meddling in general. It attempts to pinpoint when cyber election meddling amounts to one or more internationally wrongful acts, that is, when it is unlawful under international law and identifies responses available to the target State under international law.

Such internationally wrongful acts consist of two elements.[8] First, there must be a breach of a State's legal obligation through either commission or omission. Second, the act in question must be attributeable to the State concerned pursuant to the law of State responsibility. Following the examination of these two issues as applied to cyber operations, the article turns to possible responses under international law by a State that is the target of cyber election meddling. Determining that many cyber operations lie within a grey zone of legal uncertainty, particularly with respect to the applicable legal thresholds for unlawfulness,[9] it concludes with the author's reflections on the consequences of this uncertainty vis-à-vis cyber election meddling.

## The context

The most professional and thorough open-source analysis of the Russian influence campaign is the summary of a classified report on the matter prepared by the U.S. Central Intelligence Agency (CIA), Federal Bureau of Investigation (FBI), and the National Security Agency (NSA) under the auspices of the Office of the Director of National Intelligence (ODNI).[10] Released less than two weeks before President Trump's inauguration, the report's key findings, offered with a high degree of confidence,[11] were straightforward:

> Russian President Vladimir Putin ordered an influence campaign in 2016 aimed at the U.S. presidential election. Russia's goals were to undermine public faith in the U.S. democratic process, denigrate Secretary Clinton, and harm her electability and potential presidency. We further assess Putin and the Russian Government developed a clear preference for President-elect Trump.[12]

The CIA and FBI concurred, also with a high degree of confidence, that Putin and the Russian Government aspired to help President-elect Trump's election chances when possible by discrediting Secretary Clinton and publicly contrasting her unfavorably to him.[13] The NSA agreed, but only with a moderate degree of confidence.[14] Interestingly, once it appeared that Clinton would prevail, the goal of the Russian operations shifted from supporting Trump to undermining the coming Clinton presidency.[15] According to the report, the Russian cyber influence campaign, which was approved at the highest levels of the Russian government, was multifaceted.[16]

In terms of Russian legal responsibility, the most significant operations were mounted by Russian military intelligence, the General Staff Main Intelligence Directorate or GRU. The GRU hacked into personal email accounts of Democratic Party officials and other political figures and exfiltrated a great deal of data from the Democratic National Committee (DNC) in March 2016.[17] It then utilized the Guccifer 2.0 persona, DCLeaks.com, and WikiLeaks to distribute the material, including through various exclusive releases to the media.[18] Additionally, the Russian efforts included hacking into state and local boards of election to acquire a capability to exploit them, although apparently no votes were affected.[19]

During this period, an active Russian propaganda campaign involving numerous media outlets, including RT and Sputnik, was also underway.[20] More legally significant than this classic form of political propaganda were the social media activities of quasi-government trolls who amplified stories of scandals about Secretary Clinton and the role of WikiLeaks in the election campaign.[21]

The troll farm, known as the Internet Research Agency, was financed by a close Putin ally with ties to Russian intelligence.[22] Although the organizations mission was to support the Russian domestic and international political agenda, the extent of control the government exercised over the Internet Research Agency remains unclear; a fact that, as will be explained, hinders legal attribution of its operations to the State.[23]

**188** Michael Schmitt

Consisting of over ninety trolls, the Internet Research Agency spent in excess of two million dollars to purchase anti-Clinton and pro-Trump advertising on social media plat forms such as Twitter, Facebook, and Instagram.[24] Using more than 120 groups and social media accounts, the objective was not only to convince individuals how to vote, but also to keep certain voters from the polls. For example, some messaging claimed that Hillary Clinton doesn't deserve the black vote![25] Trolls also leveraged social media to encourage nearly forty anti-Clinton protests and pro-Trump rallies in swing states.[26]

The following year, ODNI released its annual Worldwide Threat Assessment, which warned that [f]foreign elections are critical inflection points that offer opportunities for Russia to advance its interests both overtly and covertly, and that [t]he 2018 U.S. mid-term elections are a potential target for Russian influence operations.[27] Three days later, the grand jury in Special Counsel Robert Muellers investigation indicted thirteen individuals and three companies associated with the trolling operations.[28]

Those indicted worked for the Internet Research Agency and were accused of con-spiring with each other and with persons known and unknown to defraud the U.S. by impairing, obstructing, and defeating the lawful functions of the government through fraud and deceit for the purpose of interfering with the U.S. political and electoral processes, including the presidential election of 2016.[29] In line with the 2017 intelligence commu-nities assessment, the indictment alleged that by early to mid-2016, Defendants operations included supporting the presidential campaign of the candidate Donald J. Trump and disparaging Hillary Clinton.[30] They also involved the use of social media to criticize Republican candidates Ted Cruz and Marco Rubio, as well as to support the Bernie Sanders campaign.[31]

Of particular importance with regard to international law and the issue of legal attribution that is discussed below is the allegation that the defendants posed as Americans, created false American personas, and stole the identities of real Americans in the effort to leverage social media.[32] At times, some of the defendants even traveled to the U.S. and used U.S.-based cyber infrastructure to mask the Russian origin of their activities.

The week after the indictments were issued, President Trump took to Twitter to claim that "[t]he results of the 2016 election were not impacted or changed" and to allege "[c]ollusion between Russia and Crooked H, the DNC and the Dems."[33] Heal so chastised then-National Security Adviser H.R. McMaster for failing to make the same claim during his address to the Munich Security Conference.[34]

The U.S. is not alone in falling victim to election cyber meddling. A sampling of such cyber operations signals their growing appeal to States wishing to manipulate foreign elec-tions. Most well known are the 2014 Cyber Berkut (a group of Russian hacktivists) op-erations targeting the Ukrainian Central Election Commission. Elements of the Commissions network were down for nearly twenty hours and on election day a false winner was an-nounced.[35] Two years later, the GRU, specifically its APT-28 or Fancy Bear hacking unit, targeted the German Bundestag, Germany's Foreign and Finance Ministries, and the Christian Democratic Unions (the party of Chancellor Angela Merkel) systems.[36] Likewise, in 2017, Emmanuel Macron's campaign for the French Presidency was the object of cyber operations that some experts attribute to the GRU.[37] The operations involved phishing attacks meant to implant malware on the campaigns website. Reportedly, the operations digital fingerprints resembled those of the operations against the U.S. Democratic National Committee and Angela Merkels campaign the previous year.[38]

In November 2017, such activities led U.K. Prime Minister Theresa May—just a week after Trump stated that he believed Putin's denial of meddling—to announce,

> We know what you are doing and you will not succeed because you underestimate the resilience of our democracies, the enduring attraction of free and open societies and the commitment of Western nations to the alliances that bind us.[39]

At the same time, the U.K. Electoral Commission opened an investigation into whether the Brexit vote had been targeted.[40]

Even Russia purportedly was victimized by cyber meddling during its presidential election. In 2018, RT News reported a distributed denial of service attack on the Russian Central Election Commission that originated from locations in fifteen countries.[41] The Commission Chairperson stated that the attack had no effect, as its automated election system is not connected to the global network.[42]

The U.S. does not come to the table with clean hands, having aggressively engaged in covert operations to influence elections from the 1950s through the 1980s, including such notable examples as Guatemala, Iran, Chile, and Nicaragua. More recently, the U.S. offered economic aid to Russia in an attempt to bolster support for Boris Yeltsin during his 1996 reelection campaign.[43] The U.S. employed the same technique in support of Fatah in the 2006 Palestinian elections, and during the 2005 Iraqi elections Congress blocked a plan to covertly fund certain candidates.[44]

Four years later, the U.S. unsuccessfully tried to prevent the reelection of Afghan President Hamid Karzai.[45] An Afghan Supreme Court justice, who was one of the two Afghans on the five member Electoral Complaints Commission, resigned his post in protest over foreign interference.[46] Indeed, there is a long- standing U.S. practice of supporting both opposition and civic groups active in mobilizing voters, as in the 2000 re-election campaign of Slobodan Milosevic and on a recurring basis in Belarus in an effort to weaken President Alexander Lukashenko.[47] As Loch Johnson, has observed:

> We've been doing this kind of thing since the C.I.A. was created in 1947. We've used posters, pamphlets, mailers, banners—you name it. We've planted false information in foreign newspapers. We've used what the British call King Georges cavalry: suit cases of cash.[48]

And, as in Russia, the effort extends beyond dejure organs of government. In 2016, for instance, the National Endowment for Democracy, a private non–profit organization based in Washington, D.C., awarded nearly $7,000,000 to Russian activists and civic organizations.[49]

Still, some scholars maintain that there is a notable difference between the American and Russian approaches to electoral interference. For example, Thomas Carothers argues that post-Cold War U.S. influence activities are distinguishable from Russia's interference in Western elections, stating:

> [U]nlike Russian electoral meddling, U.S. democracy promotion does not seek to exacerbate sociopolitical divisions, systematically spread lies, favor particular candidates, or undercut the technical integrity of elections. On the whole, it seeks to help citizens

exercise their basic political and civil rights in electoral processes, enhance the technical integrity of such processes, and increase electoral transparency.[50]

Regardless of whether this argument is convincing, the question remains as to whether attempts to influence elections, especially in light of current and emerging cyber technologies, comport with international law in general.

## Breach of legal obligation

The Obama Administration, despite publicly pointing the finger at Russia for engaging in election meddling, never asserted that the actions violated any primary rule of international law.[51] Instead, when imposing sanctions, President Obama merely cited Russia's efforts to undermine established international norms of behavior, and interfere with democratic governance.[52] Similarly, the report issued by his intelligence agencies failed to allege that the Russian efforts were unlawful under international law. Unsurprisingly, given President Trumps skepticism about the Russian operations, the current administration has remained silent as to whether Russian actions violated internationally binding norms.

This reticence begs the question of the legal character of cyber election meddling. A number of possibilities, examined below, dominate discussion. The two most prominent are violation of the target State's sovereignty and intervention into the internal affairs of the State holding the elections. A third possibility that is often ignored is breach of the obligation to exercise due diligence that the State's territory is not used as the location from which non-State actors or other States launch the cyber meddling operations.

### *Violation of sovereignty*

In the case of election meddling, the likeliest breach by a State of its international law obligations is violation of the target State's sovereignty. Before turning to the merits of that possibility, it is first necessary to address a recent dispute over whether sovereignty is a primary rule of international law or merely a foundational principle from which primary rules such as the prohibitions on intervention and the use of force emanate.[53] This is a key point because if sovereignty is not a primary rule of international law, then election meddling cannot qualify as an internationally wrongful act in that context.

Until very recently, and as illustrated below, there appeared to be broad consensus that sovereignty is both a principle and a primary rule of international law. As a principle, the concept denotes international laws acknowledgment that States are primarily responsible for what happens on their territory and that other States should respect aid competence. On this basis, sovereignty is the fount from which various primary rules, like the prohibition on intervention into the internal affairs of other States, emerged. At the same time, sovereignty was also understood to be a primary rule of international law that is itself susceptible to violation. For instance, States have often accused other States of violating their sovereignty. The classic examples are non-consensual penetration of national airspace or territorial waters by government aircraft or vessels, respectively. In fact, at times, a single act might breach both the obligation to respect another State's sovereignty and a different primary rule derived from the principle of sovereignty, as when a State violates another State's sovereignty by unlawfully employing force within the latter's territory.

This approach had apparently been embraced by the U.N. Group of Governmental Experts on Developments in the Field of Information and Telecommunications, a body consisting of State representatives tasked to assess norms in cyberspace. In its 2015 consensus report, it concluded: State sovereignty and international norms and principles that flow from sovereignty apply to the conduct by States of ICT-related activities and to their jurisdiction over ICT infrastructure within their territory.[54]

Sovereignty as both a principle and rule position was unanimously adopted by the International Group of Experts (IGE) that prepared the Tallinn Manual 2.0 on the International Law Applicable to Cyber Operations, the product of a seven-year project to determine how international law applies in the cyber context.[55] The IGE consisted of two groups of twenty international experts, and its conclusions were vetted by scores of peer reviewers. Nor did the premise of sovereignty as a primary rule encounter serious pushback from States during the Hague Process, which brought together fifty delegations, along with representatives from a number of international organizations, to consider drafts of the manual prior to publication.

Finally, adherence to the premise that sovereignty may be violated appeared to be the established U.S. position, as indicated in remarks by Department of State Legal Adviser Harold Koh at a 2012 interagency legal conference held at U.S. Cyber Command:

> States conducting activities in cyberspace must take into account the sovereignty of other States, including outside the context of armed conflict. The physical infra-structure that supports the internet and cyber activities is generally located in sovereign territory and subject to the jurisdiction of the territorial State.[56]

The position of most other countries is in accord. For instance, at the European launch of Tallinn Manual 2.0, Dutch Foreign Minister Bert Koenders noted that we mustn't be naive. Cyber operations against institutions, political parties, and individuals underline why we need the international legal principles of sovereignty and nonintervention in the affairs of other states.[57]

Indications began to surface in 2016 that certain U.S. officials tasked with rendering legal advice concerning cyber operations had adopted a different view. This view was set forth most fully in an *American Journal of International Law Unbound* article by Colonel Gary Corn, the Staff Judge Advocate of U.S. Cyber Command, and Robert Taylor, a recently retired senior attorney from the Department of Defenses Office of General Counsel. According to Corn and Taylor:

> Some argue that limitations imposed by the concept of sovereignty fill this normative space—that sovereignty is itself abiding rule of international law that precludes virtually any action yon estate in the territory of another that violates the domestic law of that other state, absent consent. However, law and state practice instead indicate that sovereignty serves as a principle of international law that guides state interactions, but is not itself a binding rule that dictates results under international law. While this principle of sovereignty, including territorial sovereignty, should factor into the conduct of every cyber operation, it does not establish an absolute bar against individual or collective state cyber operations that affect cyberinfrastructure within another state, provided that the effects do not rise to the level of an unlawful use of force or an unlawful intervention.[58]

Corn and Taylor's assertions are both counter-factual and counter-normative. First, those taking the opposing view do not argue that any non-consensual cyber operation contravening the target State's domestic law also amounts to a violation of sovereignty. For instance, they are of the view that remote cyber activities that violate domestic law on espionage would not, in themselves, violate international law.[59] Indeed, violation of a State's domestic legal regime seldom bears on the breach of a primary rule of international law. Nor do those viewing sovereignty as a primary rule of law suggest that sovereignty constitutes an absolute bar to cyber operations conducted by other States. Instead, as will be explained, proponents assert that the nature of the cyber activity and its attendant consequences determine whether a violation of sovereignty has occurred. Despite such inaccuracies, it is essential to understand that by adopting the Corn–Taylor approach, election meddling by cyber means would never amount to a violation of the target States sovereignty, for only the breach of an obligation contained in a primary rule of international law qualifies as an internationally wrongful act.

The opposing approach was set forth in a *Texas Law Review* article in which the author and a colleague surveyed treatment of the matter by international tribunals, States, international organizations, and academics.[60] We concluded that sovereignty has been treated for decades as a primary rule of international law, and we could identify no basis for treating the concept differently in the context of cyberspace.[61] For us, and for the majority of States and international law experts, the question that presents itself is whether are mote cyber operation such as election meddling rises to the level of a violation of sovereignty.[62] As Brian Eagan, then the Department of States Legal Adviser, noted during a 2017 Berkeley Law School address:

> The very design of the Internet may lead to some encroachment on other sovereign jurisdictions. Precisely when a nonconsensual cyber operation violates the sovereignty of another State is a question lawyers within the U.S. government continue to study carefully, and it is one that ultimately will be resolved through the practice and opinio juris of States.[63]

The 1928 Island of Palmas arbitration sets forth the classic definition of sovereignty: "[s]overeignty in the relations between States signifies independence. Independence in regard to a portion of the globe is the right to exercise therein, to the exclusion of any other State, the functions of a State."[64] This definition signals the two critical aspects of sovereignty: territoriality and State functions. It also confirms that only States violate sovereignty, either directly, such as by virtue of cyber operations conducted by its organs, or by attribution of a non-State actor's cyber operation pursuant to the law of State responsibility, an issue examined in further detail below.

As noted, it is well-accepted that a State's non-consensual, physical penetration of another State's territory, or even unconsented to and adverse presence thereon, amounts to a violation of sovereignty. The question is when should a remotely conducted cyber operation by, or attributable to, one State that manifests on cyber infrastructure in another's territory be treated as analogously running afoul of the obligation to respect the sovereignty of other States.

The Tallinn Manual 2.0 experts struggled mightily with this issue. They built a rough consensus around two situations. First, the experts agreed, based on the right of a State to control access to its territory, that a violation of sovereignty may result from an infringement on a State's territorial integrity. In this regard, they generally agreed that a remotely conducted cyber operation causing physical damage either to the targeted cyber infrastructure (as was the case with the Stuxnet operation) or objects reliant thereon, or injury to persons, violates sovereignty.[65] It makes no difference whether the damaged cyber infrastructure is private or governmental, for the crux of the violation is the causation of consequences upon the State's territory.

It is unlikely that a State would engage in election meddling by causing physical damage to cyber infrastructure, if only because lesser means would usually suffice to achieve its objective. The more likely scenario is a cyber operation designed to induce a loss of functionality of either election systems or cyber infrastructure with a nexus to the election, such as the servers of a political party. The Tallinn Manual 2.0 experts extended the notion of damage to loss of functionality on the basis that it should not matter whether targeted systems are physically damaged or simply rendered inoperative, for the effect is usually the same the system no longer works.[66] As an example, the 2012 cyber operations against Saudi Aramco necessitated the replacement of affected computers and therefore, if conducted by another State as is suspected, amounted to a violation of sovereignty even though the systems suffered no physical damage.[67] Treating the loss of functionality as the equivalent of physical damage comports with the object and purpose of the rule of sovereignty: to afford the territorial State control over consequential activities on its territory.

By this teleological approach, a malicious cyber operation that causes any election-related cyber infrastructure on a State's territory to cease to operate would qualify as a sovereignty violation. As an example, a foreign State's operation that disabled the computer systems of a political action committee or media organization that favored one candidate would breach sovereignty. The critical point is not that there was a nexus between the targeted system and the election, but instead simply that the operation resulted in the requisite harm—a loss of functionality.

It must be cautioned that the Tallinn Manual 2.0 experts could not achieve consensus as to the precise meaning of loss of functionality. For some, the notion implies an irreversible loss of function. For others, it extends to situations in which physical repair, as in replacement of a hard drive, is necessary. A number of Tallinn Manual 2.0 experts would treat the need to replace the operating system or bespoke data upon which the functioning of the system relies as a loss of functionality.[68] The author sympathizes with the latter position because the essence of sovereignty is control by the State over activities on its territory; remote cyber operations that necessitate reloading or replacement represent a significant intrusion on that legal prerogative.

The most legally unsettled situations with respect to sovereignty, however, are those cyber operations that manifest on another State's territory without causing physical damage or serious loss of functionality. It was difficult to identify majority and minority views amongst the Tallinn Manual 2.0 experts on the subject. Even those experts willing to consider the possibility that a violation of sovereignty is possible in such scenarios took contrasting positions. Among the activities proffered by one or more of them as sovereignty violations were:

> a cyber operation causing cyber infrastructure or programs to operate differently; altering or deleting data stored in cyber infrastructure without causing physical or

functional consequences, as described above; emplacing malware into a system; installing backdoors; and causing a temporary, but significant, loss of functionality, as in the case of a major DDoS operation.[69]

In the author's view, an operation rendering cyber infrastructure incapable of performing its functions in the manner intended qualifies as a sovereignty violation. One that causes election machinery to misreport results, for example, would fall into this category, as would one that renders machinery incapable of transmitting valid elections results.

Interestingly, and despite disagreement over these diverse examples, each expert tended to justify his or her position by reference to the object and purpose of the principle of sovereignty that affords States the full control over access to and activities on their territory.[70] In light of this confusing mélange of views, it is impossible to draw definitive red lines regarding cyber election meddling in the context of the territorial aspect of sovereignty, except with respect to situations causing physical damage or at least a significant impact on functionality. Since most operations are unlikely to reach this threshold, a grey zone of normative uncertainty looms when assessing such interference in a foreign State's elections. It accordingly would be difficult to make the case that the Russian cyber operations constituted a violation of U.S. sovereignty solely on the basis that they manifested on U.S. territory.

A more fertile ground for finding a violation of sovereignty vis-à-vis remote cyber operations affecting another State's elections is interference with, or usurpation of, inherently governmental functions.[71] Such activities, which need not cause damage or loss of functionality, violate sovereignty because States enjoy the exclusive right to perform inherently governmental activities on their territory. The inherently governmental function concept lacks granularity, although some cases are clear. On the one hand, purely commercial activities, even if engaged in by State-owned enterprises, do not qualify, for they obviously are not within the exclusive purview of a State. On the other hand, law enforcement and defense of the State from external attack are inherently governmental in character.

Between these extremes lies a great deal of uncertainty. Fortunately, for our purposes, a paradigmatic example of an inherently governmental function is the holding of elections. This being so, the issue is whether cyber activities qualify as interference or usurpation by virtue of their effect on an election. Interference denotes activities that disturb the territorial State's ability to perform the functions as it wishes. By contrast, usurpation involves performing an inherently governmental function on another State's territory without its consent. In both examples, an external actor is disrupting the ability of the target State to perform its governmental functions.

While the usurpation criterion has little relevance in the election meddling context, cyber operations may well be employed to interfere with another State's elections. Certain operations would plainly qualify, as in the case of a cyber operation that altered election data or a temporary distributed denial of service attack against election machinery that rendered it impossible for voters in a particular district to cast their votes. In States with online voting, the implantation of malware in private computers that blocks voting likewise would constitute interference, as would using cyber operations to alter voter registration numbers.

It is equally clear that merely engaging in election propaganda does not amount to interference, at least as a matter of law. This conclusion is supported by the extensive State practice of engaging in both truthful and untruthful propaganda during foreign elections. Of course, such activities may be condemned, as the efforts of RT and Sputnik and the purchase of advertising on social media were in the ODNI Report,[72] but such condemnation is seldom based on assertions of a breach of international law, specifically the obligation to respect sovereignty. This paucity of opinion juris and surfeit of contrary practice corroborates the conclusion that election propaganda by cyber means does not violate a target State's sovereignty.[73]

Other Russian activities likewise failed to reach the level of interference. Although the financial sums spent by Russia and its supporters in attempting to influence the U.S. elections were large, international law imposes no monetary threshold at which the financing of election activities in another State constitutes interference, even though as a practical matter foreign financing can determine the outcome of an election. The penetration by Russian hackers of local boards of election similarly failed to qualify as interference, for there was no subsequent activity that exploited the access to affect the elections. As such, interference did not occur. Moreover, even though Russian operations encouraged protests and rallies, these acts do not qualify as interference because, so long as they are peaceful, they are a regular feature in many democratic elections.

Russian operators succeeded by avoiding both ends of this legal spectrum and instead operated adroitly in the legal grey zone lying between them. Consider the messaging conducted by Russian trolls. The difference between their activities and those of a State or State-supportive media outlet that conducts an open propaganda campaign, even one involving disinformation, is the ability of the electorate to consider the source of the information. Indeed, recall that in order to enhance their efforts, the trolls created fake identities in which they masqueraded as Americans, sometimes even impersonating actual Americans. Thus, in addition to conveying a message to the electorate, the trolls sought to bolster that message by feigning the source thereof. Arguably, this manipulation of voters' ability to assess the messages in coming to their own decision tipped the scales and therefore constituted unlawful interference.

Another Russian activity within this grey zone was the hacking into various servers containing, inter alia, email traffic. As noted, the mere fact that the systems were penetrated does not suffice to qualify the hacking as interference with the election any more than espionage involving government systems is unlawful. In certain cases, however, the operations involved exfiltration of data and its weaponization through release at critical points in the election.[74] An assertion that the exfiltration and subsequent release were materially more aggravated than mere propaganda or disinformation, such that the operations qualified as interference, is at least somewhat supportable.

Note, in this regard, that whether the operations successfully swayed the election has no bearing on their lawfulness, as the essence of a sovereignty violation is the fact of interference. That said, there must be a degree of interference even if it does not achieve its desired objective. For example, a cyber operation that attempts to alter election returns, but which is foiled by effective point defenses in the targeted system, lacks the element of interference.[75]

Taken together, the most legally sustainable and persuasive position is that aspects of the Russian influence campaign violated U.S. sovereignty.[76] Yet, this conclusion is far from unassailable. As noted above, an argument, albeit not widely held, holds that sovereignty may never be violated because it is not a primary rule of international law. Moreover, even if sovereignty serves as a primary rule, there was no damage or substantial loss of functionality to any cyber infrastructure related to the U.S. election. Likewise, the Russian operations cleverly avoided actions, such as creating flawed returns, that would unmistakably amount to interference by taking on an inherently governmental function. Although the influence campaign was condemnable, it must be acknowledged that Russia conducted its operations in the grey zone of the law of sovereignty, thereby complicating potential U.S. responses and avoiding the international community's opprobrium for violating international law.

## *Intervention*

The other breach of an international law obligation most likely to be committed through election meddling is unlawful intervention into the internal affairs of another State.[77] Sovereignty is the foundational principle from which this primary rule of customary law derives.[78] As noted by Lassa Oppenheim, the obligation not to intervene is the corollary of every State's right to sovereignty, territorial integrity, and political independence.[79] Accordingly, States must respect the right of other States to exercise control over certain activities occurring on their territory. Note that like the violation of sovereignty, only States can engage in unlawful intervention, either directly through the actions of their organs or indirectly through instructions to, or control over, non-State actors such as IT companies, hacker groups, or terrorist organizations. And, as with sovereignty violations, cyber operations targeting both private and government infrastructure can qualify as intervention.[80]

Two elements must be satisfied before a cyber operation qualifies as wrongful intervention. The operation must affect a State's domaine réservé and it must be coercive.[81] Absent one of these elements, the operation may constitute interference, but it will not rise to the level of unlawful intervention.

With respect to the first element, the difference between an inherently governmental function in the context of sovereignty and the domaine réservé is subtle; the two categories often overlap. The former denotes an activity reserved for the government alone, while the latter refers to one that has not been committed to international law by either treaty or customary law. In its Nicaragua judgment, the International Court of Justice (ICJ) explained that a prohibited intervention must ... be one bearing on matters in which each State is permitted by the principle of sovereignty, to decide freely.[82] The Court went on to highlight the choice of a political ... system as a clear-cut example of a domaine réservé.[83]

The conduct of elections is both an inherently governmental act and within the State's domaine réservé. Some limited carve-outs of this domaine réservé exist, principally with respect to human rights norms such as self-determination, a topic briefly mentioned below. But, as a general matter, the process by which a State selects its officials is left to the determination of that State and is broadly unregulated by international law. Accordingly, cyber activities by foreign States that affect either the process by which elections are conducted or their outcome qualify as prohibited intervention, so long as the second prong of the intervention test, coercion, is satisfied.[84]

In the election context, the determinative factor distinguishing external influence on an election (which may be unlawful in the context of a sovereignty violation involving an inherently governmental function) from prohibited intervention is the element of coercion. Referring to the right of a State to choose its own political system, the ICJ observed in Nicaragua, intervention is wrongful when it uses methods of coercion in regard to such choices, which must remain free ones.[85] According to the Court, the element of coercion ... defines, and indeed forms the very essence of, prohibited intervention.[86]

The question is therefore what type of election meddling can be said to be coercive. Although international law provides no conclusive definition of the term, the Declaration on Friendly Relations provides that [n]o State may use or encourage the use of economic political or any other type of measures to coerce another State in order to obtain from it the subordination of the exercise of its sovereign rights and to secure from it advantages of any kind.[87] Drawing on this text, the Tallinn Manual 2.0 experts agreed that coercion refers to an affirmative act designed to deprive another State of its freedom of choice, that is, to force that State to act in an involuntary manner or involuntarily refrain from acting in a particular way.[88]

Some election meddling certainly would reach this threshold. As Brian Egan noted while serving as Department of State Legal Adviser, a cyber operation by a State that interferes with another country's ability to hold an election or that manipulates another country's election results would be a clear violation of the rule of non-intervention.[89] Blocking voting by cyber means, such as by disabling election machinery or by conducting a distributed denial of service attack, would likewise be coercive. In both of these situations, the result of the election, which is the expression of the freedom of choice of the electorate, is being manipulated against the will of the electorate.

At the other end of the spectrum are cyber operations designed to influence decisions in the target State without reaching the threshold of coercion. As explained in the Tallinn Manual 2.0:

> [C]oercion must be distinguished from persuasion, criticism, public diplomacy, propaganda, retribution, mere maliciousness, and the like in the sense that, unlike coercion, such activities merely involve either influencing (as distinct from factually compelling) the voluntary actions of the target State or seek no action on the part of the target State at all.[90]

Therefore, those actions described as lawful in the context of sovereignty violations, like espionage, slanted media reporting by Russian controlled media, and the purchase of advertising to sway the electorate in favor of a particular candidate, are similarly not coercive and do not qualify as a prohibited intervention.

As with sovereignty violations, a significant grey zone of normative uncertainty exists between the two ends of the influence–intervention continuum. Again, the Russian cyber meddling exploited this grey zone, thereby frustrating the ability of U.S. officials to characterize it as unlawful and thereby have the grounds for fashioning a robust response. The two best prospects for qualifying Russian operations as intervention were the cyber activities that feigned American citizenship and the hacking and subsequent release of private data.

At its core, a coercive action is intended to cause the State to do something, such as take a decision that it would otherwise not take, or not to engage in an activity in which it would otherwise engage. Thus, coercion can be said to subordinate the sovereign will of the target State.[91] In the case of elections, this might manifest in the election of a candidate who otherwise would not win, the weakening of a successful candidate's political base, or the strengthening of an unsuccessful candidate's base in anticipation of future elections.

Arguably, the covert nature of the troll operation deprived the American electorate of its freedom of choice by creating a situation in which it could not fairly evaluate the information it was being provided. As the voters were unaware that they were being manipulated by a foreign power, their decision making, and thus their ability to control their governance, was weakened and distorted. The deceptive nature of the trolling is what distinguishes it from a mere influence operation. And it can be argued that the hacking and release tainted the electoral process by introducing information that, albeit genuine, was acquired by means that are expressly prohibited under U.S. domestic law, as well as the law of most other States—namely, the unlawful penetration and exfiltration of private data.[92] In this sense, the electorate's freedom of choice was being thwarted.

These conclusions are by no means unassailable. In particular, it remains unresolved whether coercion requires a direct causal nexus between the act in question and the coercive effect, as in the case of changing election results.[93] A number of Tallinn Manual 2.0 experts took this position.[94] However, a majority of them, including the author, was of the view that indirect causation of coercive effect suffices.[95] This is an essential distinction because both of the aforementioned Russian activities were indirect in the sense that, while they may have affected the voters' choice of candidates, or even their decision to vote at all, the operations did not in themselves alter the result. Because indirect causation moves the activity along the continuum in the direction of interference and away from intervention, to survive as intervention it is critical to highlight the centrality of the covert nature of the Russian operations and the extent to which they distorted the accepted U.S. electoral dynamic.

If indirect causation satisfies the causal facet of coercion, the fact that intervention need not be directed against governmental election infrastructure is of particular importance, for it means that cyber operations directed against a political party could qualify. An example would be a denial of service attack against the party's website, blog, email, or other forms of online campaigning at a critical juncture in the election.[96] A cyber operation that generated false messages purportedly from the party and attempted to sway votes or alter the party's actual messaging in a significant way also would qualify.

President Trump has repeatedly suggested that any election meddling that might have occurred did not affect the outcome. However, whether this is true as a matter of fact is irrelevant as a matter of law. The internationally wrongful act of prohibited intervention does not require that the cyber operations in question be successful. It only requires that they be intended to have a coercive effect with respect to a domaine réservé, in this case elections.

As should be apparent, the prohibition of intervention in the context of election meddling, like the violation of sovereignty, is characterized by substantial uncertainty.[97] Fortunately, there is no disagreement over whether the prohibition comprises a primary rule of international law. But, while there are clear-cut cases that either do or do not breach the meddling States obligations vis-à-vis intervention, a significant grey zone lies between the easy cases, particularly with respect to indirect coercion.[98] This grey zone creates legal uncertainly and affords States fertile ground in which to meddle in each other's political activities.

## Due diligence

In some cases, a lack of sufficient evidence will preclude officials from concluding that another State conducted cyber election meddling, or that the operations were otherwise attributable to it, as discussed below. However, if it can be established that they were mounted from the territory of a particular State, the possibility that the territorial State may be in breach of its due diligence obligation arises.[99]

The principle of due diligence obligates States to ensure that their territory is not used as a location from which cyber operations having serious adverse consequences for the target State are launched.[100] The ICJ acknowledged the principle of due diligence and the legal obligation it creates in its first case, Corfu Channel.[101] In the judgment, the court observed that it is every State's obligation not to knowingly allow its territory to be used for acts contrary to the rights of other states.[102] Judge John Basset Moore of the Permanent Court of Justice had earlier recognized the duty in the celebrated Lotus case, where, writing in dissent, he stated, "It is well settled that a State is bound to use due diligence to prevent the commission within its dominions of criminal acts against another nation or its people."[103]

During consultations regarding drafts of the Tallinn Manual 2.0, some States expressed a tentative view that despite the notable lineage of the rule, it was of a *lex ferenda* character.[104] Indeed, when the issue of due diligence arose during U.N. GGE deliberations regarding its 2013 and 2015 reports, all that could be agreed upon was a hortatory statement to the effect that States should take actions that are necessary to put an end to harmful cyber operations occurring from their territory.[105]

The Tallinn Manual 2.0 experts carefully considered this matter, particularly since the principle had been applied principally in the context of transboundary environmental harm.[106] Although they agreed that the principle was a primary rule of international law applicable in cyberspace, they framed a number of strict limitations on its application. First, the due diligence obligation is one of conduct, not result. Thus, so long as a State is taking all feasible measures to put an end to the harmful cyber operations, it is in compliance with the obligation.[107] Second, a majority of the experts took the position that the obligation only requires a State to take action in the face of ongoing harmful cyber activities, or ones in which a material step has been taken towards execution.[108] It imposes no preventative duty to take measures to preclude future deleterious cyber activities from its territory or to monitor its cyberspace for ongoing ones.[109] Third, borrowing from international environmental law, the experts agreed that the obligation only attaches when the consequences for the victim State are serious.[110] Relatedly, they concluded the cyber activity in question must be contrary to the rights of the target State in the sense that if it had been conducted by, or was attributable to, another State, the operation would have qualified as an internationally wrongful act.[111]

Despite these limitations, the principle of due diligence nevertheless acts to relieve a target State of having to attribute election meddling to another State in order to claim that it is the victim of an internationally wrongful act. So long as the former can establish that the cyber operations would breach a legal obligation had they been attributable to a State, for instance by violating sovereignty or qualifying as a prohibited intervention, the State from whose territory the operations are being launched shoulders a legal duty to take feasible measures to put an end to the operation. The cyber operations must have serious adverse consequences, but interfering with another State's national elections will usually reach that threshold.

In the Russian meddling situation, it may be, as explained below, difficult to attribute the action of non-State actors, especially the Internet Research Agency, to Russia, a necessary step in finding Russia legally responsible for their actions. However, so long as Russia was aware of the troll farm's operations, it is responsible for failing to put an end to these operations, at least to the extent they would have violated international law had they been committed by organs of the Russian State, such as its intelligence agencies. While it is hard to imagine that the Russian authorities were unaware of the trolling, it is difficult to say with

## Other breaches of international law

Some scholars have raised other possibilities for how Russian election meddling may have breached international law. Particularly creative is Professor Jens Ohlin's assertion that it may have implicated self-determination, which grants a people the right to determine their political arrangements (at a systemic level) and their future destiny (at a more granular level of policy).[112] Recognized in the first article of both the International Covenant on Civil and Political Rights (ICCPR) and the International Covenant on Economic, Social and Cultural Rights, the right of self-determination is generally recognized as customary international law.[113] The identical articles provide that by virtue of that right they freely determine their political status.

However, as Ohlin himself notes, there are numerous reasons why international lawyers might hesitate to take this position. They include the fact that arguments based on self-determination typically appear when groups are trying to create a State, perhaps through succession, and that the will of the people cannot be determined with any degree of certainty before an election.[114] But the best response against application is that self-determination is simply not meant to apply to a situation where the people are all citizens of a State rather than a distinct group therein that is denied the right to govern itself, as in the case of colonialism, apartheid, alien subjugation, and perhaps occupation.

Somewhat more promising is Ohlin's examination of the possibility that the Russian operations may have violated the right to privacy under international human rights law. The right to privacy is secured by Article 17 of the ICCPR, which provides that no one shall be subjected to arbitrary or unlawful interference with his privacy, family, home or correspondence, nor to unlawful attacks on his honor and reputation.[115] Russia is also a party to the European Convention on Human Rights, Article 8(1) of which states that [e]veryone has the right to respect for his private and family life, his home and his correspondence.[116] The right is generally considered to be customary in nature and applicable to cyber correspondence, such as email.[117]

Ohlin highlights a series of obstacles to a finding that the Russian operations violated the human rights of affected individuals. He notes, for instance, that human rights were originally conceived as applicable to a State's own citizens and points to the extensive practice of espionage that States have not characterized as a violation of the right to privacy.[118] The most significant obstacle, however, is the open question of whether international human rights obligations are extraterritorial in nature, an issue directly on point with respect to cyber operations mounted remotely from outside a State's territory. As Ohlin observes,[119] there has been significant disagreement within the U.S. government over the extraterritorial applicability of the ICCPR.[120]

The broader question is the extraterritorial applicability of human rights obligations generally, including customary law rights such as that requiring respect for the right of privacy.[121] Although the prevailing view is that treaty law (absent a provision to the contrary) and customary human rights law apply extraterritorially, such obligations attach only when the State exercises power or effective control either over the foreign territory on which the individual owed the obligation is located or over the individual concerned.[122] Occupation of enemy territory exemplifies the former, whereas detention of the individual abroad illustrates the latter.

In the case of remote cyber operations, the State enjoys neither. An argument nevertheless can be made that a State conducting a remote cyber operation can sometimes control the exercise or enjoyment of a human right.[123] In the Russian cyber operations, for instance, remote non-consensual intrusion into databases containing personal data and the subsequent release of that data arguably deprived the individuals affected of the enjoyment of their right to privacy. Although this is an appealing argument, it is thus far unsupported by either State practice or expressions of opinio juris. The approach might amount to laudable lex ferenda, but it is not lex lata.

Finally, any assertion that the activities underlying the election meddling were unlawful under international law because they constituted espionage can be quickly discarded. Cyber espionage is an act undertaken clandestinely or under false pretenses that uses cyber capabilities to gather, or attempt to gather, information, whether that information be private or governmental in nature.[124]

The GRU's cyber activities in the Russian case, such as the exfiltration of email traffic, clearly constituted espionage. Similarly, collection operations targeting U.S. primary campaigns, think tanks, and lobbying groups [that were] viewed as likely to shape future U.S. policies qualify as espionage.[125]

Espionage, per se, does not violate of international law.[126] Thus, the mere fact that Russian intelligence agencies were conducting cyber espionage involving the U.S. elections did not render them unlawful. That is not to say that an espionage operation never violates international law, as the means by which the information is gathered may amount to an internationally wrongful act. For instance, if a government aircraft flying in the national airspace of the target country conducts cyber operations designed to access selection-related cyber infrastructure, doing so arguably violates the State's sovereignty by virtue of the unconsented-to presence of the aircraft.

## Attribution

In a press statement made in the twilight of his presidency, President Obama suggested that Russia's data theft and subsequent disclosure were of a nature that the highest levels of the Russian government must have ordered them.[127] The intelligence community likewise concluded that Putin ordered an influence campaign in 2016 aimed at the U.S. presidential election.[128] Specifically, it found that the effort consisted of covert and overt activities by Russian government agencies, State-funded media, third-party intermediaries, and paid social media users or trolls.[129]

Predictably, Russia demanded that the U.S. provide the evidence to support these allegations.[130] Although the indictment brought by Special Counsel Robert Mueller does contain an account of some alleged Russian activities, a granular U.S. reply is unlikely, in great part because providing this evidence would reveal sensitive cyber capabilities.[131] Moreover, there is no obligation under international law for one State accusing another State of unfriendly—or even unlawful—conduct to reveal the information on which it bases these accusations.[132]

Still, the U.S. government's naming of Russia as the actor behind the influence campaign does raise the issue of the attribution. Recall that an act or omission only qualifies as an internationally wrongful act if it both breaches an obligation under international law and is attributable to a State. In this regard, factual attribution must be distinguished from legal attribution. The former refers to the level of certainty that a cyber operation was conducted by a particular individual, group, organization, or State. As a general matter, factual attribution under international law is subject to a reasonableness standard.[133] With the notable exception of attribution for the purpose of taking countermeasures,[134] international law generally does not require States to be correct in their determinations; rather, they must be reasonable when making them.

Legal attribution, by contrast, deals with the condition's precedent to a finding that a State is responsible for a cyber operation pursuant to the secondary rules of international law set forth in the law of State responsibility. The International Law Commission has authoritatively restated this body of law in its Articles on State Responsibility.[135] Legal attribution plays an essential role in ascertaining the lawfulness of cyber meddling because a finding that cyber election meddling constituted an internationally wrongful act requires both that the cyber operations involved have breached an obligation owed by the meddling State (the responsible State in the law of State responsibility) to the target State (the injured State) and that the operations were attributable to the former as a legal matter.

The most straightforward form of attribution is on the basis that an organ of the State, like the GRU or other intelligence agency, conducted the cyber operation in question.[136] Such operations are attributable to the State even when they are ultra vires, that is, beyond the assigned responsibility of the organ.[137] As an example, if the activities of the Russian intelligence agencies with respect to the U.S. elections were unauthorized, Russia would nevertheless bear responsibility under international law. The key is whether the organ is acting in an apparently official capacity or a purely private one.[138] Engaging in private criminal activity for personal gain would be an example of the latter.

To qualify as an organ of the State, the entity must either enjoy that status under the State's domestic laws or factually act as an instrument of, and in complete dependence on, the State.[139] The inclusion of de facto organs precludes a State from escaping responsibility for a breach of its international obligations by simply failing to designate as such an entity that is acting as an organ of the State. For instance, by setting up an extra-legal cyber intelligence organization that operates entirely for State purposes and at its direction, a State does not evade legal responsibility for its operations.[140]

By these standards, Russia is responsible for any aspect of the cyber election meddling conducted by its intelligence agencies that amounted to a violation of an international law prohibition, as arguably was the case vis-à-vis the hacking and release operation. However, the activities of State-owned entities present a more complicated situation. The fact that an entity is State-owned does not suffice in itself for attribution of its activities to the State.[141] Rather, it must be determined whether the entity, despite being owned by the State, engages in undertakings that are solely private in nature, such as commerce. If so, its actions are not attributable to the State simply on the basis that it is an organ of the State.

Particularly problematic is the case of State-owned media, for the media sometimes serve governmental purposes like conveying government information to the public or serving as a surrogate of the State internationally in public diplomacy, propaganda, or disinformation activities. Yet, State-owned media may also, despite government ownership, act independently, much like a private media company. In terms of attribution, the key is whether the State was using its ownership interest in or control of a corporation specifically in order to achieve a particular result.[142] According to the ODNI Report, this was the case with respect to RT and Sputnik because they contributed to the digital part of the influence campaign.[143]

However, even if the actions of these and other Russian media might be attributable to the State, it is difficult to style their activities as a breach of any obligation Russia owed the U.S.

As illustrated in the case of U.S. election meddling, the relevant cyber operations may be conducted by actors other than organs of the State, as with the Internet Research Agency's troll farm. Because the nexus to the State is more attenuated in these situations, the threshold for attribution is more demanding than that applicable to organs of the State. For instance, the State is not responsible for ultra vires activities of the non-State actors like private companies, patriotic hacker groups, or hacktivists.[144]

The key normative hurdle to attribution, however, is that the State is only responsible for the cyber operations of a non-State actor when the actions taken are pursuant to the instructions of, or under the direction or control of the State,[145] or when the State acknowledges and adopts the operations as its own post factum.[146] The likelihood that a State might acknowledge and adopt a non-State actor's cyber meddling in another State's elections is slim. Therefore, the crux of the matter is the meaning of the terms instructions, direction, and control.

Both the International Law Commission and legal scholars have struggled to describe the difference between the three terms with meaningful granularity.[147] Their failure has signaled a definitional grey zone no less dense than those described earlier in the context of breaches of obligations, and no less susceptible to leveraging by a State wishing to meddle in foreign elections.

The International Law Commission's commentary to the Articles on State Responsibility suggests that instruction denotes a situation in which the non-State actor functions as the State's auxiliary.[148] Restated, a State instructs a non-State actor when it directs the non-State actor to perform a particular cyber operation, Including election meddling, on its behalf. There is no requirement that the non-State actor be compensated for the activity involved, although the possibility is not excluded. For instance, a hacker group could execute a cyber operation on the instructions of a State intelligence agency solely out of patriotism. Likewise, a criminal organization could carry out the same operation solely for financial gain. So long as the State told the group to conduct it, motivation is irrelevant.

Although the International Law Commission's commentary suggests that the terms direction and control are to be understood in the disjunctive,[149] it goes on to treat the ensemble as effective control,[150] a standard articulated by the ICJ in Nicaragua[151] and subsequently confirmed in its Genocide judgment.[152] In the latter case, the Court explained:

> It is not necessary to show that the persons who performed the acts alleged to have violated international law were in general in a relationship of completed dependence on the respondent State; it has to be proved that they acted in accordance with that State's instructions or under its effective control. It must however be shown that this effective control was exercised, or that the State's instructions were given, in respect of each operation in which the alleged violations occurred, not generally in respect of the overall actions taken by the persons or groups of persons having committed the violations.[153]

Perhaps the best way to think of effective control in the context of attribution for cyber election meddling is a de facto ability on the part of the State to cause the non-state group in question to launch a cyber operation that it would otherwise not launch or to refrain from one in which it desires to engage. It need not instruct the group to engage in a particular operation, but the relationship between the State and the group must be such that the State can, if it wishes, compel the non-State group to desist in the operation or alter the conduct thereof.

Unfortunately, the effective control test raises as many questions as it answers. For instance, with what degree of granularity must the State be aware of the operation in question to exercise effective control over it? And by what means may effective control be established? If a State provides all of the funding that makes the group's cyber operations possible, but the group develops its own operational design, is sufficient control in place to attribute the group's cyber activities to the State?

By outsourcing aspects of its interference campaign to private entities and individuals, Russia again found a grey zone of international law that allowed it safe haven to carry out its activities, for it is much more difficult to ascertain legal attribution in such cases than in those situations involving the State's organs. The U.S. intelligence community may have felt comfortable in attributing the operations of the Intelligence Research Agency and other non-State actors to Russia, but in doing so it was not applying the strict legal tests set for the law of State responsibility. Indeed, based on the information contained in their 2017 report and other open source material, it is difficult to conclusively attribute these actions to Russia as a matter of law, although it would seem self-evident that those actions were carried out as a matter of fact in support of Russian governmental objectives. The best that can be said is that it might be reasonable to attribute them to Russia.

## Responses

Responding to the Russian cyber operations, and as the Trump inauguration loomed, the Obama Administration imposed sanctions on the GRU and Federal Security Service (FSB), four GRU intelligence officers, and three companies that had supported the GRUs operations. The Secretary of the Treasury designated two Russians as having used cyber-enabled means to cause misappropriation of funds and personal identifying information, while the Department of State shuttered two Russian compounds used for intelligence purposes and declared thirty-five Russian intelligence operatives persona non grata.[154]

In March 2018, the Trump Administration finally announced sanctions on Russia after much foot-dragging following the passage of sanctions legislation in July 2017.[155] This was the first time that the administration had officially acknowledged Russia's involvement in the operations. Of particular note were sanctions on the IRA, as well as Russians indicted by Special Counsel Robert Mueller. The FSB and GRU were also sanctioned.[156] Further sanctions, also tied to the legislation, were announced the following month.[157] Under international law, there are four categories of responses available to States facing hostile cyber operations.[158] The measures taken by the Obama and Trump Administrations fall into the category of retorsion. An act of retorsion is an unfriendly, but not otherwise unlawful measure,[159] with sanctions and expulsion of diplomatic personnel being the most emblematic and frequent.[160] The cyber operations to which an act of retorsion responds need not constitute an internationally wrongful act, although they may. That both administrations limited their responses to retorsion suggests that they were hesitant to characterize the Russian operations as breaches of international law attributable to Russia. If this was the case, the Russian tactic of operating within the grey zone proved partially successful.

If the cyber operation to which the target State wishes to respond qualifies as an internationally wrongful act, countermeasures may be taken. Countermeasures are measures that would be unlawful, either as a breach of treaty law or of customary international law, but for the fact that they are a response to another State's internationally wrongful act.[161] They must be proportionate to the internationally wrongful act, and, within the cyber context, be designed to cause the other State to desist in its ongoing unlawful cyber operations or to provide assurances, guarantees, or reparations.[162] The classic example is an active defense cyber operation, typically a hack back designed to end a malicious cyber operation launched by another State.[163]

Although there are numerous other limitations on the taking of countermeasures, the option allows for flexibility in two regards. First, countermeasures need not be directed at the entity that launched the initial unlawful cyber operation.[164] As an example, unlawful cyber election meddling could be addressed by conducting hack backs against government ministries, or even private cyber infrastructure, so long as the purpose of doing so is to apply pressure to end the meddling; retaliation or punishment are not permissible purposes. Second, countermeasures need not be in kind. Thus, cyber election meddling could be addressed by engaging in non-cyber measures that would otherwise be unlawful, such as imposing trade sanctions that are contrary to a treaty between the two States.[165]

A third response is based upon the plea of necessity. States may engage in cyber or non-cyber activities that would otherwise be unlawful when their essential interests face grave and imminent peril and taking the responsive measures is the only way to defend the interest.[166] In such cases, there is no requirement that the situation to which the response is taken either constitutes breach of a legal obligation or be attributable to a State. This dispenses with much of the grey zone discussed earlier. In the Russian case, for example, the U.S. would not have needed to conclude that the influence campaign violated any primary rule of international law or establish that the nexus between the Russian government and those conducting the operations satisfies the attribution tests set out in the law of State responsibility.

However, those grey zone issues are replaced by others resident in the plea of necessity. The determinative issue is whether the integrity of the election system amounts to an essential interest of the State. Although it is reasonable to hold that the fair and credible election of high-level government officials, especially the President, is an essential interest of the State, whereas the election of local officials might not be, the threshold of essentiality is indistinct. Moreover, the situation must be ongoing or imminent and the threat posed must be extremely serious. Minor cyber election meddling, even in national elections, would not merit a response based on the plea, while meddling that threatened the outcome of an election might be characterized as grave. Determining when the peril posed by cyber election meddling in other cases qualifies as grave is more challenging.

The final response option is the use of cyber or non-cyber force in self-defense pursuant to Article 51 of the U.N. Charter and customary international law. The textual condition precedent for self-defense is an armed attack.[167]

Unfortunately, the threshold at which a cyber operation qualifies as an armed attack is unsettled.[168] Certainly, a cyber operation that causes significant physical damage or injury suffices, although consequences at this level are highly unlikely with respect to cyber election meddling. Whether nondestructive or injurious consequences that are severe would merit the use of force in self-defense is highly questionable. In the authors opinion, it is difficult to envision even internationally unlawful cyber election meddling that would, without more, allow the target State to resort to force in order to put an end to the operations.

## Reflections on the grey area

Cyber election meddling presently exists within the grey zone of international law. This zone of normative uncertainty presents a tempting environment for States that are not fully committed to the international rule of law. By operating within the grey zone, these States can avoid consensus condemnation of their cyber operations as violations of binding international legal norms. Moreover, absent a clear violation of international law attributable to the State launching the operations—and as the U.S. responses to date have demonstrated—victim State responses will generally be limited to acts of retorsion.

As the international community struggles to identify how extant norms such as respect for sovereignty, the prohibition of intervention, and due diligence obligations apply to cyber operations, some of those involved in cyber law and policy are attempting to limit the reach of international law into cyberspace. For instance, the recent failure of the U.N. GGE to agree upon text for its aborted 2017 report concerning such basic matters as applicability of the law of self-defense and international humanitarian law, topics that they had addressed in previous reports, marks a major step backwards.[169] That opposition to the text included Russia and China does not bode well for global cyber security or the rule of law more generally. Clearly, certain States are embracing legal ambiguity as a force multiplier in their cyber operations. In the realm of cyber election meddling, the ambiguity stretches from an existential threat to sovereignty as a primary rule of law to confusion over the application of the coercion criterion to voting behavior. This ambiguity represents a troubling threat to the democratic process.

Some States are taking the lead in attempting to shrink the grey zone. Efforts to bring like-minded States together to craft consensus are laudable. So too are cyber law capacity-building efforts such as the Netherlands Hague Process, in which the Netherlands sponsors regional training in collaboration with other States to construct common ground for future negotiations over the content, shape, and vector of international cyber law.[170]

Ultimately, States need to make a choice. The grey zone represents both opportunity and threat. Until States exercise their prerogative to develop new norms and interpret existing ones in the context of cyber operations, those States that are not committed to a rule-based international order will enjoy an asymmetrical advantage over those that are dedicated to compliance with the law. And foreign elections will continue to represent a lucrative target in the strategies of the former.

## Notes

1 Press Release, White House, Statement by the President on Actions in Response to Russian Malicious Cyber Activity and Harassment (Dec. 29, 2016), https://perma.cc/3XXD-8K5C [hereinafter Obama Press Release]; OFF. OF THE DIR. OF NATL INTELLIGENCE, ICA 2017–01D, ASSESSING RUSSIAN ACTIVITIES AND INTENTIONS IN RECENT US ELECTIONS (Jan. 6, 2017) [hereinafter ODNIREPORT].

2 0, supra note 53, atr. 32.

3 Mark Landler & Michael D. Shear, Indictment Makes Trumps Hoax Claim Harder to Sell, N.Y. TIMES (Feb. 16, 2018), www.nytimes.com/2018/02/16/us/politics/a-hoax-indictments-make-trumps-claim-even-harder-to-maintain.html.

4 Linda Qui, How Trump Has Split with His Administration on Russian Meddling, N.Y. TIMES (Mar. 16, 2018), www.nytimes.com/2018/03/16/us/politics/trump-russia-administration-fact-check.html.

5 Ishaan Tharoor, The Long History of the U.S. Interfering with Elections Elsewhere, WASH.

POST (Oct. 13, 2016), www.washingtonpost.com/news/worldviews/wp/2016/10/13/the-long-history-of-the-u-s-interfering-with-elections-elsewhere.

6 Andy Greenberg, Everything We Know About Russia's Election-Hacking Playbook, WIRED (June 9, 2017), perma.cc/UU3W-NUGV.

7 Indictment, *United States v. Internet Research Agency, No. 1:18-cr-00032*, 2018 WL 914777, (D.D.C. Feb.16, 2018)

8 Intl Law Commn, Rep. on the Work of Its Fifty-Third Session, Draft Articles on Responsibility of States for Internationally Wrongful Acts, pt. 1, art. 2, U.N. Doc. A/56/10, at 26 (2001), reprinted in [2001] 2 Y.B. Intl L. Commn 32, U.N. Doc. A/CN.4/SER.A/2001/Add.1 (Part 2).

9 On grey zones in international cyber law generally, see Michael N. Schmitt, Grey Zones in the International Law of Cyberspace, 42 YALE J. INTL L. ONLINE, no. 2, 2017, at 1–21.

10 ODNIREPORT, supra note 1. See also the chronology of matter at 2016 Presidential Campaign Hacking Fast Facts, CNNLIBRARY (Feb. 21, 2018), https://perma.cc/BYR2-WFVR. On the use of cyberspace as a tool of influence, see PIRET PERNIK, INTL CTR. FOR DEF. AND SECURITY, HACKING FOR INFLUENCE: FOREIGN INFLUENCE ACTIVITIES AND CYBER-ATTACKS (2018), https://perma.cc/VZP4-4L9G.

11 High confidence generally indicates that judgments are based on high-quality information from multiple sources. High confidence does not imply that the assessment is a fact or a certainty; such judgments may be wrong. ODNIREPORT, supra note 1, at 13.

12 Id. at ii.

13 Id.

14 Moderate confidence generally means that the information is credibly sourced and plausible but not of sufficient quality or corroborated sufficiently to warrant a higher level of confidence. Id. at 13.

15 Id at ii.

16 Id. at 1.

17 Id.

18 Id. at 2–3. On tying Guccifer 2.0 to the Russian government, see Kevin Poulsen and Spencer Ackerman, Lone DNC Hacker Guccifer 2.0 Slipped up and Revealed He Was a Russian Intelligence Officer, DAILY BEAST (Mar. 22, 2018), https://perma.cc/V6W9-TG6N.

19 ODNIREPORT, supra note 1, at 3; Joseph Tanfani, Russians Targeted Election Systems in 21 States, but Didn't Change Any Results, Officials Say, L.A.TIMES (June 21, 2017), http://perma.cc/R7WJ-H3N7.

20 ODNIREPORT, supranote1, at 3–4.

21 Id. at 4.

22 Id. That ally was Yevgeny Prigozhin, a Russian oligarch who both financed and controlled the Internet Research Agency. Neil Mac Farquhar, Yevgeny Prigozhin, Russian Oligarch Indicted by U.S., Is Known as Putin's Cook, N.Y. TIMES (Feb. 16, 2018), www.nytimes.com/2018/02/16/world/europe/prigozhin-russia-indictment-mueller.html. Trolls are individuals who post offensive, inflammatory, derogatory, false, or controversial comments online, often in the hope of inciting a reaction. The name of the activity, Trolling, is derived from the fishing term that referring to drawing a baited line through the water. On trolls, see Zoe Williams, What is an Internet Troll?, THE GUARDIAN (June 12, 2012), https://perma.cc/7G2M-B7JC.

23 Adrian Chen, The Agency, N.Y. TIMES MAG. (June 2, 2015), www.nytimes.com/2015/06/07/magazine/the-agency.html; Adrian Chen, What Mueller's Indictment Reveals about Russia's Internet Research Agency, NEW YORKER (Feb. 16, 2018), https://perma.cc/DCF4-LY7L; Krishnadev Calamur, What is the Internet Research Agency?, ATLANTIC (Feb. 16, 2018), https://perma.cc/WW4E-DJ9W.

24 Oliver Carroll, St. Petersburg 'Troll Farm' Had 90 Dedicated Staff Working to Influence US Election Campaign, INDEPENDENT (Oct. 17, 2017), https://perma.cc/BL34-WK9F.

25 Dave Lee, The Tactics of a Russian Troll Farm, BBC (Feb. 16, 2018), https://perma.cc/T3L5-KA4J.

26 See id. As an example of encouraging rallies, one troll using a false U.S. persona Facebook account sent a message to the Florida for Trump account stating: 'Hi there! I'm a member of Being Patriotic online community. Listen, we've got an idea. Florida is still a purple state and we need to paint it red. If we lose Florida, we lose America. We can't let it happen, right? What about organizing a YUGE pro-Trump flash mob in every Florida town? We are currently reaching out

to local activists and we've got the folks who are okay to be in charge of organizing their events almost everywhere in FL. However, we still need your support. What do you think about that? Are you in?' Indictment, supranote 7, at 26.

27 Worldwide Threat Assessment of the U.S. Intelligence Community: Hearing Before the S. Select Comm. on Intelligence, 115th Cong. 11 (2018) (Statement of Daniel R. Coats, Dir. of Natl Intelligence), https://perma.cc/2J27-8AE5. At a hearing before the Senate Intelligence Committee on February 13, the leaders of the intelligence community made the same assertions. All of the malsore affirmed the conclusions contained in the 2017 ODNIREPORT, supra note 1. See Miles Parks, Russian Threat to Elections to Persist through 2018, Spy Bosses Warn Congress, NATL PUB. RADIO (Feb. 13, 2018), https://perma.cc/W7U9-3KSE.

28 Indictment, supranote 7.

29 Id. at 2–3.

30 Id. at 4.

31 Id. at 17.

32 See also Scott Shane, The Fake Americans Russia Created to Influence the Election, N.Y. TIMES (Sept. 7, 2017), www.nytimes.com/2017/09/07/us/politics/russia-facebook-twitter-election.html.

33 Donald J. Trump (@realDonaldTrump), TWITTER (Feb. 17, 2018, 8:22 PM), https://perma.cc/M4HG-UJR6.

34 Id.

35 Nikolay Koval, Revolution Hacking, in CYBER WAR IN PERSPECTIVE: RUSSIAN AGGRESSION AGAINST UKRAINE 55, 56–58 (Kenneth Geers ed., 2015); See also Mark Clayton, Ukraine Election Narrowly Avoided Wanton Destruction from Hackers, CHRISTIAN SCI. MONITOR (June 17, 2014), https://perma.cc/N9UE-TVE6.

36 Sumi Somaskanda, The Cyber Threat to Germany's Elections Is Very Real, ATLANTIC (Sept. 20, 2017), https://perma.cc/5KA4-MJCR.

37 Eric Auchard, Macron Campaign Was Target of Cyber Attacks by Spy-Linked Group, REUTERS (Apr. 24, 2017), https://perma.cc/6FJH-L9LL.

38 Id.; see also Laura Daniels, How Russia Hacked the French Election, POLITICO (Apr. 23, 2017), https://perma.cc/F3X6-DZVG.

39 Theresa May Accuses Vladimir Putin of Election Meddling, BBC (Nov. 14, 2017), https://perma.cc/HJ5P-5NAF.

40 Id.

41 Russian Central Election Commission Comes under Cyberattack, RT NEWS (Mar. 18, 2018), https://perma.cc/D634-SBWL.

42 Id.

43 See generally Thomas Carothers, Is the U.S. Hypocritical to Criticize Russian Election Meddling?, FOREIGN AFFAIRS (Mar.12,2018), https://perma.cc/WU6L-4XJ5.

44 Id.; see also Scott Shane, Russia Isn't the Only One Meddling in Elections. We Do It, Too, N.Y.TIMES (Feb. 16, 2018), www.nytimes.com/2018/02/17/sunday-review/russia-isnt-the-only-one-meddling-in-elections-we-do-it-too.html.

45 Sabrina Taverniseetal, With New Afghan Vote, Path to Stability Is Unclear, N.Y.TIMES (Oct.20,2009), www.nytimes.com/2009/10/21/world/asia/21afghan.html.

46 Afghan Quits Election Complaints Commission, CNN (Oct. 13,2009), https://perma.cc/3AUV-J7V3.

47 Carothers, supranote 43.

48 Shane, Russia Isn't the Only One, supranote 44.

49 Russia 2016, NATL ENDOWMENT FOR DEMOCRACY (Aug. 16, 2017), https://perma.cc/N4RW-PFEN. The endowment no longer reports its recipients in light of new laws making the receipt of foreign funding unlawful.

50 Carothers, supranote 43.

51 Primary rules of international law impose obligations on States, whereas secondary rules set forth the general conditions under international law for the State to be considered responsible for wrongful actions or omissions, and the legal consequences which flow therefrom. Intl Law Commn, Draft Articles on Responsibility of States for Internationally Wrongful Acts, supranote 8.

52 Obama Press Release, supranote 1.

53 On intervention, see Section III.B, infra, and accompanying notes. The prohibition on the use of force is set forth in U.N. Charter article 2(4) and reflects customary international law. The Tallinn

Manual 2.0 experts concurred that cyber operations are capable of violating the prohibition, even when not accompanied by kinetic operations. TALLINN MANUAL 2.0 ON THE INTERNATIONAL LAW APPLICABLE TO CYBER OPERATIONS 168 (Michael N. Schmitt & Liis Vihuleds., 2017) [hereinafter TALLINN MANUAL 2.0]. However, because of the relatively high consequential threshold for violation, it is unlikely, although not inconceivable, that cyber election meddling would qualify as an unlawful use of force. On the subject of cyber uses of force, see Michael N. Schmitt, The Use of Cyber Force and International Law, in OXFORD HANDBOOK ON THE USE OF FORCE IN INTERNATIONAL LAW 1110 (Marc Weller ed. 2015).

54 Rep. of the Group of Governmental Experts on Dev. in the Field of Info. and Telecomm. in the Context of Intl Security, 15, U.N. Doc. A/70/174 (July 22, 2015) [hereinafter U.N. GGE 2015 Report]. See also Rep. of the Group of Governmental Experts on Dev. in the Field of Info. and Telecomm. in the Context of Intl Security, 19, U.N. Doc. A/68/98 (June 24, 2013) [hereinafter U.N. GGE 2013 Report].

55 There have been two editions of the book, each prepared by different IGEs. Both treat sovereignty as a primary rule. Compare TALLINN MANUAL ON THE INTERNATIONAL LAW APPLICABLE TO CYBER WARFARE r. 1 (Michael N. Schmitt gen. ed., 2013) with TALLINN MANUAL 2.0, supra note 53, rr. 1–4.

56 Harold Hongju Koh, Legal Adviser, U.S. State Dept, Remarks at the U.S. Cyber Command Inter- Agency Legal Conference (Sept. 18, 2012). On the Koh statement, see Michael N. Schmitt, International Law in Cyberspace: The Koh Speech and Tallinn Manual Juxtaposed, 54 HARV. J. INTL L. ONLINE 13 (2012). See also Applicability of International Law to Conflicts in Cyberspace, 2014 DIGEST OF UNITED STATES PRACTICE IN INTERNATIONAL LAW, ch.18,§ A(3)(b), at737.

57 Bert Koenders, Foreign Minister, Neth., Remarks at The Hague Regarding Tallinn Manual 2.0 (Feb. 13, 2017) (on file with author).

58 Gary P. Corn & Robert Taylor, Sovereignty in the Age of Cyber, 111 AM. J. INTL L. UNBOUND 207, 208–09 (2017). For a reply explaining the opposing position, see Michael N. Schmitt & Liis Vihul, Sovereignty in Cyberspace: Lex Lata Vel Non?, 111AM. J. INTL L. UNBOUND 213 (2017).

59 See, for example, Schmitt & Vihul, Sovereignty in Cyberspace, supranote 58, at 217–18; TALLINN MANUAL 2.0, supra note 53, atr. 32.

60 Michael N. Schmitt & Liis Vihul, Respect for Sovereignty in Cyberspace, 95 TEX. L. REV. 1639 (2017).

61 Id. at 1650–68.

62 Id. at 1647; TALLINN MANUAL 2.0, supranote 53, at 18–27.

63 Brian J. Egan, Legal Adviser, U.S. Dept of State, Remarks at Berkeley Law School on International Law and Stability in Cyberspace (Nov. 10, 2016), https://perma.cc/B6TH-232L.

64 Island of Palmas (Neth. v. U.S.), 2 R.I.A.A. 829, 838 (Perm. Ct. Arb.1928).

65 TALLINN MANUAL 2.0, supranote 53, at 20.

66 Id. at 20–21.

67 Nicole Perlroth, In Cyberattack on Saudi Firm, U.S. Sees Iran Firing Back, N.Y.TIMES (Oct. 23, 2012), www.nytimes.com/2012/10/24/business/global/cyberattack-on-saudi-oil-firm-disquiets-us.html.

68 TALLINN MANUAL 2.0, supranote 53, at 21.

69 Id.

70 Id.

71 Id. at 21–22.

72 ODNIREPORT, supranote 1, at 3.

73 On propaganda and sovereignty, see TALLINN MANUAL 2.0, supranote 53, at 26.

74 ODNIREPORT, supranote 1, at 2–3.

75 Id. at 24.

76 Interestingly, the Russian operations would appear to violate a 2015 revision to the Shanghai Cooperation Organizations (of which Russia is a key member together with China) own Code of Conduct, which prohibits using information and communications technology to ... interfere in the internal affairs of other States or [u]ndermine ... political, economic, and social stability. Permanent Reps. of China, Kaz., Kyrg., Russ.,Taj., and Uzb. to the U.N., Letter dated Jan. 9, 2015 from the Permanent Reps. of China, Kazakhstan, Kyrgyzstan, the Russian Federation,

## 210 Michael Schmitt

Tajikistan, and Uzbekistan to the United Nations addressed to the Secretary-General, arts. 2(3), 2(5), U.N. Doc. A/69/723 (Jan. 13, 2015).

77 Corfu Channel Case (U.K. v. Alb.), Judgment, 1949 I.C.J. Rep. 4, 35 (Apr. 9); Military and Paramilitary Activities in and Against Nicaragua (Nicar. v. U.S.), Judgment, 1986 I.C.J. Rep. 14, 202, 205, 251 (June 27); Armed Activities on the Territory of the Congo (Dem. Rep. Congo v. Uganda), Judgment, 2005 I.C.J. Rep. 168, 161–65 (Dec.19); G.A. Res. 2625 (XXV), Declaration on Principles of International Law Concerning Friendly Relations and Co-operation among States in Accordance with the Charter of the United Nations, 3, (Oct. 24, 1970); TALLINN MANUAL 2.0, supra note 53, at r. 66. For an extensive list of examples of States styling activities as intervention, and thereby supporting the premise that the prohibition enjoys customary law status, see TALLINN MANUAL 2.0, supra note 53, fn. 761. On intervention in the cyber context, see Sean Watts, Low-Intensity Cyber Operations and the Principle of Non-Intervention, in CYBER-WAR: LAW AND ETHICS FOR VIRTUALCONFLICTS 249 (Jens David Ohlin, Kevin Govern, & Claire Finklestein eds., 2015); Terry D. Gill, Non-Intervention in the Cyber Context, in PEACETIME REGIME FOR STATE ACTIVITIES IN CYBERSPACE 217 (Katharina Ziolkowski ed., 2013). On intervention generally, see OPPENHEIM'S INTERNATIONAL LAW 428–51 (Robert Jennings & Arthur Watts eds., 9th ed. 1992).

78 Nicar. v. U.S., 1986 I.C.J., supranote 77, at 202.

79 OPPENHEIM, supra note 77, at 428.

80 TALLINN MANUAL 2.0, supranote 53, at 315.

81 Nicar. v. U.S., 1986 I.C.J., supranote 77, at 205; see also TALLINN MANUAL 2.0, supranote 53, at 314–17.

82 Nicar. v. U.S., 1986 I.C.J., supra note 77, at 205; see also Nationality Decrees Issued in Tunis and Morocco, Advisory Opinion, 1923 P.C.I.J. (ser. B) No. 4, at 24 (Feb. 7) (referring to matters not, in principle, regulated by international law).

83 Nicar. v. U.S., 1986 I.C.J., supranote 77,at 205.

84 The Declaration on the Inadmissibility of Intervention, albeit not necessarily declaratory of customary international law, sets out certain parameters with respect to permissible State actions. It notes that States must refrain from any action or attempt to destabilize the political system and refrain from the promotion, encouragement or support, direct or indirect, of any action which seeks to disrupt the unity or undermine or subvert the political order of other States. G.A. Res. 36/103, annex, Declaration on the Inadmissibility of Intervention and Interference in the Internal Affairs of States, at II(e)–(f) (Dec. 9, 1981).

85 Nicar. v. U.S., 1986 I.C.J., supranote 77, at 205.

86 Id. See also Maziar Jamnejad & Michael Wood, The Principle of Non-Intervention, 22 LEIDEN J. INTL L. 345, 348 (2009) (Thus the essence of intervention is coercion .... Only acts of a certain magnitude are likely to qualify as coercive, and only those that are intended to force a policy change in the target state will contravene the principle.).

87 G.A. Res. 2625 (XXV), supranote 77, at 3.

88 TALLINN MANUAL 2.0, supranote 53, at 317.

89 Egan, supranote 63.

90 TALLINN MANUAL 2.0, supranote 53, at 318–19.

91 Jamnejad & Wood, supra note 86, at 381.

92 Computer Fraud and Abuse Act, 18 U.S.C.§ 1030 (2016).

93 In this regard, it must be cautioned that intervention may be direct or indirect, as in the case of financing insurgents. Nicar.v.U.S.,1986 I.C.J., supranote 77, at 205, 228; G.A. Res. 2625 (XXV), supra note 77, at 3; G.A. Res. 36/103, annex, supra note 84, at pmbl. The issue being examined here, however, is whether the effect that qualifies as coercive (for example, a change in election results) must be directly caused by the cyber meddling.

94 TALLINN MANUAL 2.0, supranote 53, at 320.

95 Id.

96 For an innovative, albeit somewhat overbroad, call for application of the principle of non- intervention to DDoS attacks, see William Mattessich, Note, Digital Destruction: Applying the Principle of Non-Intervention to Distributed Denial of Service Attacks Manifesting No Physical Damage, 54 COLUM. J. TRANSNATL L. 873 (2016).

97 This uncertainty was acknowledged during a 2017 workshop of the European Leadership Network tasked with assessing key concepts and norms in Russia–West relations: A destabilizing

factor affecting relations between Russia and the West have been the accusations over suspected interference in elections, both the US elections last year and the Russian elections in 2011. While the text of the non-intervention principle makes no explicit reference to elections, its remit covers direct and indirect activities that breach national and political independence, challenge political stability or change political systems. Events of the past year and a half highlight the incomplete nature of these prohibitions. The conduct of political campaigns, their direct and indirect support by foreign nationals, external governments, and the funding of parties and lobby groups by foreign states highlight the weakness of the Helsinki sixth principle. In addition, the market features of normal politicking, including where sponsored political advertisements and private fundraising enterprises act as the bedrock of so much national political activity, have circumvented the non-intervention restrictions. The outcome of an electoral process directly affects a state's political independence and stability, yet the modern-day conduct of elections is not adequately safeguarded against the involvement of foreign actors, and the international normative framework remains incomplete. DENITSA RAYNOVA, TOWARDS A COMMON UNDERSTANDING OF THE NON-INTERVENTION PRINCIPLE: EUROPEAN LEADERSHIP NETWORK POST-WORKSHOP REPORT 1, 6 (Oct. 2017).

98  For an argument that the Russian operations qualify as coercive intervention on the basis of the nature of state interests, see Steven J. Barela, Zero Shades of Grey: Russian-Ops Violate International Law, JUST SECURITY (Mar. 29, 2018), https://perma.cc/85QN-UUQC. The author finds Barela's suggestion interesting, but unreflective of lex lata.

99  See generally Michael N. Schmitt, In Defense of Due Diligence in Cyberspace, 125 YALE L.J.F. 68 (2015).

100  TALLINN MANUAL 2.0, supra note 53, at r. 6. For an excellent survey of the obligation of due diligence, see INTL L. ASSN, STUDY GROUP ON DUE DILIGENCE IN INTERNATI-ONAL LAW: FIRST REPORT (Mar. 7, 2014).

101  U.K. v. Alb.,1949 I.C.J., supranote 77.

102  Id. at 22; see also Neth. v. U.S., 2 R.I.A.A., supranote 64, at 839 (Territorial sovereignty … involves the exclusive right to display the activities of a State. This right has as corollary a duty: the obligation to protect within the territory the rights of other States.).

103  S.S. Lotus (Fr. v. Turk.), Judgment, 1927 P.C.I.J. (ser. A) No. 10, at 88 (Sept. 7) (separate opinion by Moore, J.).

104  The author served as Director of the project and was present at all meetings.

105  U.N. GGE 2013 Report, supranote 54, 23; U.N. GGE 2015 Report, supranote 54, 13(c).

106  See, for example, Trail Smelter (U.S. v. Can.), 3 R.I.A.A. 1905, 1965 (1941); U.N. Conference on the Human Environment, Declaration of the United Nations Conference on the Human Environment, prin. 21, U.N. Doc. A/CONF.48/14/Rev.1 (June 16, 1972); U.N. Conference on Environment and Development, Rio Declaration on Environment and Development, prin. 2, U.N. Doc. A/CONF.151/26/Rev.1 (Vol. I), annex I (Aug. 12, 1992).

107  TALLINN MANUAL 2.0, supranote 53, at 47.

108  Id. at 43–44.

109  Id.

110  Id. at 34 (drawing from the Trail Smelter Case, supra note 106, at 1965); see also Intl Law Commn, Rep. on the Work of Its Fifty-Third Session, Draft Articles on Prevention of Transboundary Harm from Hazardous Activities, art. 2, 4, 6 of commentary, U.N. Doc. A/56/10 (2001), reprinted in [2001] 2 Y.B. Intl L. Commn 32, U.N. Doc. A/CN.4/SER.A/2001/Add.1 (Part 2) (using the terms significant and substantial).

111  TALLINN MANUAL 2.0, supranote 53, at 34.

112  Jens David Ohlin, Did Russian Cyber Interference inthe2016 Election Violate International Law?, 95 TEX. L. REV. 1579, 1580 (2017).

113  International Covenant on Civil and Political Rights art. 1(1), Dec. 16, 1966, 999 U.N.T.S. 171 [hereinafter ICCPR]; International Covenant on Economic, Social and Cultural Rights art. 1(1), Dec. 16, 1966, 993 U.N.T.S. 3; see also G.A. Res. 2625 (XXX), supra note 77, at 5; East Timor (Port. v. Austl.), 1995 I.C.J. Rep. 90, 28 (June30) (finding self-determination to have an erga omnes character).

114  Ohlin, supranote 112, at 1596–

115  ICCPR, supranote 113, at art.17.

116  Convention for the Protection of Human Rights and Fundamental Freedoms art. 8(1), Nov. 4, 1950, 213 U.N.T.S. 221.

# 212 Michael Schmitt

117 TALLINN MANUAL 2.0, supra note 53, at 189. This conclusion is based in part on the fact that the right is found in Universal Declaration of Human Rights art. 12. G.A. Res. 217 (III) A, (Dec. 10, 1948).

118 Ohlin, supranote 112, at 1584–85.

119 Id. at 1585–87.

120 In particular, the U.S. has long taken the position that the ICCPR obligations do not apply extraterritorially. See, for example, U.N. Hum. Rts. Commn, Consideration of Reports Submitted by States Parties Under Article 40 of the Covenant, 469, U.N. Doc. CCPR/C/USA/3 (Nov. 28, 2005). Interestingly, the State Departments Legal Adviser issued a 2010 memo to the effect this position was incorrect as a matter of law. U.S. Dept of State, Office of the Legal Adviser, Memorandum Opinion on the Geographic Scope of the International Covenant on Civil and Political Rights, at 4 (Oct. 19, 2010). That memo did not mature into the U.S. position.

121 For comprehensive treatment of the subject, see MARKO MILANOVIC, EXTRATERRIT-ORIAL APPLICATION OF HUMAN RIGHTS TREATIES: LAW, PRINCIPLES, AND POLICY ch. IV (2011).

122 TALLINN MANUAL 2.0, supra note 53, at 183–84. The Tallinn Manual 2.0 experts drew the term power or effective control from Hum. Rts. Comm., General Comment No. 31: The Nature of the General Legal Obligation Imposed on States Parties to the Covenant, 10, U.N. Doc. CCPR/C/21/Rev.1/Add.13 (Mar. 29, 2004). With regard to European Court of Human Rights juris prudence in this context, see Al-Skeiniv. United Kingdom, 2011-IV Eur. Ct. H. R. 99, 130–39; Catan v. Moldova & Russia, 2012-V Eur. Ct. H. R. 309, 105.

123 TALLINN MANUAL 2.0, supranote 53, at 185.

124 Id. at 168.

125 ODNIREPORT, supranote 1, at 2.

126 TALLINN MANUAL 2.0, supranote 53, at r. 32.

127 Obama Press Release, supranote 1.

128 ODNIREPORT, supranote 1, at ii.

129 Id. at 2.

130 Putin Tells U.S. to Send Evidence of Vote Meddling, REUTERS (Mar. 3, 2018), https://perma.cc/N2AY-G56Y.

131 See, for example, David E. Sanger & Martin Fackler, N.S.A. Breached North Korean Networks Before Sony Attack, Officials Say, N.Y. TIMES (Jan. 18, 2015), https://perma.cc/WY9C-J45T (explaining U.S. unwillingness to reveal the way it was able to attribute the 2014 Sony hack to North Korea).

132 This was the conclusion of the Tallinn Manual 2.0 IGE. TALLINN MANUAL 2.0, supranote 53, at 83. Although there is no legal obligation to do so, the U.N. GGE has encouraged States to provide such evidence when cyber operations are at issue. U.N. GGE 2015 Report, supra note 54, at 15.

133 TALLINN MANUAL 2.0, supra note 53, at 81–82. Fact-finding bodies like tribunals, arbitral panels, domestic courts and the like must abide by the standards and burdens of proof applicable in proceedings before them. These may differ, as in the case of criminal trials imposing a higher standard of proof than applicable in civil proceedings.

134 Intl Law Commn, Draft Articles on Responsibility of States for Internationally Wrongful Acts, supranote 8, 3 of commentary to art. 49; TALLINN MANUAL 2.0, supranote 53, at 116. A State that misattributes a cyber operation upon which a countermeasure is based commits an internationally wrongful act.

135 Intl Law Commn, Draft Articles on Responsibility of States for Internationally Wrongful Acts, supranote 8.

136 Id., art. 4(1); TALLINN MANUAL 2.0, supranote 53, at r. 15.

137 And even in the face of contrary direction from superiors. See Intl Law Commn, Draft Articles on Responsibility of States for Internationally Wrongful Acts, supra note 8, at 13 of commentary to art. 4.

138 Id.

139 Id. at 11 of commentary to art. 4; see also Application of the Convention on the Prevention and Punishment of the Crime of Genocide (Bosn. & Herz. v. Serb. & Montenegro), Judgment, 2007 I.C.J. Rep. 43, 392–93 (Feb. 26).

140 Person or entities that do not qualify as de jure or de facto State organs may nevertheless be

empowered under domestic law to exercise elements of governmental authority. If so, their activities, including those that are ultra vires, are attributable to the State. Intl Law Commn, Draft Articles on Responsibility of States for Internationally Wrongful Acts, supranote 8, art. 5; TALLINN MANUAL 2.0, supra note 53, at r. 15. Because of the requirement for authorization under law and the limitation to activities that are by nature elements of government authority, attribution on this basis is unlikely in the case of cyber election meddling. A possible exception would be a secret contract to engage in offensive cyber operations during foreign elections.

141 Intl Law Commn, Draft Articles on Responsibility of States for Internationally Wrongful Acts,

142 Id. at 6 of commentary to art. 8 (citing *Foremost Tehran, Inc. v. Islamic Republic of Iran*, 10 Iran–U.S.Cl. Trib. Rep. 228 (1986); American Bell International Inc. v. Islamic Republic of Iran, 12 Iran–U.S. Cl. Trib. Rep. 170 (1986)).

143 ODNIREPORT, supranote 1, at 3.

144 Intl Law Commn, Draft Articles on Responsibility of States for Internationally Wrongful Acts, supranote 8, at 7–8 of commentary to art. 8.

145 Id. at art. 8; TALLINN MANUAL 2.0, supranote 53, at r. 17(a).

146 Intl Law Commn, Draft Articles on Responsibility of States for Internationally Wrongful Acts, supra note 8, art. 11; TALLINN MANUAL 2.0, supra note 53, r. 17(b). Acknowledgment and adoption were illustrated in the actions of the Iranian government following the 1979 occupation of the U.S. Embassy and consulates in Iran and the decision of the Ayatollah Khomeini to perpetuate those activities, including keeping U.S. personnel hostage therein. The International Court of Justice later found Iran responsible on this basis. United States Diplomatic and Consular Staff in Tehran (U.S. v. Iran), Judgment, 1980 I.C.J. Rep. 3, 74 (May 24).

147 Intl Law Commn, Draft Articles on Responsibility of States for Internationally Wrongful Acts, supranote 8, 2–5 of commentary to art. 8; see also Kubo Ma ák, Decoding Article 8 of the International Law Commission's Articles on State Responsibility: Attribution of Cyber Operations by Non-State Actors, 21 J. CONFLICT & SECURITY L.405 (2016).

148 Intl Law Commn, Draft Articles on Responsibility of States for Internationally Wrongful Acts, supranote 8, at 2 of commentary to art. 8.

149 Id. at 7 of commentary to art. 8.

150 Id. at 4–5 of commentary to art. 8.

151 Nicar. v. U.S., 1986 I.C.J., supranote 77, at 115.

152 Bosn. & Herz. v. Serb. & Montenegro, 2007 I.C.J., supra note 139, at 400.

153 Id.

154 White House, Fact Sheet: Actions in Response to Russian Malicious Cyber Activity and Harassment (Dec. 29, 2016), https://perma.cc/C83Z-SQSL; Obama Press Release, supra note 1; David E. Sanger, Obama Strikes Back at Russia for Election Hacking, N.Y. TIMES (Dec. 29, 2016), www.nytimes.com/2016/12/29/us/politics/russia-election-hacking-sanctions.html.

155 Peter Baker, White House Penalizes Russians over Election Meddling and Cyberattacks, N.Y.TIMES (Mar. 15, 2018), www.nytimes.com/2018/03/15/us/politics/trump-russia-sanctions.html.

156 Id.; Laura Smith-Spark & Radina Gigova, Russia to Expand American Blacklist after New US Sanctions, CNN (Mar. 16, 2018), https://perma.cc/DY52-LW48. For a list of individuals and entities sanctioned, see U.S. DEPT OF TREASURY, CAATSA—Russia-Related Designations, Cyber-Related Designations and Designations Updates, Russia/Ukraine-Related Designations Updates, Issuance of Cyber-Related General License 1A, Updated FAQs (Mar. 15, 2018), https://perma.cc/LD9M-NGJM.

157 Gardiner Harris, Trump Administration Imposes New Sanctions on Putin Cronies, N.Y. TIMES (Apr. 6, 2018), www.nytimes.com/2018/04/06/us/politics/trump-sanctions-russia-putin-oligarchs.html.

158 See generally Michael N. Schmitt, Peacetime Cyber Responses and Wartime Cyber Operations under International Law: An Analytical Vade Mecum, 8 HARV. NATL SECURITY J. 239 (2017); see also Sean Watts, International Law and Proposed U.S. Responses to the D.N.C. Hack, JUST SECURITY (Oct. 14, 2016), https://perma.cc/Q8L5-C432.

159 TALLINN MANUAL 2.0, supranote 53, at 112.

160 As noted by Professor Sean Murphy in his Statement of Defense of the United States, every state has the right to grant or deny foreign assistance, to permit or deny exports, to grantor deny loans or credits, and to grant or deny participation in national procurement or financial management, on

214  Michael Schmitt

such terms as it finds appropriate. Sean Murphy, Statement of Defense of the United States, Iran–United States Claims Tribunal, Claim No. A/30, at 57 (1996), https://perma.cc/W92E-3LLM. In support, he cites Iran v. United States, AWD No. 382-B1-FT, 62, 19 Iran–US Cl. Trib. Rep. 273,

161 Intl Law Commn, Draft Articles on Responsibility of States for Internationally Wrongful Acts,

162 Id. at arts. 49–53; TALLINN MANUAL 2.0, supra note 53, at rr. 20–25, 27–29; see also Michael N. Schmitt, Below the Threshold Cyber Operations: The Countermeasures Response Option and International Law, 54 VA. J. INTL L. 697 (2014). Assurances are a communication by the responsible State that the unlawful act will cease and not be repeated, whereas a guarantee is a measure designed to ensure non-repetition, such as removing providing information that enables the injured State to locate and remove malware. Reparations may take the form of restitution, compensation, and satisfaction (apology).

163 On active defense in the cyber context and the recently adopted U.S. policy of facilitating active defense by the private sector, see Morgan Chalfant, DHS Giving Active Defense Cyber Tools to Private Sector, Secretary Says, THE HILL (Jan. 16,2018), https://perma.cc/2ERH-HULF.

164 TALLINN MANUAL 2.0, supranote 53, at 112–13.

165 Unless the treaty sets for the remedy for, or process to handle, a breach of its terms.

166 Intl Law Commn, Draft Articles on Responsibility of States for Internationally Wrongful Acts, supranote 8, at art. 25; TALLINN MANUAL 2.0, supranote 53, at r. 26.

167 U.N. Charter art. 51.

168 TALLINN MANUAL 2.0, supranote 53, at 340–44; Michael N. Schmitt, Cyber Operations and the Jus Ad Bellum Revisited, 56 VILL. L. REV. 569, 586–603 (2011).

169 Michael N. Schmitt & Liis Vihul, International Cyber Law Politicized: The U.N. GGEs Failure to Advance Cyber Norms, JUST SECURITY (June30, 2017), https://perma.cc/3EXH-VYE8.

170 Personal knowledge of the author; training conducted in collaboration with Cyber Law International.

# 13

# STIGMATIZING CYBER AND INFORMATION WARFARE

## Mission impossible?

*Brian M. Mazanec and Patricia Shamai*

## Introduction

The 2018 US World Wide Threat Assessment of the US Intelligence Community, identified that

> The potential for surprise in the cyber realm will increase in the next year and beyond as billions more digital devices are connected – with relatively little built in security – and both nation states and malign actors become more emboldened and better equipped in the use of increasingly widespread cyber tool kits.[1]

This statement is echoed in other studies addressing the increasing threats posed by cyber weapons. In particular, in 2014, the Center for the Study of Weapons of Mass Destruction at US National Defense University published the results of a study into the future nature and role of weapons of mass destruction (WMD) in 2030. The study found that, as a future challenge to security,

> New forms of WMD beyond chemical, biological, radiological and nuclear weapons are unlikely to emerge by 2030, but cyber weapons will probably be capable of inflicting such widespread disruption that the United States may become as reliant on the threat to impose unacceptable costs to deter a large-scale cyber-attack as it is currently to deter the use of WMD.[2]

Indeed, the summary of the 2018 US Department of Defense (DOD) Cyber Strategy states that "competitors deterred from engaging the United States and our allies in an armed conflict are using cyberspace operations to steal our technology, disrupt our government and commerce, challenge our democratic processes, and threaten our critical infrastructure."[3] The threat of cyber-attack poses serious risk to the US and its allies. Why then, have cyber weapons—or the broader information warfare (IW) context within which they fall—not been proscribed by the international community as have WMD?[4]

What are the international norms associated with these weapons and how have they evolved?

Today, relatively early in the age of cyber conflict, cyber and novel IW weapons are appropriately considered emerging-technology weapons. Within this chapter, we reaffirm that developing constraining norms for emerging-technology weapons promotes the perception among powerful or relevant states that such norms are in their national self-interest.[5] Our argument builds on this argument by focusing on the issue of stigma and the role that it plays in norm development. The international stigma associated with a weapon is a key variable that influences states' perceptions of self-interest. We further argue that the nature of the cyber threat is diffuse, secretive and lacks a clear definition. The cyber threat is broad and complicated by a wide array of types of potential attacks, including, computer network attack (CNA), computer network exploitation (CNE), computer network defense (CND), cyber-crime, and hacktivism.[6] Further, secrecy and anonymity muddy the waters regarding attack and actor identification. These challenges complicate the emergence of a cyber stigma and thus efforts to proscribe these weapons. Pursuing measures to enhance the stigmatization of the cyber threat may be a means to further develop global norms towards the cyber threat. By examining the process of normative evolution, and in particular the norms leading to the branding of specific methods of warfare as stigmatized, we argue that at present a stigma does not exist towards the threat of CNA-style cyber warfare, despite recognition of the increasing importance of this threat. This is due to the problems associated with proscribing these weapons and their varied nature.

In order to demonstrate this argument, we identify the study of norm evolution and link this to research into the stigmatization of WMD. A comparison is made between the evolution of norms proscribing nuclear, chemical and biological weapons, commonly categorized as WMD and the prospects for those relating to cyber warfare. We identify that the process of stigmatization of WMD has been a reflective process; it is socially constructed, therefore subject to change and is shaped by the strategic and ethical perception of these specific methods of warfare. Comparing the WMD norms with the current norms associated with cyber weapons, we demonstrate that in order for the cyber threat to become stigmatized, greater effort and attention needs to be paid to the shared perception of the strategic and ethical nature of this threat. The cyber threat is not clearly defined, thus at present, the cyber stigma is not absolute.

In our opinion, cyber weapons do matter and greater attention needs to be paid to ways in which norms proscribing these weapons can be developed to prevent future cyber security threats.

## The cyber threat

In February 2018 US Director of National Intelligence Daniel Coats testified that "The potential for surprise in the cyber realm will increase in the next year and beyond as billions more digital devices are connected" and that "both nation states and malign actors become more emboldened and better equipped in the use of increasingly widespread cyber toolkits."[7] Today, early into the age of cyber warfare, many hold a view regarding the inevitability of significant use of force in cyberspace (e.g. CNA-style attack) similar to that held soon after the advent of nuclear weapons. For example, early in the age of nuclear weapons, Lt. Gen. James Gavin expressed the contemporary wisdom when he wrote, "Nuclear weapons will become conventional for several reasons, among them cost, effectiveness against enemy weapons, and ease of handling."[8]

However, as the nuclear era advanced, a constraining norm developed that made states reluctant to possess or use nuclear weapons. This chapter seeks to explain how cyber warfare stigma—a key ingredient for the emergence of constraining norms for cyber warfare—might develop.

Cyber weapons are emerging-technology weapons and have existed for a relatively short time. Emerging-technology weapons are weapons based on new technology or a novel employment of older technologies to achieve certain effects. Given that technology is constantly advancing, weapons that initially fall into this category will eventually be re-categorized as still newer technologies develop. For example, the gunpowder-based weapons that began to spread in fourteenth-century Europe would clearly have been classified as emerging-technology weapons in that century and perhaps in the fifteenth century, but eventually those weapons were no longer novel and became fairly ubiquitous.[9] There is relative secrecy surrounding most cyber operations with no extensive record of customary practices of states.[10] Forsyth and Pope make this point when they highlight that cyberspace has resulted in a new form of war that "no one can see, measure, or presumably fear."[11] While much of the hostile cyber activity to date is not true cyber warfare, but instead is CNE-style activity and cyber-crime, this should not be interpreted as evidence of a norm against conducting CNA-style cyber-attacks.[12] Instead, it is evidence of how early we are in the cyber era. Advanced cyber warfare is only now becoming possible and a robust target set is emerging as societies become more immersed and dependent on cyberspace. In the absence of firmly established norms governing cyber warfare, states may also be exhibiting an abundance of caution as they slowly test the limits of what the international community deems acceptable behavior in cyberspace.

## Understanding norms

In order to examine the prospect of the emergence of a cyber stigma that fosters the development of constraining norms, it is necessary to gain collective insight into the normative understanding of these weapons. How is the threat of cyber warfare perceived? Is there a common, shared understanding of this threat? In order to address these questions, it is necessary to define our understanding of the term "norms." Norms are "intersubjective beliefs about the social and natural world that define actors, their situations, and the possibilities of actions."[13] For norms to be intersubjective, they are formed through social practice and therefore are socially constructed. In order to examine the effects of norms, we adopt a constructivist approach. Constructivism moves away from a structural approach to international relations and instead highlights the causal force of material interests and power, arguing that "shared ideas and knowledge are very important building blocks of international reality."[14] The focus is upon shared understandings and the process through which decisions are made, rather than material forces. As a result of this, attitudes and interests are not predictable. As Alexander Wendt has stated, "anarchy is what states make of it."[15] Wendt notes that, "Power is dependent upon the intersubjective understandings and expectations, on the distribution of knowledge that constitutes their (states) conception of self and other."[16] Knowledge is socially formed; he uses the example of the former Soviet Union and the US, arguing that if both states "decide that they are no longer enemies, then the cold war is over." Identity is therefore relational.[17] If we use this approach when considering normative understandings of the threat of cyber weapons, we are focusing our attention towards shared understandings of these weapons, how their image is formed and collective understanding of the threats posed by potential cyber warfare.[18]

## Constitutive and regulative norms

Norms as standards of behavior are continuously "out there" within society. For a particular practice to become elevated into domestic and international attention, the specific quality or issue must build momentum, there needs to be an increasing awareness of its distinct nature. There are different effects and standards of norms, these fall into predominantly two categories, regulative or constitutive norms. Regulative norms regulate and constrain behavior. Constitutive norms "create new actors, interests or categories of action."[19] For the purpose of this study, we are focusing upon the constraining norms that relate to cyber warfare. We are looking at how specific weapons are perceived. In order to understand this further, it is necessary to examine how norms become internationalized. How do some specific standards of behavior emerge as distinct from others?

## Norm evolution: the norm life cycle

In order for specific practice to be recognized as distinct, the norms associated with it must emerge within society and must be considered a "legitimate"[20] behavioral claim. This occurs through communication, debate, political action, and fundamentally, understanding of the consequences of a particular practice.[21] Martha Finnemore and Katherine Sikkink identify that norms form a patterned life cycle and different behavioral logics dominate different segments of the cycle.[22] Norms first emerge within the domestic arena. For a particular practice to be highlighted as distinct it is communicated and elevated by domestic norm entrepreneurs, the role of the entrepreneur is to highlight and promote the practice as distinct. Jeffrey Checkel argues that norms emerge onto the domestic arena through a means of empowerment. Empowerment occurs when "prescriptions embodied in a norm first become, through changes in discourse or behavior, a focus of domestic political attention or debate. This process involves elite policymakers and other societal actors as well."[23] The norm entrepreneur can be an individual or (non-state actor) or network. The norm entrepreneur's role is to "mobilize and coerce decision makers."[24]

The first stage of the norm's life cycle is that it emerges at a domestic level. It is then accepted at this level and adopted into law. The norm is then propelled onto the international arena by the norm entrepreneurs. Norm entrepreneurs work from a platform, either an institution or non-governmental organization to promote the norm. Having reached a tipping point of interest, the norm then becomes socialized at an international level. This is the second stage of the life cycle of the norm.

Finally, the norm becomes institutionalized in specific sets of international rules and organizations.[25] The normative practice becomes so accepted that it is "taken for granted."[26] This is the third and final stage of the life cycle of the norm. Using constructivist principles, it is possible to examine how and why specific methods of warfare emerge as distinct and become proscribed by the international community. The norms associated with cyber warfare can be unraveled further by exploring the significance of norm evolution theory.

## Norm evolution theory for emerging technology weapons

By examining norm evolution theory in association with constructivism, it is possible to develop a picture of how and why specific methods of warfare, in particular, emerging-technology weapons have received international condemnation, and in turn, international action. This helps to form a picture of normative approaches towards the threat of cyber and information warfare and provides greater insight into the significance of stigma enhancing norms. While general norm evolution theory is useful for predicting and explaining the development and evolution of international norms, it was in large part developed using case studies unrelated to warfare, such as social issues involving women's rights, protecting the environment, or encouraging free trade.[27] As such, it is not specifically developed nor tailored for norms for weapons and warfare, particularly those involving emerging technology. As has been noted, emerging-technology weapons are weapons based on new technology or a novel employment of older technologies to achieve certain effects. Today cyber weapons used to conduct CNA-style cyber-attacks are emerging-technology weapons. Previous study has identified that the primary hypothesis of norm evolution theory for emerging-technology weapons is that a state's self-interest will play a significant role and a norm's convergence with perceived state self-interest will be important to achieving norm emergence and a state acting as a norm leader.[28] *This theory further argues* that norms are more likely to emerge when vital actors are involved, specifically key states acting as norm leaders, and norm entrepreneurs within organizations.

## *The case for norm evolution theory for emerging-technology weapons*

What does norm evolution theory for emerging-technology weapons predict regarding the development of constrictive international norms? The examples of chemical and biological weapons and nuclear weapons (which eventually became known and stigmatized collectively as WMD) are particularly salient historic case studies when considering norm evolution for cyber warfare.

Chemical and biological weapons and cyber weapons are both non-conventional weapons that share many of the same special characteristics with significant international security implications. They include challenges of attribution following their use, attractiveness to weaker powers and non-state actors as asymmetric weapons, use as a force multiplier for conventional military operations, questionable deterrence value, target and weapon unpredictability, potential for major collateral damage or unintended consequences due to "borderless" domains, multi-use nature of the associated technologies, and the frequent use of covert programs to develop such weapons.[29] Due to these characteristics, both of these weapons are also attractive to non-state actors or those seeking anonymity resulting in a lack of clarity regarding the responsible party.

Nuclear weapons, like airpower before it and perhaps cyber weapons today, presented states with the challenge of a completely new and emerging war fighting technology. Nuclear weapons and cyber weapons, like the other emerging-technology case studies, share many of the same special characteristics with significant international security implications. These include the potential for major collateral damage or unintended consequences (due to fallout, in the case of nuclear weapons) and covert development programs. Because of these common attributes, lessons regarding norm development can be learned and a framework developed that is applicable to predicting the prospects of constraining norms as a tool to address the use of cyber weapons.

When the two historic case studies mentioned above, are considered, the primary reason for developing constraining norms for emerging-technology weapons is the perception among powerful or relevant states that such norms are in their national self-interest. That is, a direct or indirect alignment of national self-interest with a constraining norm leads to norm emergence and the extent to which it is aligned with key or powerful states' perception of self-interest will determine how rapidly and effectively the norm emerges. The role of national self-interest as the primary ingredient leading to norm emergence also helps explain why, when challenged with violations of a young and not-yet-internalized norm, a state is quick to abandon the norm and pursue its material interest by using the previously constrained emerging-technology weapon, as was seen with chemical weapons in World War I. The international stigma associated with a weapon is a key variable that influences states' perceptions of self-interest and this chapter builds on this prior research by more closely examining the issue of stigma.

## Stigma and its impact on norm evolution

Stigmatizing a weapon type is important within norm evolution theory. Stigmatization is a process and is based upon the perception of certain weapons types as distinct. Norm evolution theory for emerging-technology weapons also recognizes other factors beyond perception of self-interest that play a major role in norm development. Stigmatizing a weapon-type is one of these key other factors. Specifically, characterizing the weapon-type as "unconventional" or otherwise granting it a special status can accelerate norm adoption and, ultimately, the achievement of a norm cascade. By definition, emerging-technology weapons do not fit cleanly into existing conventional categories. The success of norm entrepreneurs to help categorize the weapons as "special" helps single them out for norm development and can accelerate norm development. This was seen with President Truman's decision to place nuclear weapons into civilian control rather than under military control and reserve sole discretion as to when to employ them—something that had never been done with any other type of weapon.[30] Further, this is seen with the unconventional category of WMD, including biological and chemical weapons, which are declared by international treaties to be "repugnant to the conscience of mankind."[31] However, such special categorization also runs the risk of incentivizing its proliferation by making it exotic, prestigious, or a symbol associated with modernity.[32] It was this symbolism associated with nuclear weapons which some sought to ascribe to other WMD modalities, as evidenced in 1988 when then-speaker of the Iranian Parliament, Hashemi Rafsanjani, referred to biological and chemical weapons as "the poor man's atomic bomb."[33] If this type of association develops early for an emerging-technology weapons before constraining norms develop, the benefits of such an association could be negated.

## Stigma: the manifestation of a global prohibition

In order to understand the diffuse nature of the cyber norms, and appreciate the importance of stigma fostering norms it is necessary to compare cyber norms with those of WMD. As has been noted, cyber warfare relates to a diffuse range of threats. All three methods of warfare categorized within the remit of "WMD" differ greatly from one another in scale and effect. The WMD norms have been classified as so distinct as to have created a stigma towards all three methods of warfare. The stigma has developed progressively as a reflection of shared interests and values towards the perceived destruction created by WMD. The case of the stigmatization of WMD demonstrates a development of norm evolution theory; WMD were new emerging technologies which received specific condemnation due to their perceived and actual long-term effects. Collectively, WMD have been categorized as abhorrent due to their strategic and ethical quality. By examining the stigmatizing process of WMD, it is possible to see how and why these weapons have become categorized. The categorization has enabled international efforts to control these weapons. Important lessons can be learnt from this example that can help to gauge greater understanding of future methods to address the cyber threat.

A stigma refers to a mark or branding. Ervin Goffman notes that stigma is defined as "a special discrepancy between virtual and actual social identity. The term stigma is referred to as an attribute that is deeply discrediting."[34] Rebecca Adler-Nissan adds to this definition by stating that "stigma is associated with the idea that certain individuals are to be avoided or shunned, particularly in public places, as they are seen to be 'deviant' or 'morally polluted.'"[35] Within the field of sociology, stigma refers to the exclusion of individuals and groups of individuals within society, based upon cultural and social differences. In particular, the study of stigma has been associated with mental health illness, the deaf community, Aids and HIV, and the unemployed.

The author Erving Goffman's work has examined stigma as part of a human interaction, focusing on how those stigmatized respond in the face of stigma. He argues that there are two faces to stigma, that of the stigmatized and that of society at large and how it defines normality. Stigmas are "a social label created by the 'reaction' of others in society."[36] They are based upon the impressions that we draw and the language of relationships.[37] In this way, the focus is upon the socially constructed perception of differentness between those seen to possess the stigma and others. Those stigmatized are seen as outsiders. Goffman refers to this as an attribute that makes a person different from others.[38] As this "reactionary" process is socially constructed, it is subject to change.

As has been noted, norms have been defined as "a set of inter subjective understandings readily apparent to actors that makes behavioral claims on those actors."[39] For norms to be inter subjective, they are formed through social practice and therefore are socially constructed.

Sociological research into stigma can be applied to international attitudes towards specific methods of warfare and in particular, the categorization of specific methods of warfare as uniquely "destructive." The human reaction toward WMD is represented by the societal reaction within states and is evidenced by the policies and actions of states. The two faces of stigma are highlighted through the disparate arguments concerning the possession and use of WMD and fears that the development and use of these weapons would lead to lasting destruction. The focus is upon the norms associated with the stereotyping of WMD; these include the rising political and strategic distinction between WMD and other methods of warfare, as well as the contrasting debates about the possession and use of these weapons.

The author's Link and Phelan have observed that for a stigma to emerge there must be "the convergence of inter related components; stigma exists when elements of stereotyping, separation loss and discrimination occur together in a power situation that allows them."[40] The stigma towards WMD has developed progressively through history, building in momentum over time. It has emerged and developed as a result of the responses of heads of state, scientific advisers, politicians, the media and grass roots movements. The stigma has been shaped by the interests and values of western democratic states and is a reflection of the policy concerns within the US and Europe. Initially, WMD were seen as new emerging technology weapons and condemnation, as well as desirability were fueled by national interest. The focus was upon the strategic potential of these weapons. In time, the stigma has become accepted by the international community by way of international legislation and consensus within international institutions, most prominently the United Nations.[41] An evolving perception has emerged of these weapons as indiscriminate, long lasting weapons of mass destruction. The discursive tools and tactics used by actors to stigmatize WMD have focused upon the image of these weapons as causing death and disease. This has emphasized the impression of these weapons as different from other methods of warfare, and thus tainted. Any potential use would result in complete devastation and destruction, thus increasing the distinction between WMD and other methods of warfare.

When examining the developing stigmatization of WMD, the political and strategic importance of these weapons cannot be overlooked; neither can this be distinguished from concerns about the indiscriminate and long-term destructiveness of these weapons. The combination of these concerns fueled the stigma. The political manipulation of WMD has however, been determined by pre-existing inter-subjective understandings of each weapon within this category, and of the collective impression of all three. Strategies to promote political or strategic advantage throughout the Cold War years have fueled the negative imagine of WMD. Post-Cold War, the stigma has remained and intensified due to fears of the adaptive utility of WMD. It is now feared that WMD may be acquired and developed by a small number of aggressive states. There is also concern that WMD will be used within a city or domestic arena, as a weapon of terror by non-state actors. This altered context of use heightens concerns about the destructive potential of WMD and further enhances the stigma.

### How WMD became, and remain stigmatized: an overview of the process.

As has been noted, the stigmatization of WMD first came from heads of state, policy leaders, and the scientific community. This was due to fears of the increasing destructiveness of war. Prior to World War One, The potential destruction caused by chemical weapons provoked a debate about banning the development of this method of warfare. It should be noted here that the strategic value of chemical weapons was considered of great importance. These were seen to be new emerging-technology weapons and were of national interest. At this time, within the debates during the Hague Conference (1899) it was thought by both the US and the UK that chemical weapons may provide a potential future strategic advantage over other methods of warfare. As the effects and utility of these weapons was hypothetical, and chemical weapons had not been used, the US and UK were hesitant to condemn and proscribe these weapons.[42] This view changed as a result of the evidence of the destruction caused by the actual use of these weapons. Realization of the effects of the use of these weapons formalized fears regarding their potential destruction and provoked the demarcation of chemical weapons as separate in destructive effect from other methods of warfare at this time. These early efforts indicate that chemical weapons were unique in nature. They are unseen, indiscriminate weapons which, when used, generate devastating effects. When used in 1915, chemical weapons introduced a new type of technologically advanced method of warfare. The motivation to proscribe chemical weapons was largely driven by the desire to prevent the escalation of further increasingly destructive methods of warfare. This shaped the impression of these weapons as undesirable.[43] By including biological weapons alongside chemical, the conceptual potential of these weapons was the focus. Both are potentially devastating methods of warfare and if used have the potential to create long-lasting destruction.

Scientific investigations into protective measures against the use of chemical and biological weapons highlighted that there can be limited protection against attack. Protective clothing (gas masks) can limit the effects of chemical weapons. However, it is not possible to rule out the development of new strains of poisonous gases advanced to the point where protection is ineffective.[44] As battlefield weapons, there is the potential to limit the effects of use. Outside of the battlefield, if used on non-combatants, the potential of these weapons is horrifying. In the inter-war period, the realization of this led to the development of moral opprobrium toward these weapons. This established the normative and technological distinction between chemical and biological weapons and other methods of warfare, developed at this time. This technological and normative awareness formed as a result of the association of these weapons with devastating war, accounts of the effects of these weapons, and the image and language used in relation to each. The technological and normative elements of these weapons were indistinguishable. Awareness of the destructive effects of use provoked moral opprobrium.

The early condemnation of chemical and biological weapons formed the basis for the norms toward nuclear weapons. Nuclear weapons were believed to be even more devastating methods of warfare and provided confirmation of fears throughout the inter-war years that advances in technology were leading to ever increasingly destructive methods of warfare.[45] Scientific evidence of the effects of the use of nuclear weapons in Hiroshima and Nagasaki reinforced this fear. War was becoming more and more devastating; this was the basis for the strategic concepts of deterrence and Mutually Assured Destruction (MAD). Throughout the Cold War period, the destructive potential of nuclear weapons overshadowed all other methods of warfare. Despite this, within arms control discussions, all three weapons were still perceived to be unique in destructive effect. Much of the reason for discussing all three methods of warfare collectively was due to the political and strategic interests of states, driven by the animosity between East and West during the Cold War and the political pressures associated with this. As awareness of the effects of WMD increased, so too did ethical concerns over the impression of these weapons as indiscriminate and inhumane weapons of war. All three weapons created widespread destruction and could be used on combatants and the civilian population.

The condemnation of all three methods of WMD was due to the perceived devastation caused by these weapons, as much as the actual knowledge and facts about their effects. The stigma grew and developed in momentum through time as a result of the increasingly negative imagery of these weapons and perception that WMD were undesirable. Awareness of the effects of their use and political pressures enhanced the strategic advantages that WMD could produce. A contradiction existed here between the strategic advantages that these weapons potentially provided, against the devastating consequences of wide-scale use. It was concerns about the wide-scale use of WMD and the long-term consequences of this that provoked international condemnation.

As has been noted, the condemnation of WMD, and the stigmatizing process, initially emerged as a reaction to awareness of the effects of the use of WMD, these concerns were voiced by members of the scientific community and leading political figures. In time, as communication and awareness of the potential of these weapons increased, the stigma also developed in a bottom-up fashion, from grassroots movements and the media. It should be noted that there have also been times when the top-down and bottom-up processes have merged. This has been connected with shared perceptions of the changing nature of warfare, technological advances leading to the increasing destructiveness of warfare, awareness of the vulnerability of the civilian population to a potential WMD attack, as well as utilitarian and political perceptions of the use and possession of these weapons.

## Stigmatizing cyber warfare

As discussed earlier, a key hypothesis of norm evolution theory for emerging-technology weapons is that stigmatizing a weapon-type as "unconventional" or otherwise granting it a special status can accelerate norm adoption and ultimately achievement of a norm cascade.[46] Additionally, as discussed above, a key principle of norm evolution theory for emerging-technology weapons is that the perception of state self-interest is important for norms to emerge and for a state to become a leader of a particular norm. Stigma plays a role in this key act of state calculus. Since there is generally less exposure and understanding surrounding cyber weapons as well as different rates of weapon adoption and cyber vulnerability, states will be reluctant to lead on the issue of norms because they may be unable to determine the utility (or opprobrium due to stigma) of such weapons relative to their own interests. However, such calculations are key to making important and powerful states decide to become strong norm leaders and help promote the emerging norm. Additionally, with regards to China, Russia, and the United States—the preeminent cyber actors—an analysis of their respective cyber doctrines indicates that there appears to be a perspective that each nation has more to gain from engaging in cyber warfare than from significantly restricting it or giving it up entirely.[47] There appears to be insufficient international stigma associated with CNA-style cyber-attack to change state perspectives.

However, cyber warfare does have advantages that may make its stigmatization, based on the experience of stigmatizing WMD, easier. Given the unique combination of special characteristics associated with cyber warfare and the fact that it occurs in a new and man-made domain, it is by default "unconventional." Many have suggested that cyber weapons be considered another category of unconventional WMD, such as Geoffrey Ingersoll's article in *Business Insider* titled "The next weapon of mass destruction will probably be a thumbdrive."[48] This association of cyber warfare with WMD is pervasive enough to have led the *Bulletin of Atomic Scientists* to publish an article titled "The misunderstood acronym: Why cyber weapons aren't WMD."[49] This ongoing characterization of cyber weapons as different, special, or otherwise unconventional will help isolate cyber weapons and therefore enable the development of special stigma and ultimately constraining norms of behavior.

Developing a cyber stigma will face challenges arising from both differing perspectives as to future capability as well as the prospect for threat inflation. While it is true cyber warfare has been demonstrated to some degree (e.g. Stuxnet, etc.), the hidden and secretive nature of cyberspace make the actors and their intent unclear and thus limits the true demonstrative value of recent cyber-attacks. This has the effect of creating competing theories and arguments as to future effectiveness and strategic impact. Case in point, some argue (including former US Secretary of Defense Leon Panetta) that cyber warfare poses a major threat and warn of a cyber "Pearl Harbor" or "cyber 9–11" moment when critical infrastructure is attacked. Others have argued that statements such as Panetta's are pure hyperbole and that cyber warfare poses no such dire threat and that it in fact may not even constitute warfare as properly defined.[50] In the December 2013 edition of *Foreign Affairs*, Thomas Rid argued that not only is cyber attack not a major threat, but that it will in fact "diminish rather than accentuate political violence" by offering states and other actors a new mechanism to engage in aggression below the threshold of war[51] and Erik Gartzke argued further that cyber warfare is "unlikely to prove as pivotal in world affairs ... as many observers seem to believe."[52] However, cyber security is a huge and booming business for IT-security firms, with industry market research firms predicting the global cyber security market will grow from $106.32 billion in 2015 to $170.21 billion by 2020.[53] IT-security expert Bruce Schneier has alleged that these firms benefitting from cyber growth have, along with their government customers, artificially hyped the cyber threat.[54] Some critics have gone so far as to refer to this dynamic as "cyber doom" rhetoric or a "cyber security-industrial complex" similar to the oft-derided "defense-industrial complex."[55] Norm evolution theory applied in this case indicates that these vastly different perceptions as to the impact and role of cyber warfare in international relations and conflict will impair the development of a stigma and thus norm emergence, as was the case early in the twentieth century when the role and impact of strategic airpower was highly contested.

Because the cyber threat is secretive, diffuse, and lacks a clear definition, developing a credible "mass destruction" perspective and corresponding stigma associated with cyber-attack is difficult. As long as "cyber warfare," as referenced in the media and by government officials, includes CNE, CNA, CND, and petty cyber-crime, it will be difficult for a stigma to emerge. Further, key states have very different views on cyber issues which also impedes consensus on a stigma associated with these weapons. For example, the Russian and Chinese perspective on cyber conflict includes issues such as "information operations" and national Internet sovereignty—issues that are not akin to abhorrence and opprobrium associated with WMD-like stigma.

## Conclusions and recommendations

Cyber warfare—to include cyber-enabled IW—is still in its relative infancy, and there are multiple possibilities for how this new mode of warfare will evolve over the coming decades. Major CNA-style cyber-attacks pose a real and growing threat to the US and its allies. Policymakers must look at all available options to contain this threat, including non-material solutions such as developing constraining norms for cyber warfare through fostering an international stigma associated with cyber weapons. After all, active efforts to condemn all three WMD modalities through negative imagery, awareness, and demonstration have led to strong international norms and eventually binding international arms control agreements.

However, norm evolution theory for emerging-technology weapons and a careful analysis of the emergence of WMD stigma, when applied to cyber warfare, leads one to conclude that emergence of a meaningful cyber stigma is important, but unfortunately, unlikely at least in the near term. As a result, we recommend that policymakers recognize that stigma is unlikely to be a particularly effective tool in dealing with the cyber threat. That said, there are steps that can be taken to begin to build the foundation of a future stigma associated with CNA-style cyber-attacks. We recommend policymakers and academics focus on efforts to increase the discussion and transparency of CNA in order to increase awareness and demonstration of the serious damage that can be caused by these weapons. Cyber warfare must move out of the shadows for a stigma to develop. Additionally, we recommend policymakers and academics work to develop a more precise and accurate lexicon and associated understanding of the broad continuum of cyber threats so as to avoid watering down CNA by lumping it with more perpetual and relatively mundane cyber "attacks" that dilute or water down CNA's potential perceived abhorrence—such as CNE stuff. Broad differentiation and appreciation of the diverse range of cyber threats is essential for a stigma to take root. While we predict, at present, grim prospects for the evolution of constraining cyber norms, unfortunately the threat of cyber warfare is not diminishing. Learning from the WMD stigma example and realizing that cyber stigma constraining norms are unlikely to develop into a regime that could successfully manage and contain the threat is helpful as it allows policymakers to instead focus on more fruitful strategies for addressing this growing cyber warfare threat and provides further knowledge and understanding of this increasingly important subject.

## Notes

1 Daniel R. Coats, Statement for the Record: World Wide Threat Assessment of the Intelligence Community. 13th Feb 2018. Office of the Director of National Intelligence, USA. P5.
2 John P. Caves Jr and Seth Carus. *The future of weapons of mass destruction: Their nature and role in 2030.* Centre for the Study of Weapons of Mass Destruction, National Defense University, Occasional Paper 10. June 2014.
3 US Department of Defense, Summary of Department of Defense Cyber Strategy, 2018, https://media.defense.gov/2018/Sep/18/2002041658/-1/-1/1/CYBER_STRATEGY_SUMMARY_FINAL.PDF.
4 Benjamin B. Hatch presents a detailed analysis of the argument that cyber weapons should be reclassified as weapons of mass destruction in "Defining a class of cyber weapons of mass destruction: An examination of the merits," *Journal of Strategic Security.* Vol 11: 1, Article 3 2018, pp. 43–61.
5 Brian M. Mazanec. "Constraining norms for cyber warfare are unlikely," *Georgetown Journal of International Affairs*, Georgetown University Press, 17: 3, Fall/Winter 2016, pp. 100–109.
6 For the purposes of this chapter, the cyber threat is considered part of the broader continuum of IW and the term cyber weapon or cyber warfare is intended to be inclusive of cyber-enabled IW.
7 Daniel Coats. *Statement for the record: Worldwide threat assessment of the US intelligence community*, 13th Feb. 2018. www.dni.gov/files/documents/Newsroom/Testimonies/2018-ATA---Unclassified-
8 Gavin, *War and Peace in the Space Age*. 265. Harper; 1st edition (1958) ASIN: B0006AVLH0.
9 John Norris. *Early Gunpowder Artillery: c. 1300–1600* (Ramsbury, UK: Crowood Press, 2003).
10 Garry Brown and Keira Poellet. "The customary international law of cyberspace," *Strategic Studies Quarterly* 6, issue 3(Fall 2012), pp. 129–130.
11 James Forsyth and Billy Pope. "Structural causes and cyber effects: Why international order is inevitable in cyberspace," *Strategic Studies Quarterly* 8: 4 (Winter 2014), p. 118.
12 Thomas Rid. "Cyberwar will not take place," *Journal of Strategic Studies*, 35: 1(2011), pp. 5–32.
13 Theo Farrell. "Constructivist security studies: Portrait of a research programme," *International Studies Review* 4:1. (Spring 2002), p. 49.
14 Rodger A. Payne. "Persuasion, frames and norm construction," *European Journal of International Relations*, 7:1 (2001), p. 38.
15 Alexander Wendt. "Anarchy is what states make of it: The social construction of power politics." *International Organization* 46:2 (Spring 1992), p. 395.
16 Wendt. "Anarchy is what states make of it," p. 395.
17 Wendt. "Anarchy is what states make of it," p. 397.
18 While norms are viewed differently depending on the international relations theory employed, for the purposes of this chapter it does not matter if norms are viewed as major variables that can sometimes trump or constrain state-power calculations or if they play a lesser role. Even many realists now acknowledge the role of nonmaterial factors in international affairs, which demonstrates that examining norms for how various weapons develop and grow is not only a constructivist or internationalist pursuit.
19 Martha Finnemore and Kathryn Sikkink. "International norm dynamics and political change," *International Organization*, 52:4 (Autumn 1998), p. 891.

20 Ann Florini. "The evolution of international norms," *International Studies Quarterly* 40: 3(1996), p. 365.
21 For more information about norm adoption please see: Rodger A. Payne. "Persuasion, frames and norm construction," *European Journal of International Relations*, 7:1 (March 2001), pp. 37–61. Ann. E. Towns 'Norms and social hierarchies: Understanding international policy diffusion "From Below"' *International Organization* 66, Issue 2 (April 2012): 179–209.
22 Martha Finnemore and Kathryn Sikkink, p. 888.
23 Jeffrey T. Checkel. "International norms and domestic politics: Bridging the rationalist constructivist divide," *European Journal of International Relations*, 3:4 (December 1997) p. 476.
24 Checkel, p. 476.
25 Finnemore and Sikkink, p. 900.
26 Finnemore and Sikkink.
27 For example, see Mona Lena Krook and Jacqui True. "Rethinking the life cycles of international norms: The United Nations and the global promotion of gender equality," *European Journal of International Relations* 12:1 (March 2012) pp. 103–27.
28 Brian M. Mazanec. "Constraining norms for cyber warfare are unlikely," pp. 100–109.
29 Gregory Koblentz and Brian Mazanec. "Viral Warfare: The security implications of cyber and biological weapons," *Comparative Strategy* 32:5 (November 2013), pp. 418–434.
30 Steven L. Rearden. *History of the Office of the Secretary of Defense, Volume 1: The Formative Years, 1947–1950* (U.S. Government Printing Office, 1984), pp. 425–431.
31 The Organization for the Prohibition of Chemical Weapons. List of States Parties to the Convention on the Prohibition of the Development, Production and Stockpiling of Bacteriological (Biological) and Toxin Weapons and on Their Destruction as of June 2005. www.opbw.org/ Accessed October 13, 2013.
32 Scott Sagan. "Why do states build nuclear weapons? Three models in search of a bomb," *International Security*, 21:.3 (Winter, 1996–1997), p. 74.
33 111th United States Congress. *Senate Report 111–377: WMD Prevention and Preparedness Act of 2009.* December 17, 2010.
34 Erving Goffman. *Stigma: Notes on the management of spoiled identity* (Englewood Cliffs, NJ: Prentice-Hall, 1963: Penguin Books, 1990), p. 13.
35 Rebecca, Adler-Nissen. "Stigma management in international relations: Transgressive identities, norms and order in international society," *International Organization* 68:1 (January 2014), p. 145.
36 Martin Slatterly. *Key ideas in sociology.* (Macmillan Edition Limited. 1991: Surrey, UK: Thomas Nelson and Sons, 1992.), p. 118.
37 Slatterly, p. 118.
38 Erving Goffman, *Stigma: Notes on the management of spoiled identity,* p. 12.
39 Martha Finnemore and Kathryn Sikkink, "International Norm Dynamics and Political Change," *International Organization* 52:4 (Autumn 1998), p. 891.
40 Bruce G. Link and Jo C. Phelan. "Conceptualizing stigma," *Annual Review of Sociology* 27:3 (August 2001), p. 377.
41 The classification of the term "Weapons of Mass Destruction" is an embodiment of the stigma. This was first defined within The United Nations Security Council, *Commission for Conventional Armaments Resolutions Adopted by the Commission at its 13th Meeting, 12th August 1948 and its Second Progress Report of the Commission, 18th August 1948,* s/c.3/32/Rev.1/.
42 The Avalon Project at Yale Law School, Peace Conference at the Hague 1899: *Report of Captain Mahan of the United States Commission to the International Conference at the Hague on Disarmament etc. (With reference to Navies)* www.yale.edu/lawweb/avalon/lawofwar.hague99/hag99-06.htm.
43 League of Nations, *Preparatory Commission for the Conference for the Reduction and Limitation of Armaments,* Seventh Meeting, 20th May 1926, C.425.M.158.1926 IX [C.P.D.1a] Geneva 56.
44 LoN, *Preparatory Commission for the Conference for the Reduction and Limitation of Armaments,* Series II, *Minutes for the First Session of the Preparatory Commission for the Disarmament Conference,* May 18th–26th 1926, *Fifth Meeting,* C.425.M.158.1926.1X[C.P.D.1 9(a)] August 15th 1926. Geneva, 31–36.
45 *Documents on Disarmament 1945–59, Vol.1 1945–56* "Address by the Soviet Representative (Gromyko) to the United Nations Atomic Energy Commission" June 19th 1946, doc. 5, U.N. doc. AEC/8 17.
46 Brian M. Mazanec. "Constraining norms for cyber warfare are unlikely," pp. 100–109.

47 Brian Mazanec. "Why international order in cyberspace is not inevitable," *Strategic Studies Quarterly* 9:2 (Summer 2015), pp. 78–98.
48 G. Ingersoll. "The next weapon of mass destruction will probably be a thumbdrive," *Business Insider*, 29th October, 2012. www.businessinsider.com/the-next-weapon-of-mass-destruction-will-probably-be-a-thumbdrive-2012-10.
49 Jeffrey Carr. "The misunderstood acronym: Why cyber weapons aren't WMD," *The Bulletin of Atomic Scientists* 69:5 (17th October 2013), pp. 32–37.
50 Thomas Rid. *Cyber war will not take place* (Hurst Publishers/Oxford University Press) April 2012.
51 Thomas Rid. "Cyberwar and peace: Hacking can reduce real-world violence," *Foreign Affairs*, 92:6 (November/December 2013), pp. 77–87.
52 Erik Gartzke. "The myth of cyberwar: Bringing war in cyberspace back down to earth," *International Security*, 38:2 (Fall 2013), p. 42.
53 Markets and Markets. Global Forecast to 2020. June 2015. www.marketsandmarkets.com/PressReleases/cyber-security.asp.
54 Bruce Schneier. "Threat of 'cyberwar' has been hugely hyped," *CNN*, 7th July 2010. www.cnn.com/2010/OPINION/07/07/schneier.cyberwar.hyped.
55 Jerry Brito and Tate Watkins. "Loving the cyber bomb? The dangers of threat inflation in Cybersecurity policy," *Mercatus Center George Mason University* (April 26, 2011).

**PART IV**

# The fluid shape of modern information warfare

# 14

# HOW DEEP THE RABBIT HOLE GOES

Escalation, deterrence and the "deeper" challenges of information warfare in the age of the Internet

*Christopher Whyte*

Few artifacts of modern society capture the ideational eccentricities or the complex relationships between citizens and technology that exist in the Internet-fueled world of the 21st century so clearly as does the 1999 film *The Matrix*. Today, the catalyzing choice made by the main protagonist – that one can either choose to accept the façade of lies that is modern society (i.e. "take the blue pill") or be freed by rejection thereof (i.e. "take the red pill") – reflects a pervasive reality of life in the digital age. To be sure, that reality is not that the many alternative perspectives on how the world works that are the focus of so many "red pill" (and "black pill," "green pill," etc.) Internet sub-cultures are credible; rather, it is simply that the information environment of the Internet age is so fragmented along various lines that opportunities for deception, fabrication and radicalization abound in unprecedented fashion. Whether by malicious design or natural social process, misinformation and disinformation increasingly seep into societal discourse through the cracks formed by the rise of a decentralized and relatively leaderless global media environment.

The chapters in this book have conceptualized, problematized and empirically examined the threat of information warfare (IW) in the age of cyber conflict as a blended threat to democratic countries that variously involves digital intrusion, conventional propaganda-promoting intelligence operations and the manipulation of the full range of Internet services and platforms that underwrite modern societal discourse. It is perhaps to the detriment of the whole that no substantial attention has been paid to the dynamics and scope of those Internet communities and unusual sub-cultural spaces – which are often extremely restrictive and notably conspiratorial in nature – that now dot the landscape of cyberspace in their hundreds. Though not at the heart of most influence operations seen conducted by adversarial states against the West over the past decade, they are relevant. Russian IW operations have included infiltration of communities on sites like Reddit, 4chan and 8chan in a bid to build counter-mainstream narratives that amplify the impact of content peddled to broader audiences via social media. Such spaces are also illustrative in their own right of the challenge that those hoping to deter future IW face insofar as their growth and diversification is not simply a result of the rise of the Internet, but rather of the declining ability of democracies in the 21st century to generally assure the factual and attributable qualities of information in the marketplace of ideas.

**232** Christopher Whyte

This concluding chapter takes up the daunting task of exploring what might be done about the threat of cyber-enabled information warfare from a strategic perspective. The starting point for this task is the clear conclusion one might draw from preceding chapters that countering information warfare threats in the digital age is not fully the same task as deterring cyber conflict. As was argued in an earlier section, the best approach to understanding cyber conflict is so often to look beyond "logic of the domain" arguments about interactions in cyberspace to consider digital actions in the context of the logic of other conflict processes.[1] With IW, this means thinking about the attack surface of democratic polities in informational terms and assessing the degree to which Western states are capable of addressing what seems at the moment to be a host of endemic vulnerabilities to multi-form digital attack.

The chapter begins by considering the nature of the threat to democratic states. While previous chapters have attempted in different ways to adjudicate on this exact problematic, this final entry of the book takes the high-level view that cyber-enabled IW is an evolution of the intelligence enterprise that brings with it unprecedented opportunities for militaristic escalation of hostilities in international affairs. These lateral prospects for insecurity are concerning for a number of reasons, not least because – at least on the face of it – information operations share many of the characteristics that make cyber operations so fundamentally difficult to deter. However, I argue that it *is* possible to deter cyber-enabled information warfare, though admittedly under reasonably specific conditions that will be difficult to bring about and to maintain over time.

## How cyber-enabled information warfare might lead to conflict escalation

Information warfare in the age of cyber conflict is held up by experts, pundits and lawmakers as a grave and unprecedented – at least in terms of its current expansive format – threat facing democratic polities. But what might really go wrong off the back of successful and continued attempts by foreign foes to interfere with the sociopolitical processes of Western societies? Those same public voices that cite the specter of the threat also point to the short-term skewness in political process, social divisiveness and the associated uncertainty that comes with both as the primary negative outcome involved. What's less discussed is the prospective impact on processes of international cooperation and conflict.

Answering the question of what might go wrong is fundamentally difficult, given both the diffuse nature of the threat faced with digital age IW and the dispersed nature of the attack surface of modern democracies. Were IW campaigns of the kind seen prosecuted by Russia in the West in recent years not *both* multifaceted and broadly targeted, it might be logically straightforward to simply suggest that information warfare is unlikely to lead to conflict escalation. After all, many of the same arguments surrounding cyber operations – as a standalone feature of interstate engagement – as imperfect instrument of escalation might also be said to apply to IW.[2] Above all else, information warfare operations augmented by digital activities present responding decision-makers with an attribution challenge not conducive to rapid response. This mirrors dynamics of attribution in cyberspace – particularly, of course, where cyber operations are conducted in support of IW – though the challenge with attribution of IW is arguably complicated less due to the technical function of Internet technologies and more to do with the dispersed footprint of such campaigns.

Additionally, much like cyber warfare, information warfare is often experienced in such fashions that retaliatory options – in particular those that are proportionate – might simply not exist at a time where their deployment would be most desirable. There is also a substantial degree to which there is contemporary uncertainty about what might constitute an appropriate response to cyber-enabled interference operations. There are two elements to this issue. First, it is unclear as to what foreign policy response actions might be considered proportionate to interference via political warfare activities. Even if cyber operations were conducted in aid of IW, it is not immediately clear that counteroffensive cyber operations are a reasonable response to the discovery of IW (as opposed to, say, public attribution, criminal indictments, economic sanctions, etc.). For one thing, such operations may be viewed and interpreted by different elements of an adversary state's foreign policy apparatus than was responsible for the original interference operation. This dynamic is more particularly possible in the digital age, given the manner in which operational authorization is often nested below traditional executive-level. Second, many of the foreign policy actions most likely near to IW in terms of "severity" are those that often have limited effects (e.g. cyber operations or criminal indictment) or carry with them heightened uncertainty about effects felt and the clarity of signals sent (e.g. military grandstanding, sanctions or, again, cyber operations). The result is a disincentive for strategic decision-makers to retaliate in such fashion.

Finally, there is a sizable degree of variability bound up in determining the effectiveness of information warfare operations in line with what we might see in cyber operations. The actions of not only active defenders, but also of the populations and stakeholders (e.g. a company like Twitter) affect the prospective effectiveness of ongoing operations. Defense is, thus, less of a static artifact of a given strategic situation and more of a movable and evolvable element of a given IW episode. Indeed, here above arguably any other dimension of IW are there considerable parallels to the logic of operation in cyberspace. In cyberspace, access to a system may have required significant labor and time to achieve. And yet, simple defender actions – such as applying software patches – may undo the entire effort and force attacker adaptation. With information warfare, periodic updates to a platform's terms and services or to the rules of a given social media community space might force IW operators to alter their approach to content or narrative distribution. Divisive or scandalous content injected into media discourse may lose its appeal more quickly than was desired because of one or other unpredicted development that captured the news cycle anew. In short, much as is the case with cyber operations, the operational tempo of influence campaigns is not as regular and rapid as might be conventionally assumed. This creates additional space and time within which opportunities for reasonable responses – and, particularly, for focus on defensive reactions – are likely to supersede those that emphasize escalation.

However, given that IW operations *are* both multifaceted and broadly targeted, there are non-trivial reasons to fear that either crisis escalation or a broad-scoped heightening of conflict tensions between countries might be the result of endemic foreign interference in democratic processes. Specifically, information operations conducted at scale and over lengthy periods of time may introduce various lateral pressures on both society and decision-makers that could lead to conflict escalation irrespective of the operational logics described above. It is important to remember that the intended effects of information warfare are *cognitive* and that, therefore, influence operations must be thought of in terms beyond the tit-for-tat dynamics of security interactions that are the traditional focus of much international relations research.

**234** Christopher Whyte

A few points bear particular note along these lines. First, if the intended direct effects of IW are cognitive in nature, then target selection and chosen attack vectors will often be defined by normative – rather than material – significance to national security or politics. Much of what we have discussed as IW in this volume might be categorized as *subversion*. Indeed, subversion is the characteristic of recent IW that so clearly differentiates cyber-enabled influence operations in just the past decade from the counter-command/control (C2W) warfare that received so much attention from experts through the 1980s and '90s. Subversion is the degradation of power via the targeting of underlying constituting sources and mechanisms thereof. Different from coercive efforts to degrade power that target the material bases thereof, however, subversive efforts challenge the authority and legitimacy of a prevailing power dynamic or force. Since the strategy of subversion is an inherently normative task, subversive efforts are characterized by the normative significance of targeted symbols and processes over material importance. This is evident in so much IW in just the past few years that, distinct from some activity which simply aims to induce cognitive dissonance among decision-makers, aims to discredit democratic process and introduce into the mainstream ideas that might previously have been considered taboo or extreme.

Because so much of what IW touches or portends to affect is normative, there is inevitably a degree of uncertainty surrounding the prospective reaction of democratic forces or leaders to ongoing interference. While IW prosecuted in one campaign or another may be the stuff of nuisance and may not clearly invite assertive foreign policy response on strategic grounds, so too may it loom large in the mind of political leaders for ideational or ideological reasons. Rationalists in the international relations (IR) field hold that the precepts of the bargaining theory of war are often violated due to issue indivisibility, which is the idea that some things cannot be negotiated over because they either physically or normatively cannot be divvied up (such as territory that has spiritual meaning for both sides, like the city of Jerusalem). This notion applies to the effects of IW insofar as the underlying meaning being a particular interference effort results in a disproportionately negative reaction on the part of domestic stakeholders than the material costs of disruption might suggest. This dynamic presents opportunity for unintended provocation or for political opportunism that leads to escalation, particularly under circumstances where a democracy's political forces attempt to leverage popular outrage for domestic political gain by incurring audience costs.

Second, information warfare might also lend itself to escalating hostilities where decision-makers perceive a cumulative threat rather than a punctuated series of interference actions that, in themselves, would not invite a strong response. Part of what makes information warfare in the digital age so worrying is the manner in which detection of systems failures is so inherently difficult. This is a problem often classified in computer science as "Byzantine" in nature, referring to an information security game wherein effective communications between cooperating armies is ultimately impossible because of the problem of other minds (i.e. it is never possible to know with absolute certainty what others' intentions are). The threat of IW, at least in just the past few years, is arguably most clearly defined by such a dynamic, where the exact point of failure of discursive processes of democratic society is difficult to pinpoint. As such, decision-makers will likely be inclined to consider a cross-sample of foreign interference events as evidence of a broader effort of some kind. Within such a process, uncertainty creeps in and motivation towards more assertive response than might be required becomes possible.

Third, the effects of IW are felt more broadly than just the leadership and relevant security decision-makers in a given country. Information warfare entails broad-scoped cognitive manipulation of democratic conditions. Moreover, adjunct activities that aid IW – such as cyber operations – often seem detached from the other pillars of the effort. These realities mean that there are opportunities for unintended consequences stemming from IW, including conflict escalation. Given appropriate authorization from the government, for instance, private entities caught up in a cyber intrusion might be incentivized to "hack back" against foreign actors and create new, lateral challenges for interstate security. At the same time, information warfare might sometimes involve the coercion of domestic stakeholders by example. Data breaches leading to the release of scandalous information on one political actor, for example, might implicitly motivate other actors to either stay their hand in speaking out against foreign interference or call for disproportionate response to set red lines.

Finally, regardless of the episodic dynamics of potential escalation from information warfare, there may be significant long-term effects on conflict potential stemming from the degradation of democratic process. In the era of "post-truth" or "post-fact" information environments, which information warfare has certainly contributed to the intensification of, democratic social and political process may become far less predictable and more open to manipulation than has been the case in eras past. Foreign policymakers and international relations scholars alike rely on numerous measures of democratic operation to underwrite strategic behavior in world politics. Though there is too little room here to explore the particular potential effects of democratic degradation for international interactions in detail, it does not seem unreasonable or especially controversial to suggest that skewness of democratic process across the West would likely lead to greater variation in foreign policy outcomes than we might expect. Perhaps it has already done so.

## Deterring cyber-enabled information warfare

How might Western states deter intentional manipulation of those information systems that now underwrite every function and feature of modern discursive democracy? Given the lateral opportunities for interference to lead to uncertainty and escalatory tendencies in international politics, the case for finding an effective deterrent posture vis-à-vis digital age information warfare seems arguably greater than is the case for affecting deterrence of cyber conflict as a standalone phenomenon. After all – though the line between the two phenomena is, as has been asserted from the outset of this book, admittedly blurry – much of the cyber conflict that concerns national military establishments is the punctuated compromise of systems critical to the function of government and key infrastructural assets, and is thus jurisdictionally within the traditional domain of state control. With IW, as Christopher Colligan notes in Chapter 8, Western states face the threat of societal compromise entirely via systems and processes ensconced within and protected by the expectations of democratic civil society.

### Deterrence challenges in the digital age

Conventionally, scholars hold that deterrence is not a particularly credible strategy for cyberspace for a number of reasons and, though this book has striven to highlight the differences in logic and challenge between cyber conflict and cyber-*enabled* IW, these reasons have some meaning

**236** Christopher Whyte

for us here. Deterrence is any strategy that seeks to alter the cost/benefit calculation of an adversary such that the adversary does not change its status quo behavior (i.e. your foe opts not to attack). It is the flip side of compellence, wherein use of force or threat thereof is employed to actively prompt adversaries to change their behavior. Operationally, the point of deterrence is to ensure some degree of cost is applied to any action by an adversary that involves conflictual engagement. This can take a number of forms but traditionally is brought about via either strategies of denial or punishment. Strategies of deterrence by denial impose costs on an opponent by the limitation of an adversary's ability to achieve objectives, often via defensive action or the strategic deployment of forces in key areas (e.g. "tripwire" forces deployed in allied states under threat of foreign assault). Deterrence by punishment involves imposing costs via the threat of severe penalties if some attack takes place. Punishment differs from denial distinctly in that denial is linked to the operational engagement between adversaries itself – and thus might involve punitive measures linked with, say, the deployment of the aforementioned "tripwire" forces – while punishment threatens wider response that would raise the cost of attack.

With cyberspace, experts point out that a strategic posture of deterrence by denial would require an exquisite national information defense infrastructure. The attack surface of nationals – particularly democratic states – in the digital age is expansive enough and encompasses the use of diverse information technologies at every level of society. Particularly given the legacy path dependency issues bound up in the lack of original security controls in the technologies that undergird the function of the Internet today (i.e. the Internet protocol suite), hardening entire countries against attack and building resilience to particular forms of digital disruption is a daunting prospect. As such, deterrence by denial is likely not a viable strategy, at least at this time.

As Harknett and Fischerkeller point out,[3] there are distinctly poor notions of sovereignty surrounding cyberspace. Sovereignty has conventionally been at the heart of most deterrence strategies employed by nation-states. Holding territory of an adversary at risk by positioning forces nearby or developing capabilities to effectively take foreign territory are effective ways of signaling resolve and a clear intention to use force in the event of deviant adversary behavior. In cyberspace, there is no territoriality recognized by states such that an equivalent set of thresholds for gauging the validity of force posture exists in any substantial form. As such, the question of what kinds of action *below the threshold of armed attack* (or its equivalent via use of cyber instruments) should prompt an armed response remains open.

Another reason that deterrence is not conventionally deemed to be a credible approach in cyberspace is that signaling of intent is, operationally, remarkably difficult. The attribution challenges of operation in the domain extends not only to agency, but to intent. How might responders classify cyber actions that clearly involve foreign intrusion into domestic systems, even critical ones, if the details of the attack cede no understanding of intention? Is the purpose of a given intrusion to probe defender systems, to enable espionage, to make way for a disruptive attack or even to send some kind of signal for its own sake? Moreover, the time horizons involved in effectively punishment behavior following an intrusion of some kind are extremely short, particularly given the constant nature of contact between adversaries in the domain. Even where the intention of a cyber attack is reasonably clear in the fact of particular incident outcomes, constant contact couples with intrinsic difficulties in signaling to impose temporal limitations on punishment capabilities. After all, beyond a limited time frame – and, arguably, beyond a particularly proportionate response – where retaliation clearly *is* retaliation, how might an adversary interpret attempts to punish?

This thinking on the inapplicability of deterrence to cyberspace has led to the development of strategies of "persistent engagement," a variation on traditional approaches to deterrent agenda setting that couples conventional diplomatic efforts on norm construction with direct engagement of enemy forces online wherever they might be find at an extremely high operational tempo. The idea, in short, is that many of the restraint-assuming postures associated with deterrence don't work with cyber and that the domain-specific version of the thing that might work *must* be characterized be perpetual engagement. Against the fears of policymakers past who worried that any major response to foreign cyber aggression might provoke conflict escalation, the emerging approach around persistent engagement argues that tactical calculations in cyberspace can increasingly be made with high degrees of accuracy. State responses can be tailored in their severity, can be coupled with conventional signaling, can be designed so as to be low-visibility and can be aimed so as to be reversible in terms of damage caused. And, most importantly, such responses can be employed only where defenders see the opportunity to transform tactical effects into cumulative strategic ones. In this way, practitioners and policymakers in defense establishments increasingly believe that they can overcome the inherent limitations in traditional deterrent regimes.

## Differentiating deterrence of cyber conflict and information warfare

From at least some points of view, the caveats about operation in cyberspace made by numerous experts hold some water for the discussion of prospective deterrence of information warfare in the digital age. The attack surface of states for IW is easily as broad as it is with cyber conflict. Indeed, as distinct as the two phenomena are, this is yet another area where the two are closely linked. Much as is true with cyber, additionally, IW threats in the age of the Internet manifest in complex campaigns across diverse attack vectors. This complicates the signaling challenge insofar as it reduces time horizons within which it is possible to effectively affect a punitive response.

However, cyber conflict and information operations – at least, the large-scale interference operations that are the substance of so much concern about IW in just the past decade – might be differentiated in a number of ways that cast doubt on the overall prescription that deterrent postures might not be credible for dealing with IW in the way that they are not for cyber. The most significant of these is the different nature of the infrastructure being targeted and the implications of disruption or manipulation therefor. Whereas cyber operations target information systems typically to achieve some form of conflictual or intelligence effect, information operations target cognitive outcomes. The attack surface of democracies in the digital age may be the sum of vulnerabilities bound up in cyber-physical systems, media platforms and human cognition; however, the intended effects are, as the chapters of this volume have outlined, purely informational. In other settings, scholars have recognized this fact and have even taken to labeling the socio-cognitive substrate of modern society that information warfare targets the "sixth domain" of warfare. Regardless of the suitability of such a label, this means that the operational perspective on conflict held by experts on cyber conflict may not – despite the seeming proximity of the issues that emerge from the significance of new information technologies to both – apply readily to information warfare.

Most specifically, there is arguably a silver lining in the manifestation of foreign interference that does not quite so clearly exist with the specter of much cyber conflict and crime. Some interference in democratic process may be quite desirable insofar as the function of

**238** Christopher Whyte

robust democratic institutions and norms is to adjudicate on the full spectrum of perspectives that emerge in discourse and advocacy to guide the polity towards some form of prudence (though not necessarily, as Trevor Thrall and Andrew Armstrong point out, to truth). Democratic process relies on deviation from status quo perspectives in order to not only effectively test available policy positions in the crucible of the public eye, but also to build the credibility of democratic institutions and to assure the people that discursive competition is reasonably transparent. These things are critical to the function of democracy and are themselves primary targets of sophisticated IW operations.

## Encouraging a stability–instability paradox for information warfare

This final chapter of the book is not meant to be a deep dive on the issue of deterrence for IW so much as it is an effort to present observations that have emerged in the writing of this book by numerous authors and editors. In writing this final chapter, it is hoped that the volume does not leave readers with concern quite so much as it leaves one with the idea that IW is neither an existential threat to Western society nor an insurmountable policy challenge in the foreseeable future. The Western world is in a war of sorts, one that is taking place in the minds of citizenry as much as it is taking place on media platforms and in networked computer systems. It is a war that the West did not start, nor invited. And while it may seem like democratic society in the digital age is losing this information war, that does not mean that all is lost. Indeed, the past decade has been a mere opening bout in the information wars that will characterize much of the next century. The editors and the authors of this volume believe that – given the right steps – Western society can secure itself from IW in the age of cyber conflict and relegate such campaigns, as has been done time and again in human history, to being the stuff of special circumstances.

To do this, Western policymakers must design policy and public–private relationships that address IW as a diffuse prospective threat. We argue that deterring information operations that target dispersed populations, systems and media environments, Western states might produce a situation wherein foreign aggressors are incentivized only towards IW as a limited tactic to be employed in aid of traditional security objectives. The goal should be to artificially produce a stability–instability dynamic that motivates limited conflict because the threshold above which IW holds no strategic utility for an adversary is clear. Then, given such a dynamic, those limited operations can be addressed as they have conventionally been addressed – as an expected element of intelligence campaigns or, where relevant, as a behavior to be modified and deterred by persistent engagement in cyberspace.

To deter IW in its broadest manifestations, we argue that policy and practice must focus on the development of effective system-level aids to democratic functionality. Specifically, democratic policymaking on IW should focus on ensuring several basic information criteria pertaining to the function of national media environments. Three bear particular mention. First, modern information environments should be curated and regulated towards reasonable capabilities for the average citizen to identify the origination of information. This means that political and social interlocutors should not be fundamentally able to hide their identity when speaking on issues of national significance. Anonymity has its place in democratic discourse, but time-and-place safeguards should be affected that give the average citizen the ability to gauge the factuality of underlying data or reasonably assess the origination of a piece of advocacy. Second, democratic governments should enact policy and public–private coordination towards the goal of ensuring that debate is credible – i.e. that citizens can be assured that debate *is* debate, rather than a façade. Finally, governments must take necessary steps to ensure that significant social and political debate is high quality. Democracy requires information quality sufficient to allow a reasonable ability for citizens to parse signal from noise. In the digital age, this means developing methods by which citizens can cope with information overload and cut to relevant discourse.

It seems likely that many readers will assume that government actions taken to assure these information requirements might inevitably include regulation of the almost-exclusively privately-owned attack surface of modern democratic polities. Chapter 8 of this book covers in detail the challenges awaiting democratic governments that seek to empower security forces along such lines. However, we suggest that action taken to assure information in democracies need not be heavy-handed. Much of what we suggest as necessary above might functionally be accomplished with the provision of standard metrics of quality, certitude and attribution on platforms deemed to be critical to the function of a democracy (e.g. non-personal messaging on any social media platform with at least 50 million domestic users). And the utility of such provisions would not only be defined by their functionality, but ultimately by the degree to which a population of users is used to evaluating media in the context thereof. After all, the opportunity that exists with regards to deterring broad-scoped information warfare efforts lies in the systematic fashion in which populations could prospectively be insulated from the effects thereof. If the safeguards that assure the integrity of national information environments can be implemented in core areas and in such ways that norms of "safe" information consumption can be promulgated, then opportunities for malicious influence campaigns will be increasingly relegated to the fringes of national society.

## Curiouser and curiouser: looking forward to AI-enabled information warfare

It would not do to end this volume on any other note than the admission that the phenomenon discussed here in more than a dozen chapters is liable to continue to evolve – and perhaps even transform – in shape as time goes on. This past decade has made most persons in Western societies feel suddenly like strangers in a strange land. After all, interference by the Russian Federation and other belligerent states has occurred in dispersed format and across dozens of national instances since just 2014, likely leaving many with the feeling that there could be mischievous wizards behind every curtain of modern society. Such actors have stepped into an under-realized space and acted towards the detriment of democratic process, even in those instances where only nuisance came from an attempt at interference. Our overarching message in this book has been simple: that IW is nothing new, that cyber instruments augment but do not define influence campaigns, and that deterrence of this new threat is a surmountable challenge.

This said, it seems likely that yet further Western crises of disinformation and information warfare await us. The primary development that seems likely to propel us into such crises is the advent of more sophisticated artificial intelligence (AI) technologies, specifically those related to deep learning. Though many think of Hollywood entities like Skynet or HAL 3000 when AI is invoked, these technologies are really a basket of techniques designed with narrow capabilities in mind. At present, we live at the outset of an area of limited AI systems that come nowhere near – and won't for some decades – the shape of such Hollywood specters. And the most significant developments among these AI systems pertain to machine learning, the algorithmic process by which machines are not only programmed to mimic human cognition, but can actually consider data and infer without the interference of a human designer. Machine learning has already enabled remarkable features of modern society, not least the operations of companies like Google and Amazon, Inc., and stands to revolutionize sectors of commerce and science in coming years.

With regards information warfare, the advent of AI is double-edged. Deep learning systems may make easier the tasks of broad-scoped information assurance outlined above. However, AI also offers distinct opportunities for prosecutors of IW, both in terms of the targeting of influence campaigns and in the fabrication of content so realistic that even the most well-resourced censor would fail to catch it some of the time. Perhaps the best example of this in the public eye is the DeepFake, media fabricated by artificial neural networks that employs pre-existing content as a template from which to build. Already, DeepFakes have been produced at high levels of fidelity sufficient to fool large numbers of viewers. And two features of the technique suggest that society's challenge in addressing AI-enabled information manipulation will only get worse. First, DeepFakes utilize adversarial learning algorithms, which means that *two* algorithms work in tandem to create fake content. The first algorithm creates the best fabrication it can and the second attempts to determine if that media is fake. If it can do so, the first algorithm is updated to compensate and sets about further fabrication. This goes on until the first can consistently fool the second, suggesting – naturally – that efforts to use AI to defeat media manipulation in the future might only make such manipulation more effective. Second, DeepFake production software is already freely available on the application stores of Apple and Google. Thus, though AI may sound to many like the stuff of science fiction, it is already accessible by those without any specialized skills in programming. The arsenal of information warfare is, in essence, itself being democratized.

The authors and editors of this volume do not offer answers as to the challenges of IW pursuant to yet further transformations of our information technology. However, it seems likely that the same lessons learned and explored in the course of this book will continue to apply even in an age of AI, quantum computing and yet unimagined technological revolutions. Information warfare is ages-old and is fundamentally a technique focused on socio-cognitive outcomes – on distinctly *human* processes and behaviors. As such, the sociological, political and economic opportunities for mitigation of disinformation are likely to continue to exist in perpetuity even as the path dependency and seeming determinism of technological design features conjures specters of societal doom.

## Notes

1 This approach seems uncontroversial. And yet, it is a different perspective on the question of deterrence of novel hybrid threats than is commonly taken, where scholars and practitioners couch discussion of the thing purely in the context of offensive cyber operations. See, for instance, Ajir, Media, and Bethany Vailliant. "Russian Information Warfare: Implications for Deterrence Theory." *Strategic Studies Quarterly* 12, no. 3 (2018): 70–89.
2 For perhaps the best summation of such arguments, see Borghard, Erica D., and Shawn W. Lonergan. "Cyber Operations as Imperfect Tools of Escalation." *Strategic Studies Quarterly* 13, no. 3 (2019): 122–145.
3 Fischerkeller, Michael P., and Richard J. Harknett. "Deterrence is not a credible strategy for cyberspace." *Orbis* 61, no. 3 (2017): 381–393.

# INDEX

Page numbers in italics refer to figures. Page numbers in bold refer to tables. Page numbers followed by "n" refer to notes.

4chan 103, 231
8chan 231
active defense cyber operation 205
active measures 27, 28, 99, 101, 102; and counter-information 38; modern, birth of 28–9; modern, rise of 30–3; Operation Infektion 34–6; organ trafficking rumors 36–7; Pizzagate 37; *see also* disinformation, Russian
Adamsky, Dmitry 22
Adler-Nissan, Rebecca 221
Adobe Voco 170
Afro-Asian People's Solidarity Organization 32
agency theory of civil–military relations 158
Agitprop 30, 31
Alliance for Securing Democracy 121
al Qaeda 90, 98, 116
ambiguity of information warfare 19–20, 21, 24
American Revolutionary War 3
Andrew, Christopher 32, 34
anti-vaccine movement 79
Apple, Inc. 156–7, 240
Arab Spring 92
Aristotle 76
Armstrong, Andrew 9
Arquilla, John 1
Articles on State Responsibility 202, 203
artificial intelligence (AI) 49; -driven chatbots 169–70; -enabled information warfare 239–40
attitudinally congruent information 139
attribution problem 19, 232; effective control 203–4; factual attribution 202; instruction 203; and international law 201–4; legal attribution 187, 188, 202; organ of the State, qualification of 202; State-owned media 202–3
audio forgeries 170
availability heuristic 92, 93

Baghdadi, Abu Bakr al- 99
bargaining theory of war 234
Baum, M. A. 76
Bhutto, Bilawal 64
big data 49
Bittman, Ladislav 31
Black Lives Matters (BLM) 125
Bl@ck Dr@gon 64
Boatwright, Brandon C. 117–8
Bolsheviks 29, 38
bot(s) 140; chat, AI-driven 169–70; network 89, 90, 91, *91*, 97, 100–1, 102–3, 104, 106, 107; news 91; sleeper 107; spam- 17
Boyd, John 15
Brandeis, Louis 180
Brantly, Aaron F. 8, 27
Brennan, William J., Jr. 172
Brexit 189
Broadcasting Board of Governors (BBG) 174, 177
*Buckley v. Valeo* 184n58
Bump, Philip 81–2
Bureau of International Information Programs (IIP) 173
Bureau of Public Affairs (PA) 174

Cambridge Analytica 167, 169
Carothers, Thomas 189–90
Castells, Manuel 55
Center for Strategic Counterterrorism Communications 107
Center for the Study of Weapons of Mass Destruction 215
Centers for Disease Control (CDC) 34
Central Committee of the Communist Party of the Soviet Union (CPSU) 30, 31; International Department 30, 32, 34; International Information Department 30–1, 32
Central Election Commission (Russia) 189
Central Election Commission (Ukraine) 188

**242** Index

Central Intelligence Agency (CIA) 30, 31, 32, 34, 35, 174, 177, 187
Central Military Commission (China) 48
Cernovich, Mike 104
chaos-producing operations 137, 139, 140
chatbots, AI-driven 169–70
Checkel, Jeffrey 218
chemical and biological weapons (CBW) 33–4, 35, 219, 222–3
chemical weapons 222
Chen, Adrian 100, 104
Cheney, Dick 167
China 2, 4, 8, 23, 42, 58; cyber-enabled information operations of 59, 116; existential challenge and emerging opportunities 42–4; information operations in military strategy 45–7; national power 44; political warfare in current/historical perspective 44–5; potential emerging techniques and capabilities 49–50; three warfares 47–8
China Huayi Broadcasting Corporation (CHBC) 47, 53n55
Chinese Communist Party (CCP) 42, 44; Central Committee 43
Christian Peace Conference (CPC) 32
*Citizens United v. Federal Election Commission* 184n58
civilian targets of information warfare 20–1
civil–military gap 152
civil–military relations 9–10, 149, 150; civilian control over military institutions 149–50; civil–military–society relations 158–9; control of private elements 162; driving research questions 161–2; emergent threats 150; empirics 156–7; exogenous socio-technological conditions 156; fusionist approaches 159; gap in civil–military–private actors relations 161; information revolution 163; military effectiveness 150; patterns of civil–military–society engagement 160–1; policy-oriented military 152–3; private actors/sector 154–6, 158, 159, 161, 162; problematique 151–3; problematique in digital age, altering 153–9; research agendas 160–2; scholarship 150; theories of military effectiveness in democracies 157–8
climate change 79, 80
Clinton, Bill 153
Clinton, Hillary 4, 81, 84, 102, 103, 104, 187, 188
Coats, Daniel 216
coercion, and intervention into internal affairs 196–8
cognitive/emotional level of cyberspace 136
cognitive miser 138
cold cognition 133, 134–5, 138, 139
Cold War 7, 117, 150, 222, 223

Colligan, Christopher 9, 149, 235
Comet Ping-Pong 37, 103
common knowledge 119, 122
Communications Act of 1934 177
competitive process, in marketplace of ideas 76
computer network attack (CNA) 5, 216, 219, 224, 225, 226
computer network defense (CND) 216
computer network exploitation (CNE) 5, 216, 217, 226
computer subversion, as information warfare 16–8
concordance theory of civil–military relations 157–8, 159
conflict escalation, and cyber-enabled information warfare 232–5
constitutive norms 218
contested knowledge 119
convergence of information warfare 15–6; ambiguity 19–20, 21, 24; co-mingling IW elements 22–3; computer subversion as information warfare 16–8; future of U.S. information warfare 23–4; information warfare as niche of cyber war 18–20; non-lethality 19, 21, 24; persistence of information warriors 20, 21, 24; variance 18, 20–1
convergence theory of civil–military relations 157
Corfu Channel case 199
Corn, Gary 191–2
counter-command/control warfare (C2W) 1, 3, 155, 234
countermeasures (international law) 204–5
coups 150, 152
Cozy Bear 117
Credibility Coalition 121
credibility laundering 82–3
critical thinking skills 176
Cruz, Ted 188
Cyber Berkut 188
cyber conflict 1, 232; approach of PLA to 46; and civil–military relations 154–5, 160–2; defining information warfare in the age of 4–6; deterrence of 237–8; forms of 56
cyber-crime 123, 216, 217
cyber-enabled information operations (CIO) 55, 56–7, 66, 116–8, 150, 168; and conflict escalation 232–5; cyber methods **61**; defining 55–7; deterrence of 235–9; evolving understanding of cyber operations 56; findings and analysis 59–61; high impact/low-cost opportunity 63, 64, 65; India–Pakistan cyber rivalry 64–5; information warfare 55–6; research design 57–8; response to 233; Russia *vs.* World Anti-Doping Agency 61–4, *63*, 65; state actors who launch **59**; state credibility 63, 64, 65; strategic objective 57–8, **60**; *see also* information warfare kill chain

## Index

cyber espionage 16, 18, 22, 201
cyber kill chain 115, 120, 121
cyber operations 3, 15, 88, 114–5, 132; in 2010s 128; degrading attack 56, 58; disruptive attack 56, 57–8, 60, 66; evolving understanding of 56; and information warfare 9, 10; *vs.* kinetic operations 18–9; offensive cyber operations 5, 154; People's Liberation Army 42; and PSYOPs 17, 23; Russian 2; *see also* cyber-enabled information operations (CIO)
cybersecurity: definition of 168; digital pollution 161; Secure Elections Act 167, 168; U.S. government roles/responsibilities, bubble chart for 178, *179*
cyberspace 4, 22, 132, 159, 217, 231, 232; digital pollution 160–1; logic of operation in 233; nature of threats enabled by 160; structures of 135–7; threats, ranking of 161; *see also* information warfare and information operations (IWIO)
Cyberspace Administration of China 43
cyber superpower 42, 43
cyber team 89
cyber threats 115, 160, 216–7, 225–6
cyber warfare 1, 225; norms 217, 218; Russian interference in 2016 U.S. presidential election 167; stigmatization of 224–5; *see also* information warfare (IW)
cyber warriors, social media 89, 91, 96, 97, 98, 99, 100

danger control actions 125
data mining 16, 17
Dawn of Glad Tidings app 97
DCLeaks.com 187
Deacon, Richard 108
Declaration on Friendly Relations 197
Declaration on the Inadmissibility of Intervention 210n84
deepfakes 49, 170, 240
deep learning 240
defacements, website 58, 60, 65
Defense Advanced Research Projects Agency 24
Defense for Children, International (DCI) 36
degrading attack 56, 58
deliberative democracy 76
democracy(ies): and active measures 28, 33; attack surface of 119–21, 155, 159, 232, 236, 239; and civil–military relations 152, 154, 157; conflict escalation 232–5; deliberative democracy 76; policymaking 238–9; and propaganda 73, 108; theories of military effectiveness in 157–8, 159
Democratic Congressional Campaign Committee (DCCC) 117
Democratic National Committee (DNC) 103, 168; Russian hacking of 58, 117, 128, 166, 187
denial, deterrence by 236

denial of service (DoS) 58, 60, 116, 198
Deplorable Network 103, 104, 106
deterrence of cyber-enabled information warfare 235; challenges in digital age 235–7; cyber conflict and information warfare, differentiating 237–8; signaling of intent 236; stability–instability paradox 238–9
dezinformatsiya *see* disinformation, Russian
discourse dominance 42
discourse power (*huayuquan*) 44, 45, 51n22
discursive power 51n24, 51n25
disinformation 93; campaigns, phases of 120–1; commandments (Soules) 120, *120*; disruptive events 57–8; Global Engagement Center (GEC) 176–7
disinformation, Russian 27–8, 60, 99, 107, 117; defensive counter-information 38; early post-revolutionary disinformation and propaganda 29–30; Okhrana and birth of modern active measures 28–9; Operation Infektion 34–6, 120; organ trafficking rumors 36–7; Pizzagate 37, 103; post-war period and rise of modern active measures 30–3; #PrayforMizzou 100–1; and social media 100
disruptive attack 56, 57–8, 60, 66
distributed denial of service (DDOS) attack 21, 22, 58, 189, 194, 197
Document 9, 43
domaine réservé 196
doxing 17
Drobota, Ovidiu 95
Dual Process Theory (DPT) 134–5
due diligence, and cyber election meddling 198–200
Dyadic Cyber Incident and Campaign Dataset (DCID) 57

Eagan, Brian 192
economic markets 75, 76, 77
effective control 203–4
efficacy messaging 125, 126
Egan, Brian 197
Eisenhower, Dwight 107, 179
Election Assistance Commission (EAC) 175, 177
election hacking 119
Electoral Commission (UK) 189
electromagnetic warfare 178–80
electronic warfare (EW) 15, 17–8, 19, 21, 23, 24
elite cues theory 83
Ellul, Jacques 91, 104, 108
emerging-technology weapons 217; norm evolution theory for 218–20, 224
emotions: emotionally charged information 139; emotional state, exploitation of 169; hot cognition 134; and processing of information 142–3
espionage 5, 56, 58, 128; cyber espionage 16, 18,

22, 201; and international law 201;
Okhrana 28
Etudo, Ugochukwu 9, 127, 128
European Convention on Human Rights 200
European Leadership Network 210–211n97

Facebook 2, 4, 89, 155; advertisements 127;
Cambridge Analytica 167, 169; combating
malicious use 108; engagements for top 20
election stories 95; review process 78; trends
list 90; use by Russia 81, 83, 101–2
FaceMusic 127
factual attribution 202
faked documents 169
fake news 82, 89, 92, 93, 95, 103–4, 138
Fancy Bear 62–3, 63, 117, 188
Fatah 189
fear appeals 124
fear control actions 125
Feaver, Peter 158, 159
Federal Bureau of Investigation (FBI) 187
Federal Communications Commission (FCC)
174, 177
Federal Election Campaign Act of 1971
184n58
Federal Election Commission (FEC) 174–5, 177
Federal Trade Commission (FTC) 175
Feeling of Rightness (FOR) 135
Feinstein, Dianne 167
festivals, organizational 32
Finnemore, Martha 218
First Amendment 171–2, 180, 181, 184n58
Fischerkeller, Michael P. 236
Fogarty, Stephen G. 10
Foote, Colin 7, 9, 54
foreign policy 3, 176; and civil–military relations
152, 153; and cyber-enabled information
operations 233; and marketplace of ideas 76;
and religion 32; Russian 38
Forsyth, James 217
FSB (Federal'naya sluzhba bezopasnosti
Rossiyskoy Federatsii, Federal Security Service
of the Russian Federation) 27–8, 30, 204

Galton, Francis 76
Gartzke, Erik 225
Gavin, James 216
Geneva Conventions 34, 35
Giles, Keir 22
Gingrich, Newt 84
Gjelten, Tom 5
Glass, William 25n3
Global Engagement Center (GEC) 174, 176
Godson, Roy 31, 33
Goffman, Ervin 221
Gomez, Miguel Alberto 8, 9, 132
Google 167, 240

Gorbachev, Mikhail 31, 35
Goryacheva, Svetland 37
Graham, Billy 32
Grizzly Steppe see marketplace of ideas (MOI)
Groeling, T. J. 76
GRU (Glavnoye razvedyvatel'noye upravleniye,
Main intelligence Directorate) 27, 30, 62, 187,
188, 201, 204
Guccifer 2.0 187
gun violence 79

Harknett, Richard J. 236
hashtag 90, 97, 98, 100–2
HAV (Hauptabteilung Aufklärung) 35
Help America Vote Act of 2002 175
heuristics 134, 135, 143; machine heuristic 140;
and propaganda 92, 93
HIV-1 virus 31
hoaxes, social media 100, 103, 111n42, 111n45
Hoffer, Eric 91–2
homophily within social media 93–4
Hong Kong protests (2019) 4
hot cognition 133–4, 135, 138
Howe, William 3
Hu Jintao 50n16
human cognition 133; cold cognition 133, 134–5;
hot cognition 133–4
human rights 200; obligations, extraterritorial
applicability of 200–1
Hunker, Jeffrey Allen 156
Hunt, A. R. 73
Huntington, Samuel P. 150, 157, 159, 161
hybrid warfare 22, 118
hyper-partisanship, and election
vulnerability 83

ideologically congruent information 138–9
India–Pakistan cyber rivalry 58, 60, 64–5
informational power 55
information dominance 42, 45, 46
information manipulation 27, 34, 240
information operations (IOs) 10, 55, 128; in
Chinese military strategy 45–7; see also
cyber-enabled information operations (CIO);
information warfare (IW)
information warfare (IW) 1, 2, 15, 55–6, 99, 105,
153–4, 215; ambiguity of 19–20, 21, 24; anti-
democratic 114–5; artificial intelligence-
enabled 239–40; campaigns 3–4; defining in
the age of cyber conflict 4–6; definition of 2,
5–6; detection of systems failures 234;
deterrence of 237–8; and digital age 6–7;
easiness and popularity of 2; effects of 235; and
environment 24; and global Internet usage
2–3; impact of 3, 7–8; lack of international
norms for 7; non-lethality of 19, 21, 24;
operational realities 115; operations,

effectiveness of 233; persistence of information warriors 20, 21, 24; pervasiveness and importance of 6–8; rhetoric 115–6; variance of 18, 20–1

information warfare and information operations (IWIO) 56, 132–3, 168; affective states, exploring 142–3; cognitive effects of 138–41; defense of U.S. government against 170–80; disintermediation of information 140–1; effects, containing 141–3; future cyber-enabled capabilities for 168–70; high connectivity and low cost 138–9; human cognition 133–5; importance of 166–7; information encoding, disruption of 141–2; low information latency and multiple distribution points 139–40; structures of cyberspace 135–7; typologies 137–8

information warfare kill chain 115, 125–8; advocacy of broader themes 127–8; attack surface of democracies 119–21; audience capture and growth 127; community engagement 123; constituency 122, 123; defining interference 118–9; digital means of approach to interference 123; efficacy messaging 125, 126; implications for defense and deterrence 129; narrative 125–126; operationalizing distortion 124–125; secrecy 122; shortcomings 121; threat model 118–21, 122; triggering events 125, 126; underlying assumptions 122–3

Ingersoll, Geoffrey 224

inherently governmental functions: and domaine réservé 196; interference with/usurpation of 194

Institute of Museum and Library Services (IMLS) 175, 178

intelligence, surveillance, and reconnaissance (ICR) 15, 17, 19, 23, 24

internal affairs, intervention into 196–8

International Court of Justice (ICJ) 196, 199, 203

International Covenant on Civil and Political Rights (ICCPR) 200

International Covenant on Economic, Social and Cultural Rights 200

International Group of Experts (IGE) 191

international law, and cyber election meddling 186–7; attribution 201–4; breach of legal obligation 190–201; context 187–90; due diligence 198–200; grey area 206; intervention into internal affairs 196–8; other breaches 200–1; responses 204–5; violation of sovereignty 190–6

International Law Commission 202, 203

international norms, for information warfare 7

International Olympic Committee (IOC) 62

International Organization of Journalists (IOJ) 32, 33

International Union of Students 32

Internet 2–3, 7, 89, 163; and China 42, 43; commercial services, manipulation of 155; global reach of 19; infrastructure, and civil–military relations 151, 154–5, 162; Internet service providers 156; sub-cultures 231; *see also* social media

Internet of Things 16, 17, 20–1

Internet Research Agency (IRA), Russia 81, 84, 99, 117–8, 125, 126, 127, 128, 155, 167, 187–8, 199, 203, 204

Iran 4, 7, 116, 125, 126

Islamic State (IS) 4, 88, 96–9, **97**, **99**, 107, 116

Island of Palmas case 192

Ivan the Terrible 3

*Izvestia* 36

Jamieson, Kathleen Hall 7–8, 73

Janowitz, Morris 157, 159

Jensen, Benjamin 7, 9, 117, 132

Johnson, Loch 189

Joint Task Force Computer Network Defense (JTF-CND) 158

journalists, use of social media 95–6

Kahneman, D. 134–5

Kalugin, Oleg 99

Kania, Elsa B. 8, 42

Karzai, Hamid 189

Kashmir conflict 64–5

Katz, Rita 107–8

Kaufmann, C. 76

Kelly, Walt 83

Kenez, Peter 29–30

Kennedy, Anthony 184n58

Kennedy, John F. 21

Kerr, Jaclyn 55–6, 138

KGB (Komitet Gosudarstvennoy Bezopasnosti, Committee for State Security) 27, 30, 31, 32; Department A 30, 32, 33, 34

Kilcullen, David 106

kinetic operations: *vs.* cyber operations 18–20; use of IW elements to support 20, 21

KKK 100

Koenders, Bert 191

Koh, Harold 191

Krutskih, Andrey 105

latency, information 139–40

Lavrov, Sergey 101

law of State responsibility 186, 192, 202, 204, 205

leak operations 137, 138–9

legal attribution 187, 188, 202

legal warfare 42, 44, 45, 47–8

**246** Index

Le Pen, Marine 106
Libicki, Martin C. 6, 8, 15
Lin, Herbert 10, 55–6, 138, 166
Link, Bruce G. 221
Linvill, Darren L. 117–8
Lippman, D. 84
*Literatumaya Gazeta* 35
Lockheed Martin 115
long-term espionage 58, 59
Louis XIV 3
Lukashenko, Alexander 189

Maathai, Wangari 35
McCain, John 84, 109
machine learning 240
McLuhan, Marshall 6
McMaster, H. R. 188
Macron, Emmanuel 105–6, 188
#MacronLeaks 105–6
Maduro, Nicolás 106
Malign Foreign Influence Campaign Cycle 121
malware 117, 127, 128, 155, 161, 188, 194
Mandiant 115
Maness, Ryan C. 7, 9, 132
Mao Zedong 46
marketplace of ideas (MOI) 73, 75–8, 178, 231;
    assumptions 76–7; competitive process 76; elite
    cues and credibility laundering 82–3; and First
    Amendment 171, 172; health of 75; large
    market and fierce competition 80–2; market
    failures 77, 78, 171, 172; polarization 83–4;
    Russian interference in 2016 U.S. presidential
    election 80–4; time for debate and deliberation
    76–7; truth 77
marketplace of values 78–80, 82, 85
May, Theresa 189
Mayer, J. 73
Mazanec, Brian 1, 10, 215
Ma Zhong 45
Mbeki, Thabo 35
Mercer, J. 134
Merkel, Angela 101, 188
Mill, John Stuart 75, 76, 77, 171
Milosevic, Slobodan 189
Milton, John 75, 85n1
Moore, John Bassett 199
Moscow Radio 36
motivated reasoning 133–4, 138, 139
Mtrokhin, Vasili 32, 34
Mueller, Robert 81, 82, 188, 201, 204
Murphy, Sean 213n160

Nakasone, Paul 56
Nanjing Political Institute, PLA 45, 52n33
National Defense University, PLA 45, 49
National Endowment for Democracy
    50n19, 189

National Endowment for the Humanities (NEH)
    175, 178
National Science Foundation (NSF) 175, 178
National Security Agency (NSA) 187
National Security Law (China) 43
National Security Study Memorandum 59
    (NSSM-59) 33–4
network-centric warfare 155
network infiltrations 58
network intrusions 58
neurocinematics 170
news organizations 7, 32, 82–3, 100, 101
Nixon, Richard 33
non-lethality of information warfare 19, 21, 24
norm evolution theory for emerging-technology
    weapons 218–9, 224; case for 219–20; and
    national self-interest 216, 219, 220, 224; stigma
    and its impact on norm evolution 220
norms 216; constitutive 218; constructivist
    approach 217; definition of 221; life cycle 218;
    regulative 218; understanding 217; WMD 220;
    *see also* stigmatization
North Korea 7, 22–3, 105
*Novosti* 36
Novosti Press Agency (APN) 32
nuclear weapons 216–7, 219, 223

Obama, Barack 35, 156, 170; Russian use of
    social media against 100; sanctions on Russia
    204; #StevensHeadinObamasHands 98; and
    U.S. presidential election (2016) 186, 190, 201
objective civilian control 157
offensive cyber operations (OCO) 5, 154
Office of Personnel Management (OPM) 16,
    25n6, 58
Office of the Director of National Intelligence
    (ODNI) 3, 166, 167, 168, 187, 188
Ohlin, Jens 200
Okhrana 28–9
OODA (observe, orientate, decide, act)
    loop 55
Operation Infektion 34–6, 120
opinion formation model 92, 93
#OpOlympics 62–3, 64
Oppenheim, Lassa 196
organ trafficking 36–7
Oxford Internet Institute, Unit for
    Propaganda 107

Pakistan *see* India–Pakistan cyber rivalry
Pakistani Peoples Party (PPP) 64
Panetta, Leon 224
*Patriot, The* 34, 35
Pawn Storm 58, 62
Pennycook, G. 139
People's Liberation Army (PLA) 42, 44–5,
    51–52n32; Academy of Military Science 45;

approach to cyber conflict 46; Base 311, 47–8, 53n55, 53n57; doctrine 46, 52n48; joint campaign scenarios 48; on military struggle 46; Nanjing Political Institute 45; National Defense University 45, 49; psychological warfare 47; Xi'an Political Institute 45
People's Liberation Army Strategic Support Force (PLASSF) 48
Perrow, C. 136
persistence of information warriors 20, 21, 24
persistent engagement 129, 159, 237
personal information, name-matched use of 169
Phelan, Jo C. 221
physical level of cyberspace 136
piggybacking 16
Pimen, Patriarch 32
Pizzagate 37, 103
plea of necessity (international law) 205
Podesta, John 103–4, 168
#PodestaEmail 103, 104
/pol/ (bulletin board) 103
polarization, and marketplace of ideas 78, 80, 83–4
political advertising 177
political warfare 44–5, 114
Political Work Regulations (2003), China 44
Pompeo, Mike 100
Pope, Billy 217
positive propaganda 43, 49
Posobiec, Jack 104
Posse Comitatus Act 176
Postal Service and Federal Employees Salary Act of 1962 172
*Pravda* 36
#PrayforMizzou 100–1
press: foreign, Soviet influence over 32; International Organization of Journalists 33; and social media 109; Soviet 29–30
Press Club of India (PCI) 64
Prier, Jarred, Lt Col 9, 88
principal–agent problems 151–2; *see also* civil–military relations
prior knowledge, and information processing 141
privacy, right to 200
professionalism, and civil–military relations 157, 159
propaganda 3, 17, 108; and artificial intelligence 49; China 43; digital 73, 74; election 194; existing narrative 89, 92, 96, 101, 102; Fancy Bear *63*; India–Pakistan cyber rivalry 60, 64–5; Islamic State (IS) 96, 97, 98; operations 137, 138–9; positive 43, 49; Russian 100, 101, 102, 106; social media 89–90, 91–3, *94*, 96–9; and social networks 94, 95; Soviet Union 29–30, 31, 32, 33; spread via trend *94*

psychological operations (PSYOPs) 15, 18, 173; and artificial intelligence 49; and cyber operations 17; People's Liberation Army 42
psychological warfare 42, 44, 45, 47–8
public opinion: and disinformation 34; dominance, in China 43, 49; and elites 76; warfare 42, 44, 45, 47–8; *see also* marketplace of ideas (MOI)
punishment, deterrence by 236
Putin, Vladimir 3, 21, 63, 100, 186, 187

Rafsanjani, Hashemi 220
Rand, D. G. 139
ransomware attacks 161
Rapp, D. N. 139
Rather, Dan 35
Rational Choice Theory 133, 134
recollection bias 140
Red Army 44
Reddit 2, 155, 231
Redlawsk, D. P. 139
Regional Media Hubs (Department of State) 174
regulative norms 218
Reinhardt, G. Y. 139
Reiter, D. 76
religious institutions, and Soviet active measures 32
RenRen 2
retorsion 204
revolution in military affairs (RMA) 149, 163
Rid, Thomas 132, 224–5
Rio Olympics (2016) 61, 62
Rodchenkov, Grigory 61
Rogers, Michael 25n6
Romney, Mitt 84
Ronfeldt, David 1
RT (Russia Today) 100, 101, 187, 189, 194, 202
Rubio, Marco 188
Russia 1, 7, 8, 125, 126, 127, 231; anti-immigration narrative 101; convergence of information warfare 22; cyber-enabled information operations of 54, 59–60, 66, 116–8; cyber espionage against Western targets 22; hacking of DNC 58; hybrid warfare 22; interference on European elections 188; #PrayforMizzou 100–1; and Ukraine 4, 21, 22; use of social media 99–105, 106, **106**, 108; U.S. sanctions on 204; *vs.* World Anti-Doping Agency 61–4, *63*, 65; and West, relations 210–211n97; *see also* disinformation, Russian; U.S. presidential election (2016), Russian interference in
Russian Civil War 29
Russian Empire 27, 28

**248** Index

Salovich, N. A. 139
San Bernardino terrorist attacks (2015) 156
Sanders, Bernie 102, 188
Saudi Aramco 193
Schiff, Rebecca 159
Schmitt, Michael 10, 186
Schneier, Bruce 119, 120, 121, 123, 225
search engine optimization 107
Secure Elections Act 167, 168
Segal, Jacob 35
Segal, Lili 35
self-defense, use of force in 205
self-determination, right to 200
semantic level of cyberspace 136
Senate Armed Services Subcommittee 55
Shamai, Patricia 10
Shane, Peter M. 156
sharp power 44
short-term espionage 58
Shultz, Richard 31, 33
Sikkink, Katherine 218
Silver, Nate 81
simulations 16
sleeper bots 107
Sochi Olympics (2014) 61
social media 73–4, 88–9; commanding the trend
in 88, 89, 90, 92; Islamic State (IS) 88, 96–9,
**97**, **99**, 107; propaganda 91–3, *94*; social
networks and 93–6; trend 89–91, 94, 108–9;
use by Russia 99–105, 106, **106**, 187, 188;
weaponized, future of 105–8; *see also* U.S.
presidential election (2016), Russian
interference in
social networks 93–6
soft power 44, 45, 166
Sony Studios, North Korean hacking of 105
Sotloff, Steven 98
*Sotsialistichekaya Industriya* 36
Soules, Anthony 120, *120*, 121, 122, 123
sovereignty 42, 206; definition of 192; and
deterrence 236; interference with/usurpation of
inherently governmental functions 194; and loss
of functionality 193–4, 195; as primary rule of
international law 190, 191, 192; as principle of
international law 190, 191; and private actors
156; and territorial integrity 193; violation, and
cyber election meddling 190–6, 197
*Sovetskaya Kultura* 36
*Sovetskaya Rossiya* 36
Soviet Union 7, 27, 34, 99, 107, 117; early post-
revolutionary disinformation and propaganda
29–30; post-war period and rise of modern
active measures 30–3; *see also* Russia
spam-bots 17
Sputnik 100, 187, 194, 202
Stam, A. C. 76
#StevensHeadinObamasHands 98

stigmatization 216; of chemical and biological
weapons 222–3; of chemical weapons 222;
of cyber warfare 224–5; impact on norm
evolution 220; of nuclear weapons 223;
stigma, definition of 221; unconventionality
of weapons 220, 224; of weapons of mass
destruction 220–4
Stuxnet attack 58
subjective civilian control 157
subversion 234; computer 16–8; ideological 32
Sundar, S. S. 140
Sun Tzu 3, 15, 27, 133, 137, 166
SVR (Sluzhba vneshney razvedki, Foreign
Intelligence Service of the Russian Federation)
27, 30
syntactic level of cyberspace 136

tactics, techniques and procedures (TTPs)
30, 33
Taiwan 4, 47–8, 116
Tallinn Manual 2.0 on the International Law
Applicable to Cyber Operations 191, 192–3,
197, 198, 199, 208–209n53
TASS 32, 35, 36
Taylor, Robert 191–2
*Tecugigalpa La Tribuna* 36
territorial integrity, and sovereignty 193
terrorism 21–2
"Think Again, Turn Away" campaign 107–8
Thrall, A. Trevor 1, 9, 73
time for debate/deliberation, and marketplace of
ideas 76–7
Toffler, Alvin 15
Toffler, Heidi 15
trend creation 90, 103, 106, 109
trend distribution 90, 100–1
trend hijacking 90, 97–8, 101, 106
TrendMap app 104
*Trud* 36
true believers, social media 89, 91, 92; and Islamic
State 97, 98; and Russia 100, 101, 102–3, 104
Truman, Harry 220
Trump, Donald: "Access Hollywood" tape
103; campaign expenses 81; pro-Russian
messaging of 84; sanctions on Russia 204;
supporters, Clinton on 102; support of true
believers 104; and U.S. presidential election
(2016) 8, 73, 75, 80, 85, 95, 125, 167, 186,
187, 188, 198
#TrumpWon 104
truth: and benefit, connection between 77; and
marketplace of ideas 75, 76, 77; and values 78–9
Tshabalala-Msimang, Manto 35
Twain, Mark 78
Twitter 2, 4, 7, 89, 90, 106, 155; combating
malicious use 108; Islamic State 97–9, **97**; use
by Russia 83, 99–105, 167, 168

Ukraine 4, 21, 22
U.N. Charter 182n16, 205
U.N. Group of Governmental Experts on Developments in the Field of Information and Telecommunications 191
United Nations Commission on Human Rights 36
United States 32, 156–7; bad fit of government authorities 175–80; bubble chart for cybersecurity roles/responsibilities 178, *179*; cyber-enabled information operations of 59; defense against IWIO 170–80; First Amendment 171–2; information warfare, future of 23–4; interference on foreign elections 189–90; and Operation Infektion 34–6, 120; and organ trafficking rumors 36–7; private sector 180–1; role of government departments and agencies 172–5; and Soviet Union 30
United States Agency for International Development (USAID) 175, 177
United States Information Agency (USIA) 33, 36, 38, 107
University of Missouri 100–2
unpredictability of information warfare operations 18–9, 20, 24
U.S. Biological Weapons programs 33
U.S. Cyber Command (USCYBERCOM) 5, 23, 158, 191
U.S. Department of Defense (DOD): Cyber Strategy 215
U.S. Department of Defense (DoD) 5, 6, 173, 176, 178, 179
U.S. Department of Education (ED) 173, 176
U.S. Department of Homeland Security 178
U.S. Department of Justice (DOJ) 173, 176, 178, 186
U.S. Department of State 32, 34, 35, 107, 173, 176–7, 204
useful idiots 121, 124
U.S. Intelligence Community 215
U.S. Joint Chief of Staff 55
U.S. National Defense University 215
U.S. Northern Command (USNORTHCOM) 176
U.S. presidential election (2016), Russian interference in 2, 3–4, 73, 74–5, 77, 80, 186, 187–8; attribution 201–4; campaign spending 81; as cyberwar 167; due diligence 199; elite cues and credibility laundering 82–3; espionage 201; genuinely competitive states 81–2; hacking into servers 195; human rights 200–1; indictments 81, 173, 176, 186, 188, 204; intervention into internal affairs 197–8; as IWIO 166–7, 168; large market and fierce

competition 80–2; and marketplace of values 79; messaging of trolls 195; polarization 83–4; responses to 204–5; right to privacy 200; right to self-determination 200; and social media 88–9, 102–5, 117; and Trump, Donald 84–5; and violation of sovereignty 194–6

Valeriano, Brandon 7, 9, 132
Valley Forge attack (American Revolutionary War) 3
vandalism 58, 60
variance of information warfare 18, 20–1
Vasīlév, Aleksieĭ Tīkhonovīch 28
video forgeries 170
Virilio, Paul 163

Wanamaker, John 18
Warren, Patrick L. 117–8
Washington, George 3
Watson, Paul Joseph 104
weapons of mass destruction (WMD) 215, 216; norms 220; stigmatization of 220–4; unconventionality of 220, 224
Weeks, B. E. 142–3
Weibo 2
Weiss, Michael 99
Welch, Edgar Maddison 37
Wendt, Alexander 217
*Whitney v. California* 180
Whyte, Christopher 1, 9, 10, 114, 231
WikiLeaks 100, 103, 104, 105, 187
Winkler, Jonathan 178–80
World Anti-Doping Agency (WADA), Pawn Storm's assault on 8, 61–4, *63*, 65
World Congress of Intellectuals in Defense of Peace 31
#WorldCup2014 98
World Federation of Democratic Youth 32
World Health Organization 36
World Peace Conference of Religious Workers 32
World Peace Council (WPC) 31
World War II 3
Worldwide Threat Assessment 188, 215
Wright, Jeremiah 35

Xi'an Political Institute, PLA 45
Xi Jinping 43, 44

Yeltsin, Boris 189

Zapevalov, Valentin 35
Zarqawi, Abu Musab al- 96
zero-day vulnerability 168, 182n19